STAR WARS

DARTH VADER

DARK LORD OF THE SITH

THE BURNING SEAS

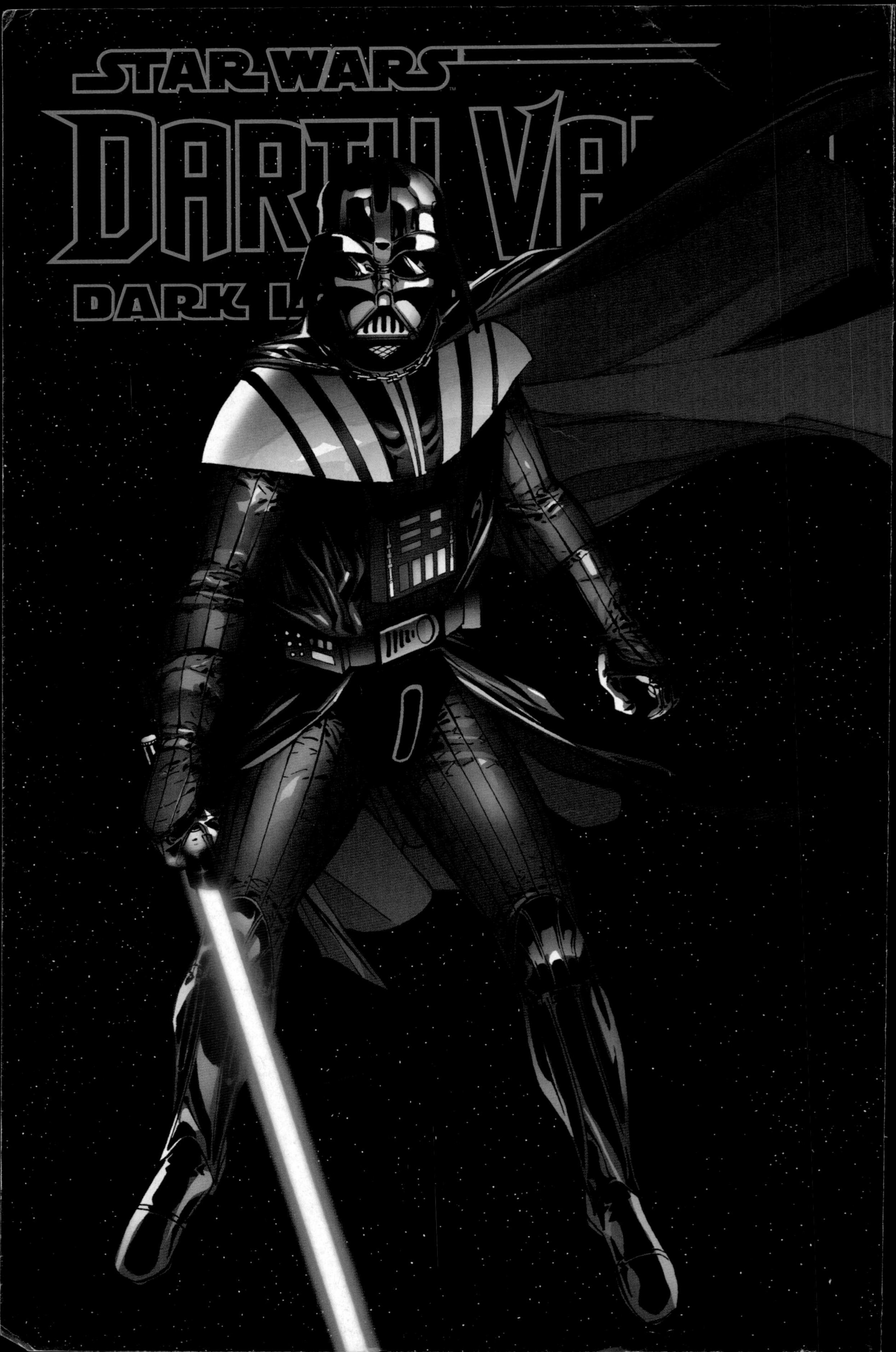
STAR WARS

THE BURNING SEAS

Writer	**CHARLES SOULE**
Penciler	**GIUSEPPE CAMUNCOLI**
Inker	**DANIELE ORLANDINI**
Colorists	**DAVID CURIEL** (#13-15, #17-18) &
	JAVA TARTAGLIA WITH **GURU-eFX** (#16)
Letterer	**VC's JOE CARAMAGNA**
Cover Art	**GIUSEPPE CAMUNCOLI & ELIA BONETTI**
Assistant Editors	**HEATHER ANTOS, CHRISTINA HARRINGTON, EMILY NEWCOMEN & TOM GRONEMAN**
Editors	**JORDAN D. WHITE** WITH **MARK PANICCIA**

ANNUAL #2

Writer	**CHUCK WENDIG**
Penciler	**LEONARD KIRK**
Inkers	**WALDEN WONG & SCOTT HANNA**
Colorist	**NOLAN WOODARD**
Letterer	**VC's JOE CARAMAGNA**
Cover Art	**MIKE DEODATO JR. & ARIF PRIANTO**
Assistant Editor	**TOM GRONEMAN**
Editors	**HEATHER ANTOS & MARK PANICCIA**

Editor in Chief	**C.B. CEBULSKI**
Chief Creative Officer	**JOE QUESADA**
President	**DAN BUCKLEY**

For Lucasfilm:

Assistant Editor	**NICK MARTINO**
Senior Editor	**ROBERT SIMPSON**
Executive Editor	**JENNIFER HEDDLE**
Creative Director	**MICHAEL SIGLAIN**
Lucasfilm Story Group	**JAMES WAUGH, LELAND CHEE, MATT MARTIN**

Collection Editor	JENNIFER GRÜNWALD	VP Production & Special Projects	JEFF YOUNGQUIST
Assistant Editor	CAITLIN O'CONNELL	SVP Print, Sales & Marketing	DAVID GABRIEL
Associate Managing Editor	KATERI WOODY	Book Designer	ADAM DEL RE
Editor, Special Projects	MARK D. BEAZLEY		

STAR WARS: DARTH VADER: DARK LORD OF THE SITH VOL. 3 — THE BURNING SEAS. Contains material originally published in magazine form as DARTH VADER #13-18 and ANNUAL #2. First printing 2018. ISBN 978-1-302-91056-3. Published by MARVEL WORLDWIDE, INC., a subsidiary of MARVEL ENTERTAINMENT, LLC. OFFICE OF PUBLICATION: 135 West 50th Street, New York, NY 10020. STAR WARS and related text and illustrations are trademarks and/or copyrights, in the United States and other countries, of Lucasfilm Ltd. and/or its affiliates. © & TM Lucasfilm Ltd. No similarity between any of the names, characters, persons, and/or institutions in this magazine with those of any living or dead person or institution is intended, and any such similarity which may exist is purely coincidental. Marvel and its logos are TM Marvel Characters, Inc. Printed in the U.S.A. DAN BUCKLEY, President, Marvel Entertainment; JOHN NEE, Publisher; JOE QUESADA, Chief Creative Officer; TOM BREVOORT, SVP of Publishing; DAVID BOGART, SVP of Business Affairs & Operations, Publishing & Partnership; DAVID GABRIEL, SVP of Sales & Marketing, Publishing; JEFF YOUNGQUIST, VP of Production & Special Projects; DAN CARR, Executive Director of Publishing Technology; ALEX MORALES, Director of Publishing Operations; DAN EDINGTON, Managing Editor; SUSAN CRESPI, Production Manager; STAN LEE, Chairman Emeritus. For information regarding advertising in Marvel Comics or on Marvel.com, please contact Vit DeBellis, Custom Solutions & Integrated Advertising Manager, at vdebellis@marvel.com. For Marvel subscription inquiries, please call 888-511-9480. Manufactured between 7/6/2018 and 8/7/2018 by LSC COMMUNICATIONS INC., KENDALLVILLE, IN, USA.

10 9 8 7 6 5 4 3 2 1

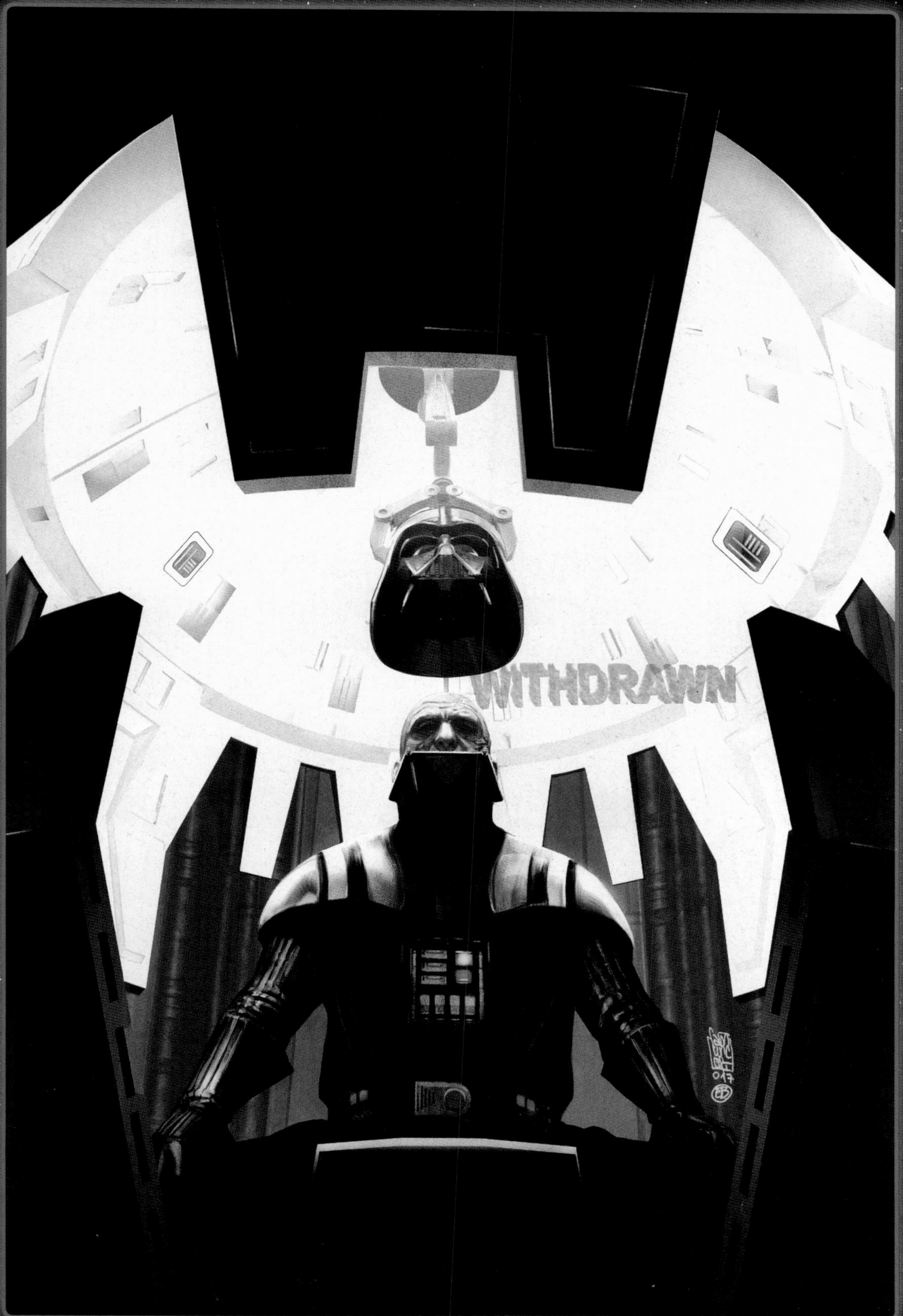

13

BURNING SEAS

Some time has passed since the ascension of Emperor Palpatine, the formation of his great Galactic Empire, and the descent of former Jedi Knight Anakin Skywalker into his new form as twisted half-man, half-machine Darth Vader – Sith apprentice to Palpatine.

Vader and his squad of evil Force-wielding hunters, the Inquisitors, have had great success seeking out the few survivors of the purge that destroyed the noble Jedi Order just prior to Palpatine's rise. Few Jedi remain in the galaxy.

But now, a threat has arisen to the Emperor's still-new, still-vulnerable regime, and Vader must confront both his past and his present....

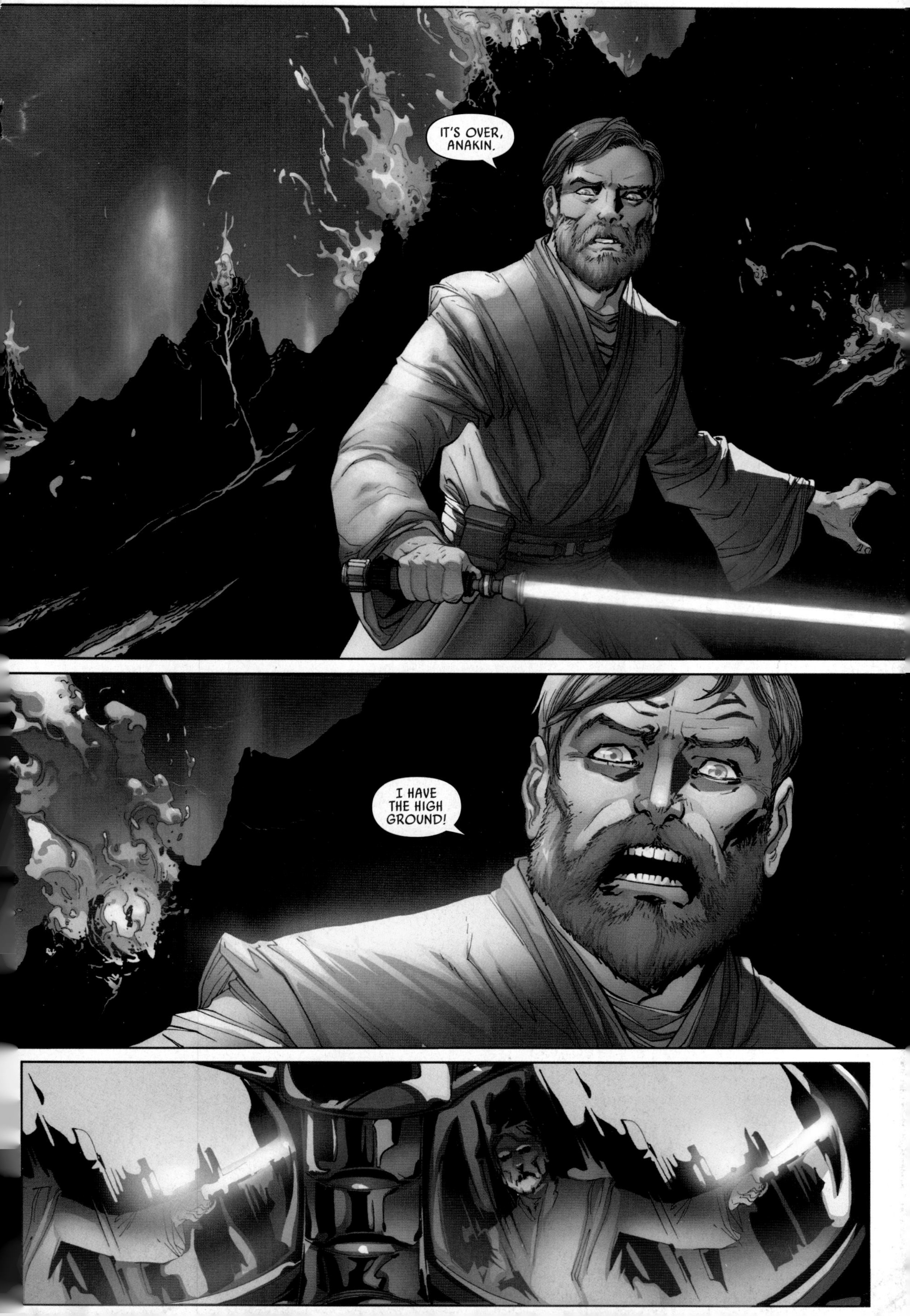
IT'S OVER, ANAKIN.
I HAVE THE HIGH GROUND!

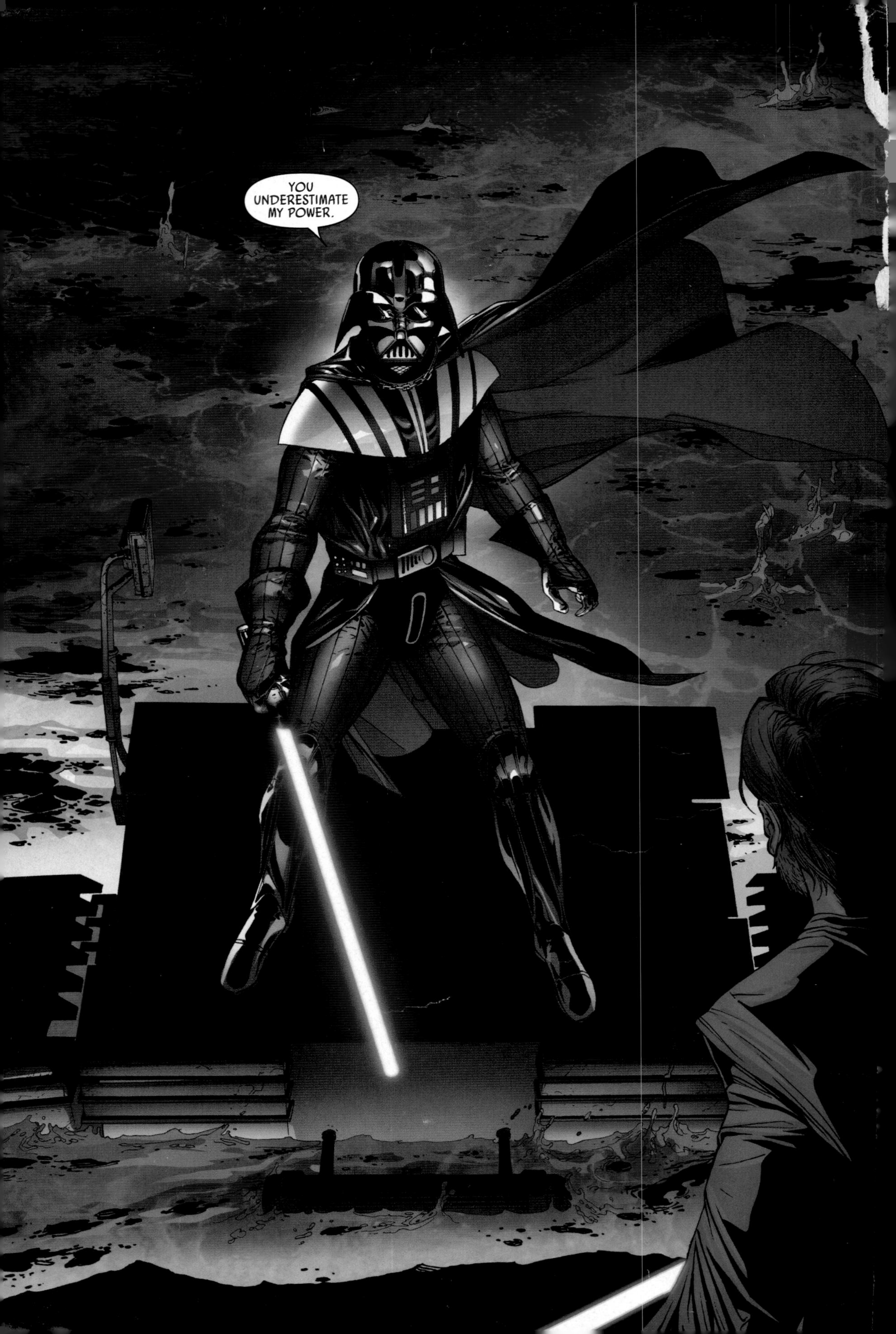
YOU UNDERESTIMATE MY POWER.

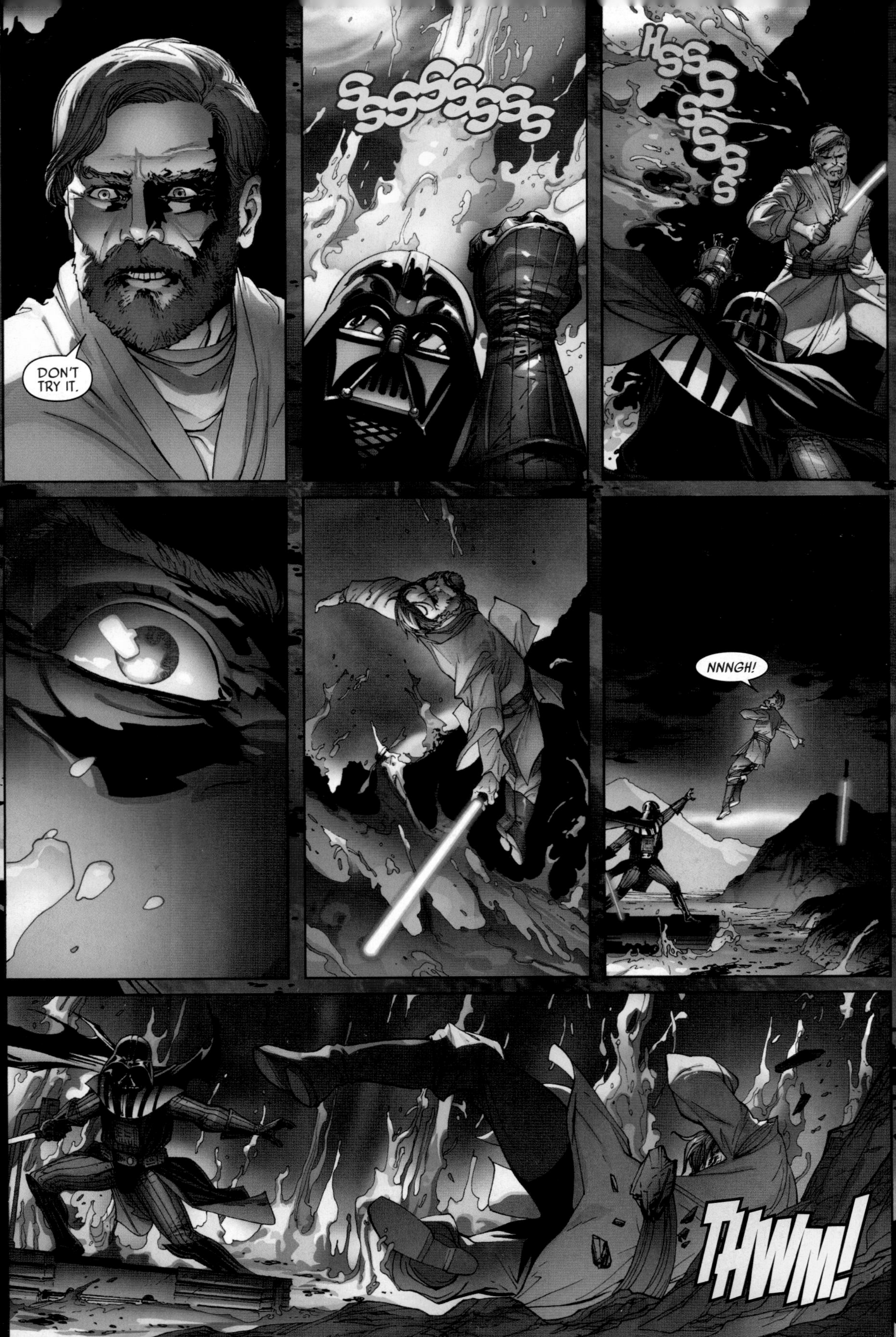
DON'T TRY IT.
SSSSSSSSS
HSSSSSSSS
NNNGH!
THWM!

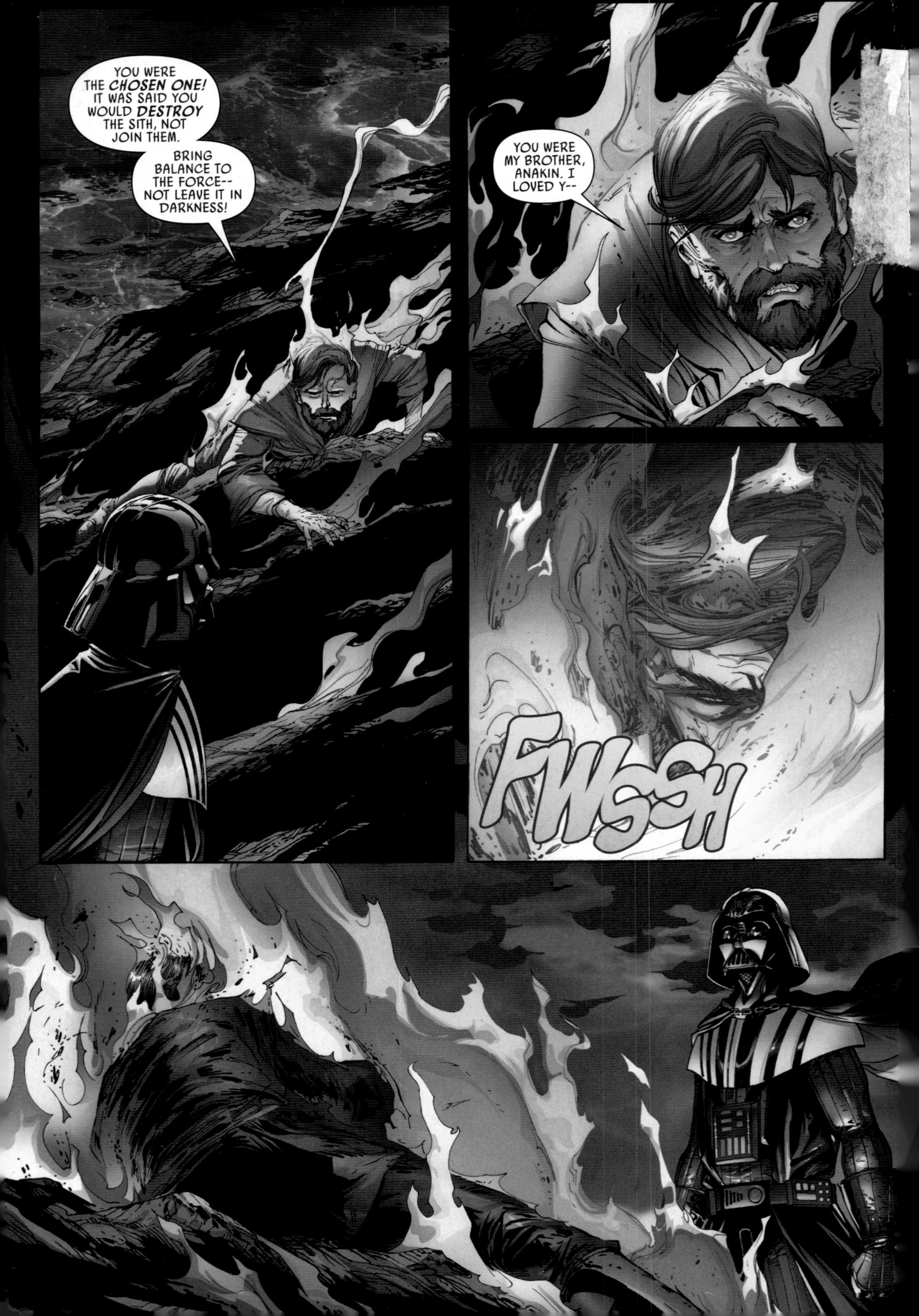
YOU WERE THE CHOSEN ONE! IT WAS SAID YOU WOULD DESTROY THE SITH, NOT JOIN THEM.
BRING BALANCE TO THE FORCE-- NOT LEAVE IT IN DARKNESS!
YOU WERE MY BROTHER, ANAKIN. I LOVED Y--
FWSSH

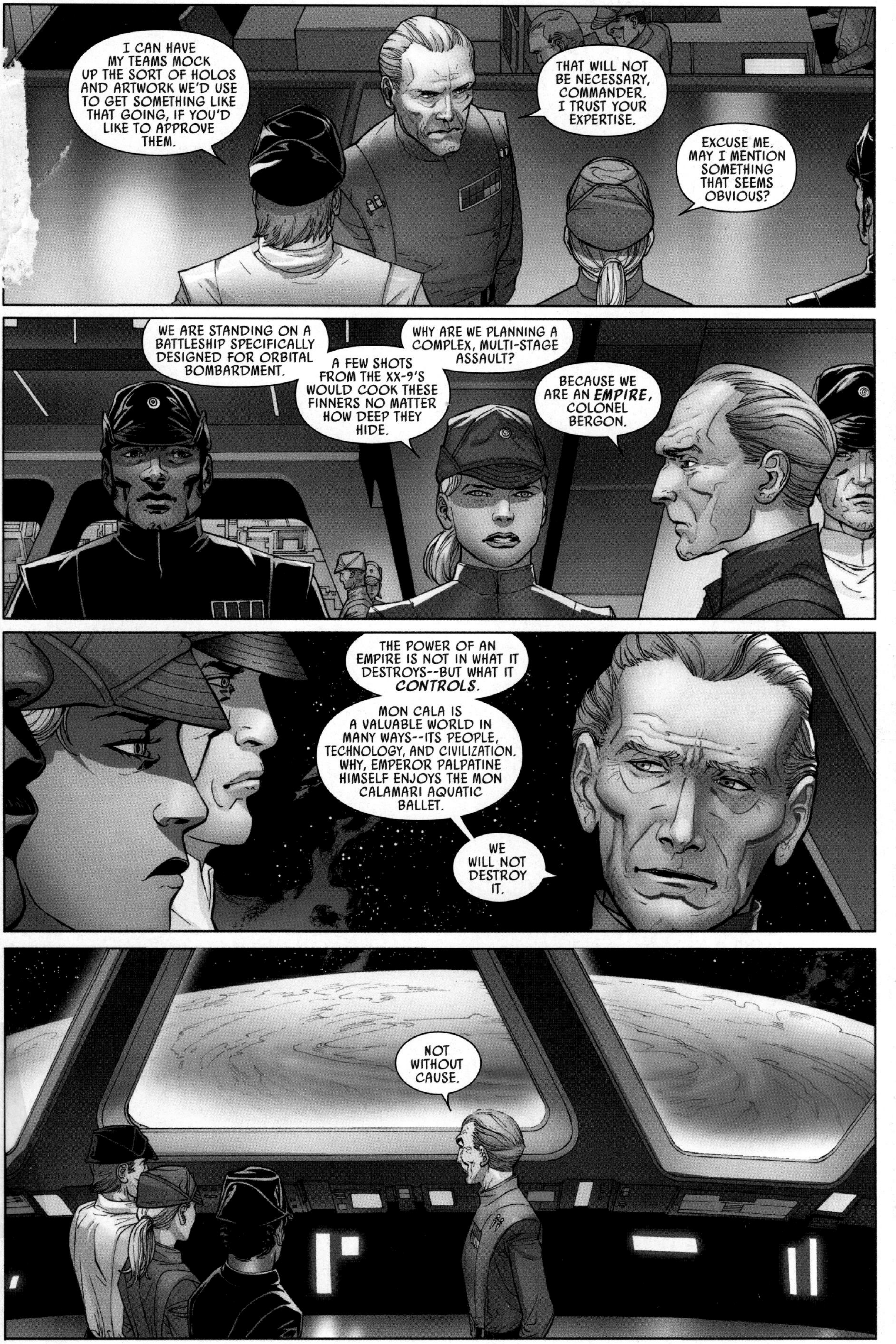
I CAN HAVE MY TEAMS MOCK UP THE SORT OF HOLOS AND ARTWORK WE'D USE TO GET SOMETHING LIKE THAT GOING, IF YOU'D LIKE TO APPROVE THEM.
THAT WILL NOT BE NECESSARY, COMMANDER. I TRUST YOUR EXPERTISE.
EXCUSE ME. MAY I MENTION SOMETHING THAT SEEMS OBVIOUS?
WE ARE STANDING ON A BATTLESHIP SPECIFICALLY DESIGNED FOR ORBITAL BOMBARDMENT.
WHY ARE WE PLANNING A COMPLEX, MULTI-STAGE ASSAULT?
A FEW SHOTS FROM THE XX-9'S WOULD COOK THESE FINNERS NO MATTER HOW DEEP THEY HIDE.
BECAUSE WE ARE AN *EMPIRE,* COLONEL BERGON.
THE POWER OF AN EMPIRE IS NOT IN WHAT IT DESTROYS--BUT WHAT IT *CONTROLS*.
MON CALA IS A VALUABLE WORLD IN MANY WAYS--ITS PEOPLE, TECHNOLOGY, AND CIVILIZATION. WHY, EMPEROR PALPATINE HIMSELF ENJOYS THE MON CALAMARI AQUATIC BALLET.
WE WILL NOT DESTROY IT.
NOT WITHOUT CAUSE.

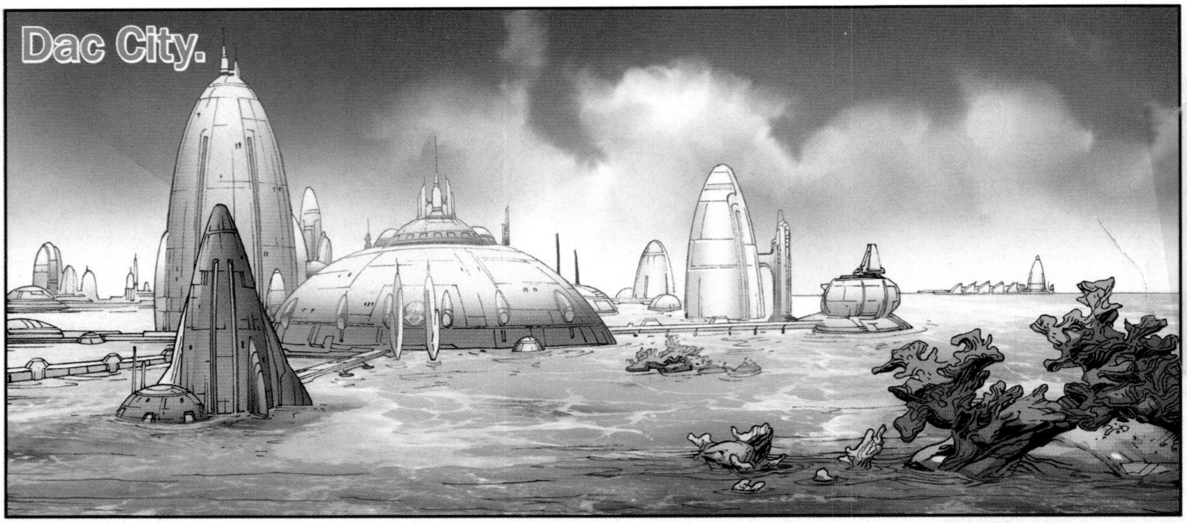
Dac City.

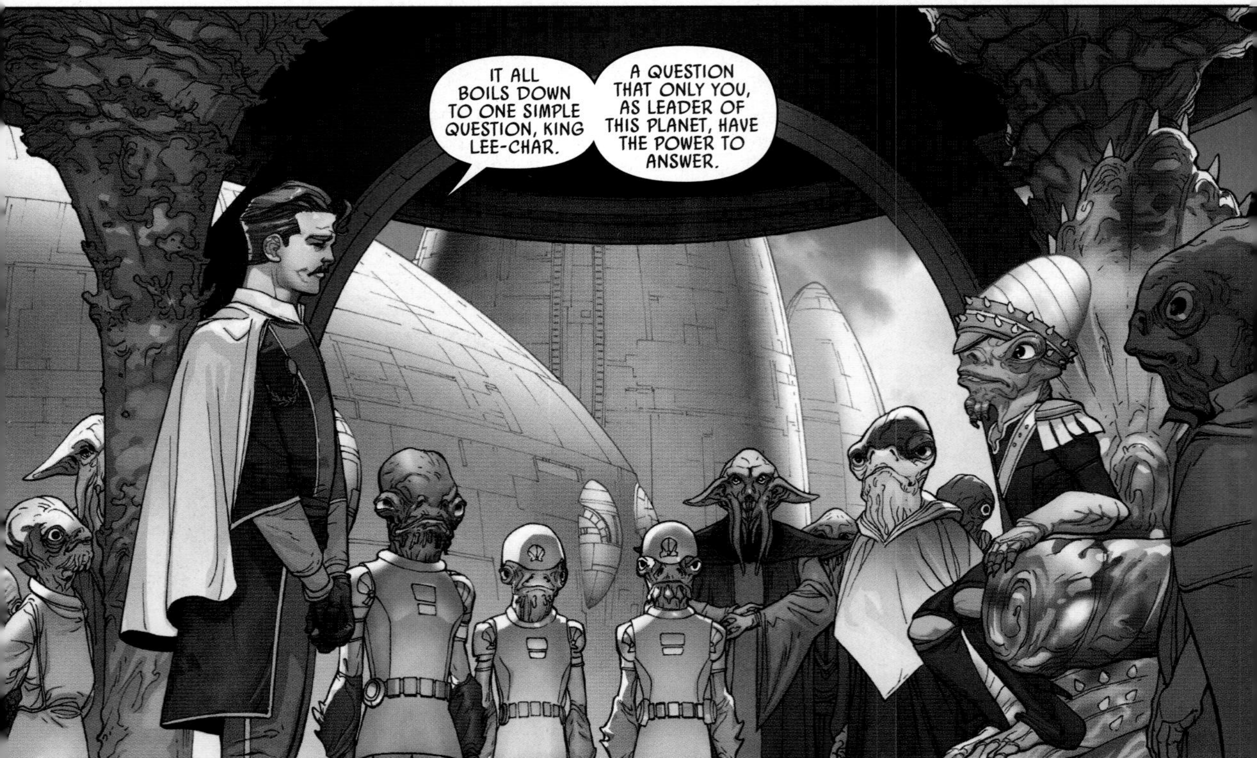
IT ALL BOILS DOWN TO ONE SIMPLE QUESTION, KING LEE-CHAR.
A QUESTION THAT ONLY YOU, AS LEADER OF THIS PLANET, HAVE THE POWER TO ANSWER.

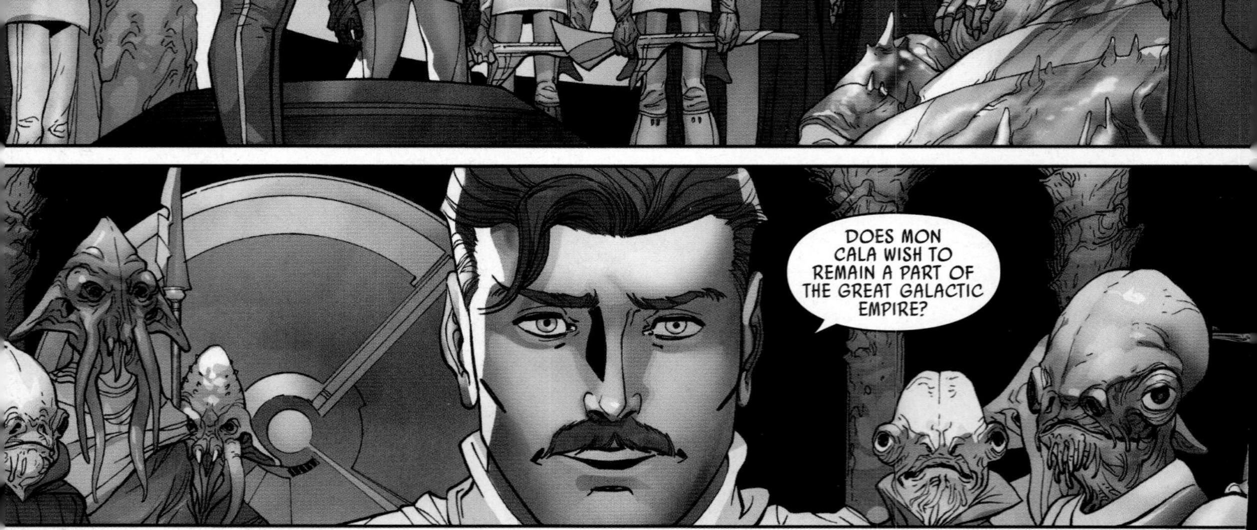
DOES MON CALA WISH TO REMAIN A PART OF THE GREAT GALACTIC EMPIRE?

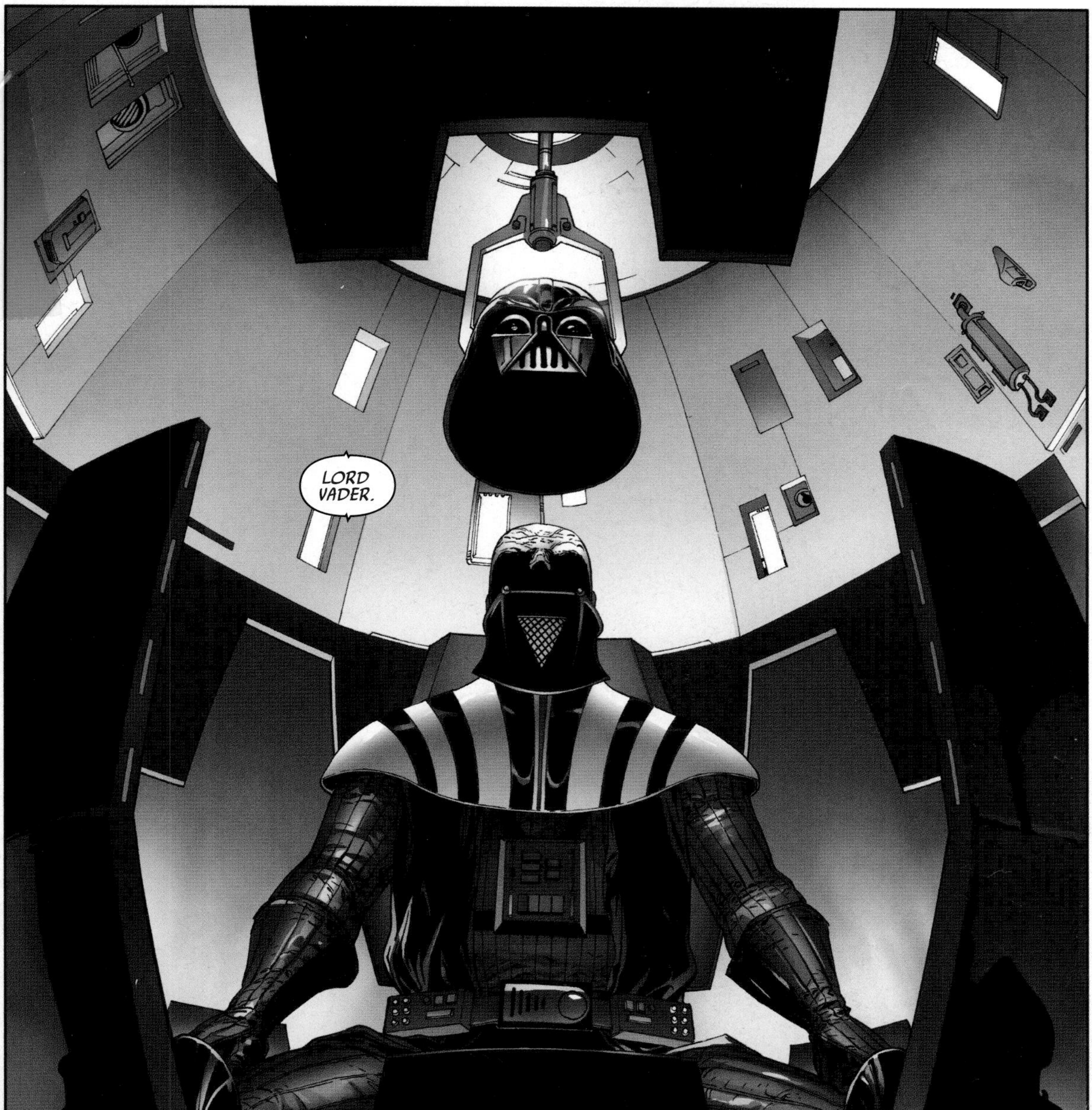
LORD VADER.

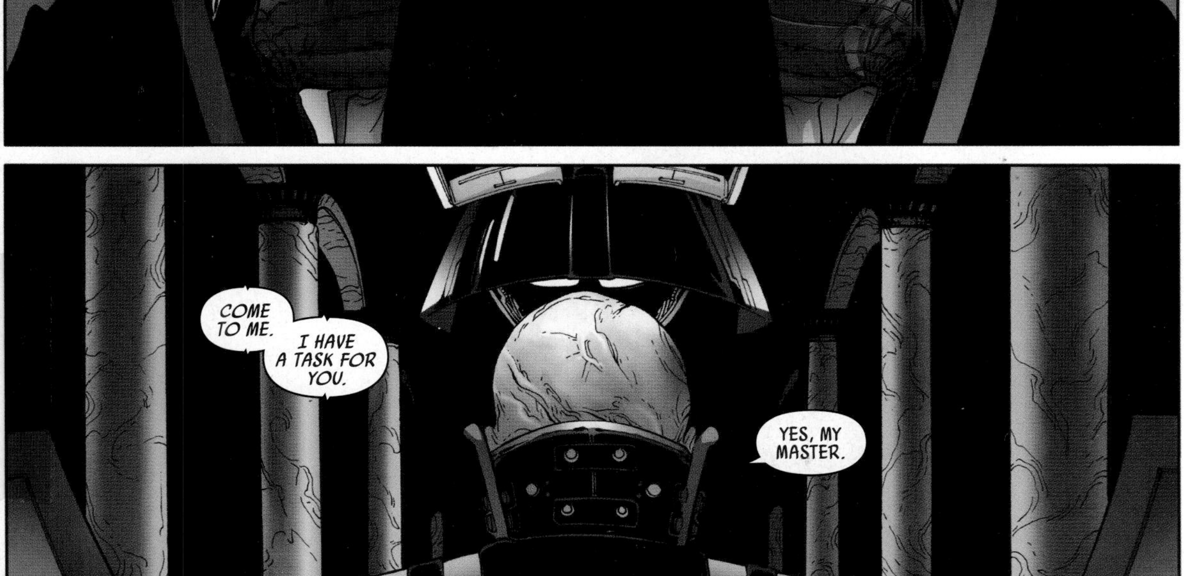
COME TO ME.
I HAVE A TASK FOR YOU.
YES, MY MASTER.

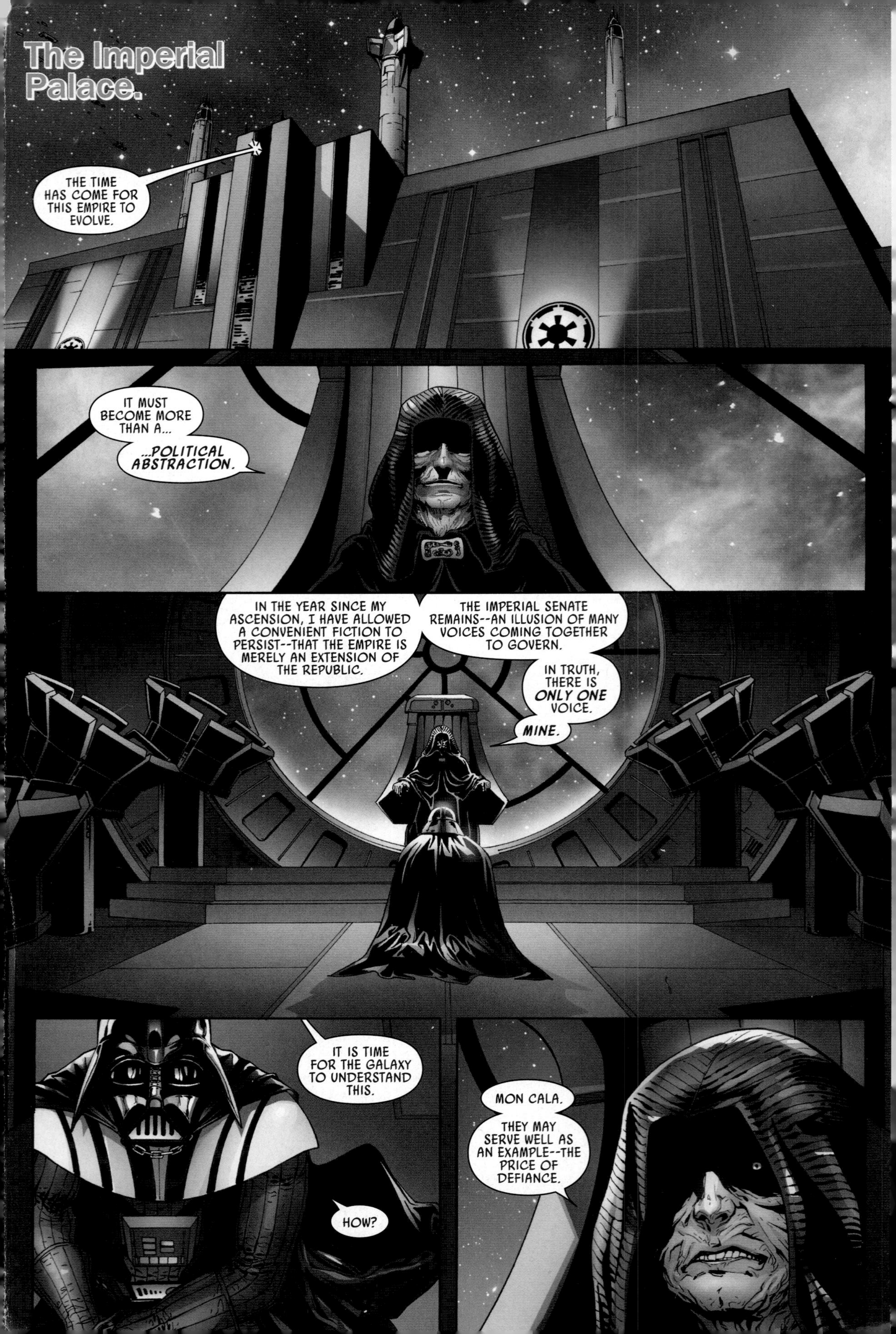
The Imperial Palace.
THE TIME HAS COME FOR THIS EMPIRE TO EVOLVE.
IT MUST BECOME MORE THAN A...
...POLITICAL ABSTRACTION.
IN THE YEAR SINCE MY ASCENSION, I HAVE ALLOWED A CONVENIENT FICTION TO PERSIST--THAT THE EMPIRE IS MERELY AN EXTENSION OF THE REPUBLIC.
THE IMPERIAL SENATE REMAINS--AN ILLUSION OF MANY VOICES COMING TOGETHER TO GOVERN.
IN TRUTH, THERE IS ONLY ONE VOICE.
MINE.
IT IS TIME FOR THE GALAXY TO UNDERSTAND THIS.
HOW?
MON CALA.
THEY MAY SERVE WELL AS AN EXAMPLE--THE PRICE OF DEFIANCE.

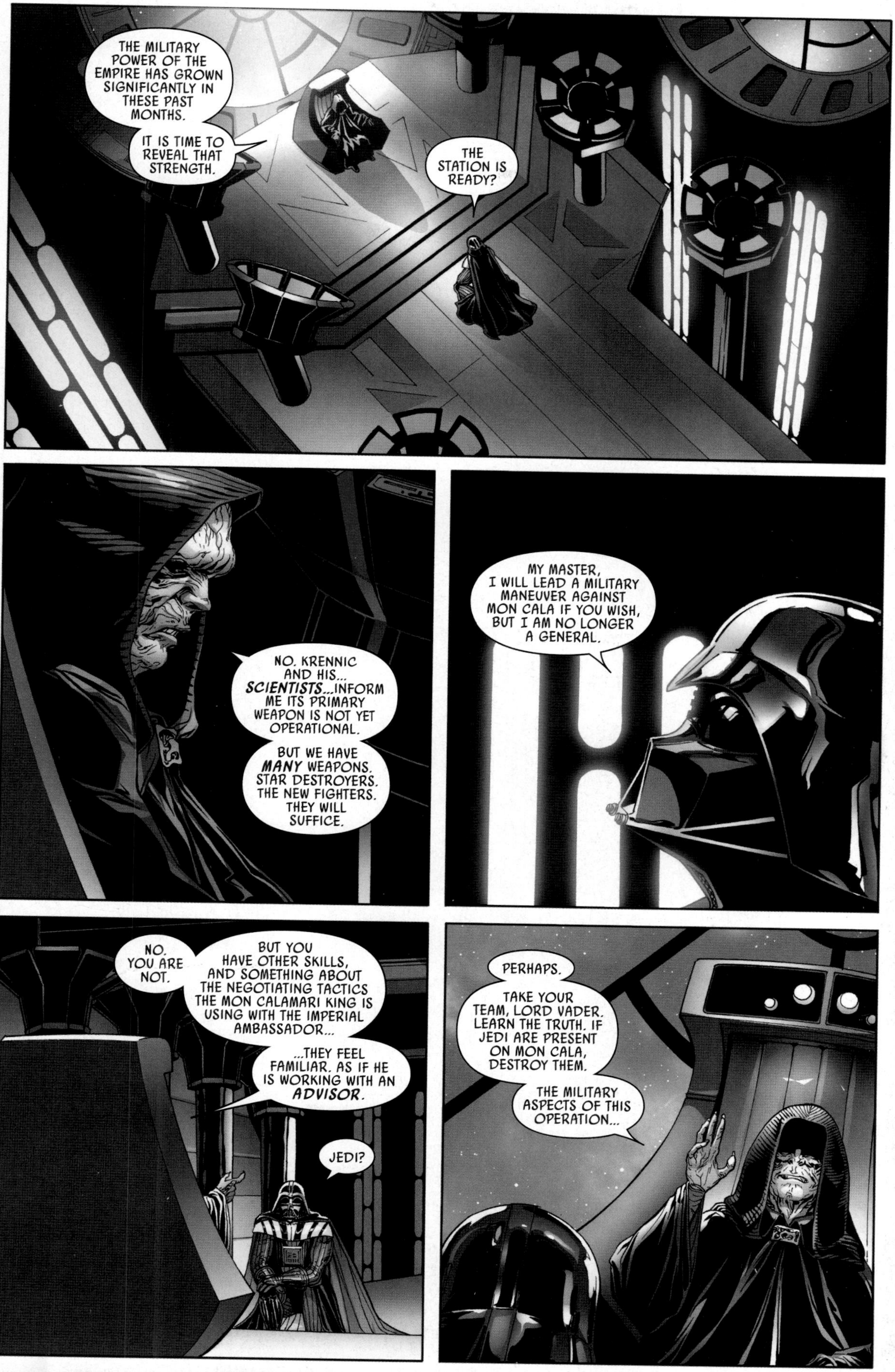

THE MILITARY POWER OF THE EMPIRE HAS GROWN SIGNIFICANTLY IN THESE PAST MONTHS.
IT IS TIME TO REVEAL THAT STRENGTH.
THE STATION IS READY?
NO. KRENNIC AND HIS... SCIENTISTS...INFORM ME ITS PRIMARY WEAPON IS NOT YET OPERATIONAL.
BUT WE HAVE MANY WEAPONS. STAR DESTROYERS. THE NEW FIGHTERS. THEY WILL SUFFICE.
MY MASTER, I WILL LEAD A MILITARY MANEUVER AGAINST MON CALA IF YOU WISH, BUT I AM NO LONGER A GENERAL.
NO. YOU ARE NOT.
BUT YOU HAVE OTHER SKILLS, AND SOMETHING ABOUT THE NEGOTIATING TACTICS THE MON CALAMARI KING IS USING WITH THE IMPERIAL AMBASSADOR...
...THEY FEEL FAMILIAR. AS IF HE IS WORKING WITH AN ADVISOR.
JEDI?
PERHAPS.
TAKE YOUR TEAM, LORD VADER. LEARN THE TRUTH. IF JEDI ARE PRESENT ON MON CALA, DESTROY THEM.
THE MILITARY ASPECTS OF THIS OPERATION...

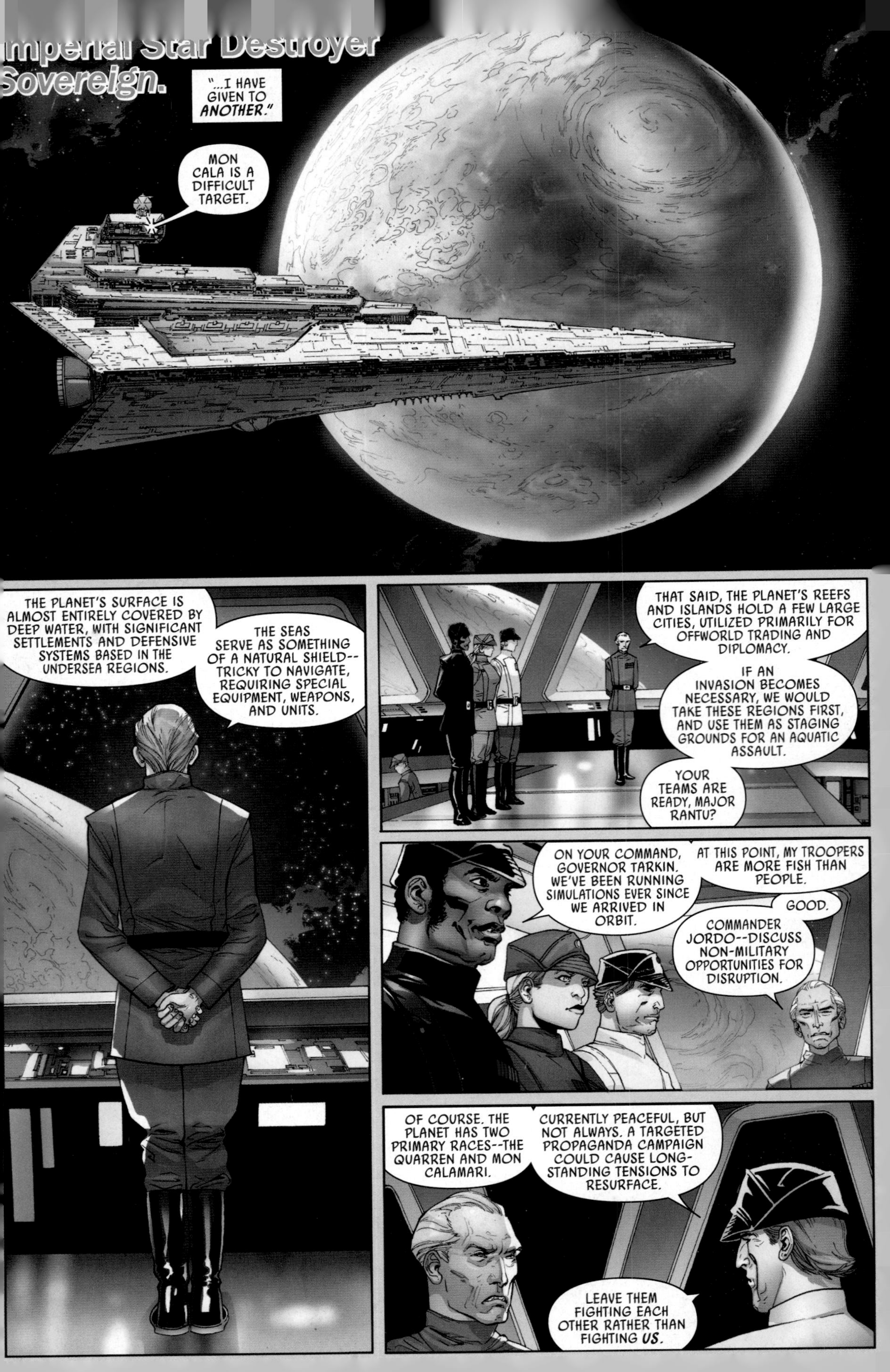
Imperial Star Destroyer Sovereign.
"...I HAVE GIVEN TO ANOTHER."
MON CALA IS A DIFFICULT TARGET.
THE PLANET'S SURFACE IS ALMOST ENTIRELY COVERED BY DEEP WATER, WITH SIGNIFICANT SETTLEMENTS AND DEFENSIVE SYSTEMS BASED IN THE UNDERSEA REGIONS.
THE SEAS SERVE AS SOMETHING OF A NATURAL SHIELD--TRICKY TO NAVIGATE, REQUIRING SPECIAL EQUIPMENT, WEAPONS, AND UNITS.
THAT SAID, THE PLANET'S REEFS AND ISLANDS HOLD A FEW LARGE CITIES, UTILIZED PRIMARILY FOR OFFWORLD TRADING AND DIPLOMACY.
IF AN INVASION BECOMES NECESSARY, WE WOULD TAKE THESE REGIONS FIRST, AND USE THEM AS STAGING GROUNDS FOR AN AQUATIC ASSAULT.
YOUR TEAMS ARE READY, MAJOR RANTU?
ON YOUR COMMAND, GOVERNOR TARKIN. WE'VE BEEN RUNNING SIMULATIONS EVER SINCE WE ARRIVED IN ORBIT.
AT THIS POINT, MY TROOPERS ARE MORE FISH THAN PEOPLE.
GOOD.
COMMANDER JORDO--DISCUSS NON-MILITARY OPPORTUNITIES FOR DISRUPTION.
OF COURSE. THE PLANET HAS TWO PRIMARY RACES--THE QUARREN AND MON CALAMARI.
CURRENTLY PEACEFUL, BUT NOT ALWAYS. A TARGETED PROPAGANDA CAMPAIGN COULD CAUSE LONG-STANDING TENSIONS TO RESURFACE.
LEAVE THEM FIGHTING EACH OTHER RATHER THAN FIGHTING US.

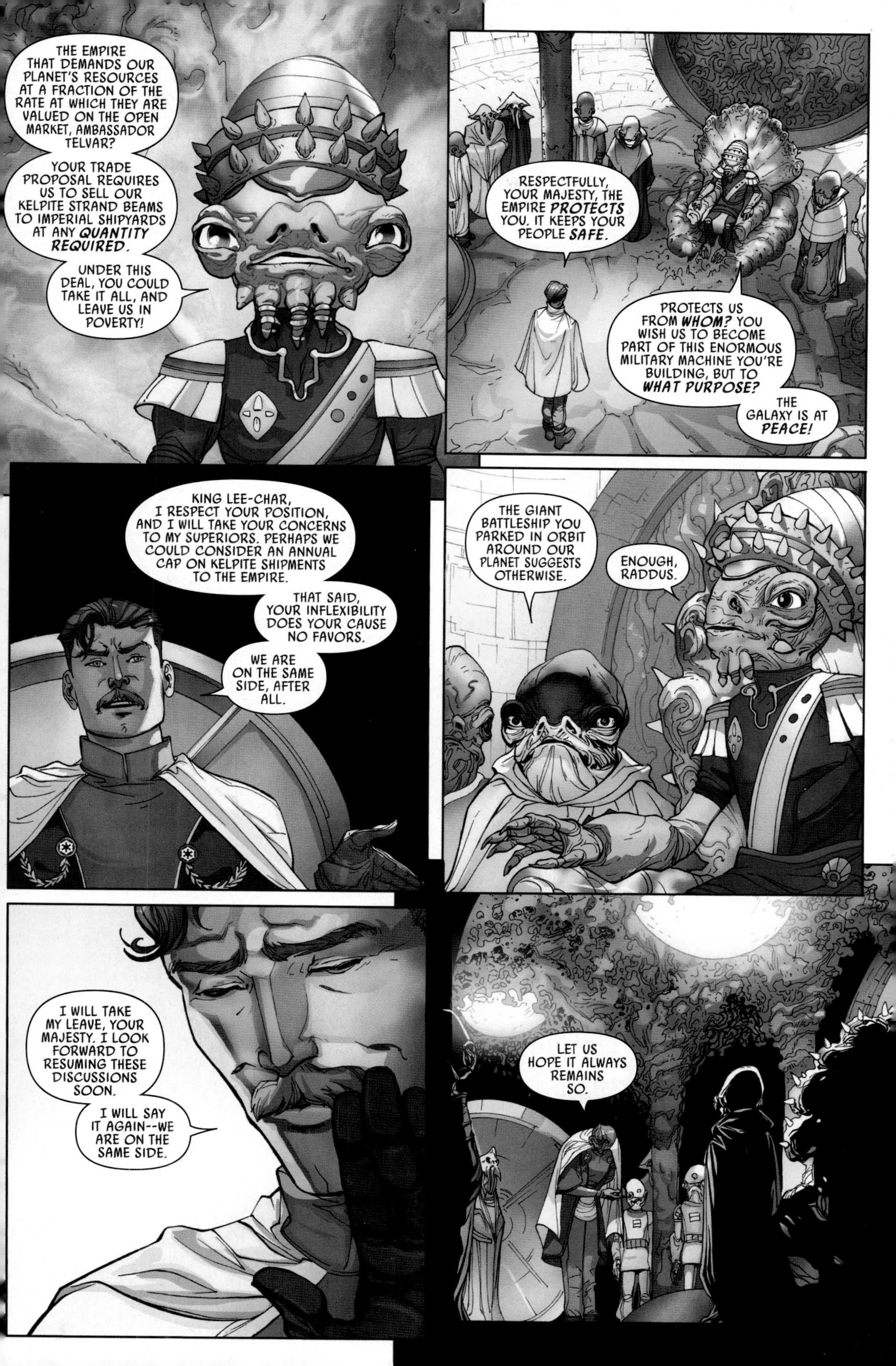
THE EMPIRE THAT DEMANDS OUR PLANET'S RESOURCES AT A FRACTION OF THE RATE AT WHICH THEY ARE VALUED ON THE OPEN MARKET, AMBASSADOR TELVAR?
YOUR TRADE PROPOSAL REQUIRES US TO SELL OUR KELPITE STRAND BEAMS TO IMPERIAL SHIPYARDS AT ANY QUANTITY REQUIRED.
UNDER THIS DEAL, YOU COULD TAKE IT ALL, AND LEAVE US IN POVERTY!
RESPECTFULLY, YOUR MAJESTY, THE EMPIRE PROTECTS YOU. IT KEEPS YOUR PEOPLE SAFE.
PROTECTS US FROM WHOM? YOU WISH US TO BECOME PART OF THIS ENORMOUS MILITARY MACHINE YOU'RE BUILDING, BUT TO WHAT PURPOSE?
THE GALAXY IS AT PEACE!
KING LEE-CHAR, I RESPECT YOUR POSITION, AND I WILL TAKE YOUR CONCERNS TO MY SUPERIORS. PERHAPS WE COULD CONSIDER AN ANNUAL CAP ON KELPITE SHIPMENTS TO THE EMPIRE.
THAT SAID, YOUR INFLEXIBILITY DOES YOUR CAUSE NO FAVORS.
WE ARE ON THE SAME SIDE, AFTER ALL.
THE GIANT BATTLESHIP YOU PARKED IN ORBIT AROUND OUR PLANET SUGGESTS OTHERWISE.
ENOUGH, RADDUS.
I WILL TAKE MY LEAVE, YOUR MAJESTY. I LOOK FORWARD TO RESUMING THESE DISCUSSIONS SOON.
I WILL SAY IT AGAIN--WE ARE ON THE SAME SIDE.
LET US HOPE IT ALWAYS REMAINS SO.

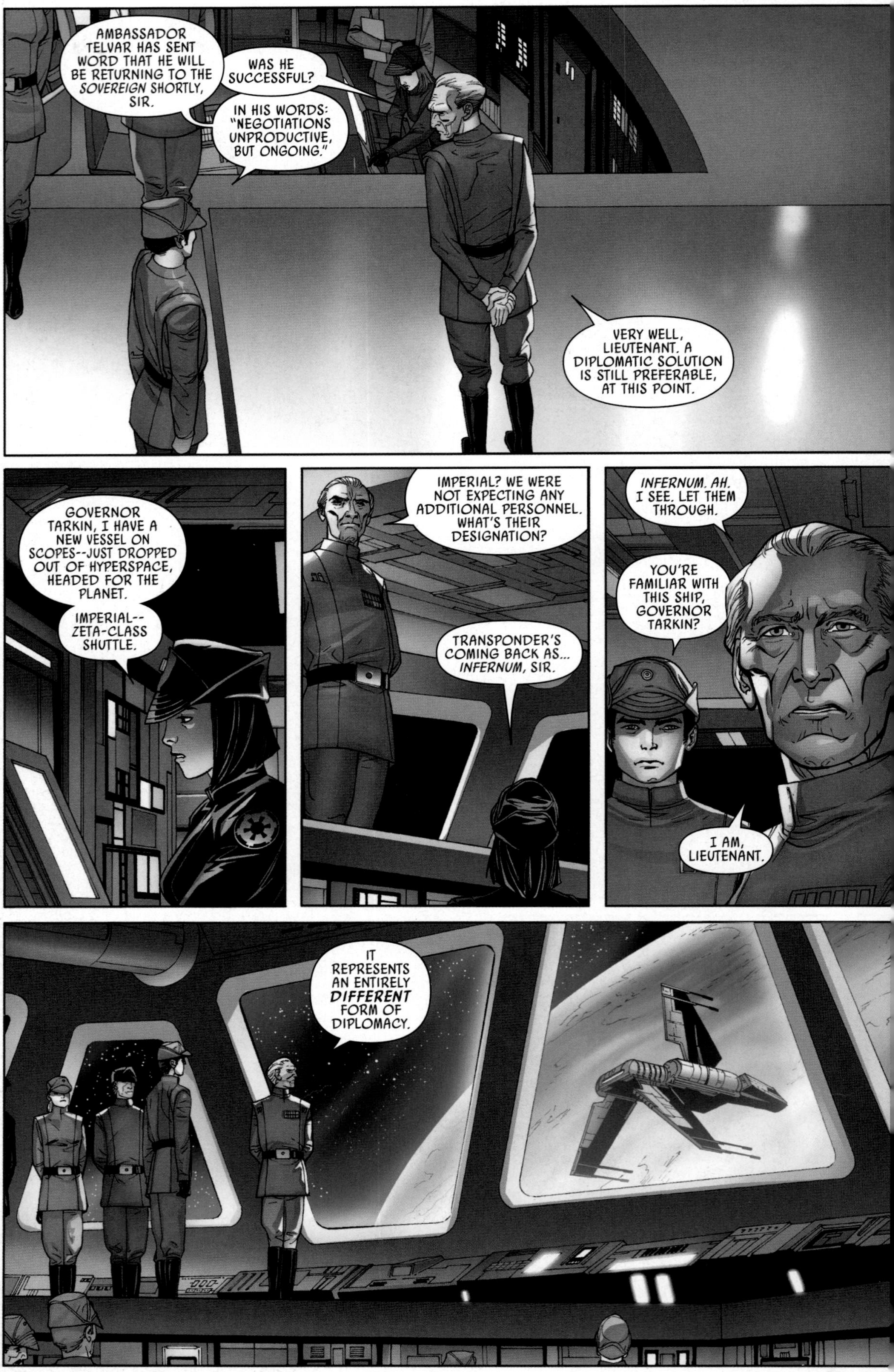
AMBASSADOR TELVAR HAS SENT WORD THAT HE WILL BE RETURNING TO THE *SOVEREIGN* SHORTLY, SIR.
WAS HE SUCCESSFUL?
IN HIS WORDS: "NEGOTIATIONS UNPRODUCTIVE, BUT ONGOING."
VERY WELL, LIEUTENANT. A DIPLOMATIC SOLUTION IS STILL PREFERABLE, AT THIS POINT.
GOVERNOR TARKIN, I HAVE A NEW VESSEL ON SCOPES--JUST DROPPED OUT OF HYPERSPACE, HEADED FOR THE PLANET.
IMPERIAL--ZETA-CLASS SHUTTLE.
IMPERIAL? WE WERE NOT EXPECTING ANY ADDITIONAL PERSONNEL. WHAT'S THEIR DESIGNATION?
TRANSPONDER'S COMING BACK AS... *INFERNUM*, SIR.
INFERNUM. AH. I SEE. LET THEM THROUGH.
YOU'RE FAMILIAR WITH THIS SHIP, GOVERNOR TARKIN?
I AM, LIEUTENANT.
IT REPRESENTS AN ENTIRELY ***DIFFERENT*** FORM OF DIPLOMACY.

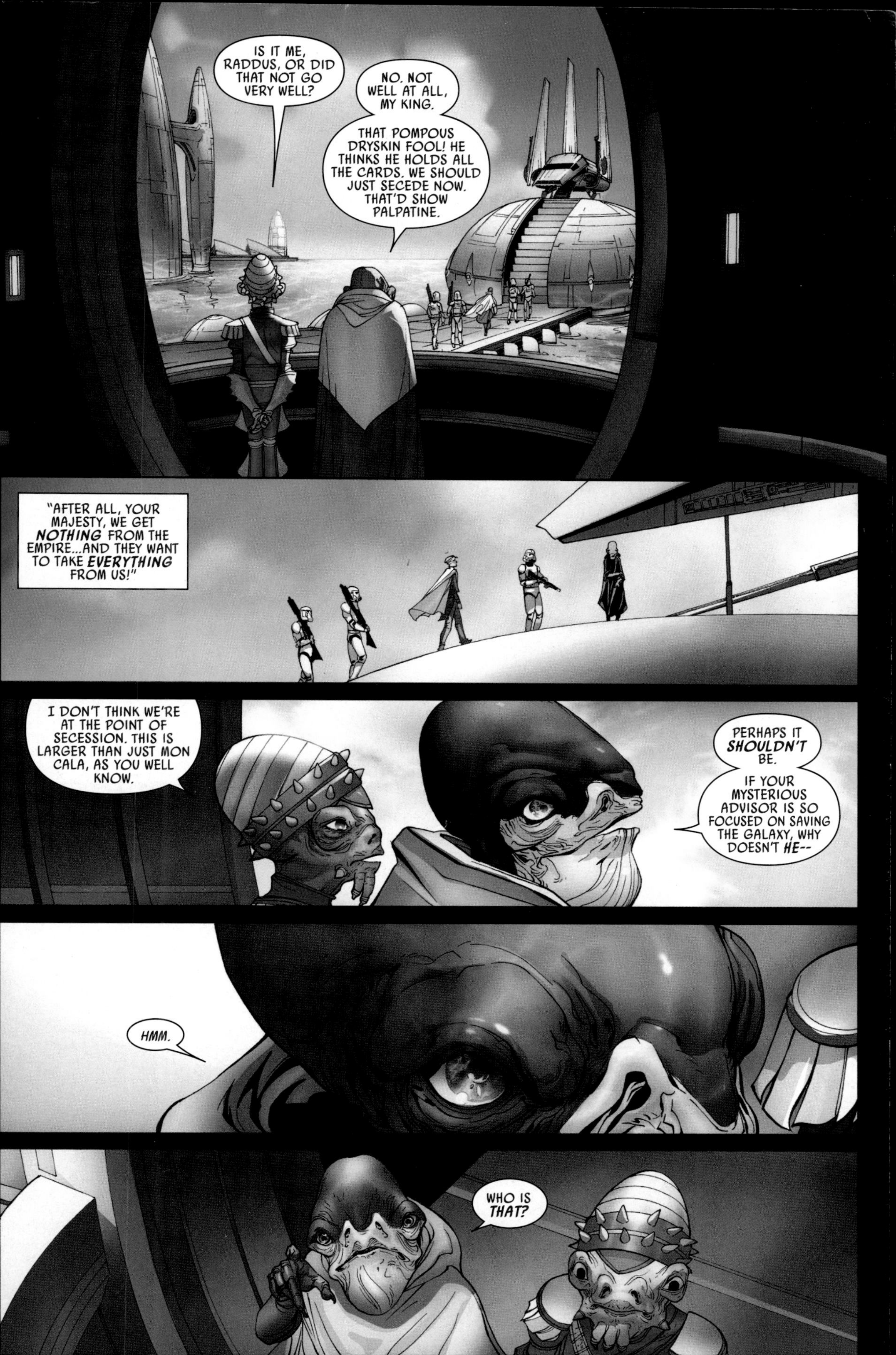
IS IT ME, RADDUS, OR DID THAT NOT GO VERY WELL?
NO. NOT WELL AT ALL, MY KING.
THAT POMPOUS DRYSKIN FOOL! HE THINKS HE HOLDS ALL THE CARDS. WE SHOULD JUST SECEDE NOW. THAT'D SHOW PALPATINE.
"AFTER ALL, YOUR MAJESTY, WE GET NOTHING FROM THE EMPIRE...AND THEY WANT TO TAKE EVERYTHING FROM US!"
I DON'T THINK WE'RE AT THE POINT OF SECESSION. THIS IS LARGER THAN JUST MON CALA, AS YOU WELL KNOW.
PERHAPS IT SHOULDN'T BE.
IF YOUR MYSTERIOUS ADVISOR IS SO FOCUSED ON SAVING THE GALAXY, WHY DOESN'T HE--
HMM.
WHO IS THAT?

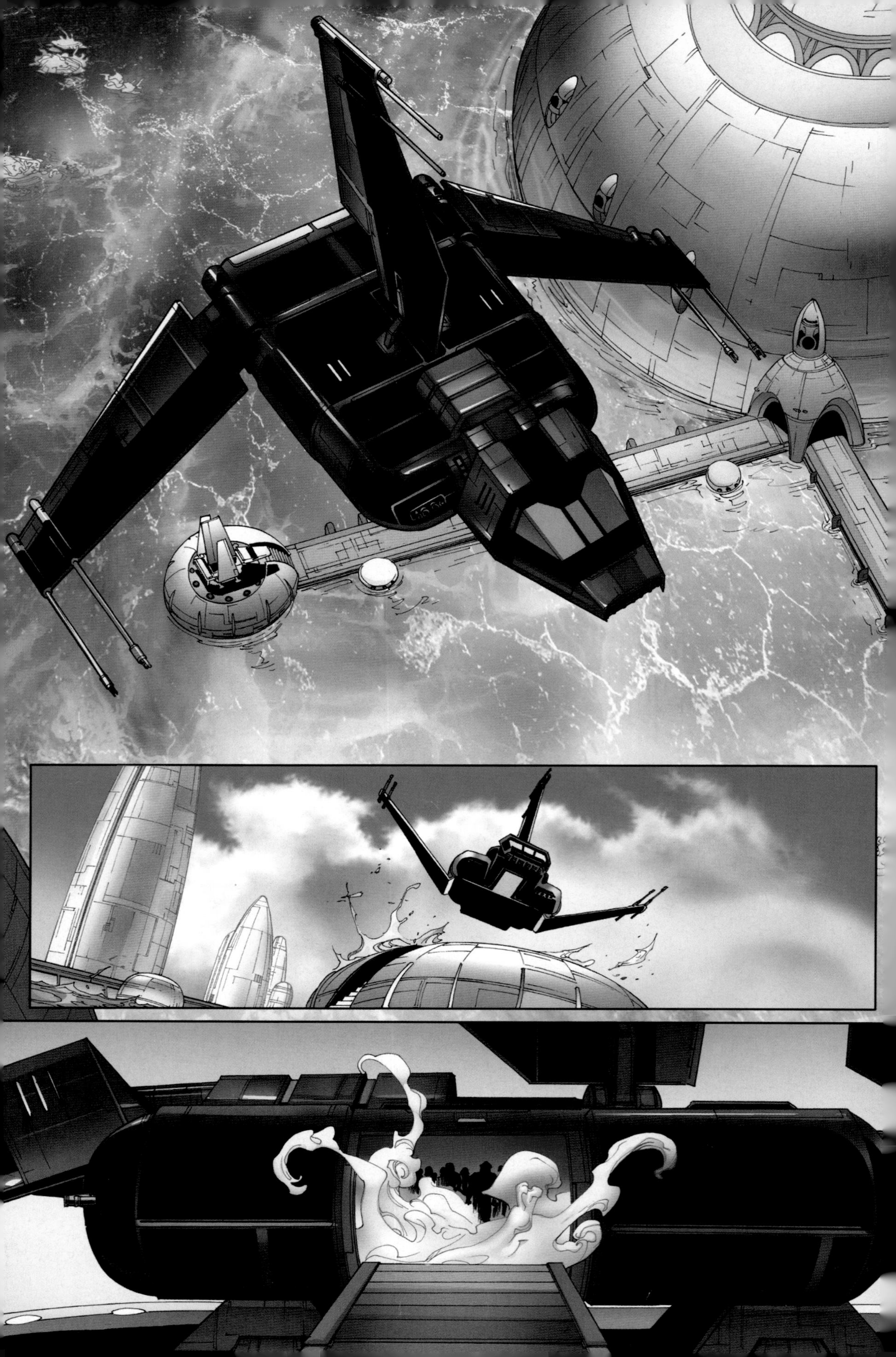

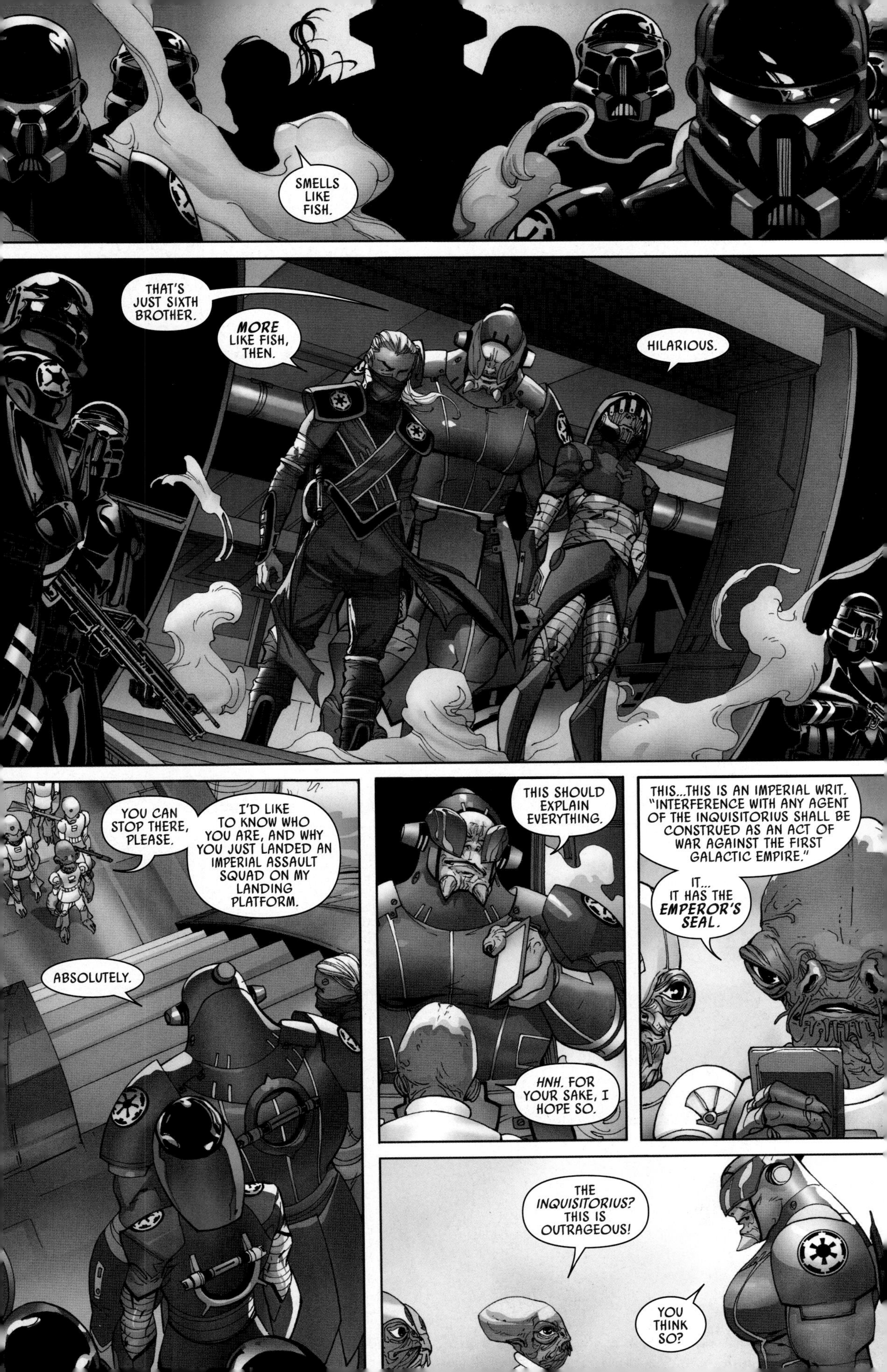
SMELLS LIKE FISH.
THAT'S JUST SIXTH BROTHER.
MORE LIKE FISH, THEN.
HILARIOUS.
YOU CAN STOP THERE, PLEASE.
I'D LIKE TO KNOW WHO YOU ARE, AND WHY YOU JUST LANDED AN IMPERIAL ASSAULT SQUAD ON MY LANDING PLATFORM.
ABSOLUTELY.
THIS SHOULD EXPLAIN EVERYTHING.
HNH. FOR YOUR SAKE, I HOPE SO.
THIS...THIS IS AN IMPERIAL WRIT. "INTERFERENCE WITH ANY AGENT OF THE INQUISITORIUS SHALL BE CONSTRUED AS AN ACT OF WAR AGAINST THE FIRST GALACTIC EMPIRE."
IT... IT HAS THE EMPEROR'S SEAL.
THE INQUISITORIUS? THIS IS OUTRAGEOUS!
YOU THINK SO?

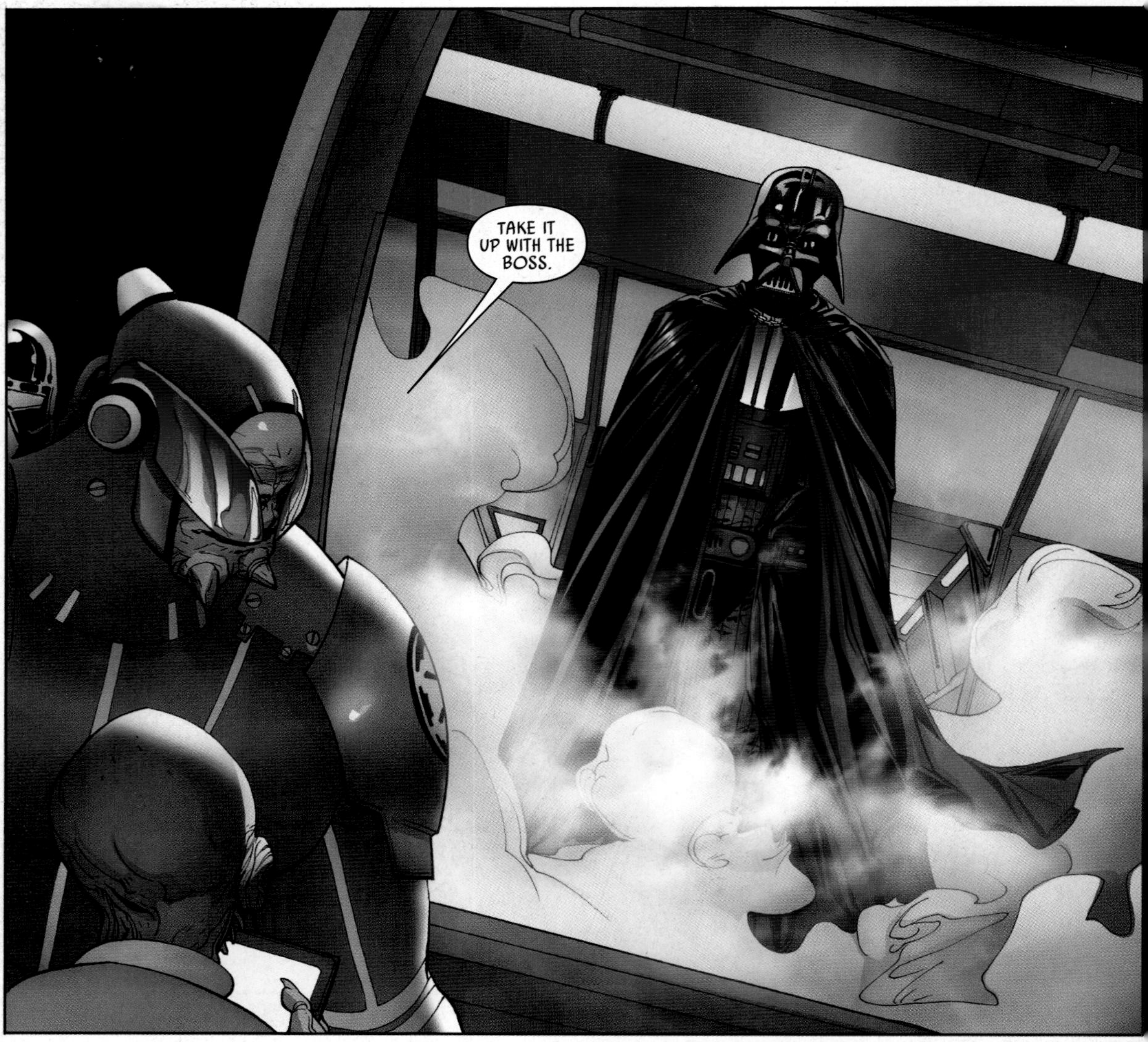
TAKE IT UP WITH THE BOSS.

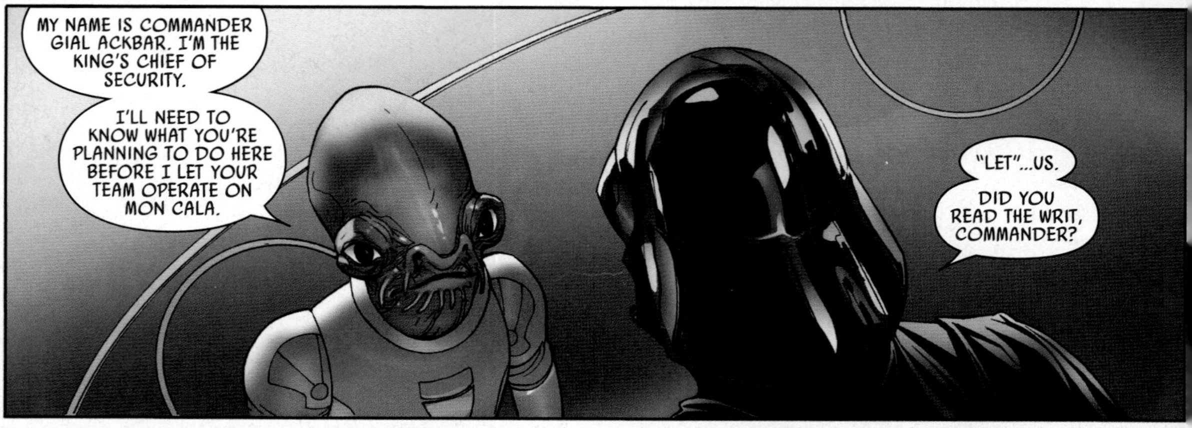
MY NAME IS COMMANDER GIAL ACKBAR. I'M THE KING'S CHIEF OF SECURITY.
I'LL NEED TO KNOW WHAT YOU'RE PLANNING TO DO HERE BEFORE I LET YOUR TEAM OPERATE ON MON CALA.
"LET"...US.
DID YOU READ THE WRIT, COMMANDER?

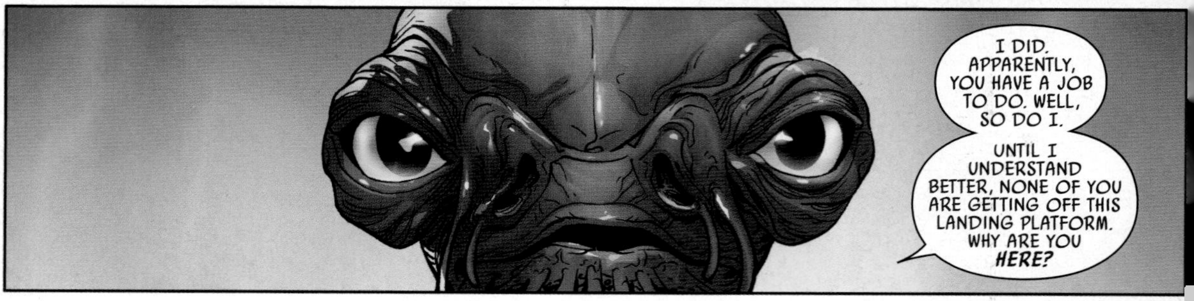
I DID. APPARENTLY, YOU HAVE A JOB TO DO. WELL, SO DO I.
UNTIL I UNDERSTAND BETTER, NONE OF YOU ARE GETTING OFF THIS LANDING PLATFORM. WHY ARE YOU *HERE?*

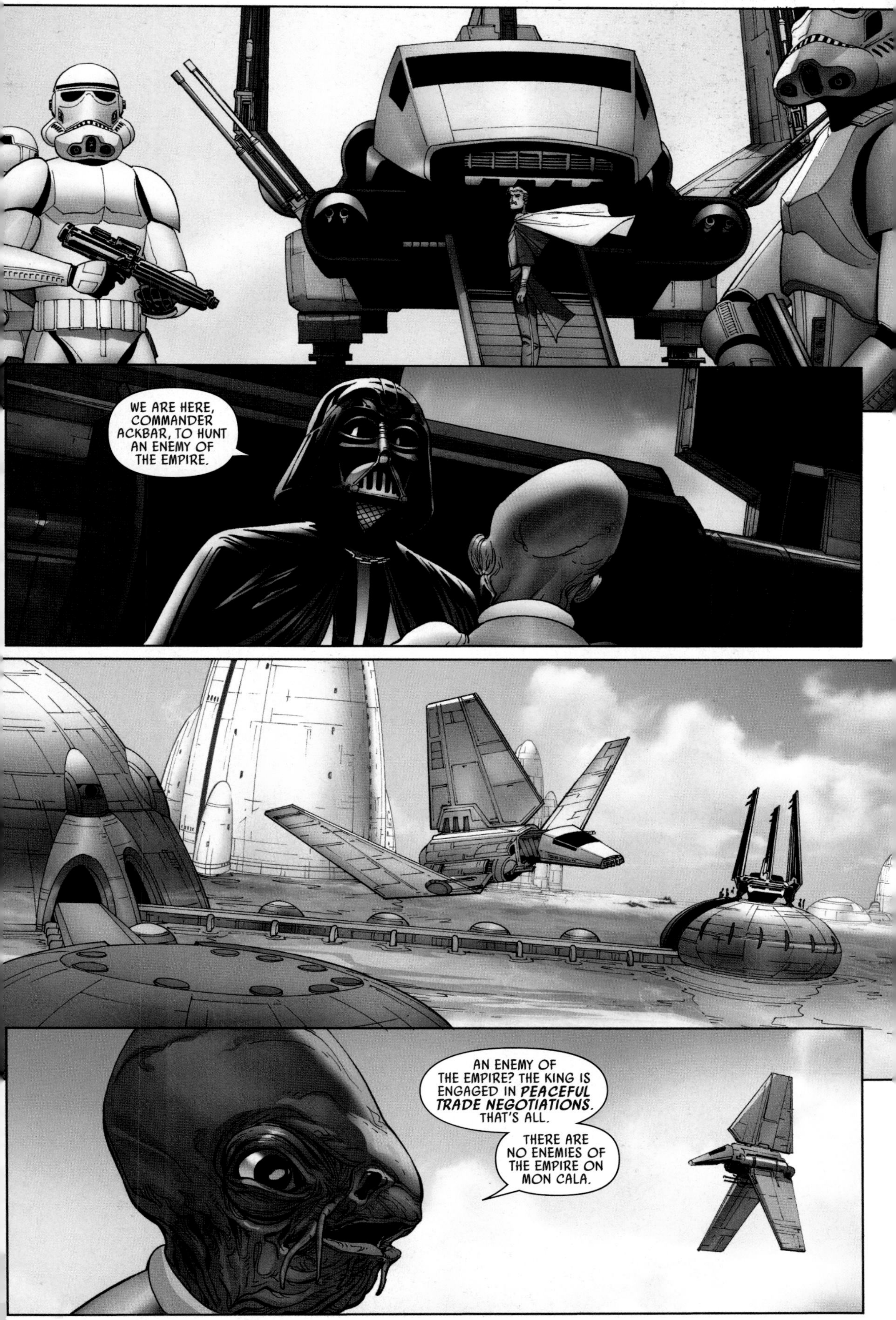
WE ARE HERE, COMMANDER ACKBAR, TO HUNT AN ENEMY OF THE EMPIRE.
AN ENEMY OF THE EMPIRE? THE KING IS ENGAGED IN *PEACEFUL TRADE NEGOTIATIONS*. THAT'S ALL.
THERE ARE NO ENEMIES OF THE EMPIRE ON MON CALA.

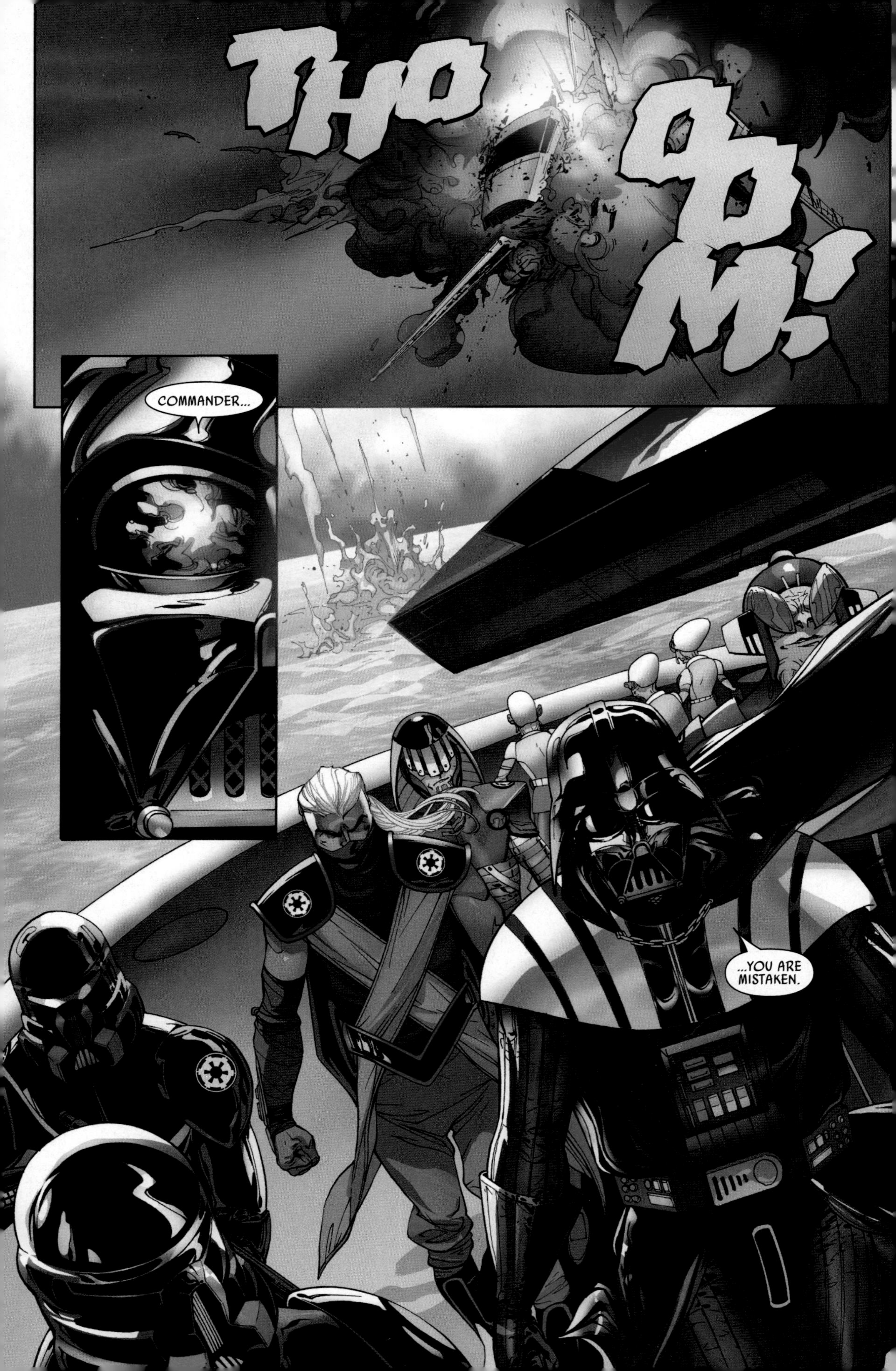
THOOOM!
COMMANDER...
...YOU ARE MISTAKEN.

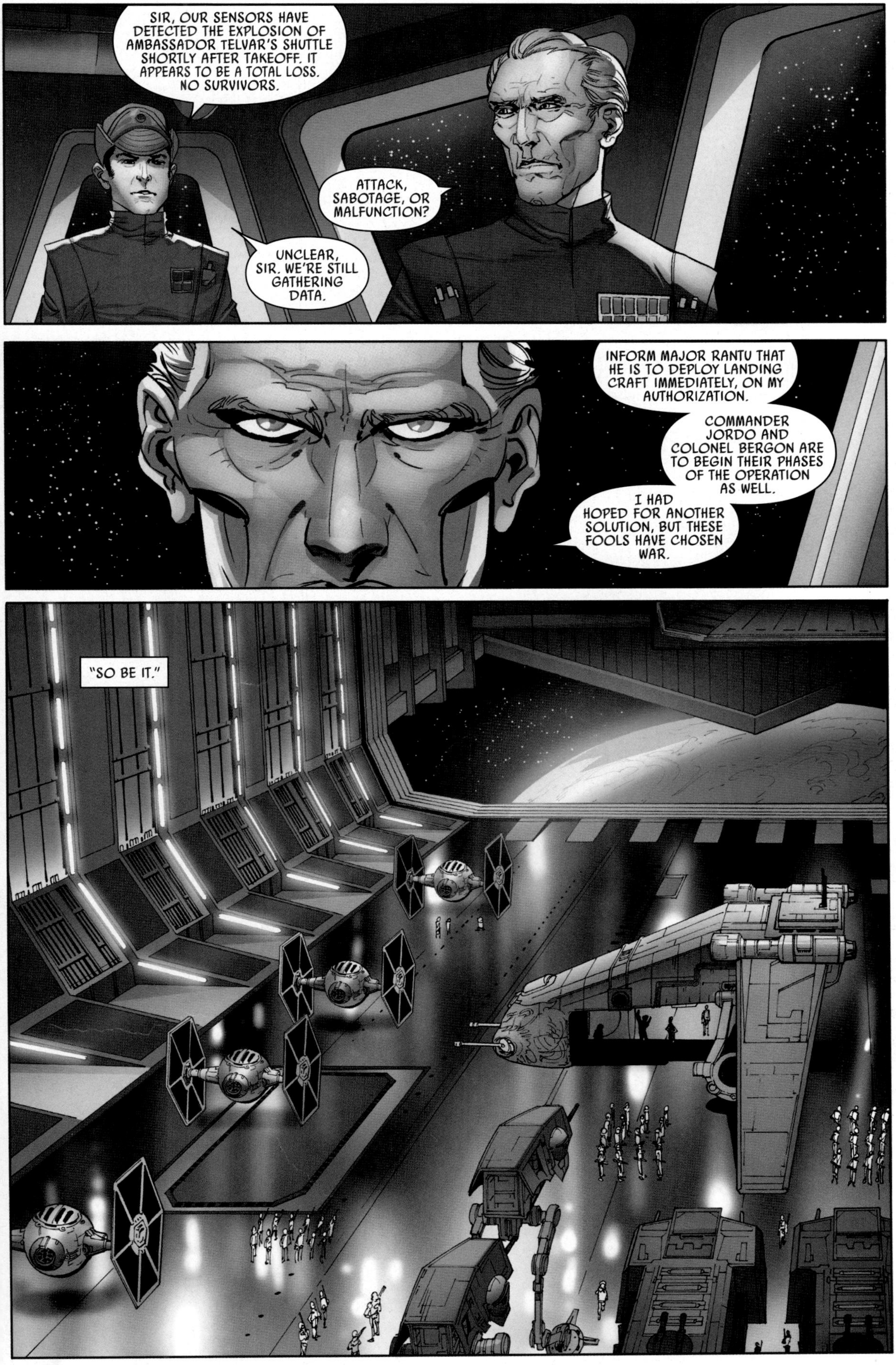
SIR, OUR SENSORS HAVE DETECTED THE EXPLOSION OF AMBASSADOR TELVAR'S SHUTTLE SHORTLY AFTER TAKEOFF. IT APPEARS TO BE A TOTAL LOSS. NO SURVIVORS.
ATTACK, SABOTAGE, OR MALFUNCTION?
UNCLEAR, SIR. WE'RE STILL GATHERING DATA.
INFORM MAJOR RANTU THAT HE IS TO DEPLOY LANDING CRAFT IMMEDIATELY, ON MY AUTHORIZATION.
COMMANDER JORDO AND COLONEL BERGON ARE TO BEGIN THEIR PHASES OF THE OPERATION AS WELL.
I HAD HOPED FOR ANOTHER SOLUTION, BUT THESE FOOLS HAVE CHOSEN WAR.
"SO BE IT."

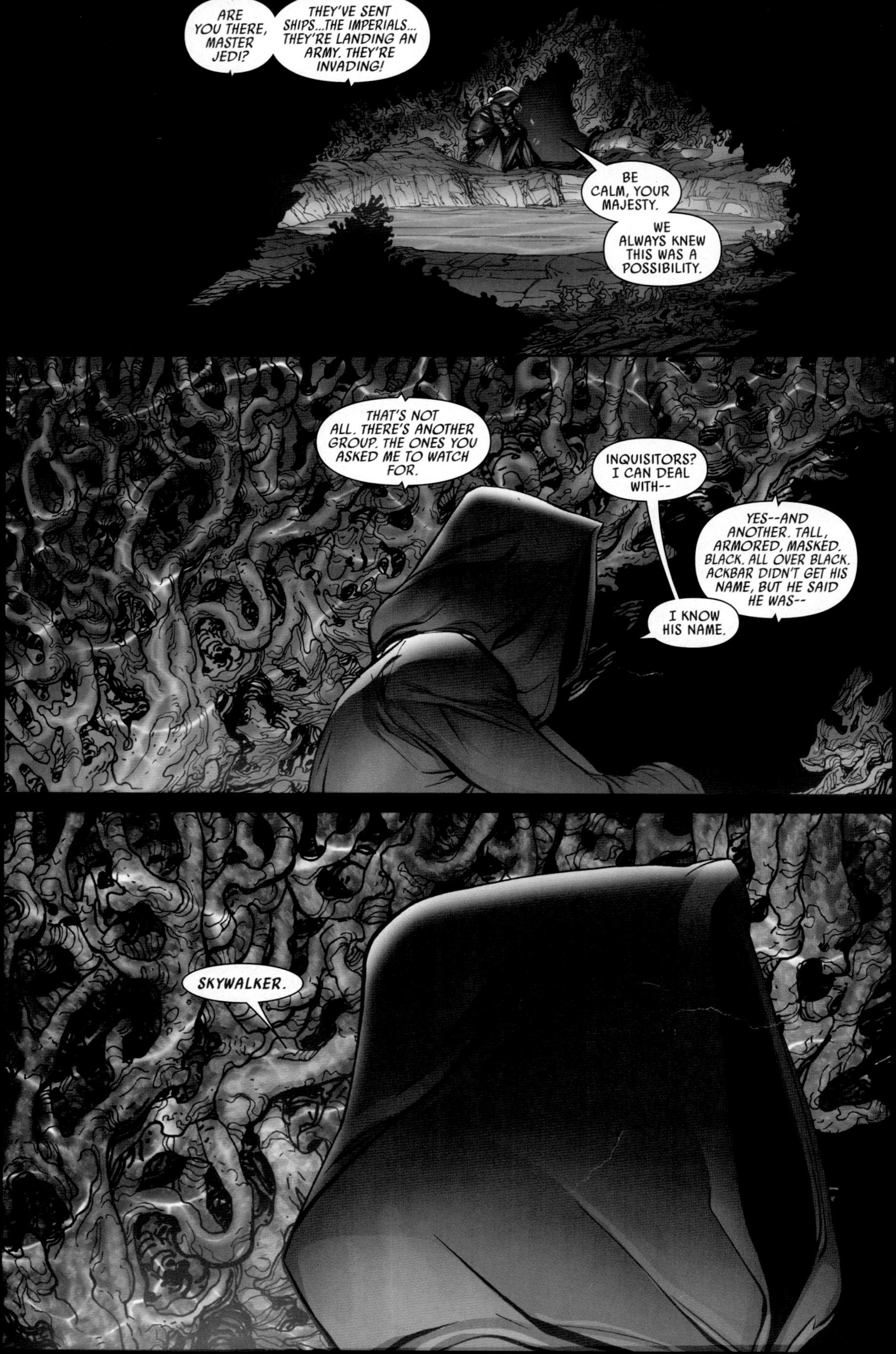
ARE YOU THERE, MASTER JEDI?
THEY'VE SENT SHIPS...THE IMPERIALS... THEY'RE LANDING AN ARMY. THEY'RE INVADING!
BE CALM, YOUR MAJESTY.
WE ALWAYS KNEW THIS WAS A POSSIBILITY.
THAT'S NOT ALL. THERE'S ANOTHER GROUP. THE ONES YOU ASKED ME TO WATCH FOR.
INQUISITORS? I CAN DEAL WITH--
YES--AND ANOTHER. TALL, ARMORED, MASKED. BLACK. ALL OVER BLACK. ACKBAR DIDN'T GET HIS NAME, BUT HE SAID HE WAS--
I KNOW HIS NAME.
SKYWALKER.

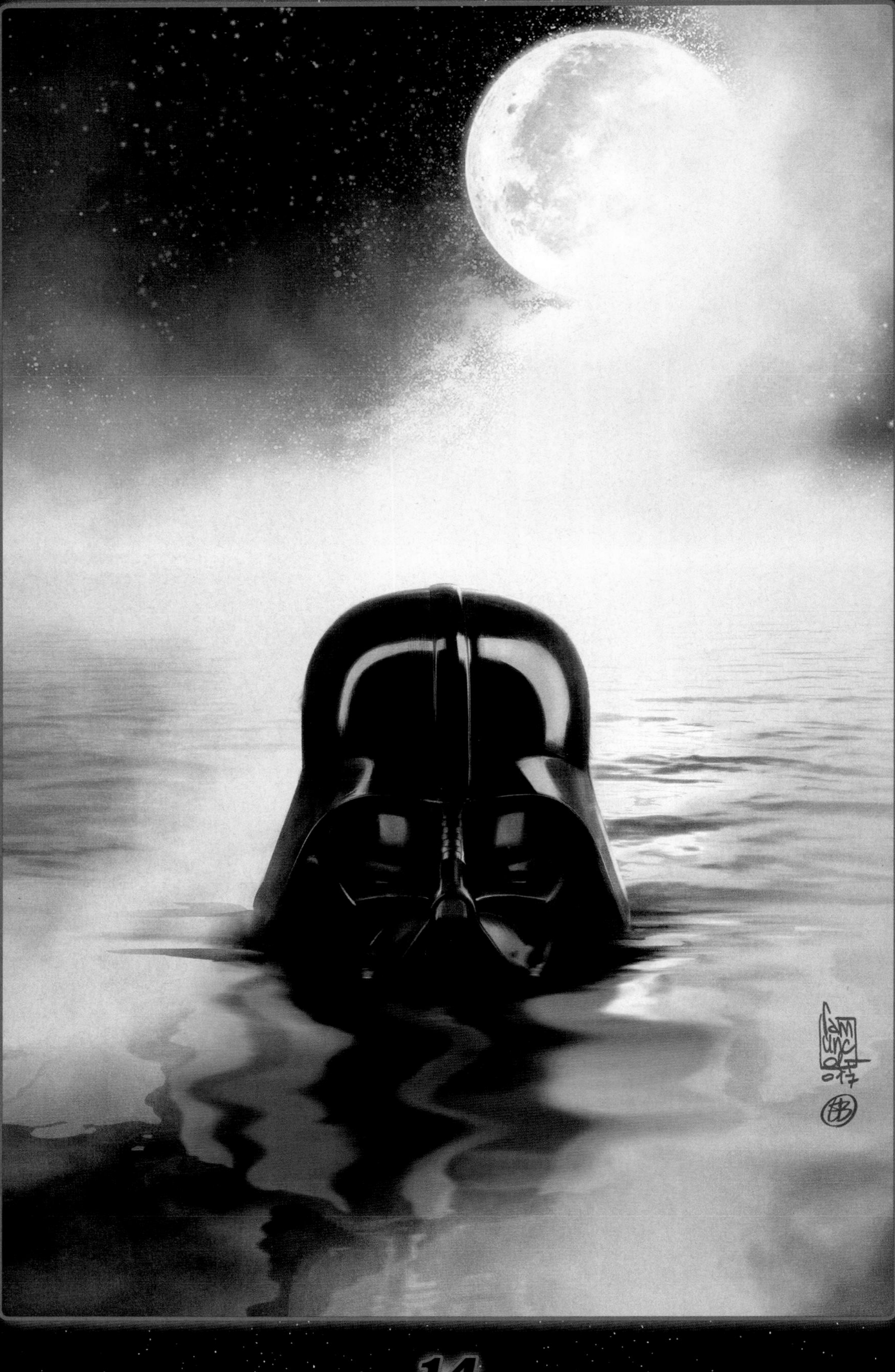

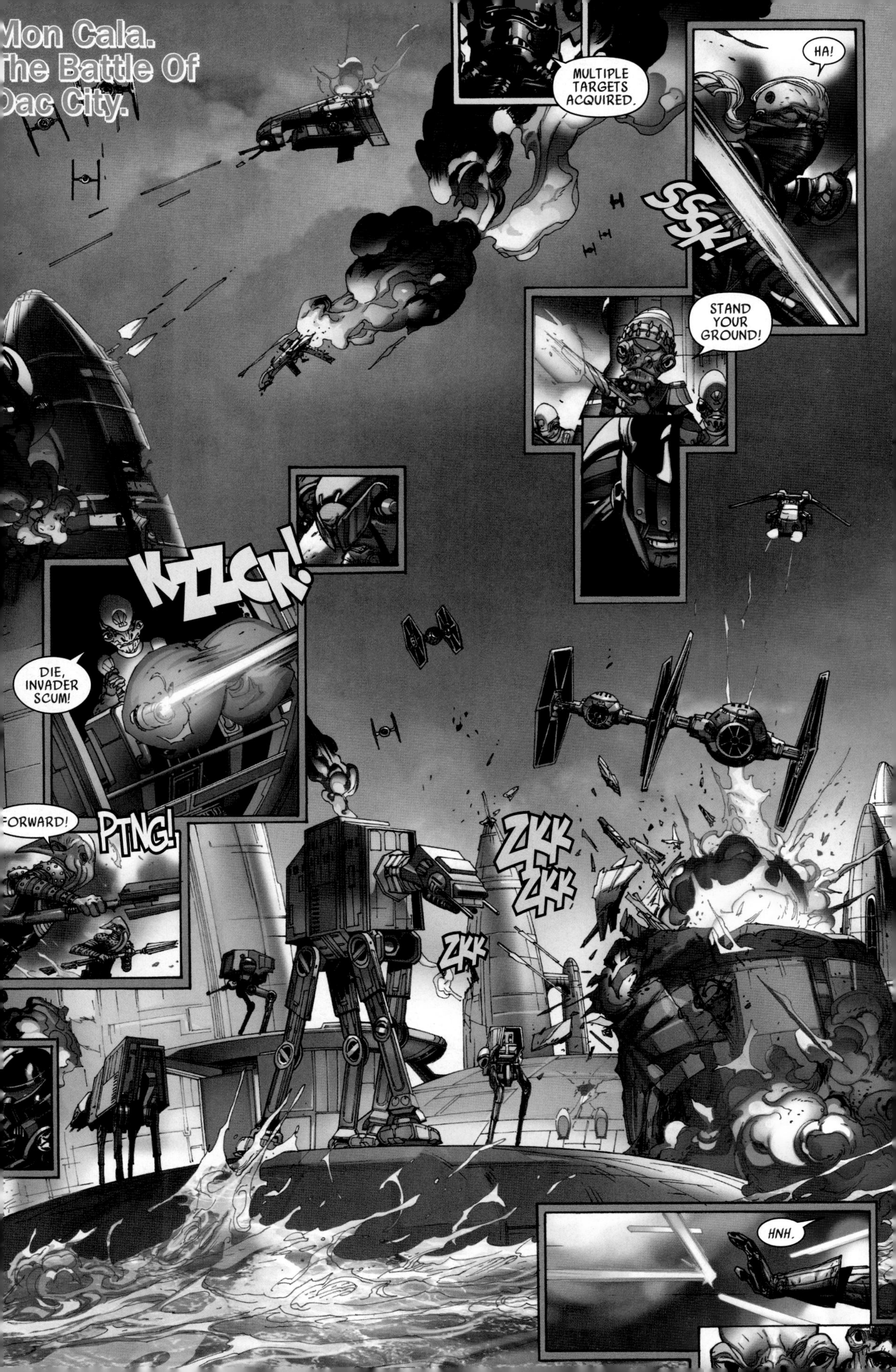
Mon Cala.
The Battle Of
Dac City.
MULTIPLE TARGETS ACQUIRED.
HA!
SSSK!
STAND YOUR GROUND!
KZZCK!
DIE, INVADER SCUM!
FORWARD!
PTNG!
ZKK
ZKK
ZKK
HNH.

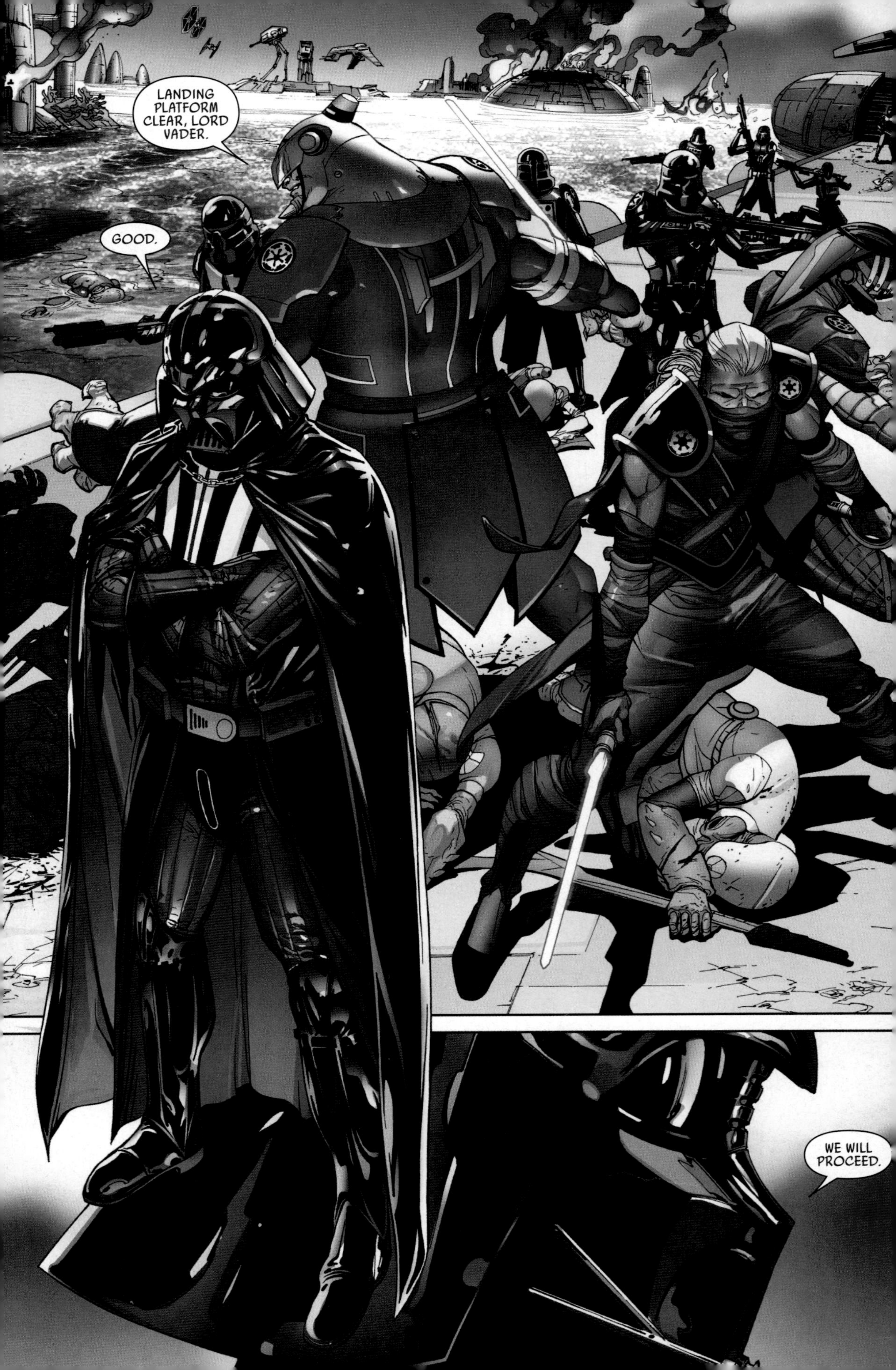
LANDING PLATFORM CLEAR, LORD VADER.
GOOD.
WE WILL PROCEED.

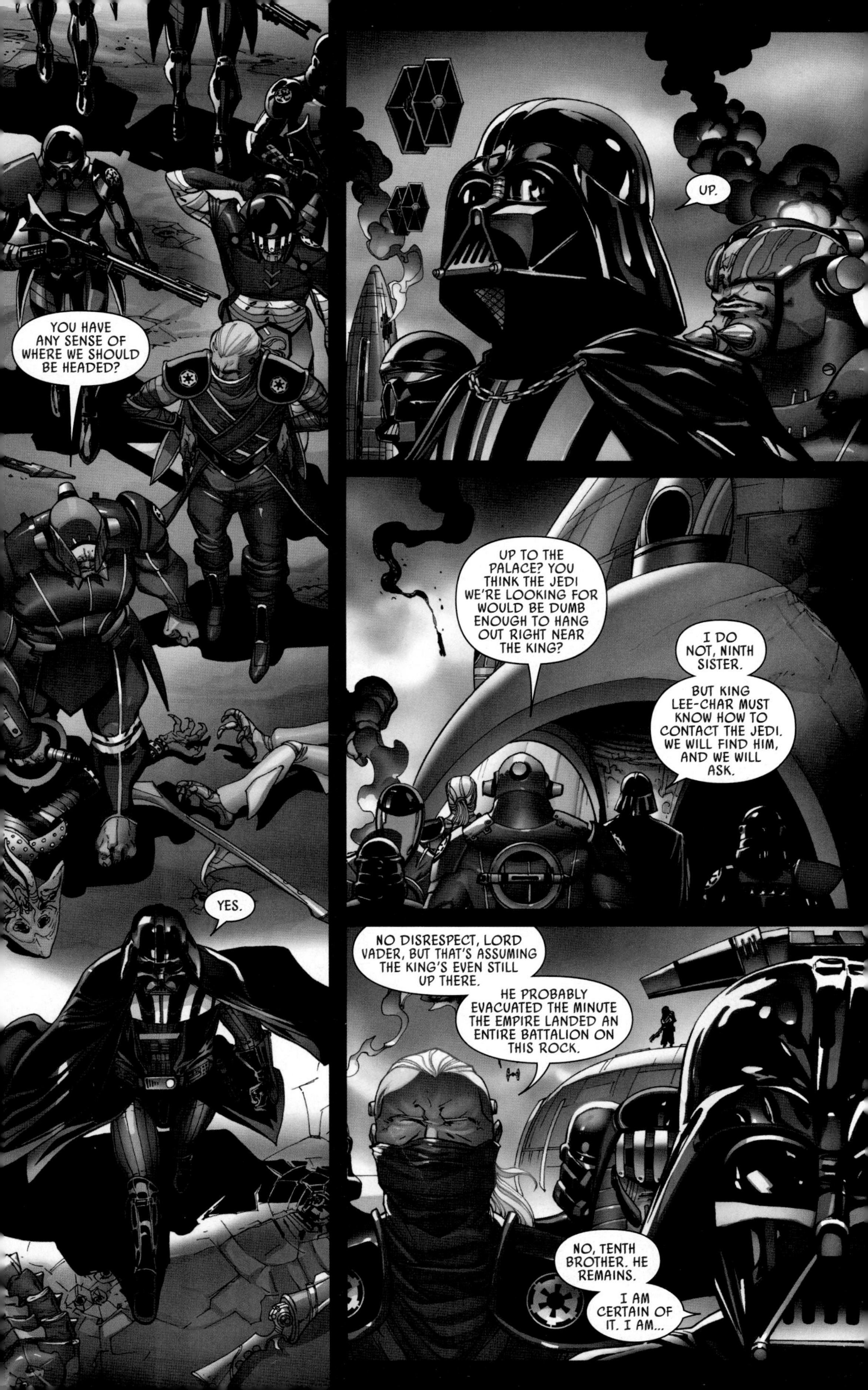
YOU HAVE ANY SENSE OF WHERE WE SHOULD BE HEADED?
UP.
YES.
UP TO THE PALACE? YOU THINK THE JEDI WE'RE LOOKING FOR WOULD BE DUMB ENOUGH TO HANG OUT RIGHT NEAR THE KING?
I DO NOT, NINTH SISTER.
BUT KING LEE-CHAR MUST KNOW HOW TO CONTACT THE JEDI. WE WILL FIND HIM, AND WE WILL ASK.
NO DISRESPECT, LORD VADER, BUT THAT'S ASSUMING THE KING'S EVEN STILL UP THERE.
HE PROBABLY EVACUATED THE MINUTE THE EMPIRE LANDED AN ENTIRE BATTALION ON THIS ROCK.
NO, TENTH BROTHER. HE REMAINS.
I AM CERTAIN OF IT. I AM...

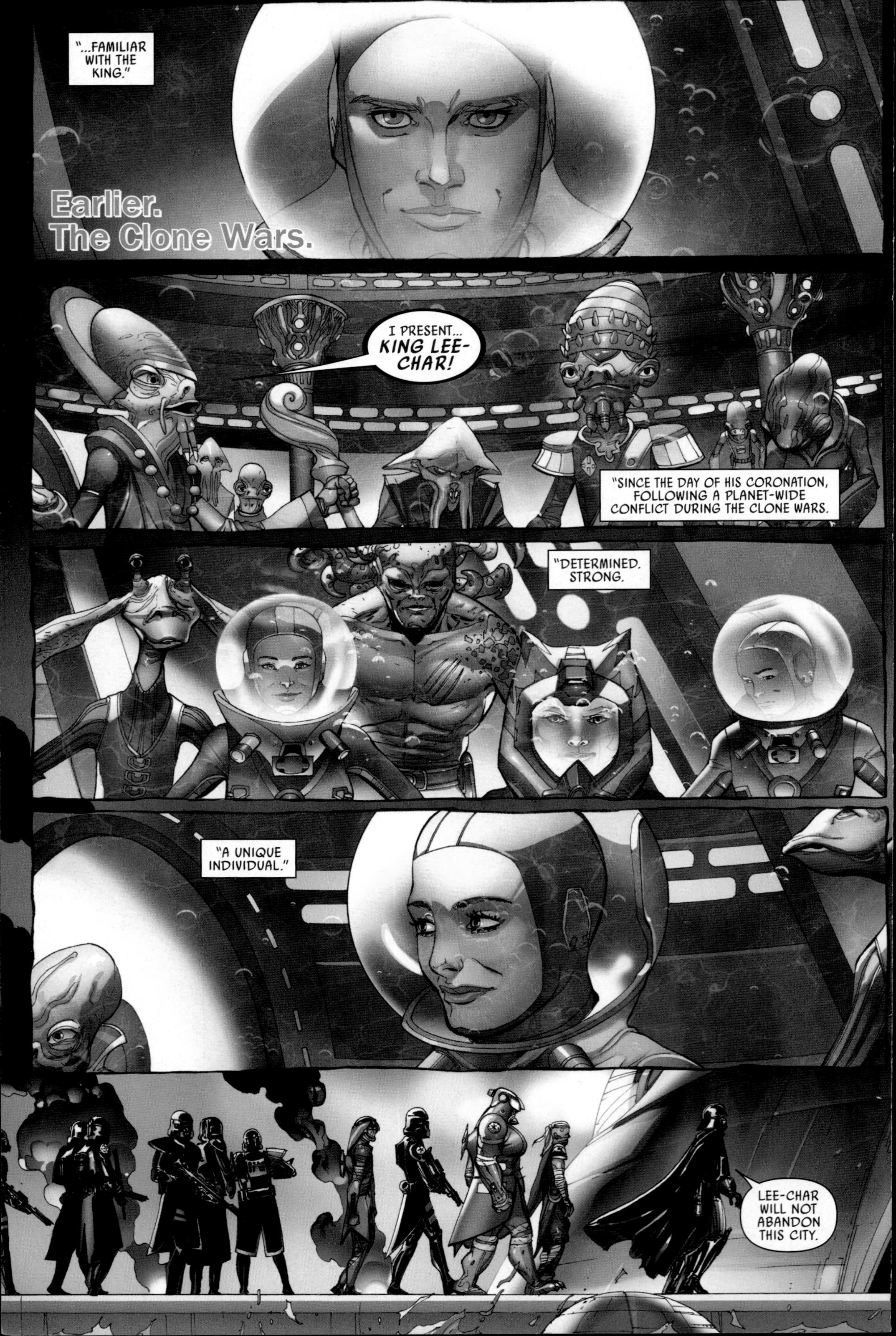
"...FAMILIAR WITH THE KING."
Earlier. The Clone Wars.
I PRESENT... KING LEE-CHAR!
"SINCE THE DAY OF HIS CORONATION, FOLLOWING A PLANET-WIDE CONFLICT DURING THE CLONE WARS.
"DETERMINED. STRONG.
"A UNIQUE INDIVIDUAL."
LEE-CHAR WILL NOT ABANDON THIS CITY.

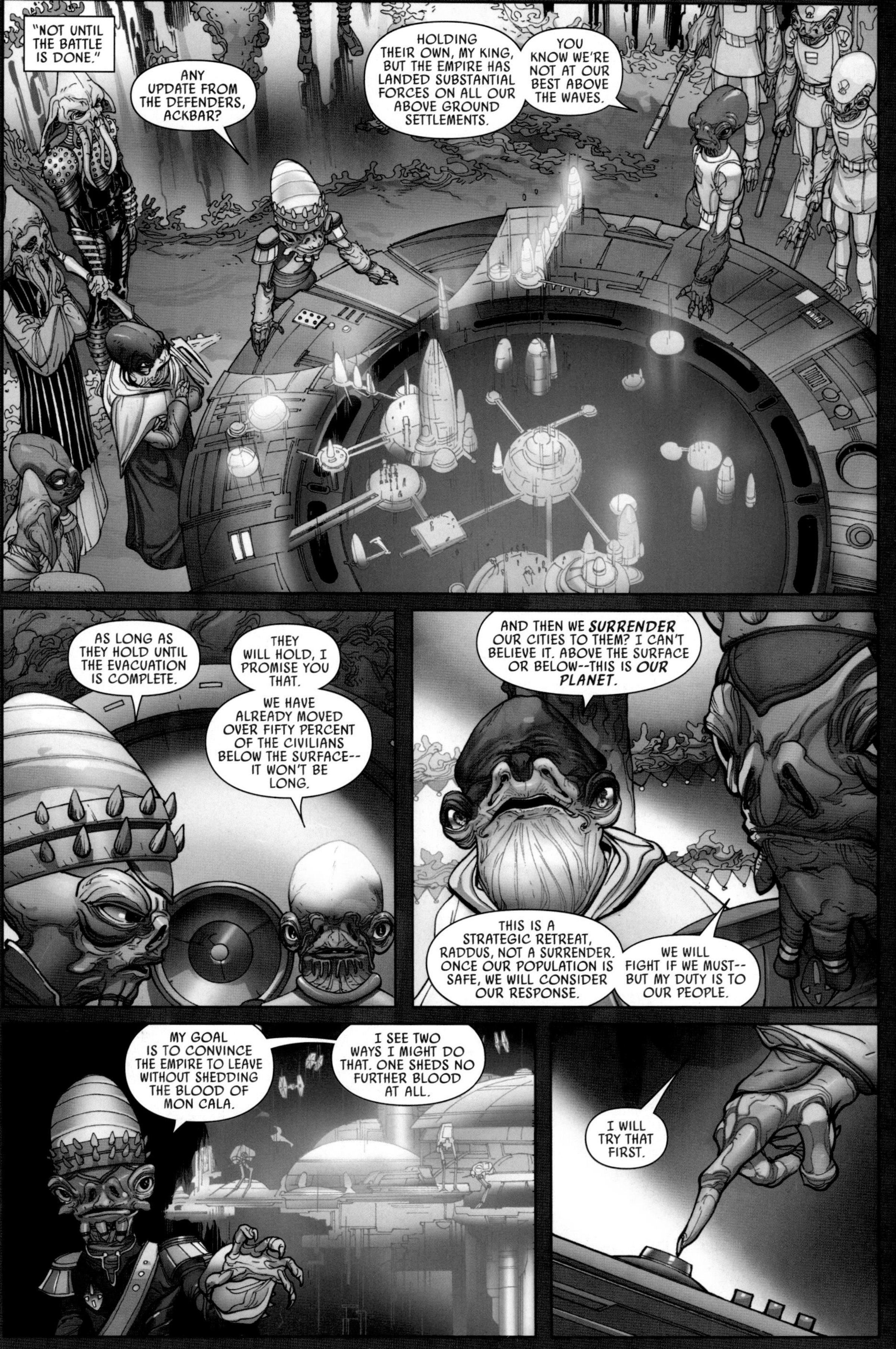
"NOT UNTIL THE BATTLE IS DONE."
ANY UPDATE FROM THE DEFENDERS, ACKBAR?
HOLDING THEIR OWN, MY KING, BUT THE EMPIRE HAS LANDED SUBSTANTIAL FORCES ON ALL OUR ABOVE GROUND SETTLEMENTS.
YOU KNOW WE'RE NOT AT OUR BEST ABOVE THE WAVES.
AS LONG AS THEY HOLD UNTIL THE EVACUATION IS COMPLETE.
THEY WILL HOLD, I PROMISE YOU THAT.
WE HAVE ALREADY MOVED OVER FIFTY PERCENT OF THE CIVILIANS BELOW THE SURFACE-- IT WON'T BE LONG.
AND THEN WE *SURRENDER* OUR CITIES TO THEM? I CAN'T BELIEVE IT. ABOVE THE SURFACE OR BELOW--THIS IS *OUR PLANET.*
THIS IS A STRATEGIC RETREAT, RADDUS, NOT A SURRENDER. ONCE OUR POPULATION IS SAFE, WE WILL CONSIDER OUR RESPONSE.
WE WILL FIGHT IF WE MUST-- BUT MY DUTY IS TO OUR PEOPLE.
MY GOAL IS TO CONVINCE THE EMPIRE TO LEAVE WITHOUT SHEDDING THE BLOOD OF MON CALA.
I SEE TWO WAYS I MIGHT DO THAT. ONE SHEDS NO FURTHER BLOOD AT ALL.
I WILL TRY THAT FIRST.

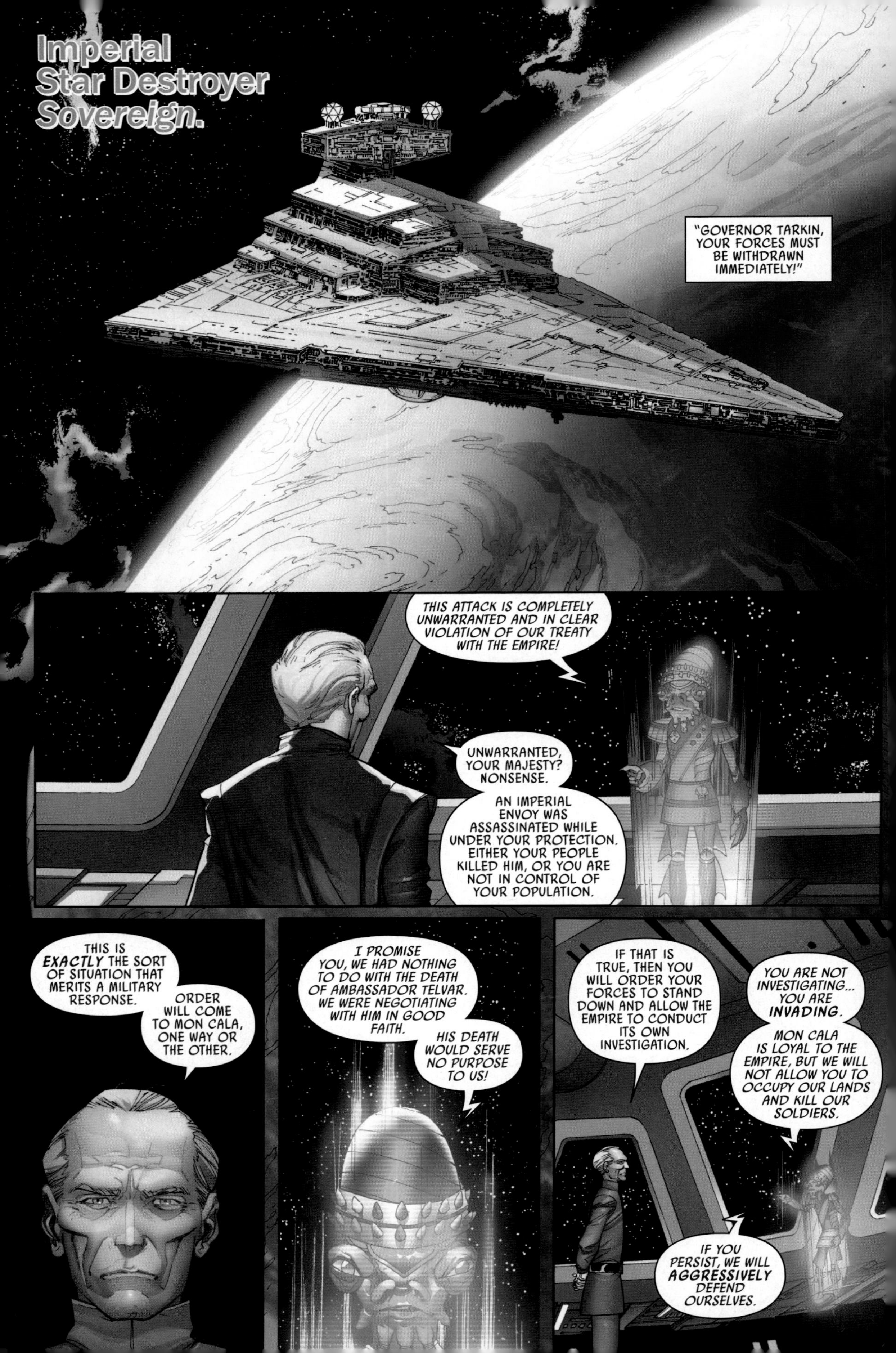
Imperial Star Destroyer Sovereign.
"GOVERNOR TARKIN, YOUR FORCES MUST BE WITHDRAWN IMMEDIATELY!"
THIS ATTACK IS COMPLETELY UNWARRANTED AND IN CLEAR VIOLATION OF OUR TREATY WITH THE EMPIRE!
UNWARRANTED, YOUR MAJESTY? NONSENSE.
AN IMPERIAL ENVOY WAS ASSASSINATED WHILE UNDER YOUR PROTECTION. EITHER YOUR PEOPLE KILLED HIM, OR YOU ARE NOT IN CONTROL OF YOUR POPULATION.
THIS IS EXACTLY THE SORT OF SITUATION THAT MERITS A MILITARY RESPONSE.
ORDER WILL COME TO MON CALA, ONE WAY OR THE OTHER.
I PROMISE YOU, WE HAD NOTHING TO DO WITH THE DEATH OF AMBASSADOR TELVAR. WE WERE NEGOTIATING WITH HIM IN GOOD FAITH.
HIS DEATH WOULD SERVE NO PURPOSE TO US!
IF THAT IS TRUE, THEN YOU WILL ORDER YOUR FORCES TO STAND DOWN AND ALLOW THE EMPIRE TO CONDUCT ITS OWN INVESTIGATION.
YOU ARE NOT INVESTIGATING... YOU ARE INVADING.
MON CALA IS LOYAL TO THE EMPIRE, BUT WE WILL NOT ALLOW YOU TO OCCUPY OUR LANDS AND KILL OUR SOLDIERS.
IF YOU PERSIST, WE WILL AGGRESSIVELY DEFEND OURSELVES.

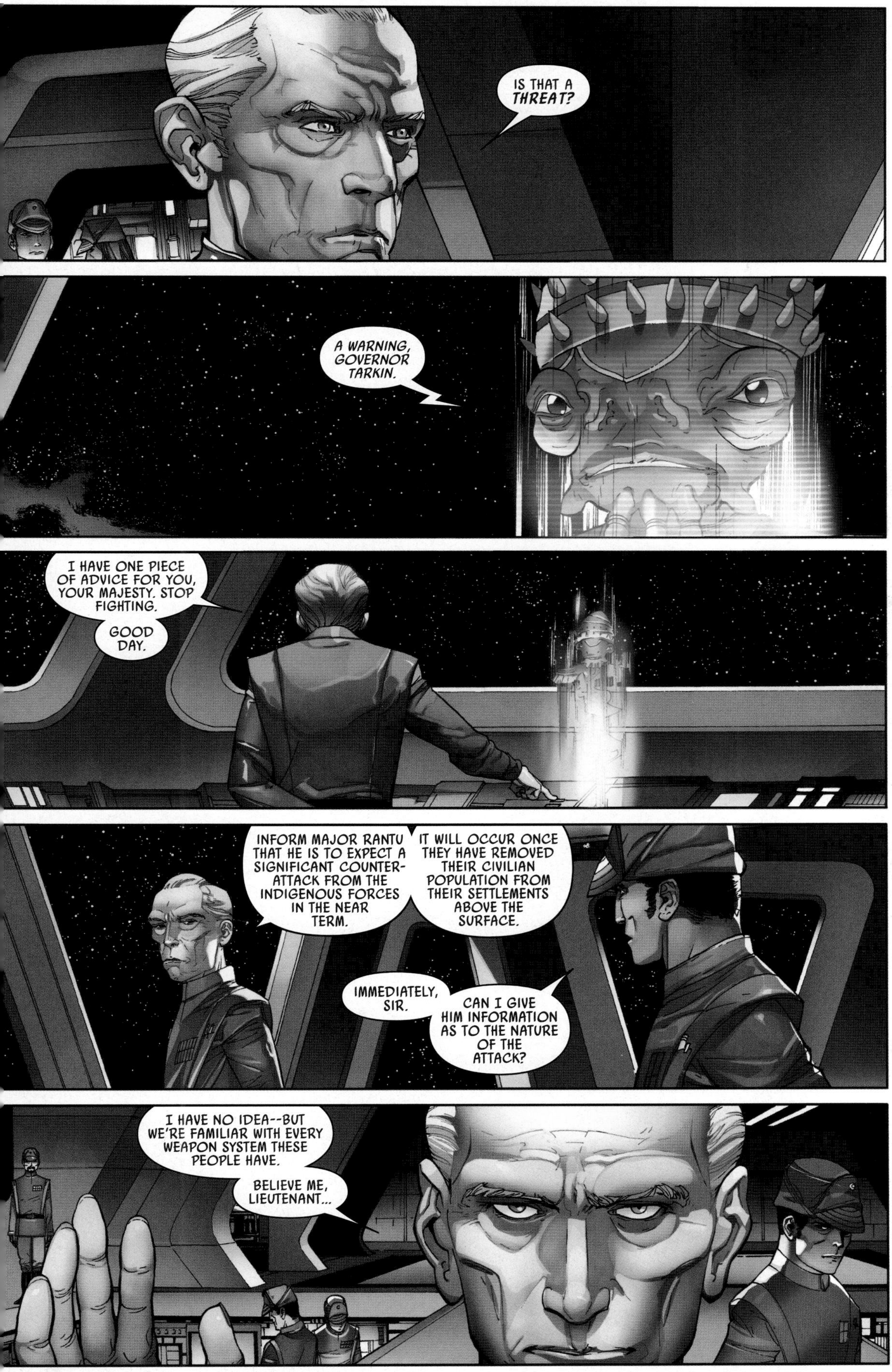
IS THAT A THREAT?
A WARNING, GOVERNOR TARKIN.
I HAVE ONE PIECE OF ADVICE FOR YOU, YOUR MAJESTY. STOP FIGHTING.
GOOD DAY.
INFORM MAJOR RANTU THAT HE IS TO EXPECT A SIGNIFICANT COUNTER-ATTACK FROM THE INDIGENOUS FORCES IN THE NEAR TERM.
IT WILL OCCUR ONCE THEY HAVE REMOVED THEIR CIVILIAN POPULATION FROM THEIR SETTLEMENTS ABOVE THE SURFACE.
IMMEDIATELY, SIR.
CAN I GIVE HIM INFORMATION AS TO THE NATURE OF THE ATTACK?
I HAVE NO IDEA--BUT WE'RE FAMILIAR WITH EVERY WEAPON SYSTEM THESE PEOPLE HAVE.
BELIEVE ME, LIEUTENANT...

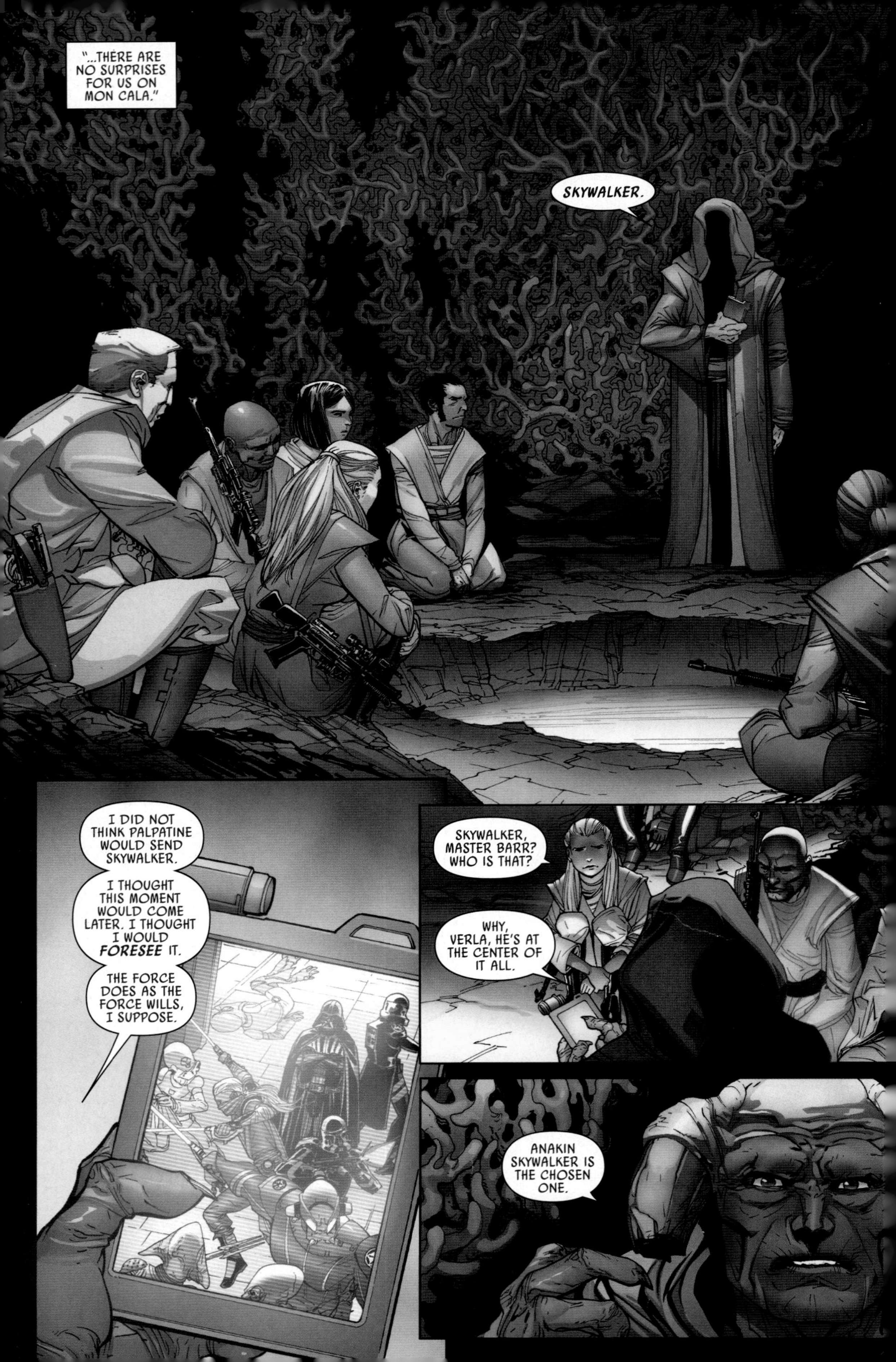
"...THERE ARE NO SURPRISES FOR US ON MON CALA."
SKYWALKER.
I DID NOT THINK PALPATINE WOULD SEND SKYWALKER.
I THOUGHT THIS MOMENT WOULD COME LATER. I THOUGHT I WOULD FORESEE IT.
THE FORCE DOES AS THE FORCE WILLS, I SUPPOSE.
SKYWALKER, MASTER BARR? WHO IS THAT?
WHY, VERLA, HE'S AT THE CENTER OF IT ALL.
ANAKIN SKYWALKER IS THE CHOSEN ONE.

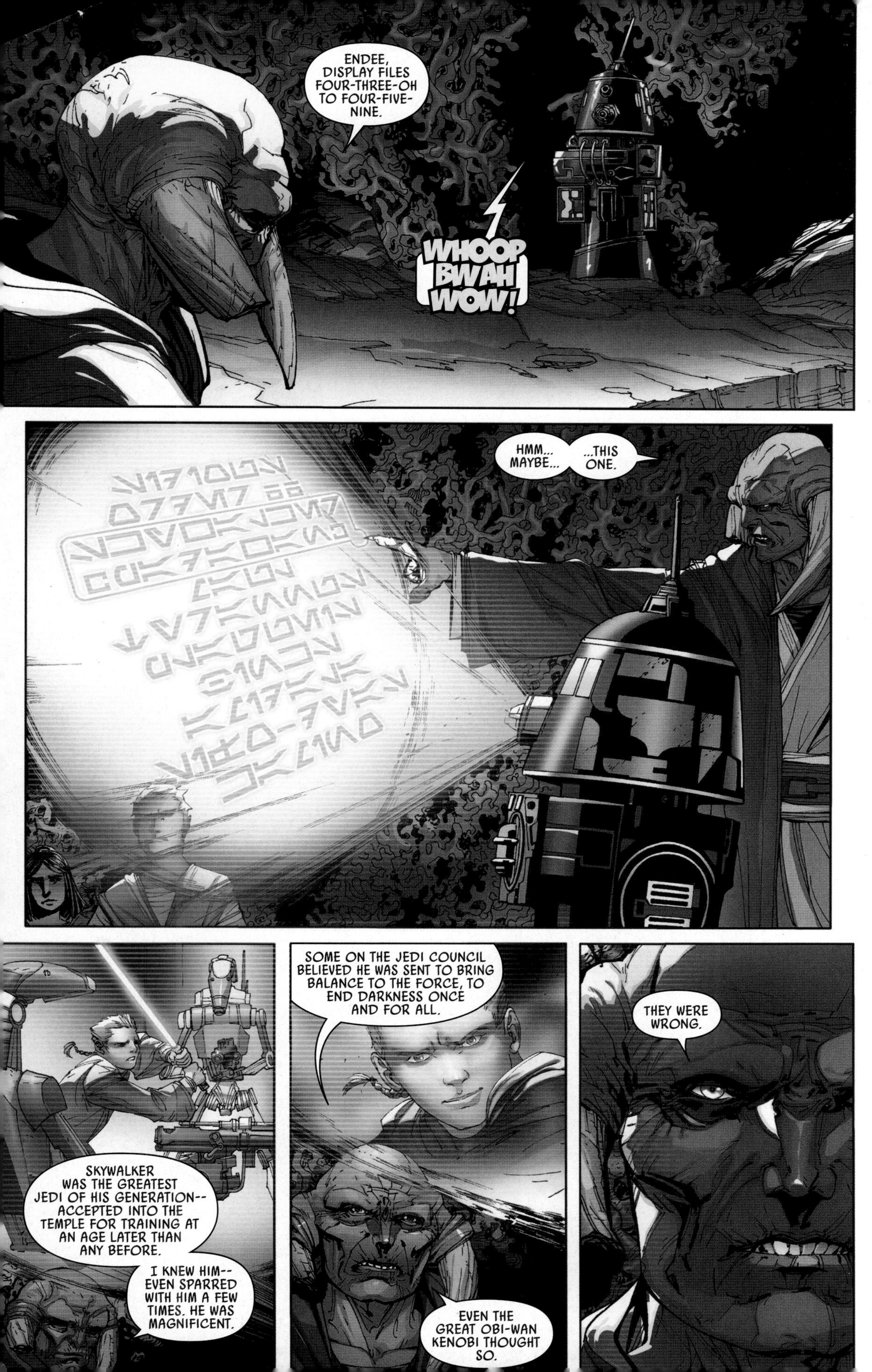
ENDEE, DISPLAY FILES FOUR-THREE-OH TO FOUR-FIVE-NINE.
WHOOP BWAH WOW!
HMM... MAYBE...
...THIS ONE.
SKYWALKER WAS THE GREATEST JEDI OF HIS GENERATION--ACCEPTED INTO THE TEMPLE FOR TRAINING AT AN AGE LATER THAN ANY BEFORE.
I KNEW HIM--EVEN SPARRED WITH HIM A FEW TIMES. HE WAS MAGNIFICENT.
SOME ON THE JEDI COUNCIL BELIEVED HE WAS SENT TO BRING BALANCE TO THE FORCE, TO END DARKNESS ONCE AND FOR ALL.
EVEN THE GREAT OBI-WAN KENOBI THOUGHT SO.
THEY WERE WRONG.

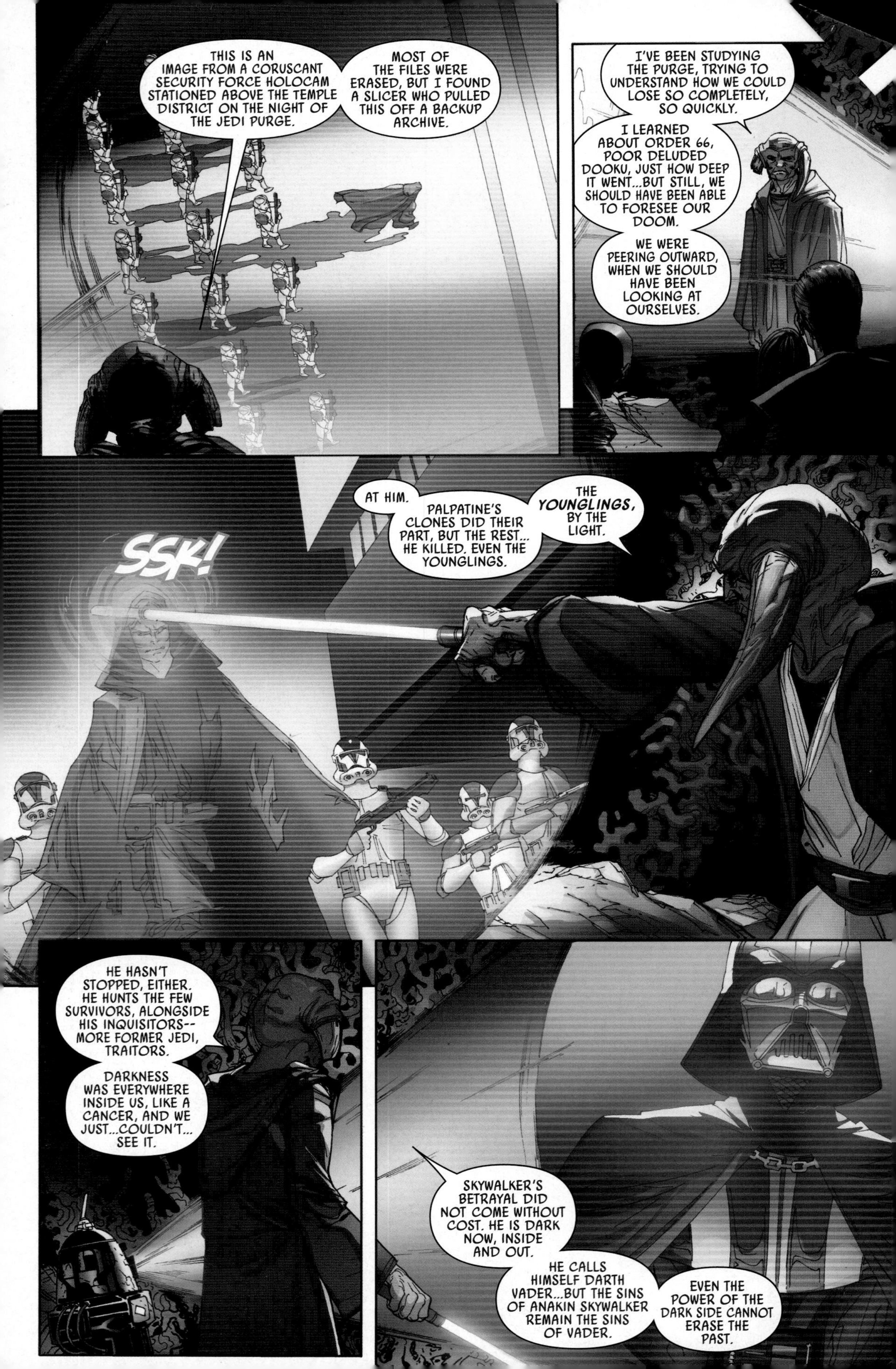
THIS IS AN IMAGE FROM A CORUSCANT SECURITY FORCE HOLOCAM STATIONED ABOVE THE TEMPLE DISTRICT ON THE NIGHT OF THE JEDI PURGE.
MOST OF THE FILES WERE ERASED, BUT I FOUND A SLICER WHO PULLED THIS OFF A BACKUP ARCHIVE.
I'VE BEEN STUDYING THE PURGE, TRYING TO UNDERSTAND HOW WE COULD LOSE SO COMPLETELY, SO QUICKLY.
I LEARNED ABOUT ORDER 66, POOR DELUDED DOOKU, JUST HOW DEEP IT WENT...BUT STILL, WE SHOULD HAVE BEEN ABLE TO FORESEE OUR DOOM.
WE WERE PEERING OUTWARD, WHEN WE SHOULD HAVE BEEN LOOKING AT OURSELVES.
SSK!
AT HIM.
PALPATINE'S CLONES DID THEIR PART, BUT THE REST... HE KILLED. EVEN THE YOUNGLINGS.
THE YOUNGLINGS, BY THE LIGHT.
HE HASN'T STOPPED, EITHER. HE HUNTS THE FEW SURVIVORS, ALONGSIDE HIS INQUISITORS-- MORE FORMER JEDI, TRAITORS.
DARKNESS WAS EVERYWHERE INSIDE US, LIKE A CANCER, AND WE JUST...COULDN'T... SEE IT.
SKYWALKER'S BETRAYAL DID NOT COME WITHOUT COST. HE IS DARK NOW, INSIDE AND OUT.
HE CALLS HIMSELF DARTH VADER...BUT THE SINS OF ANAKIN SKYWALKER REMAIN THE SINS OF VADER.
EVEN THE POWER OF THE DARK SIDE CANNOT ERASE THE PAST.

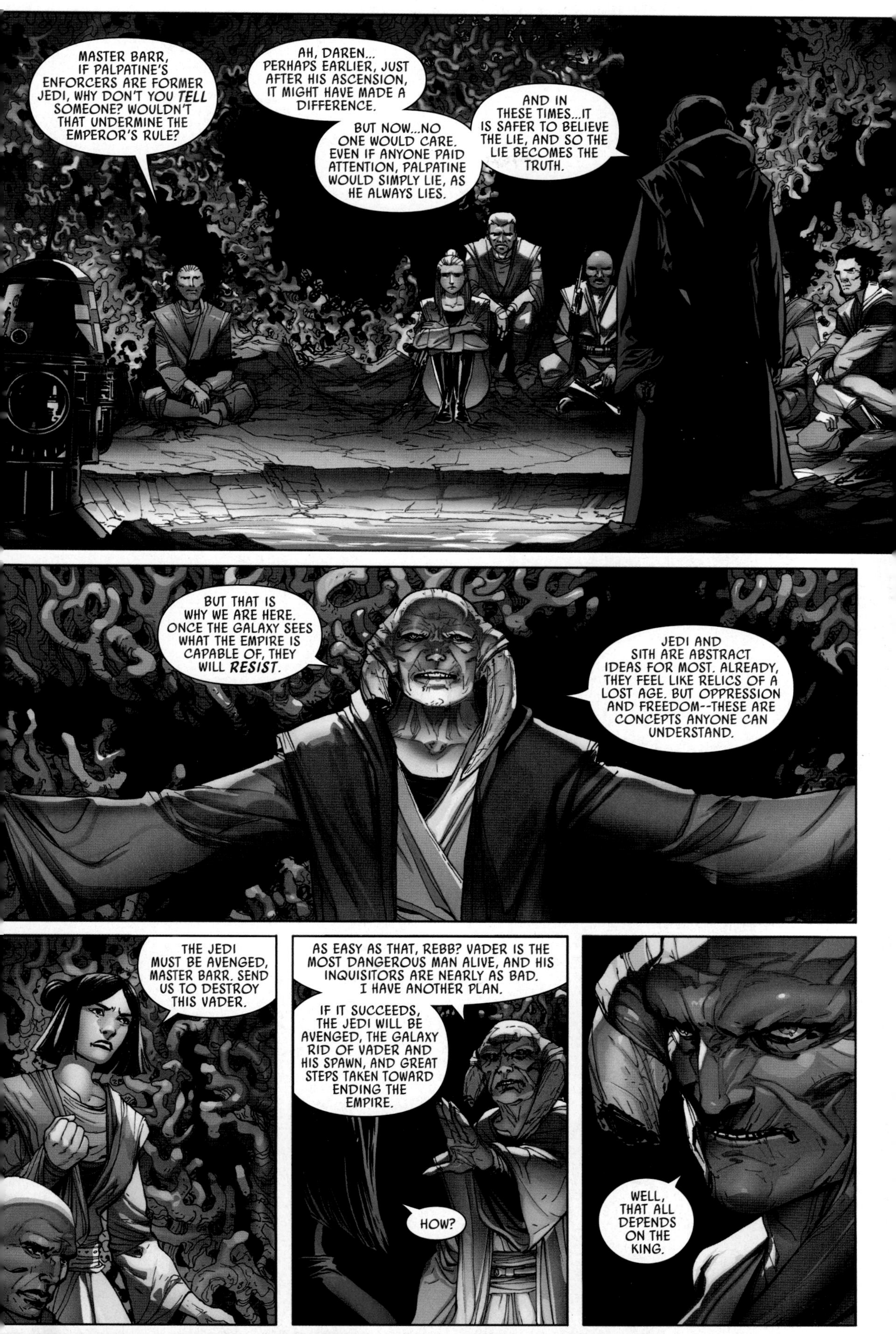
MASTER BARR, IF PALPATINE'S ENFORCERS ARE FORMER JEDI, WHY DON'T YOU TELL SOMEONE? WOULDN'T THAT UNDERMINE THE EMPEROR'S RULE?
AH, DAREN... PERHAPS EARLIER, JUST AFTER HIS ASCENSION, IT MIGHT HAVE MADE A DIFFERENCE.
BUT NOW...NO ONE WOULD CARE. EVEN IF ANYONE PAID ATTENTION, PALPATINE WOULD SIMPLY LIE, AS HE ALWAYS LIES.
AND IN THESE TIMES...IT IS SAFER TO BELIEVE THE LIE, AND SO THE LIE BECOMES THE TRUTH.
BUT THAT IS WHY WE ARE HERE. ONCE THE GALAXY SEES WHAT THE EMPIRE IS CAPABLE OF, THEY WILL RESIST.
JEDI AND SITH ARE ABSTRACT IDEAS FOR MOST. ALREADY, THEY FEEL LIKE RELICS OF A LOST AGE. BUT OPPRESSION AND FREEDOM--THESE ARE CONCEPTS ANYONE CAN UNDERSTAND.
THE JEDI MUST BE AVENGED, MASTER BARR. SEND US TO DESTROY THIS VADER.
AS EASY AS THAT, REBB? VADER IS THE MOST DANGEROUS MAN ALIVE, AND HIS INQUISITORS ARE NEARLY AS BAD. I HAVE ANOTHER PLAN.
IF IT SUCCEEDS, THE JEDI WILL BE AVENGED, THE GALAXY RID OF VADER AND HIS SPAWN, AND GREAT STEPS TAKEN TOWARD ENDING THE EMPIRE.
HOW?
WELL, THAT ALL DEPENDS ON THE KING.

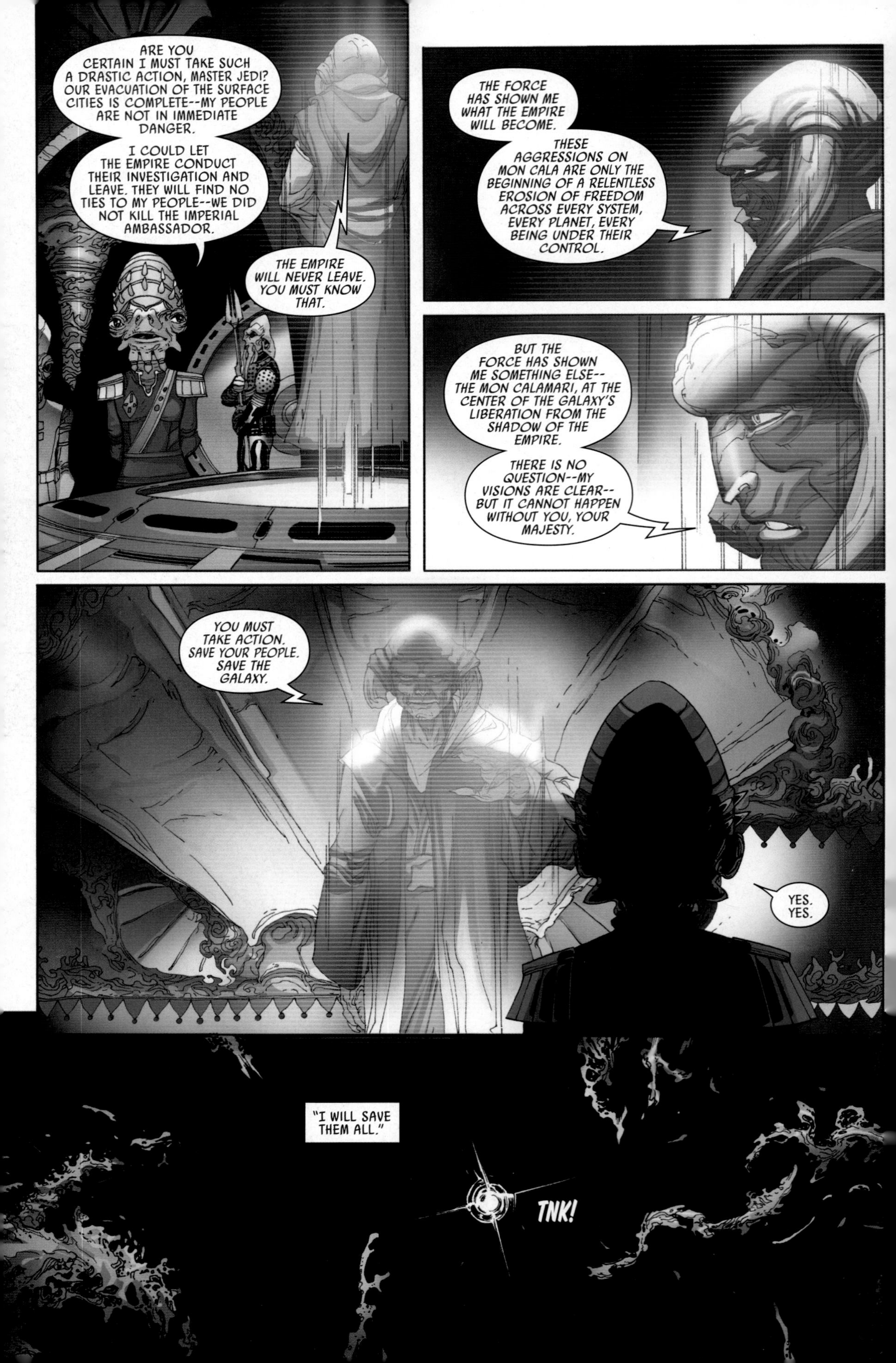
ARE YOU CERTAIN I MUST TAKE SUCH A DRASTIC ACTION, MASTER JEDI? OUR EVACUATION OF THE SURFACE CITIES IS COMPLETE--MY PEOPLE ARE NOT IN IMMEDIATE DANGER.
I COULD LET THE EMPIRE CONDUCT THEIR INVESTIGATION AND LEAVE. THEY WILL FIND NO TIES TO MY PEOPLE--WE DID NOT KILL THE IMPERIAL AMBASSADOR.
THE EMPIRE WILL NEVER LEAVE. YOU MUST KNOW THAT.
THE FORCE HAS SHOWN ME WHAT THE EMPIRE WILL BECOME.
THESE AGGRESSIONS ON MON CALA ARE ONLY THE BEGINNING OF A RELENTLESS EROSION OF FREEDOM ACROSS EVERY SYSTEM, EVERY PLANET, EVERY BEING UNDER THEIR CONTROL.
BUT THE FORCE HAS SHOWN ME SOMETHING ELSE-- THE MON CALAMARI, AT THE CENTER OF THE GALAXY'S LIBERATION FROM THE SHADOW OF THE EMPIRE.
THERE IS NO QUESTION--MY VISIONS ARE CLEAR-- BUT IT CANNOT HAPPEN WITHOUT YOU, YOUR MAJESTY.
YOU MUST TAKE ACTION. SAVE YOUR PEOPLE. SAVE THE GALAXY.
YES. YES.
"I WILL SAVE THEM ALL."
TNK!

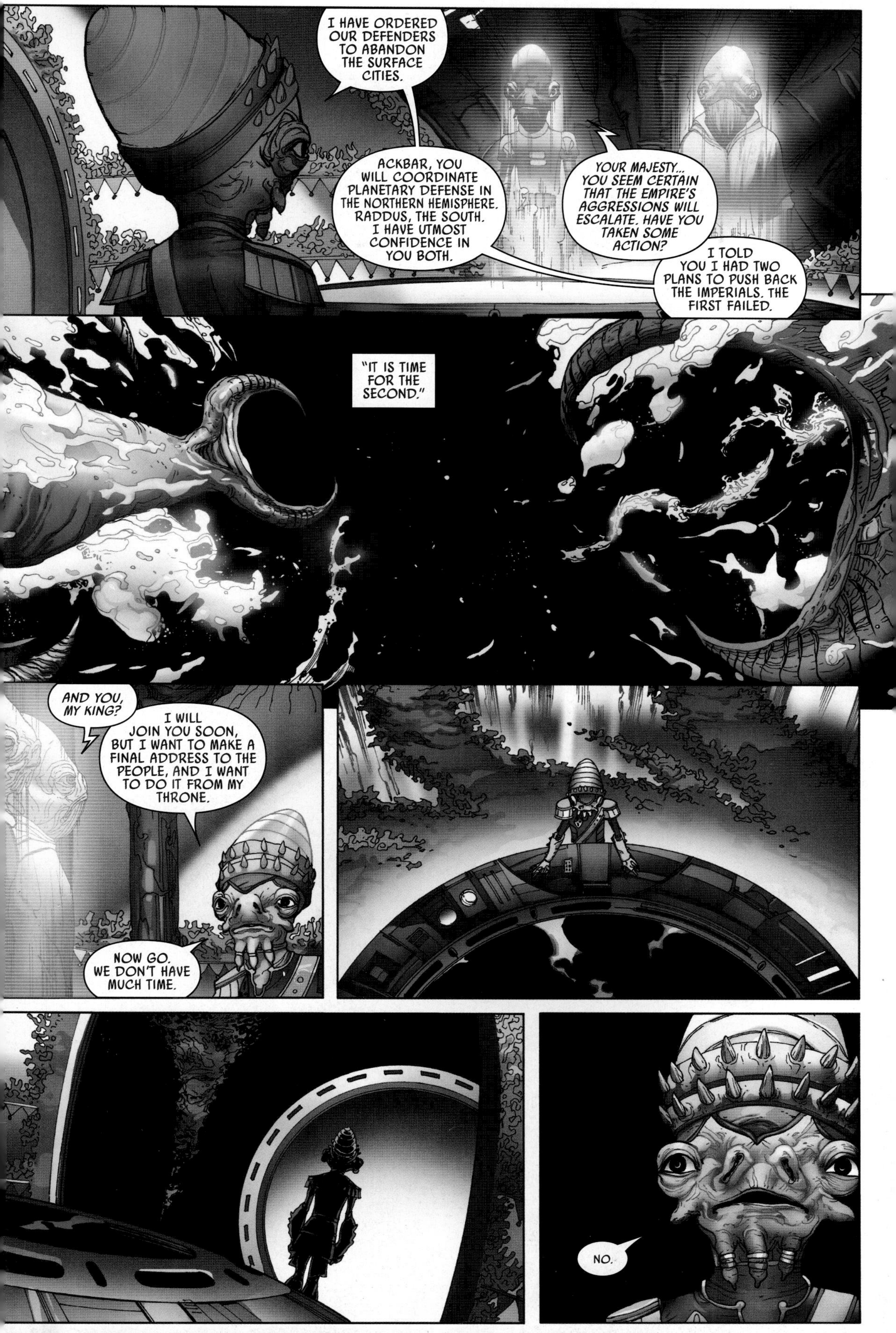
I HAVE ORDERED OUR DEFENDERS TO ABANDON THE SURFACE CITIES.
ACKBAR, YOU WILL COORDINATE PLANETARY DEFENSE IN THE NORTHERN HEMISPHERE. RADDUS, THE SOUTH. I HAVE UTMOST CONFIDENCE IN YOU BOTH.
YOUR MAJESTY... YOU SEEM CERTAIN THAT THE EMPIRE'S AGGRESSIONS WILL ESCALATE. HAVE YOU TAKEN SOME ACTION?
I TOLD YOU I HAD TWO PLANS TO PUSH BACK THE IMPERIALS. THE FIRST FAILED.
"IT IS TIME FOR THE SECOND."
AND YOU, MY KING?
I WILL JOIN YOU SOON, BUT I WANT TO MAKE A FINAL ADDRESS TO THE PEOPLE, AND I WANT TO DO IT FROM MY THRONE.
NOW GO. WE DON'T HAVE MUCH TIME.
NO.

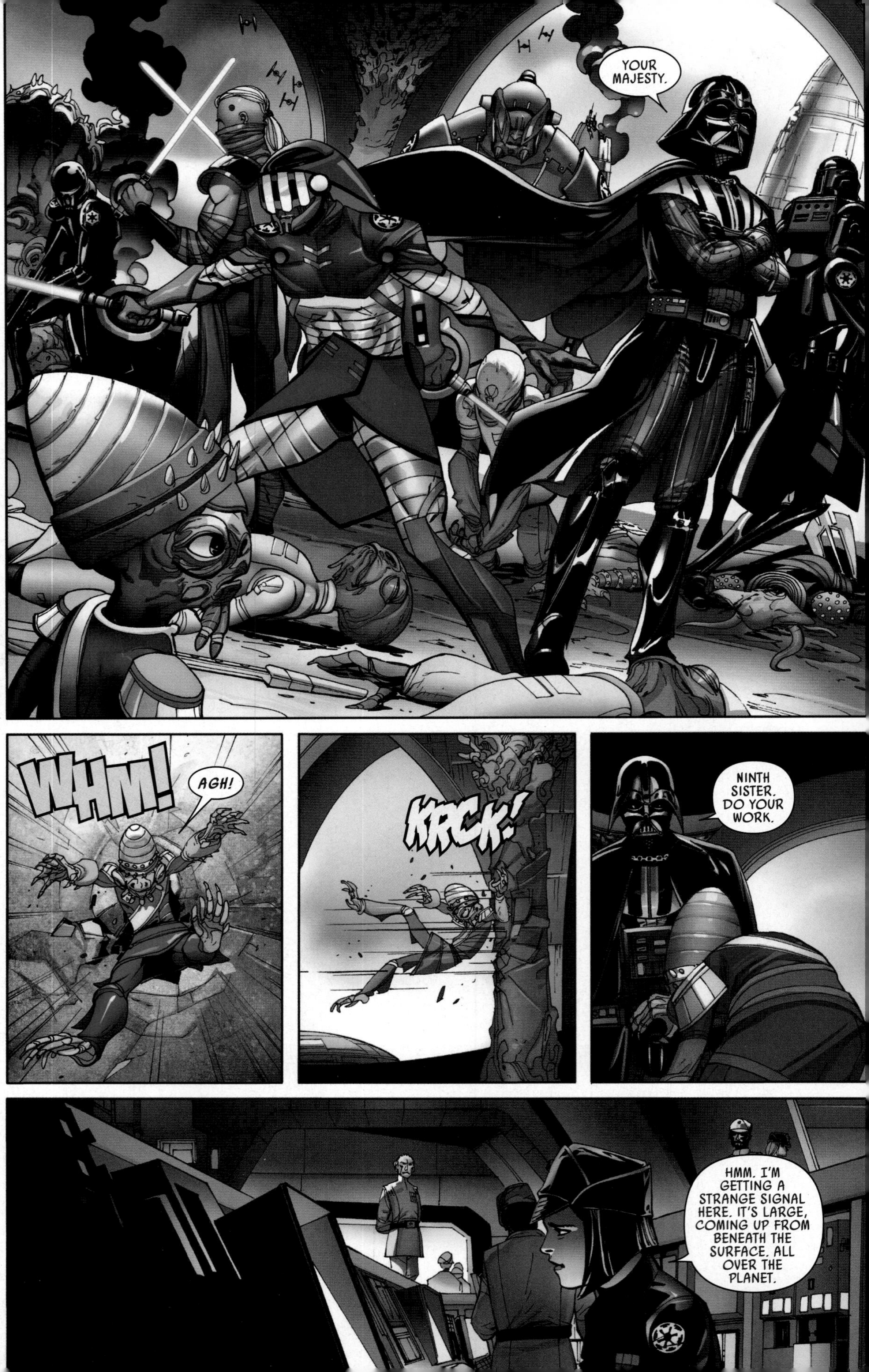
YOUR MAJESTY.
WHM!
AGH!
KRCK!
NINTH SISTER. DO YOUR WORK.
HMM. I'M GETTING A STRANGE SIGNAL HERE. IT'S LARGE, COMING UP FROM BENEATH THE SURFACE. ALL OVER THE PLANET.

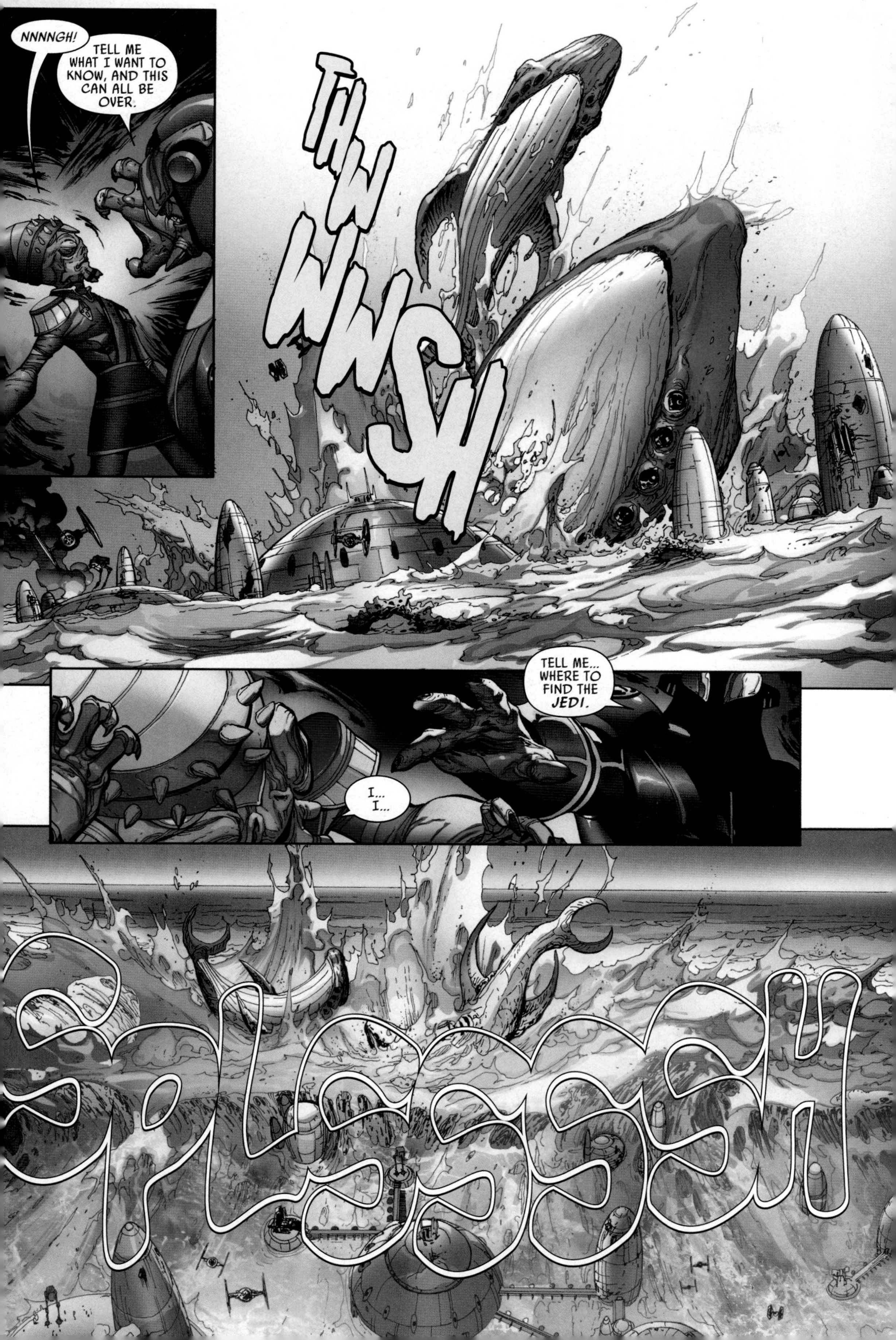
NNNNGH!
TELL ME WHAT I WANT TO KNOW, AND THIS CAN ALL BE OVER.
THWWWSH
TELL ME... WHERE TO FIND THE JEDI.
I... I...
SPLOOOSH

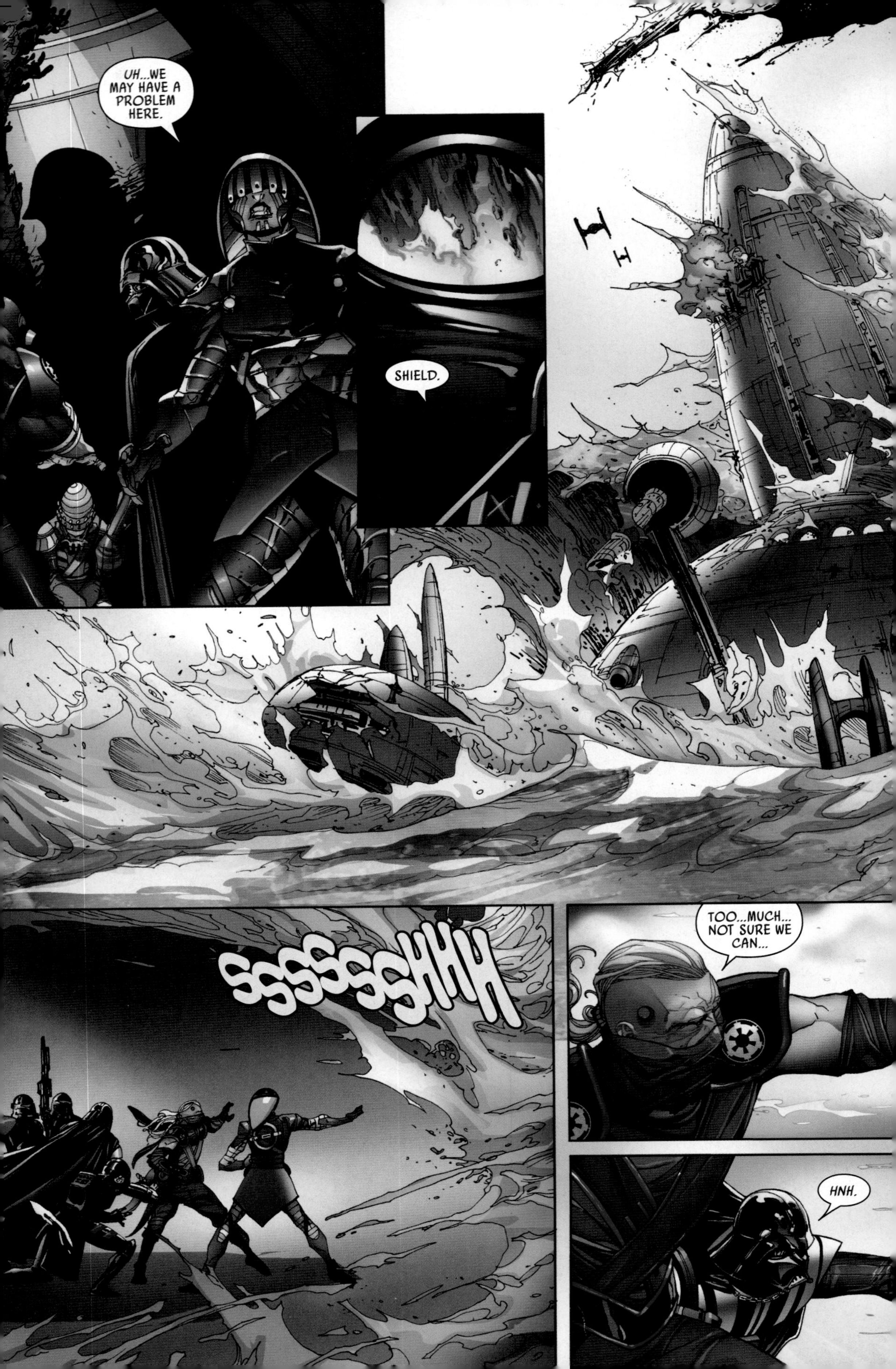

UH...WE MAY HAVE A PROBLEM HERE.
SHIELD.
SSSSSSHHHH
TOO...MUCH... NOT SURE WE CAN...
HNH.

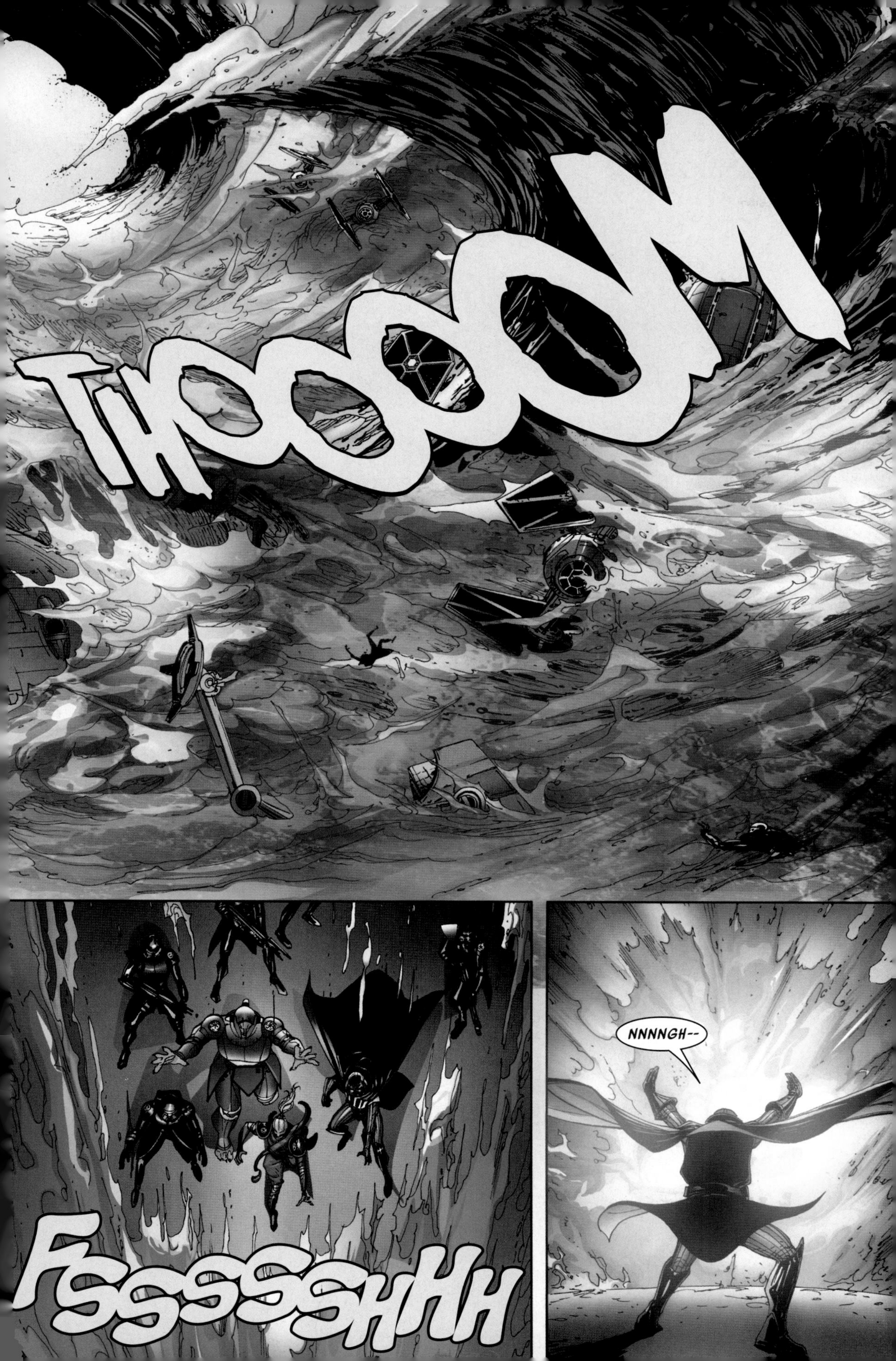
THOOOM
FSSSSSHHH
NNNNGH--

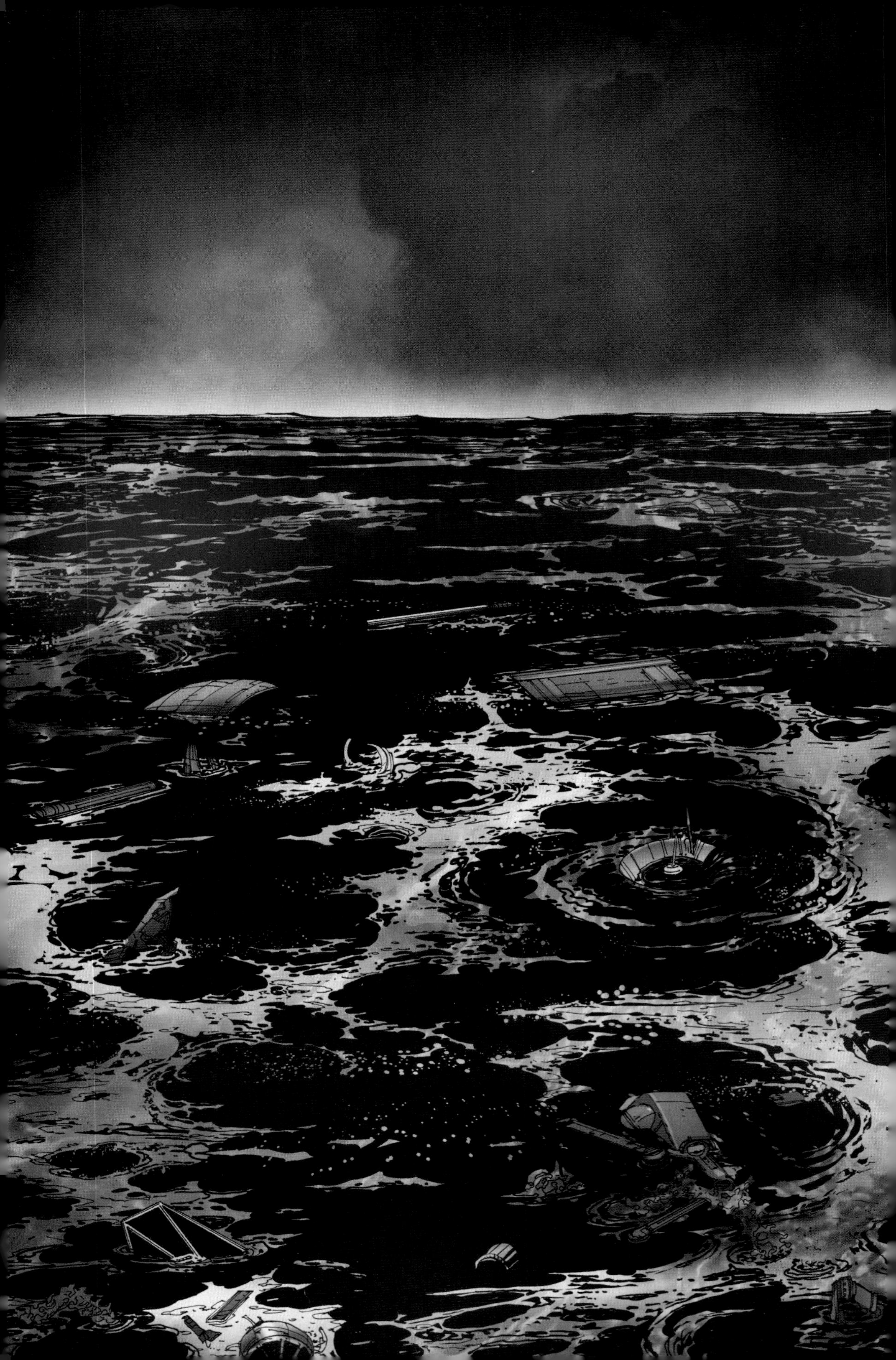

THEY...THEY DESTROYED THEIR OWN CITIES. ALL ACROSS THE PLANET, EVERYTHING ABOVE THE SURFACE... JUST *GONE*.

THEY DESTROYED *NOTHING*, COMMANDER JORDO. DAC CITY AND THE OTHERS WERE MERELY OUTPOSTS. THEIR TRUE CIVILIZATION LIES BENEATH THE SURFACE-- A THOUSAND TIMES AS EXPANSIVE.

THIS ACTION BARELY HURT THEM AT ALL, BUT IT MAKES OUR TASK INFINITELY MORE DIFFICULT. WITH THE SURFACE CITIES GONE, WE CAN NO LONGER USE THEM AS STAGING GROUNDS.

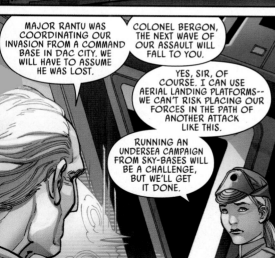

MAJOR RANTU WAS COORDINATING OUR INVASION FROM A COMMAND BASE IN DAC CITY. WE WILL HAVE TO ASSUME HE WAS LOST.

COLONEL BERGON, THE NEXT WAVE OF OUR ASSAULT WILL FALL TO YOU.

YES, SIR, OF COURSE. I CAN USE AERIAL LANDING PLATFORMS-- WE CAN'T RISK PLACING OUR FORCES IN THE PATH OF ANOTHER ATTACK LIKE THIS.

RUNNING AN UNDERSEA CAMPAIGN FROM SKY-BASES WILL BE A CHALLENGE, BUT WE'LL GET IT DONE.

COMMANDER JORDO-- WE JUST LOST SIGNIFICANT RESOURCES. YOU ARE THE IMPERIAL SECURITY BUREAU OFFICER WITH RESPONSIBILITY FOR THIS PLANET.

HOW DID WE NOT KNOW THE MON CALAMARI POSSESSED THIS CAPABILITY? HOW?

I... I HAVE NO EXPLANATION, GOVERNOR TARKIN, AND NO EXCUSE.

I WILL... I WILL *REDOUBLE* MY EFFORTS. YOU WILL SEE. I WILL REDEEM MYSELF.

SEE THAT YOU DO.

IT IS A LONG FALL TO THE OCEAN.

ANY WORD FROM LORD VADER?

I'M SORRY, SIR...

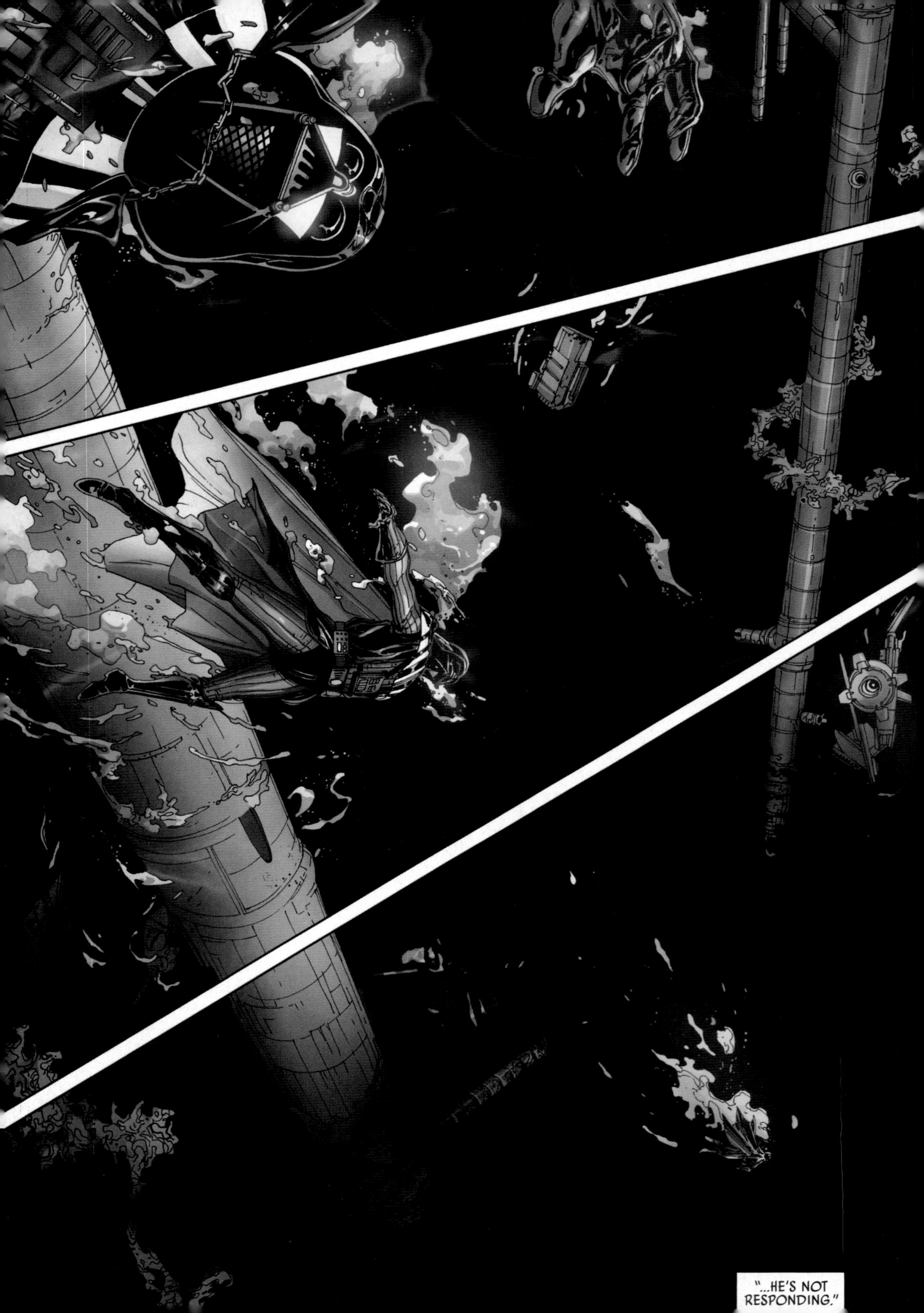
"...HE'S NOT RESPONDING."

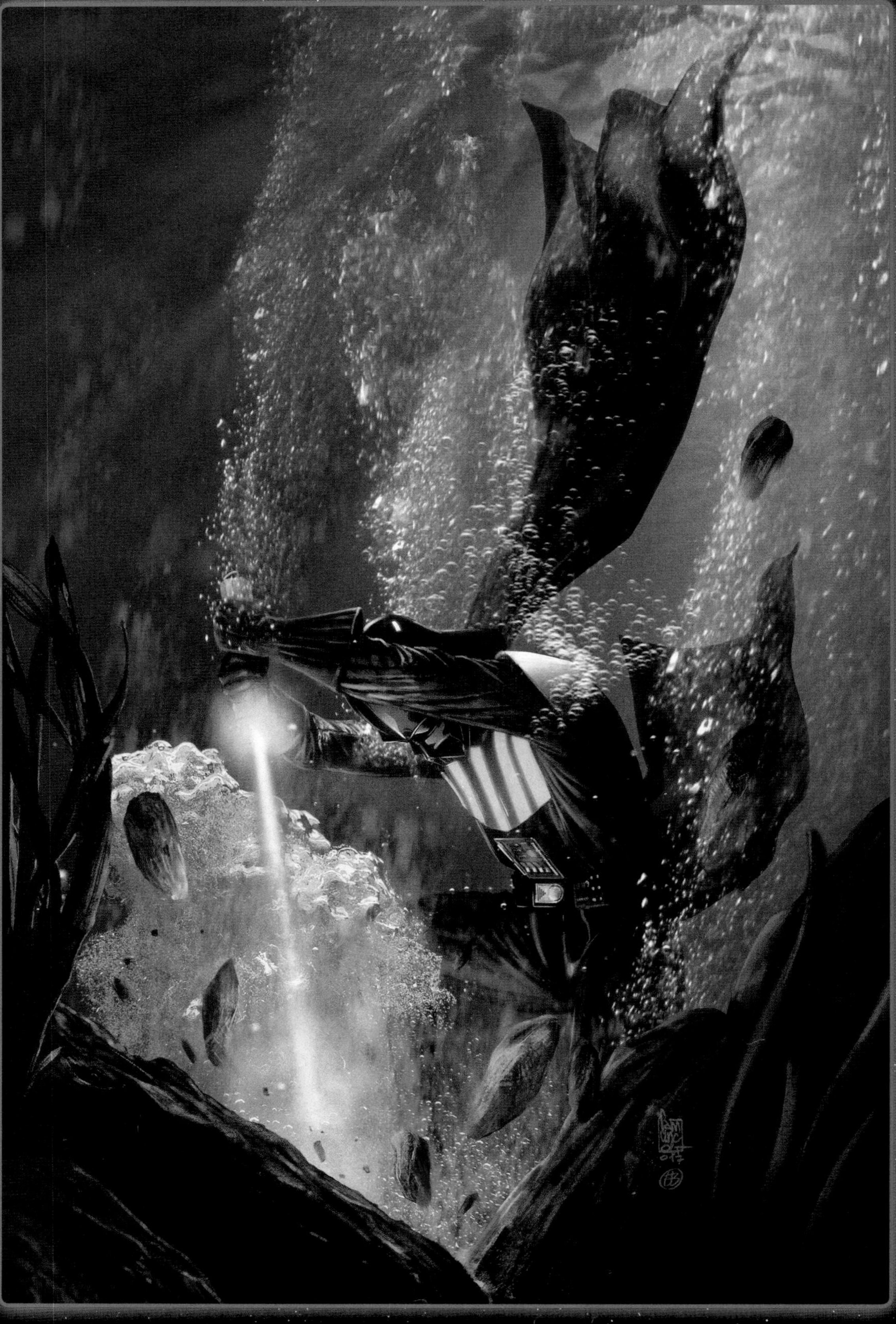

15

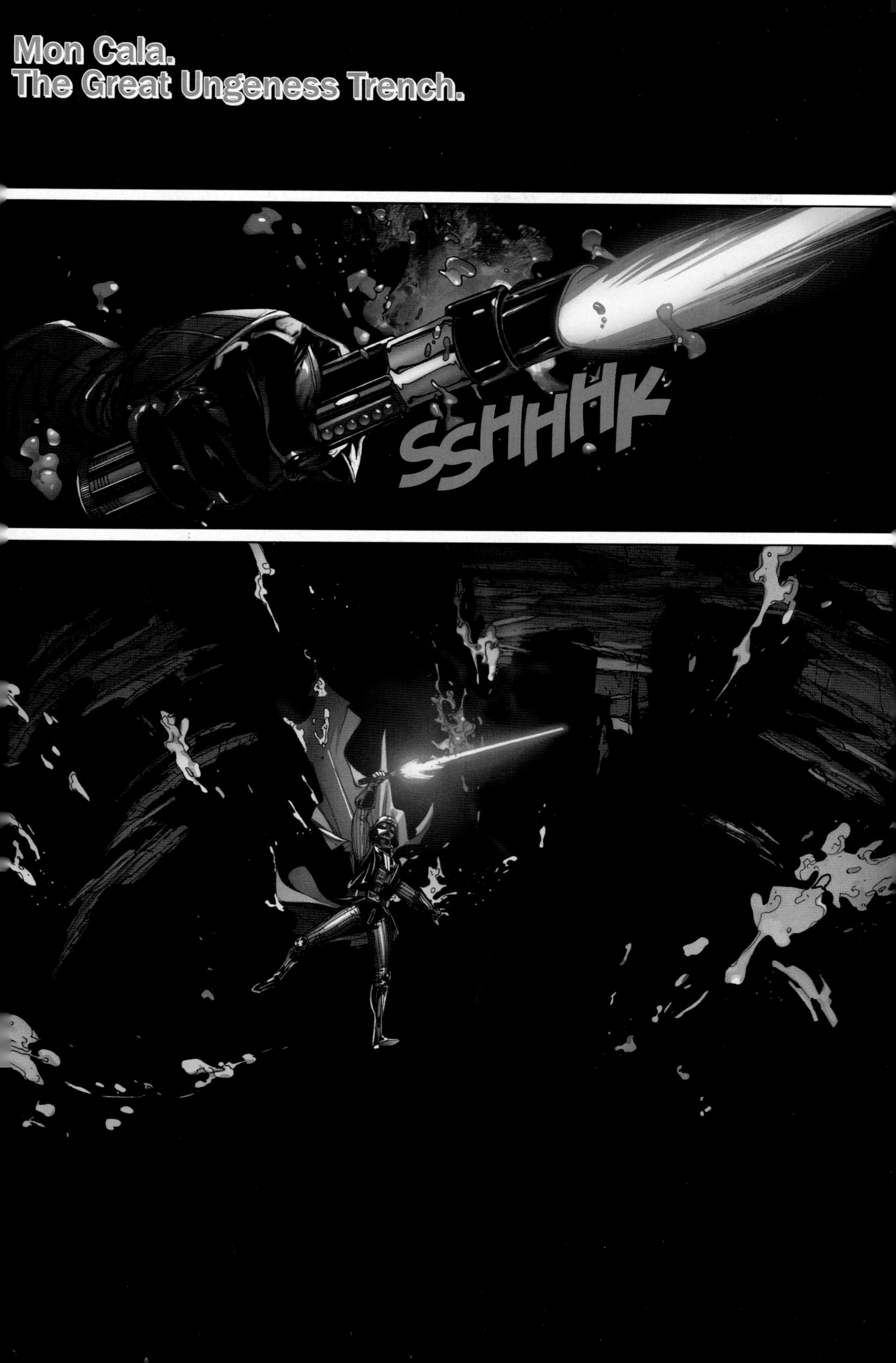
Mon Cala.
The Great Ungeness Trench.
SSHHHK

ALERT. OXYGEN RESERVES AT 30 PERCENT.

ALERT. EXTERNAL PRESSURE HAS EXCEEDED MAXIMUM SUIT TOLERANCE.

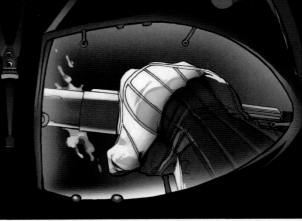

ALERT. SUIT RUPTURE IMMINENT.

RELOCATE TO SAFE ENVIRONMENT IMMEDIATELY.

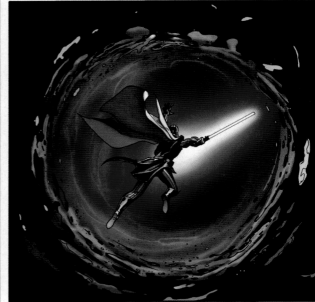

EXTERNAL PRESSURE RETURNED TO NORMAL TOLERANCES.

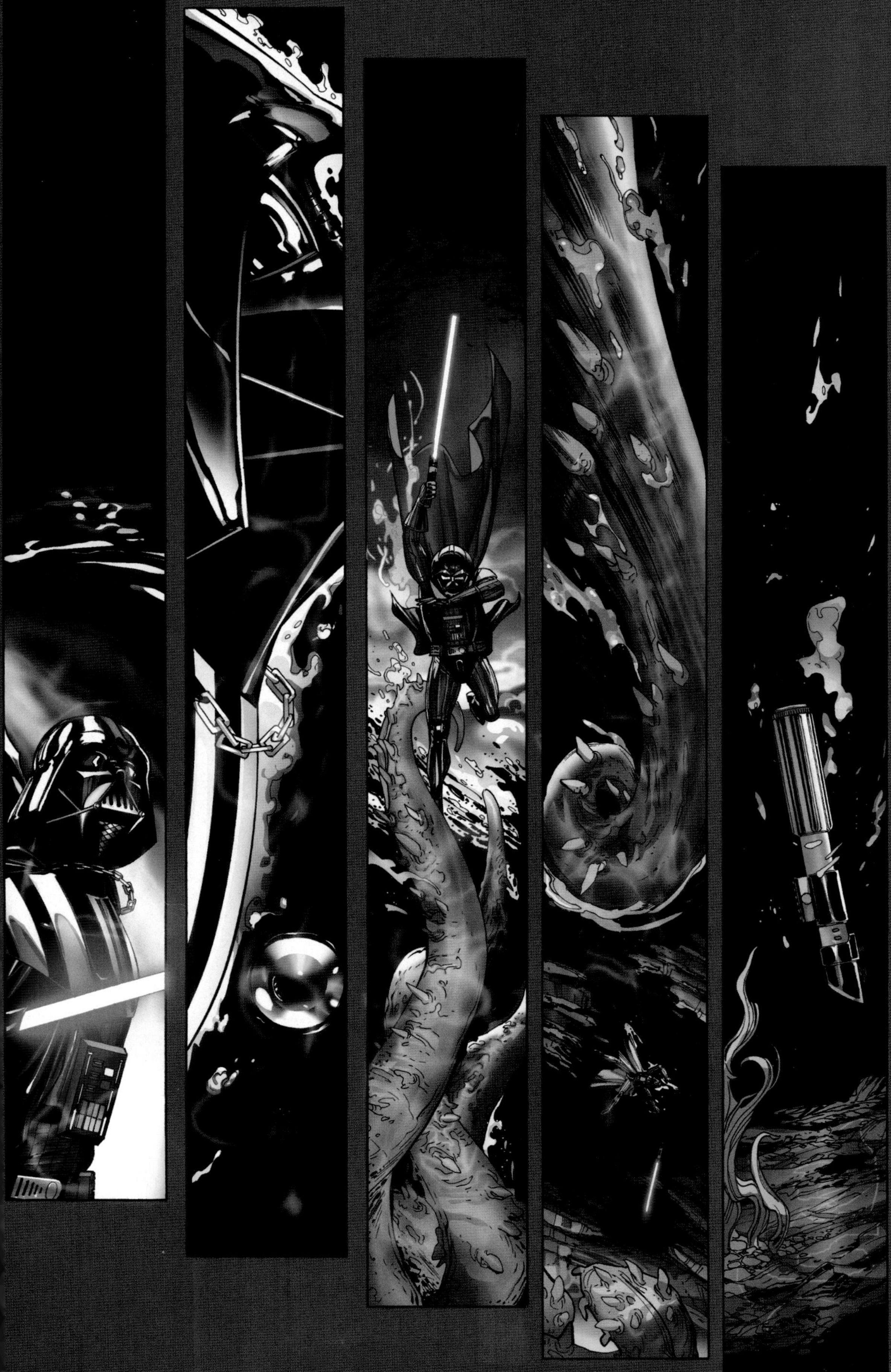

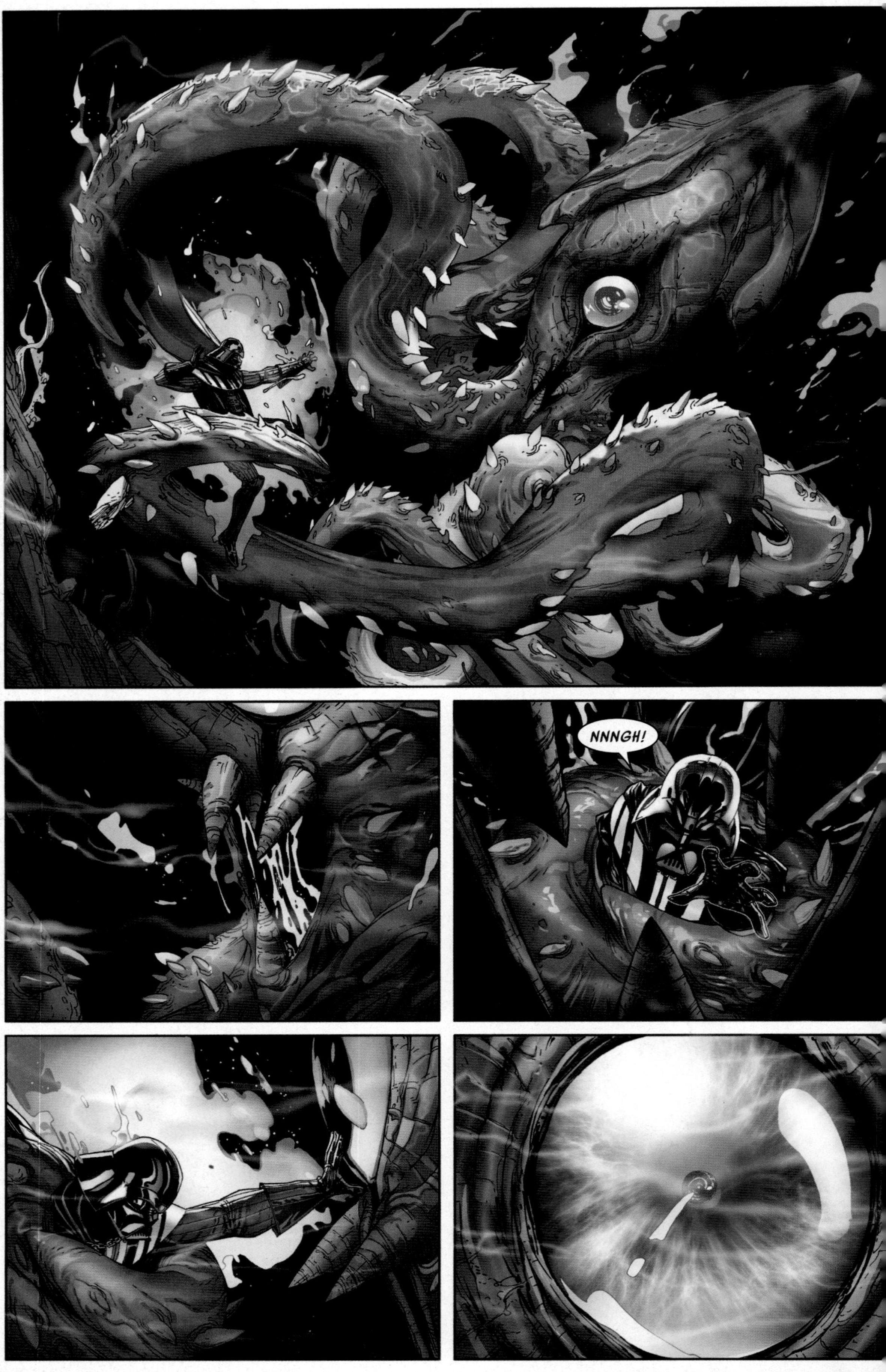
NNNGH!

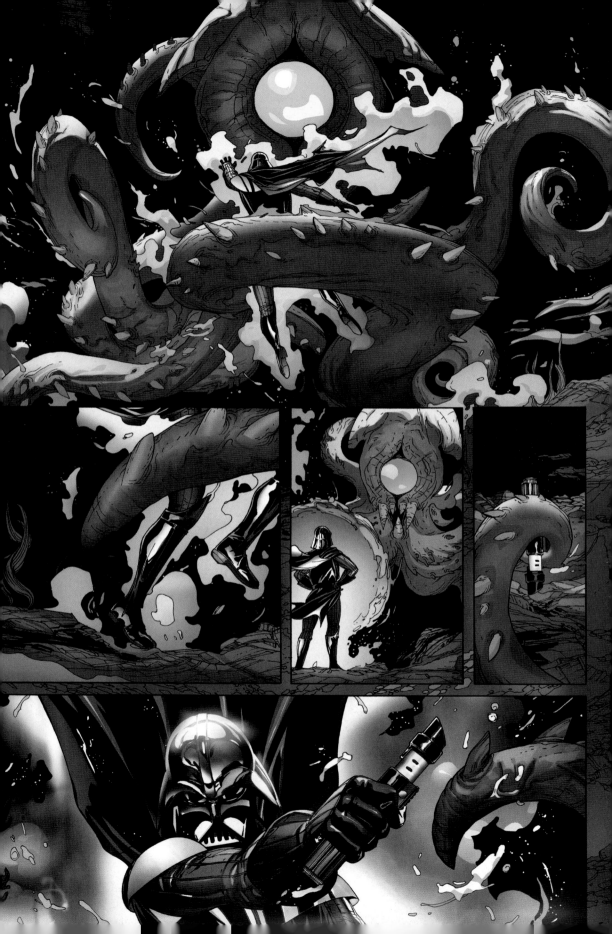

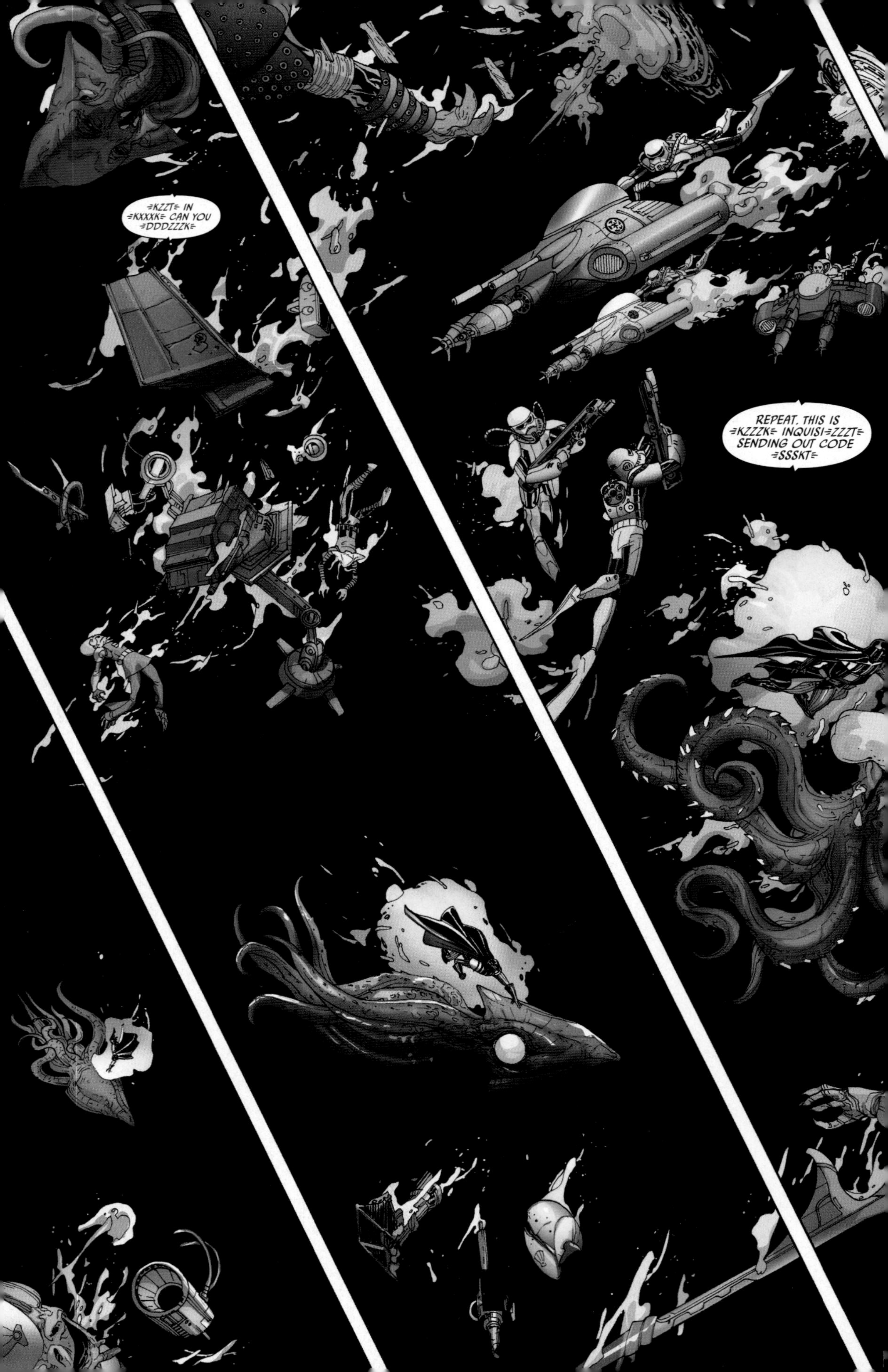

=KZZT= IN =KXXXK= CAN YOU =DDDZZZK=
REPEAT. THIS IS =KZZZK= INQUISI=ZZZT= SENDING OUT CODE =SSSKT=

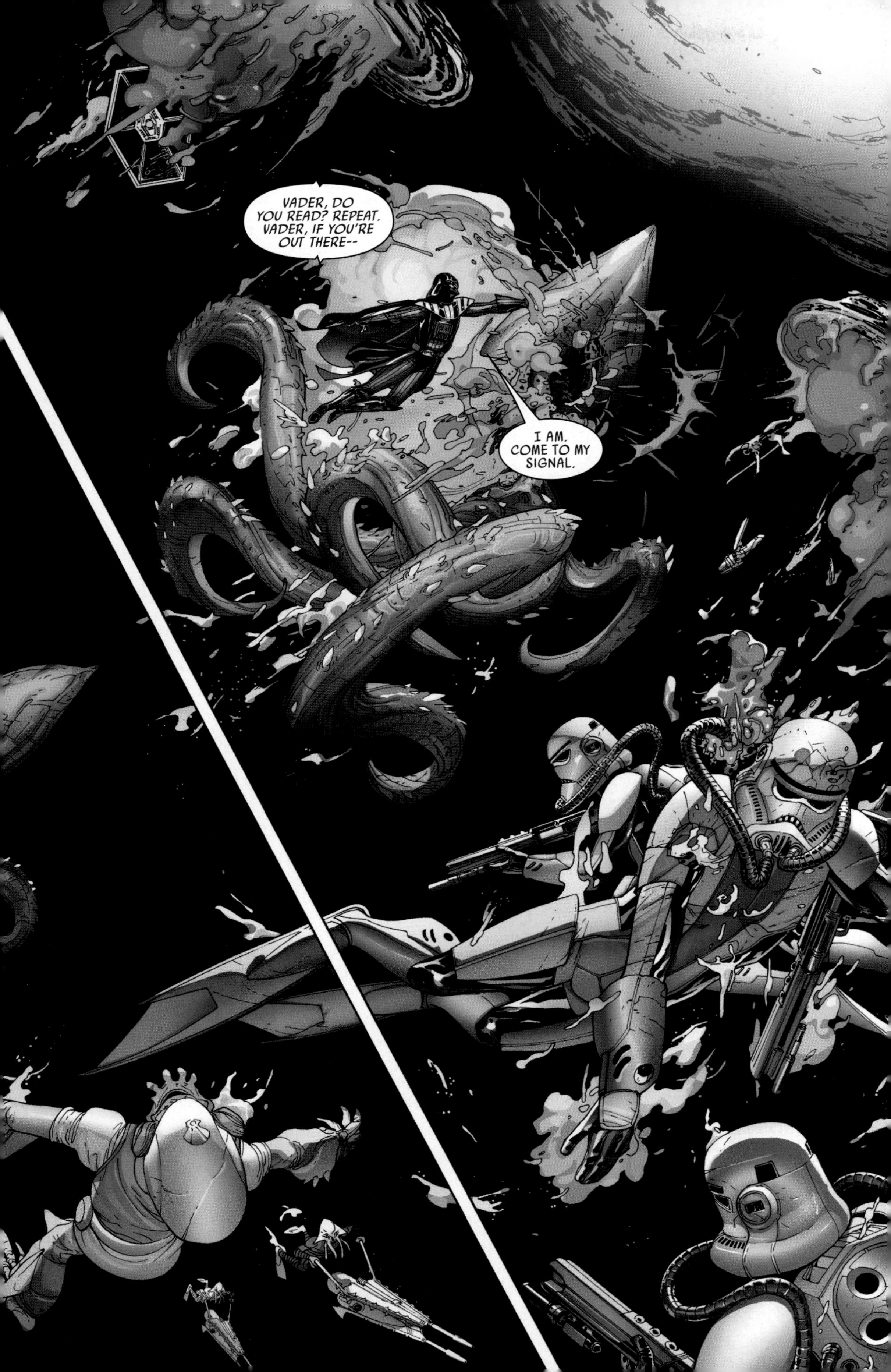
VADER, DO YOU READ? REPEAT. VADER, IF YOU'RE OUT THERE--
I AM. COME TO MY SIGNAL.

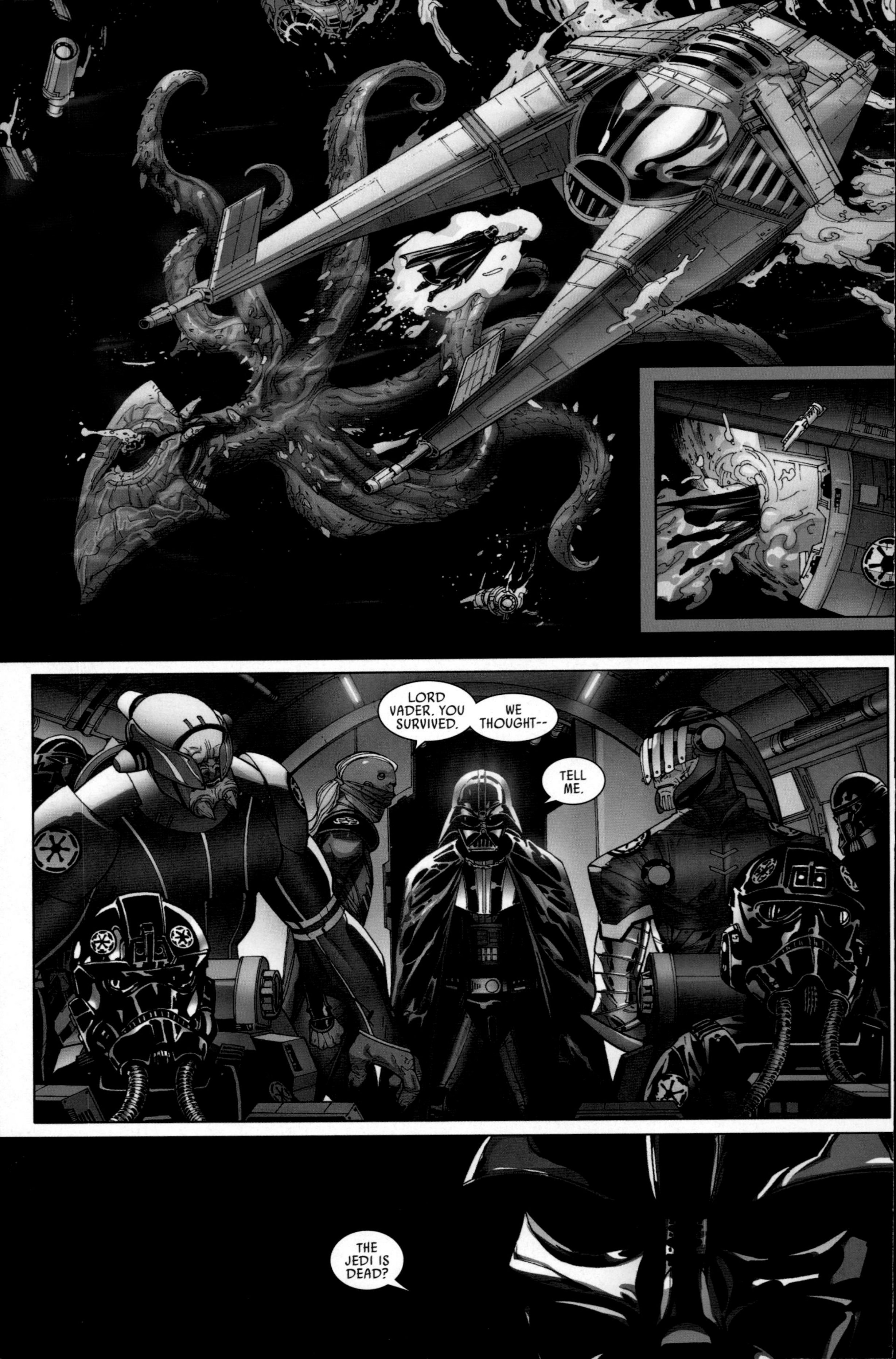
LORD VADER. YOU SURVIVED.
WE THOUGHT--
TELL ME.
THE JEDI IS DEAD?

NO... NOT YET. BUT WE--

THE KING, THEN, IS LEE-CHAR DEAD?

WE...DON'T KNOW.

THE KING WAS SWEPT AWAY WHEN THE TIDAL WAVE HIT.

BUT IT'S NOT ALL BAD. I GOT LEE-CHAR TO GIVE ME THE JEDI'S LOCATION.

WE KNOW EXACTLY WHERE TO GO.

WE BARELY SURVIVED THE WAVE OURSELVES--LOST TWO CLONES.

ONCE WE PULLED OURSELVES TOGETHER, WE REQUISITIONED THIS SUB AND CAME LOOKING FOR YOU.

WHY?

YOUR EMPEROR ASSIGNED YOU A TASK, SIXTH BROTHER. IF THAT TASK IS NOT YET COMPLETE, YOU HAVE FAILED.

BUT... I MEAN... WE RESCUED YOU, LORD VADER.

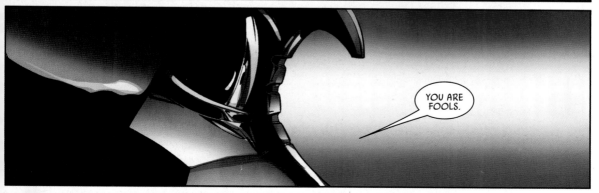

YOU ARE FOOLS.

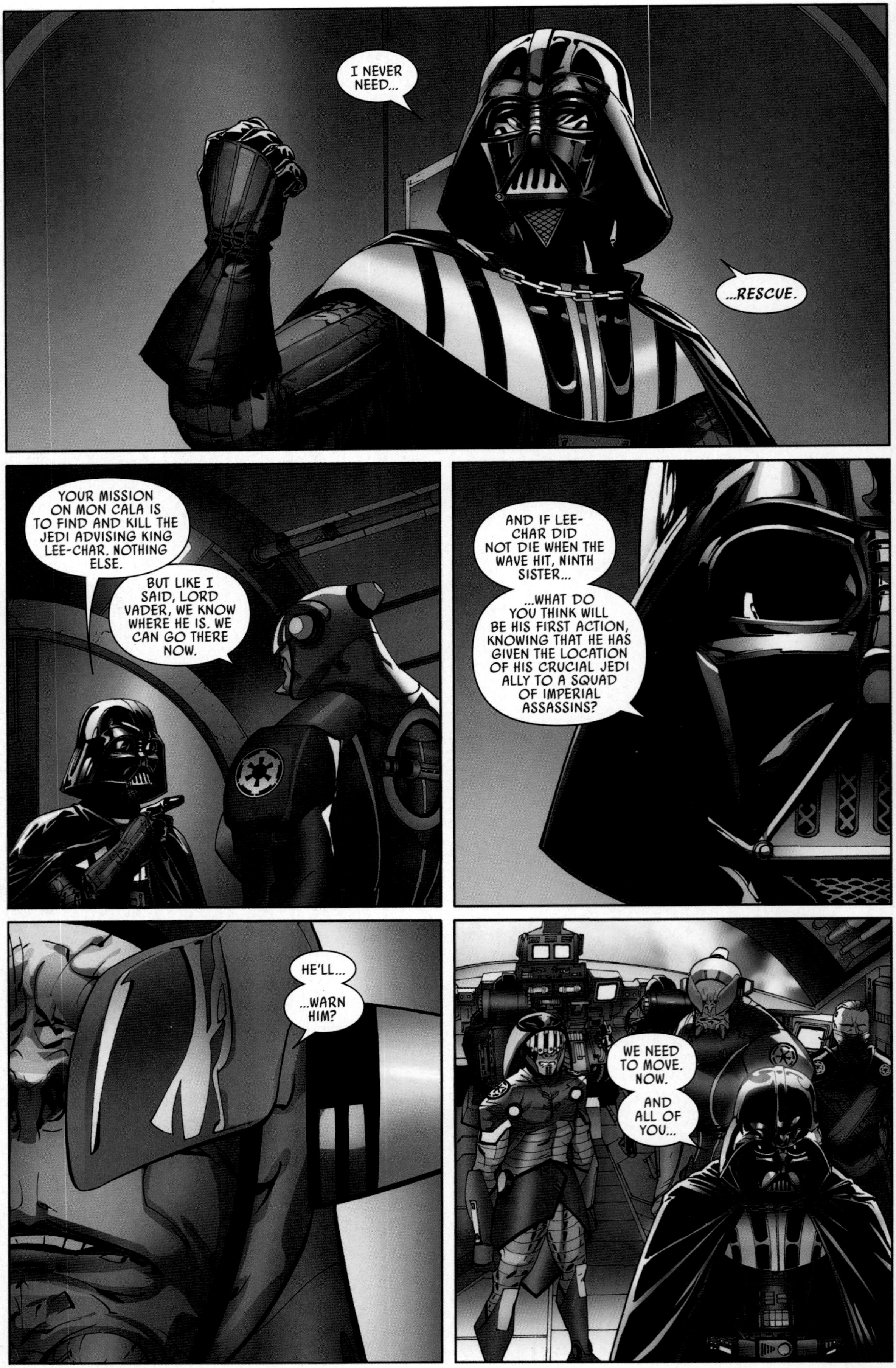

I NEVER NEED...
...RESCUE.
YOUR MISSION ON MON CALA IS TO FIND AND KILL THE JEDI ADVISING KING LEE-CHAR. NOTHING ELSE.
BUT LIKE I SAID, LORD VADER, WE KNOW WHERE HE IS. WE CAN GO THERE NOW.
AND IF LEE-CHAR DID NOT DIE WHEN THE WAVE HIT, NINTH SISTER...
...WHAT DO YOU THINK WILL BE HIS FIRST ACTION, KNOWING THAT HE HAS GIVEN THE LOCATION OF HIS CRUCIAL JEDI ALLY TO A SQUAD OF IMPERIAL ASSASSINS?
HE'LL...
...WARN HIM?
WE NEED TO MOVE. NOW.
AND ALL OF YOU...

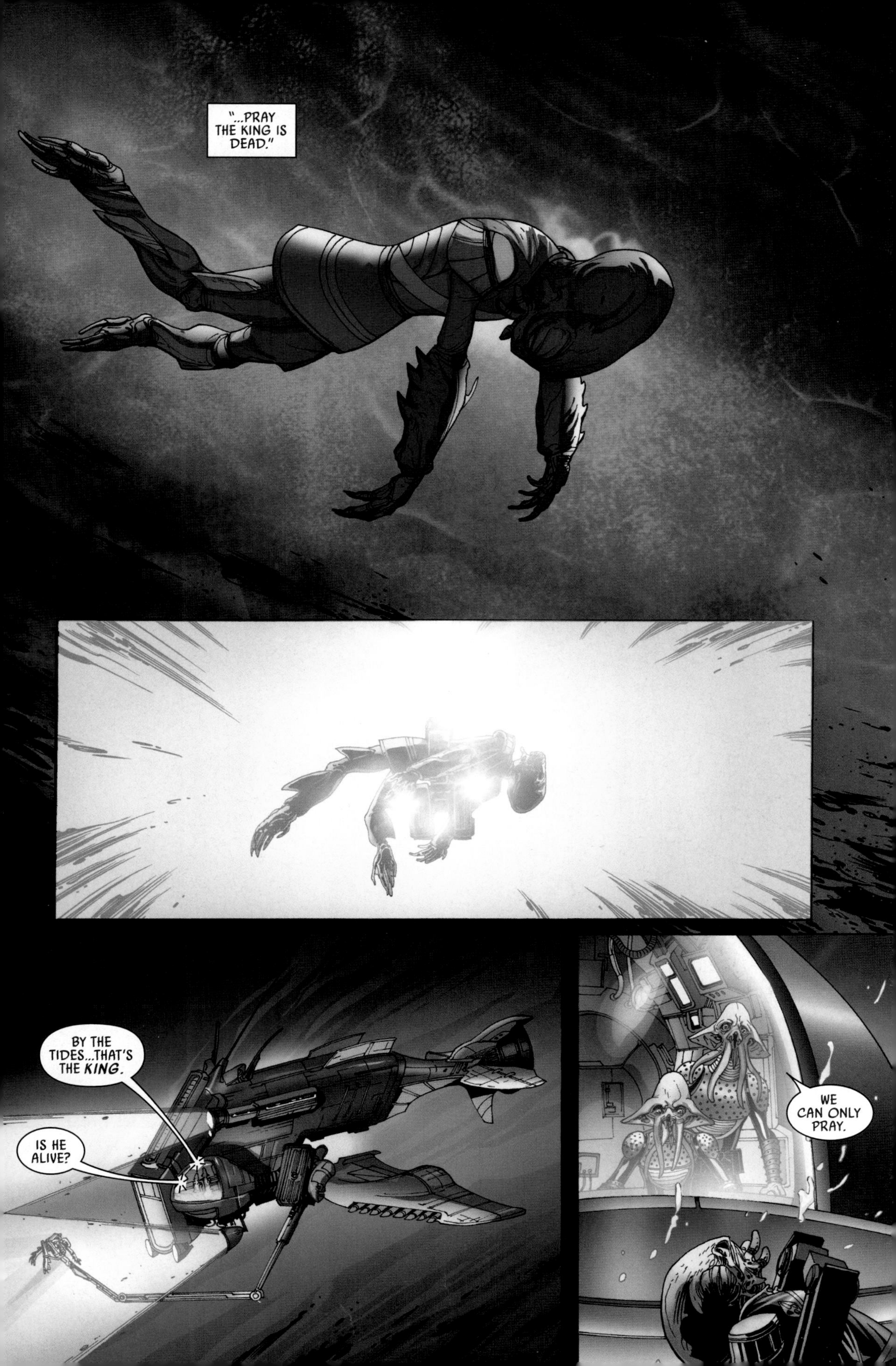
"...PRAY THE KING IS DEAD."
BY THE TIDES...THAT'S THE *KING*.
IS HE ALIVE?
WE CAN ONLY PRAY.

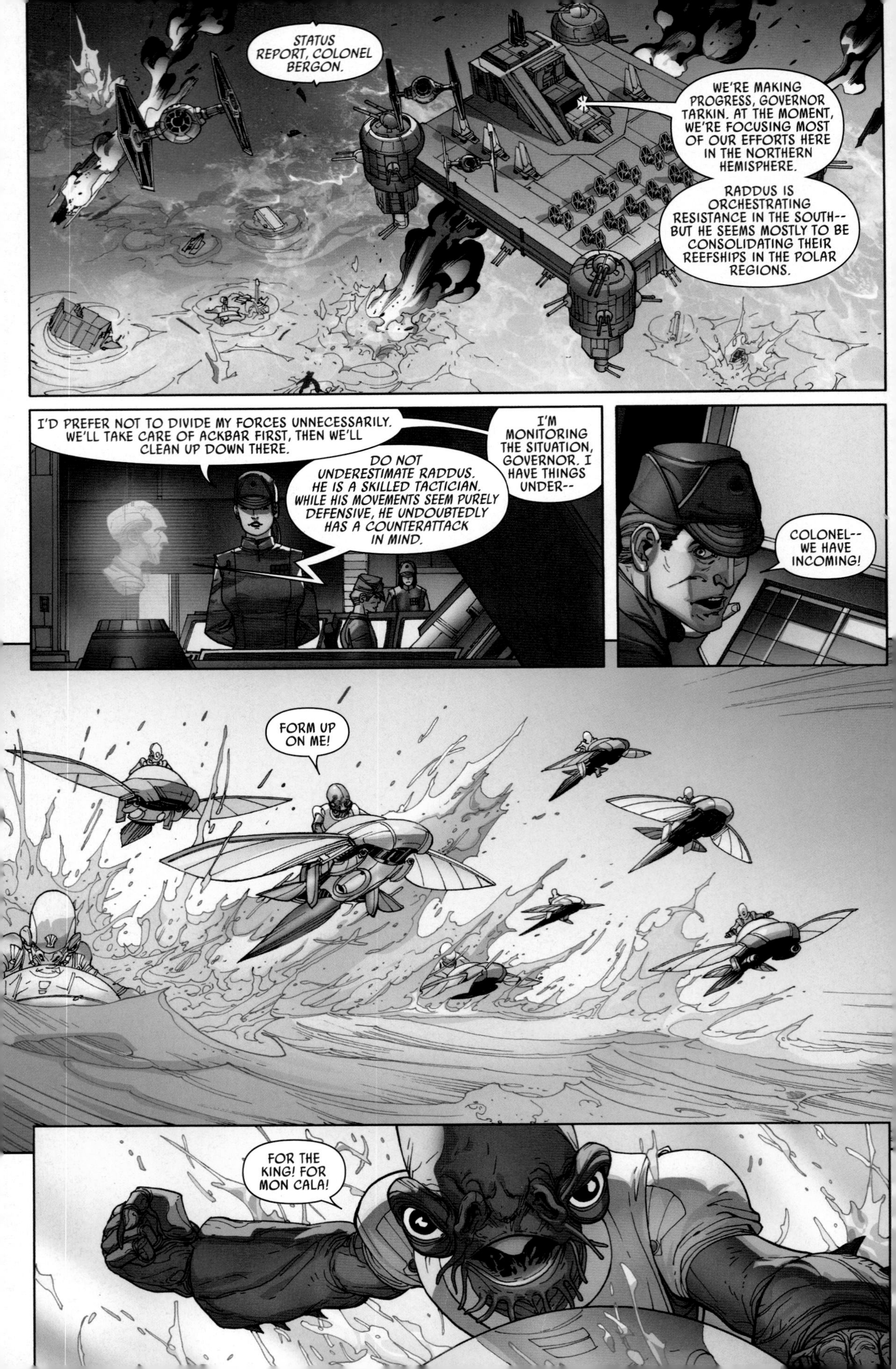
STATUS REPORT, COLONEL BERGON.
WE'RE MAKING PROGRESS, GOVERNOR TARKIN. AT THE MOMENT, WE'RE FOCUSING MOST OF OUR EFFORTS HERE IN THE NORTHERN HEMISPHERE.
RADDUS IS ORCHESTRATING RESISTANCE IN THE SOUTH--BUT HE SEEMS MOSTLY TO BE CONSOLIDATING THEIR REEFSHIPS IN THE POLAR REGIONS.
I'D PREFER NOT TO DIVIDE MY FORCES UNNECESSARILY. WE'LL TAKE CARE OF ACKBAR FIRST, THEN WE'LL CLEAN UP DOWN THERE.
DO NOT UNDERESTIMATE RADDUS. HE IS A SKILLED TACTICIAN. WHILE HIS MOVEMENTS SEEM PURELY DEFENSIVE, HE UNDOUBTEDLY HAS A COUNTERATTACK IN MIND.
I'M MONITORING THE SITUATION, GOVERNOR. I HAVE THINGS UNDER--
COLONEL--WE HAVE INCOMING!
FORM UP ON ME!
FOR THE KING! FOR MON CALA!

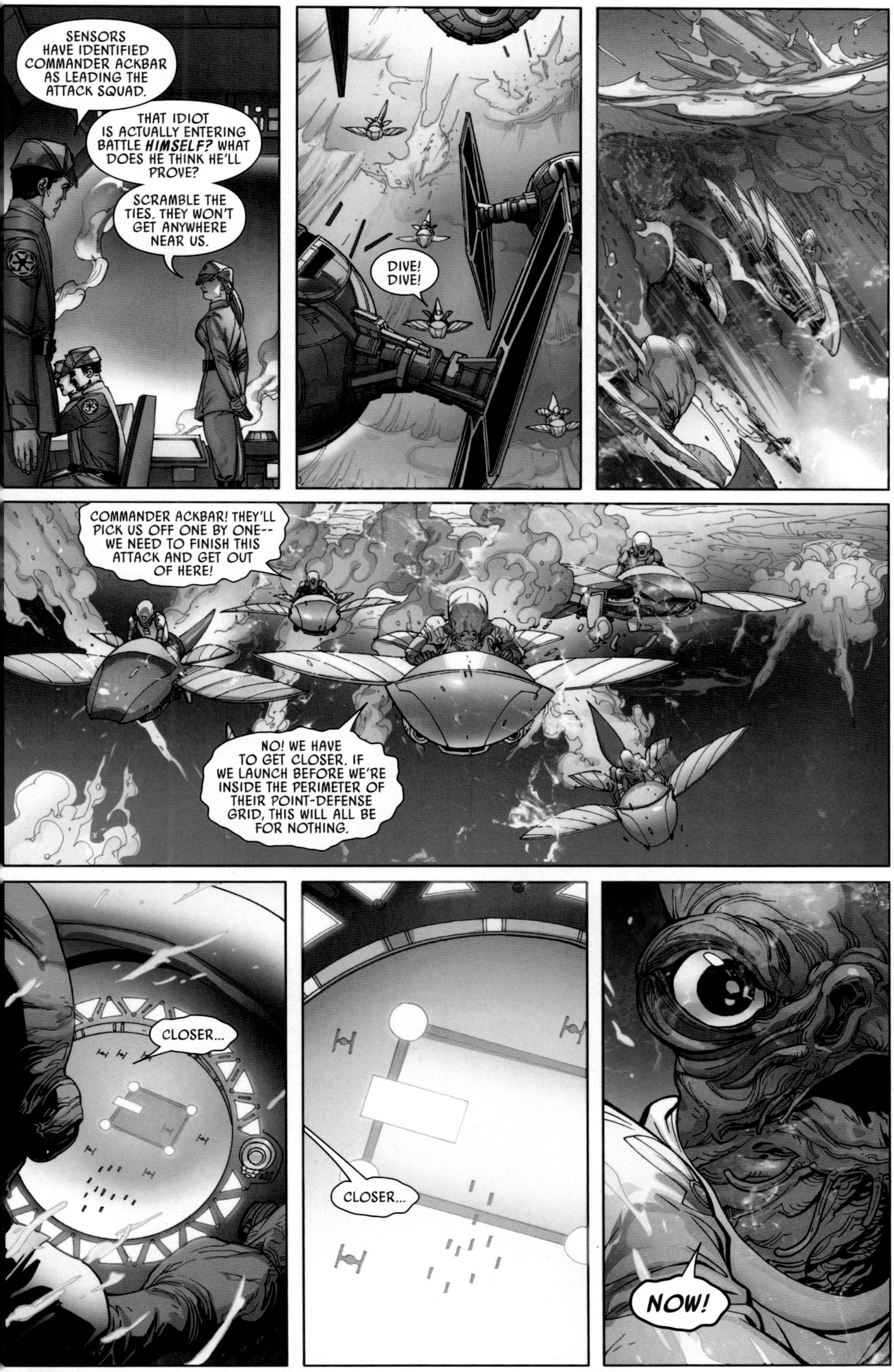
SENSORS HAVE IDENTIFIED COMMANDER ACKBAR AS LEADING THE ATTACK SQUAD.
THAT IDIOT IS ACTUALLY ENTERING BATTLE HIMSELF? WHAT DOES HE THINK HE'LL PROVE?
SCRAMBLE THE TIES. THEY WON'T GET ANYWHERE NEAR US.
DIVE! DIVE!
COMMANDER ACKBAR! THEY'LL PICK US OFF ONE BY ONE-- WE NEED TO FINISH THIS ATTACK AND GET OUT OF HERE!
NO! WE HAVE TO GET CLOSER. IF WE LAUNCH BEFORE WE'RE INSIDE THE PERIMETER OF THEIR POINT-DEFENSE GRID, THIS WILL ALL BE FOR NOTHING.
CLOSER...
CLOSER...
NOW!

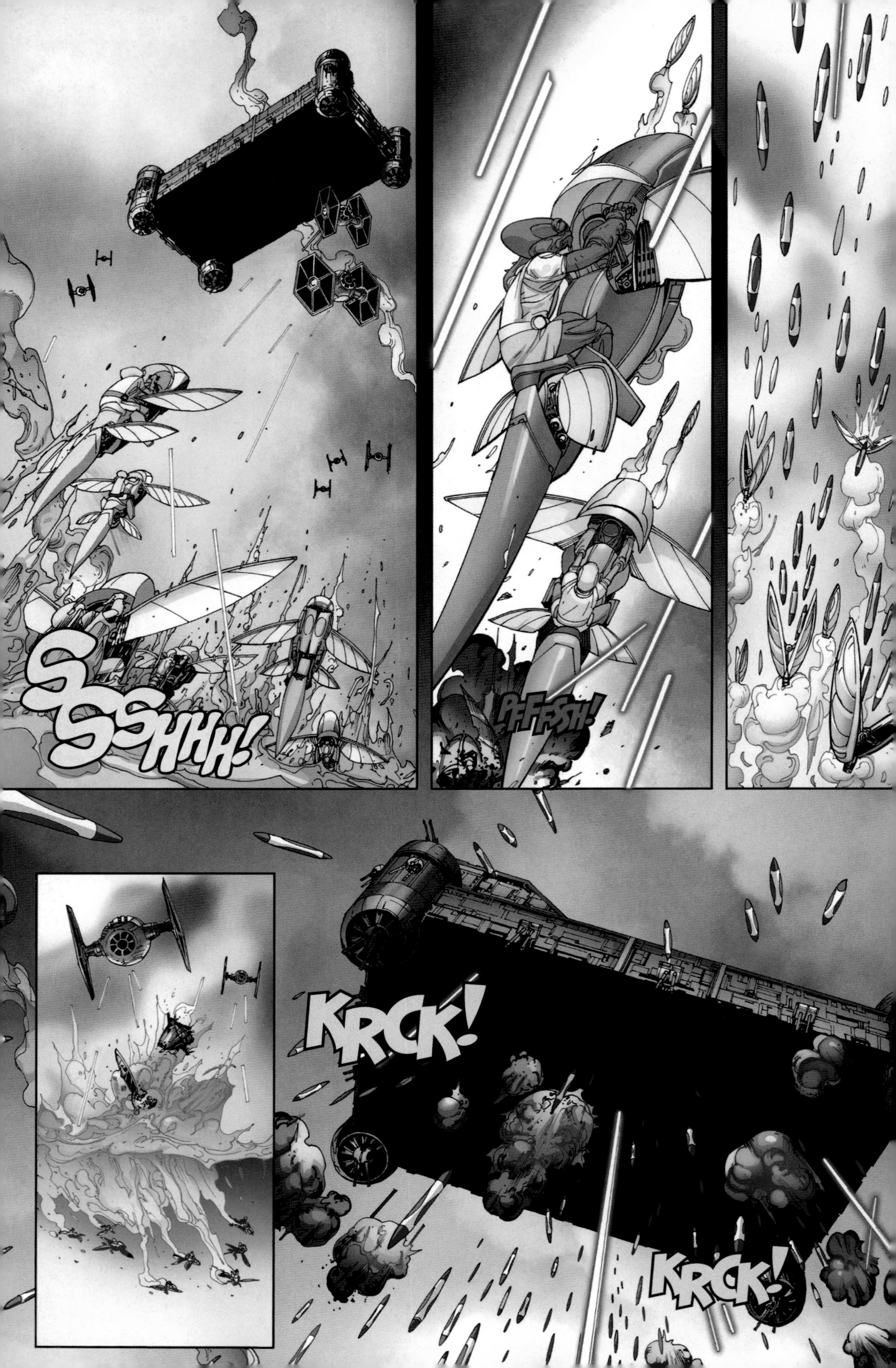
SSSHHH!
PFFFSH!
KRCK!
KRCK!

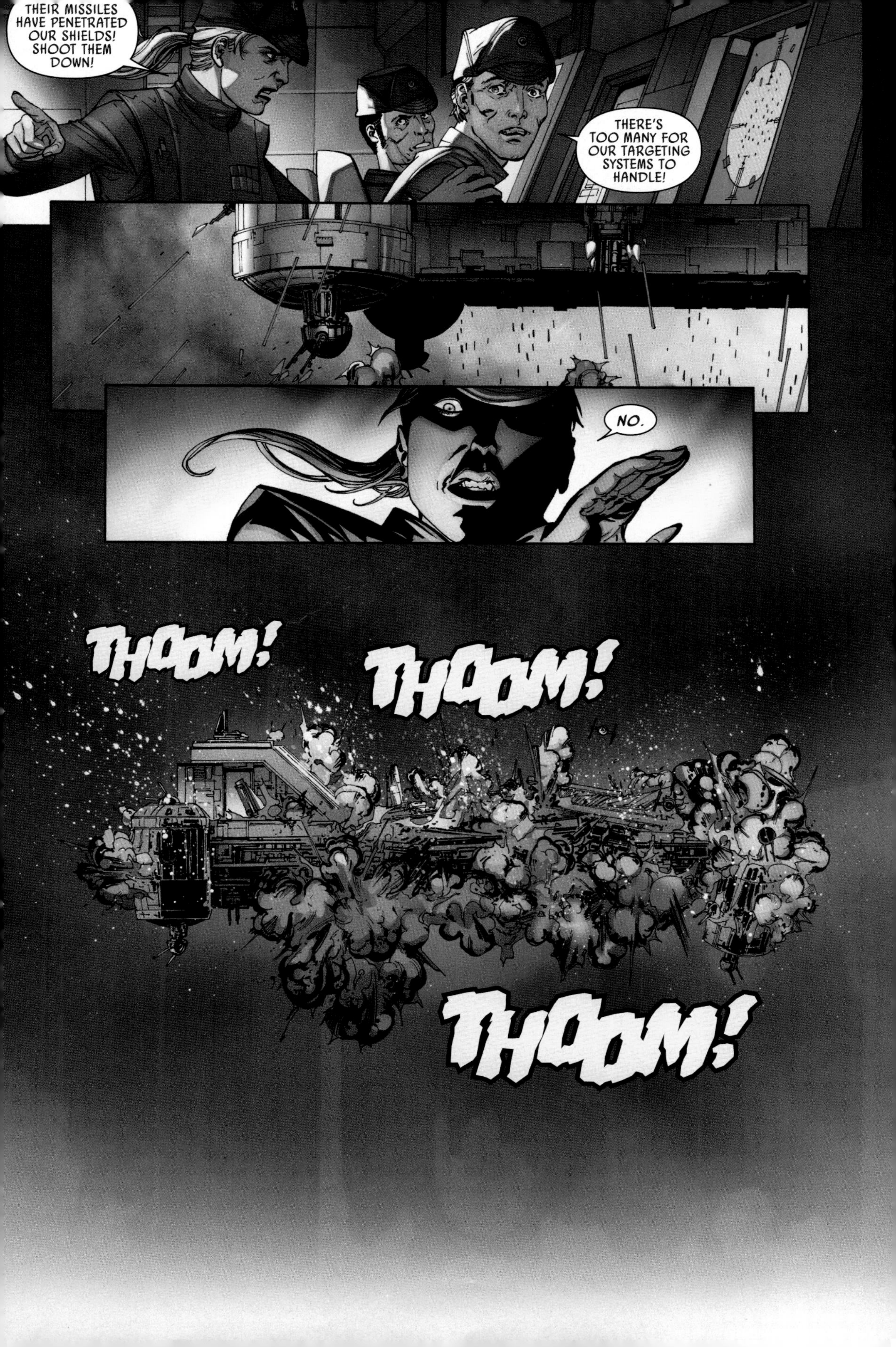
THEIR MISSILES HAVE PENETRATED OUR SHIELDS! SHOOT THEM DOWN!
THERE'S TOO MANY FOR OUR TARGETING SYSTEMS TO HANDLE!
NO.
THOOM!
THOOM!
THOOM!

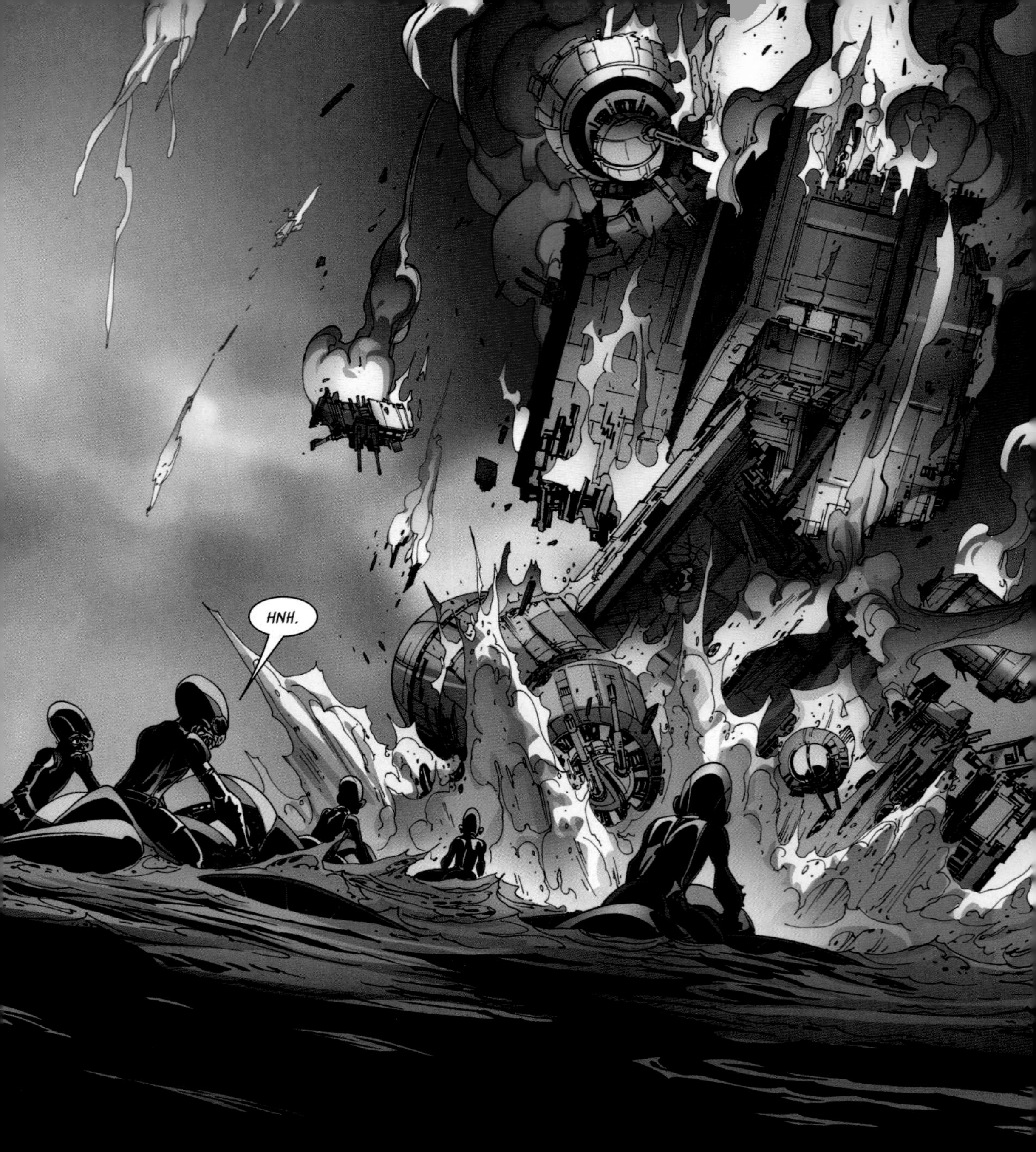
HNH.

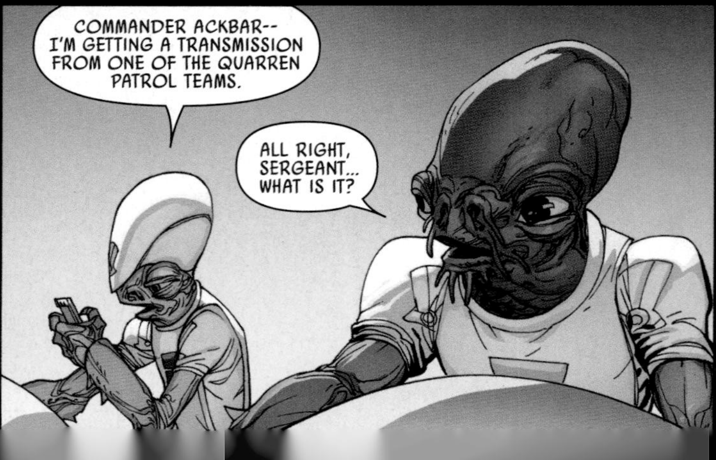
COMMANDER ACKBAR-- I'M GETTING A TRANSMISSION FROM ONE OF THE QUARREN PATROL TEAMS.
ALL RIGHT, SERGEANT... WHAT IS IT?

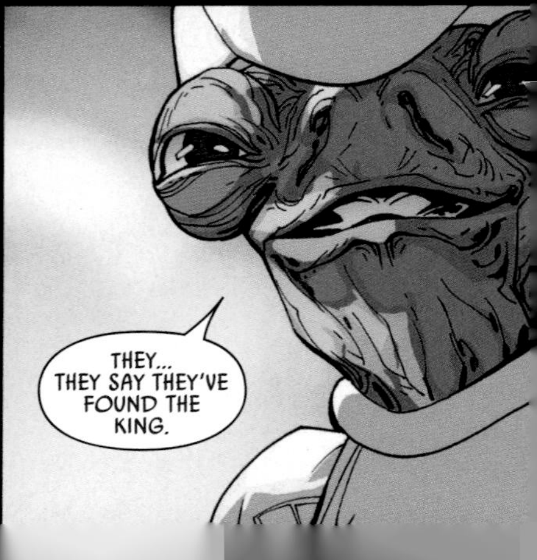
THEY... THEY SAY THEY'VE FOUND THE KING.

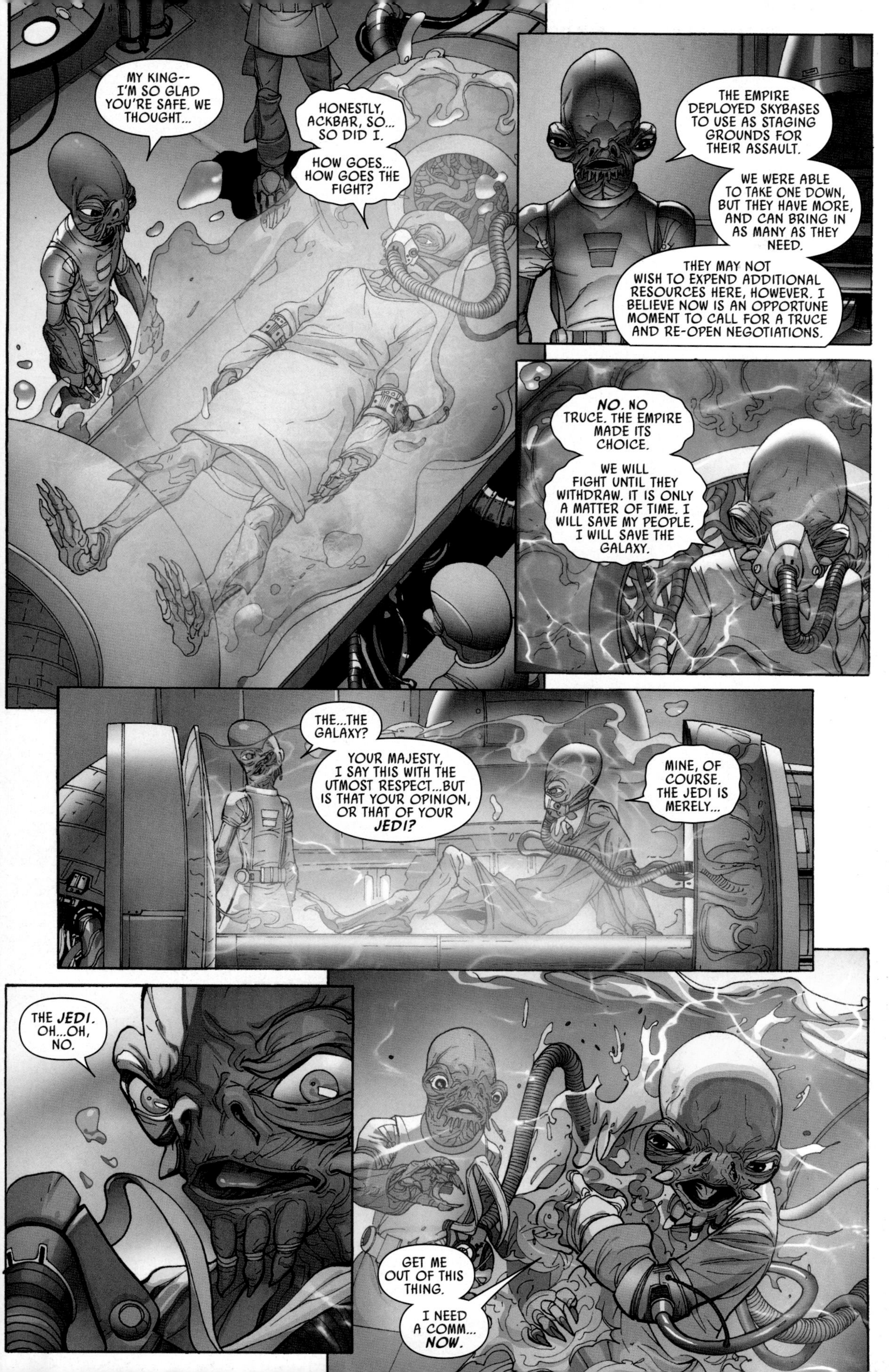
MY KING-- I'M SO GLAD YOU'RE SAFE. WE THOUGHT...
HONESTLY, ACKBAR, SO... SO DID I.
HOW GOES... HOW GOES THE FIGHT?
THE EMPIRE DEPLOYED SKYBASES TO USE AS STAGING GROUNDS FOR THEIR ASSAULT.
WE WERE ABLE TO TAKE ONE DOWN, BUT THEY HAVE MORE, AND CAN BRING IN AS MANY AS THEY NEED.
THEY MAY NOT WISH TO EXPEND ADDITIONAL RESOURCES HERE, HOWEVER. I BELIEVE NOW IS AN OPPORTUNE MOMENT TO CALL FOR A TRUCE AND RE-OPEN NEGOTIATIONS.
NO. NO TRUCE. THE EMPIRE MADE ITS CHOICE.
WE WILL FIGHT UNTIL THEY WITHDRAW. IT IS ONLY A MATTER OF TIME. I WILL SAVE MY PEOPLE. I WILL SAVE THE GALAXY.
THE...THE GALAXY?
YOUR MAJESTY, I SAY THIS WITH THE UTMOST RESPECT...BUT IS THAT YOUR OPINION, OR THAT OF YOUR ***JEDI?***
MINE, OF COURSE. THE JEDI IS MERELY...
THE ***JEDI.*** OH...OH, NO.
GET ME OUT OF THIS THING.
I NEED A COMM... ***NOW.***

Elsewhere.

THE MON CALAMARI AND QUARREN ARE PUTTING UP A GOOD FIGHT, MASTER BARR.

I EXPECTED NO LESS, VERLA. THIS PLANET'S PEOPLE SEE THEMSELVES AS STRONG AND FREE. THEY WILL NOT SUBMIT EASILY TO THE EMPIRE.

BUT PALPATINE CAN'T AFFORD TO LET THEM *WIN*, RIGHT? DO YOU THINK THEY WILL ACTUALLY SUCCEED IN LIBERATING THEIR PLANET?

EITHER WAY.

BLEET BLEEP WHIRRR

AH. THE KING SURVIVES. GOOD. PUT HIM THROUGH, ENDEE.

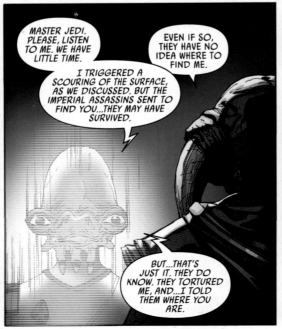

MASTER JEDI. PLEASE, LISTEN TO ME. WE HAVE LITTLE TIME.

EVEN IF SO, THEY HAVE NO IDEA WHERE TO FIND ME.

I TRIGGERED A SCOURING OF THE SURFACE, AS WE DISCUSSED. BUT THE IMPERIAL ASSASSINS SENT TO FIND YOU...THEY MAY HAVE SURVIVED.

BUT...THAT'S JUST IT. THEY DO KNOW. THEY TORTURED ME, AND...I TOLD THEM WHERE YOU ARE.

THEY'RE PROBABLY COMING FOR YOU RIGHT NOW.

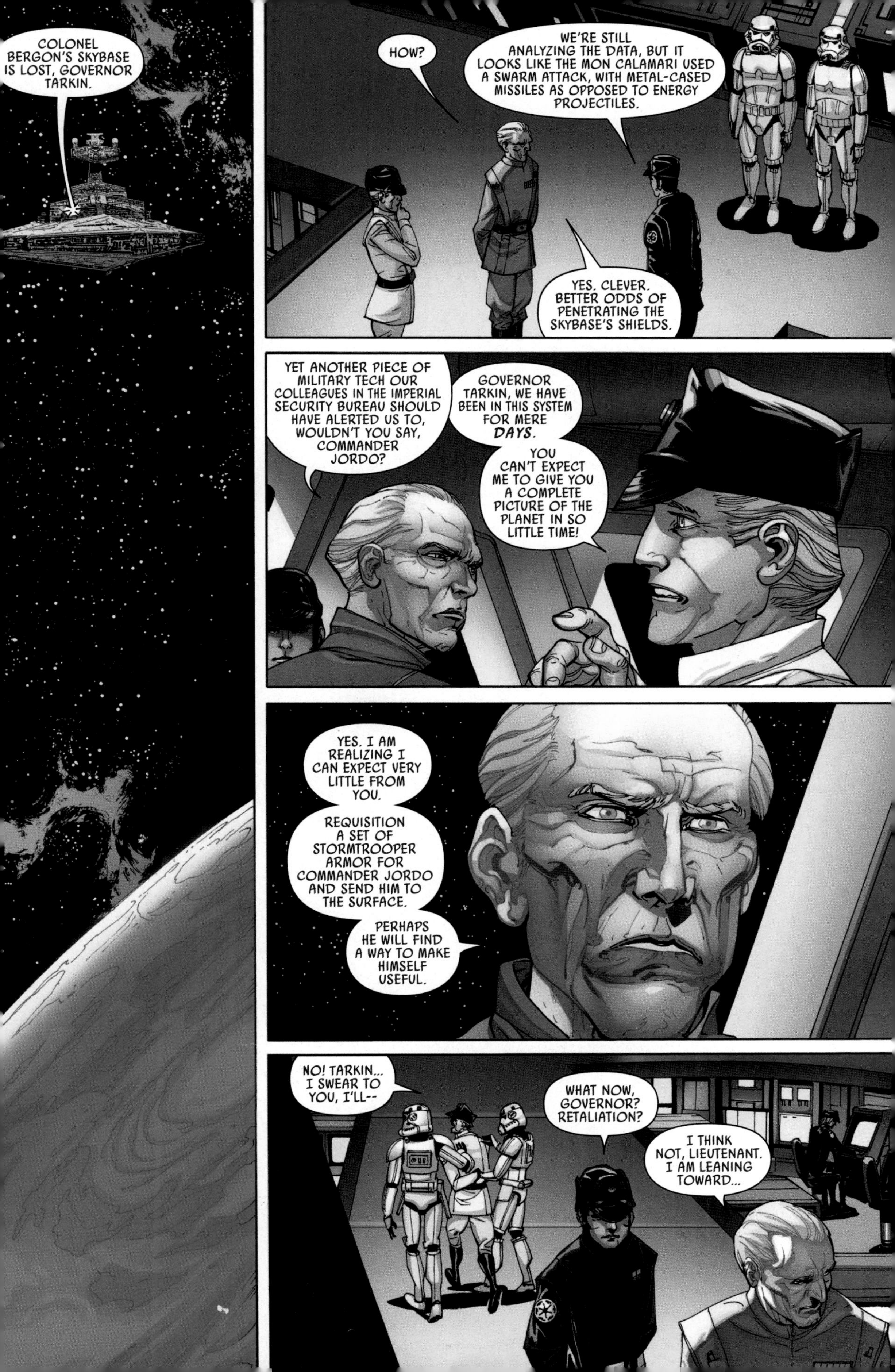
COLONEL BERGON'S SKYBASE IS LOST, GOVERNOR TARKIN.
HOW?
WE'RE STILL ANALYZING THE DATA, BUT IT LOOKS LIKE THE MON CALAMARI USED A SWARM ATTACK, WITH METAL-CASED MISSILES AS OPPOSED TO ENERGY PROJECTILES.
YES. CLEVER. BETTER ODDS OF PENETRATING THE SKYBASE'S SHIELDS.
YET ANOTHER PIECE OF MILITARY TECH OUR COLLEAGUES IN THE IMPERIAL SECURITY BUREAU SHOULD HAVE ALERTED US TO, WOULDN'T YOU SAY, COMMANDER JORDO?
GOVERNOR TARKIN, WE HAVE BEEN IN THIS SYSTEM FOR MERE *DAYS*.
YOU CAN'T EXPECT ME TO GIVE YOU A COMPLETE PICTURE OF THE PLANET IN SO LITTLE TIME!
YES. I AM REALIZING I CAN EXPECT VERY LITTLE FROM YOU.
REQUISITION A SET OF STORMTROOPER ARMOR FOR COMMANDER JORDO AND SEND HIM TO THE SURFACE.
PERHAPS HE WILL FIND A WAY TO MAKE HIMSELF USEFUL.
NO! TARKIN... I SWEAR TO YOU, I'LL--
WHAT NOW, GOVERNOR? RETALIATION?
I THINK NOT, LIEUTENANT. I AM LEANING TOWARD...

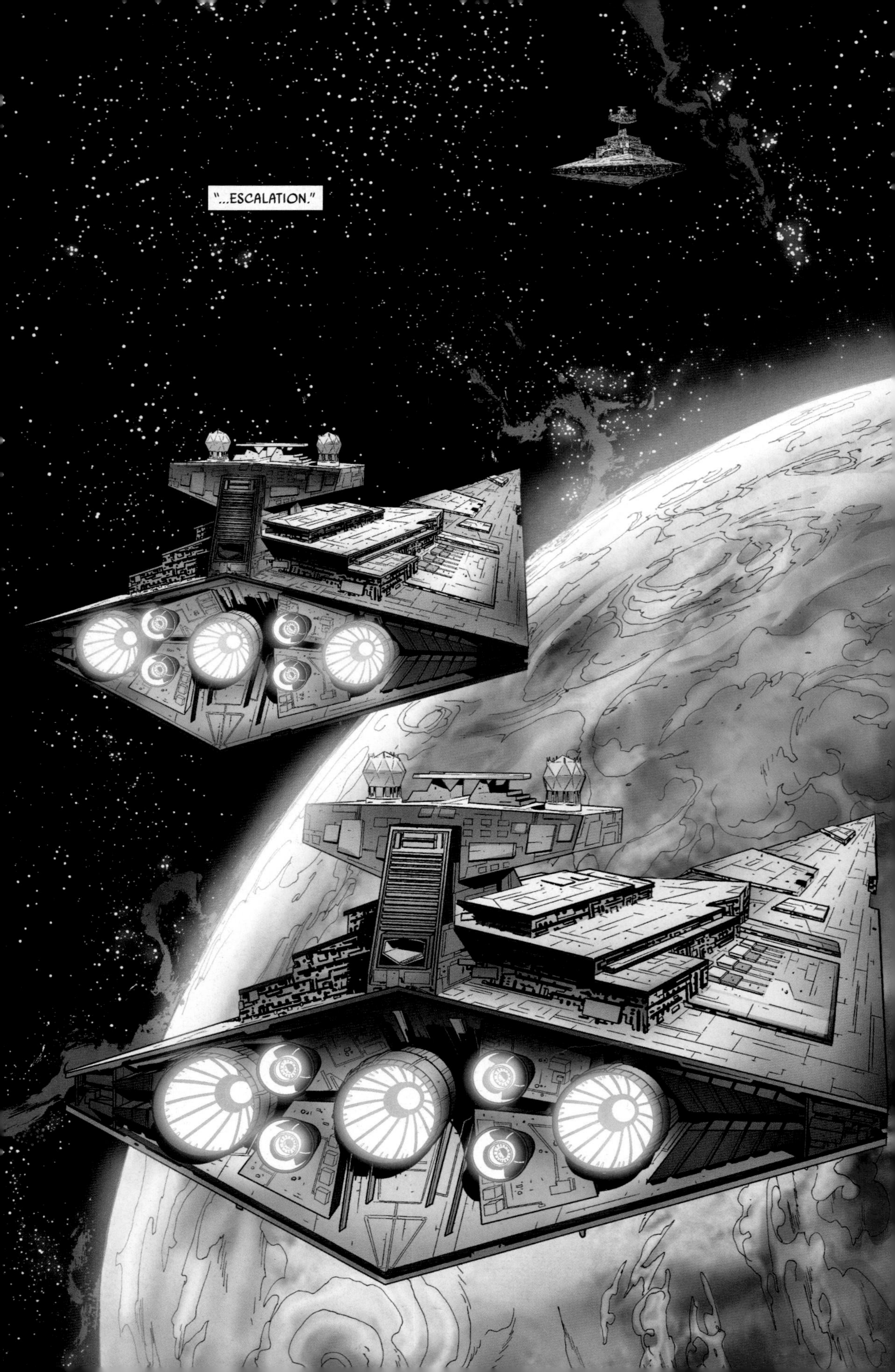
"...ESCALATION."

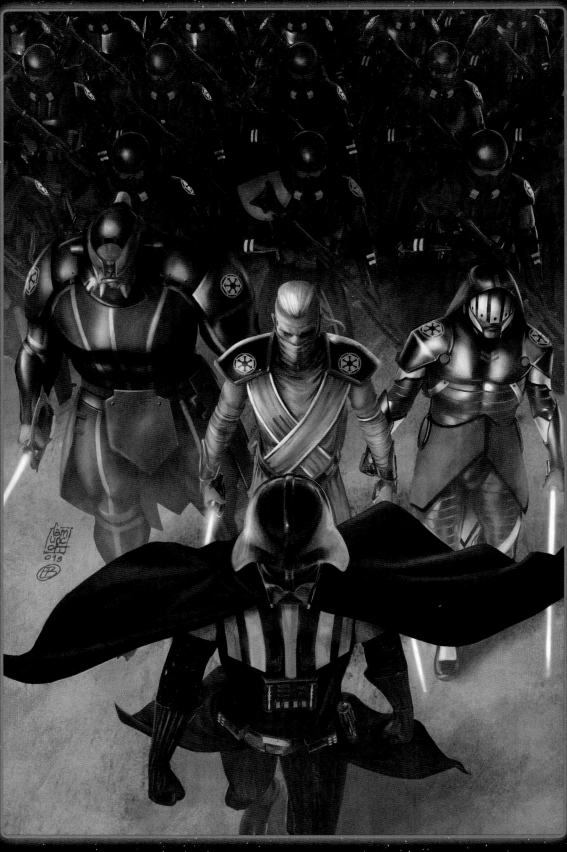

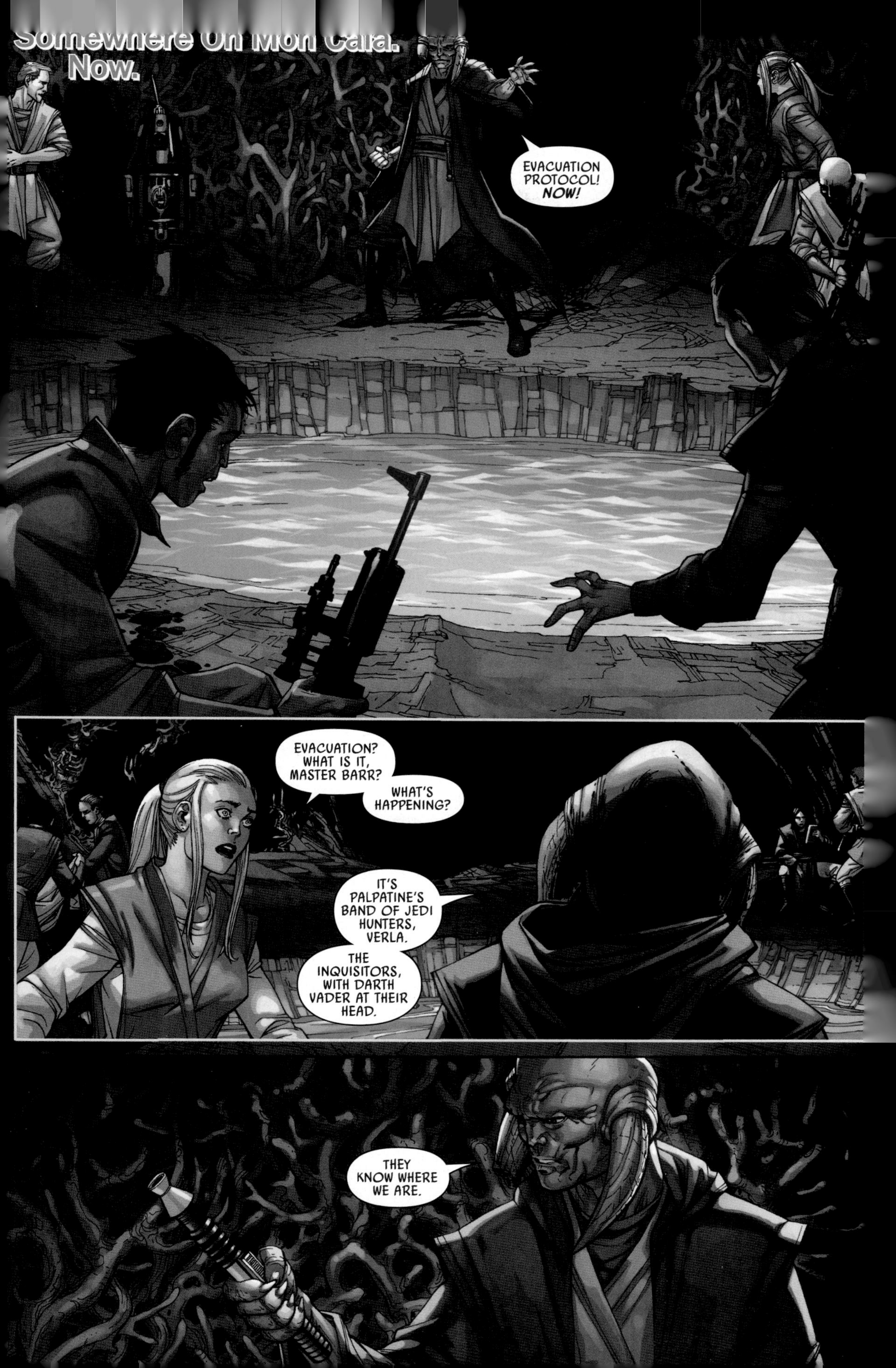

Somewhere On Mon Cala.
Now.
EVACUATION PROTOCOL! NOW!
EVACUATION? WHAT IS IT, MASTER BARR?
WHAT'S HAPPENING?
IT'S PALPATINE'S BAND OF JEDI HUNTERS, VERLA.
THE INQUISITORS, WITH DARTH VADER AT THEIR HEAD.
THEY KNOW WHERE WE ARE.

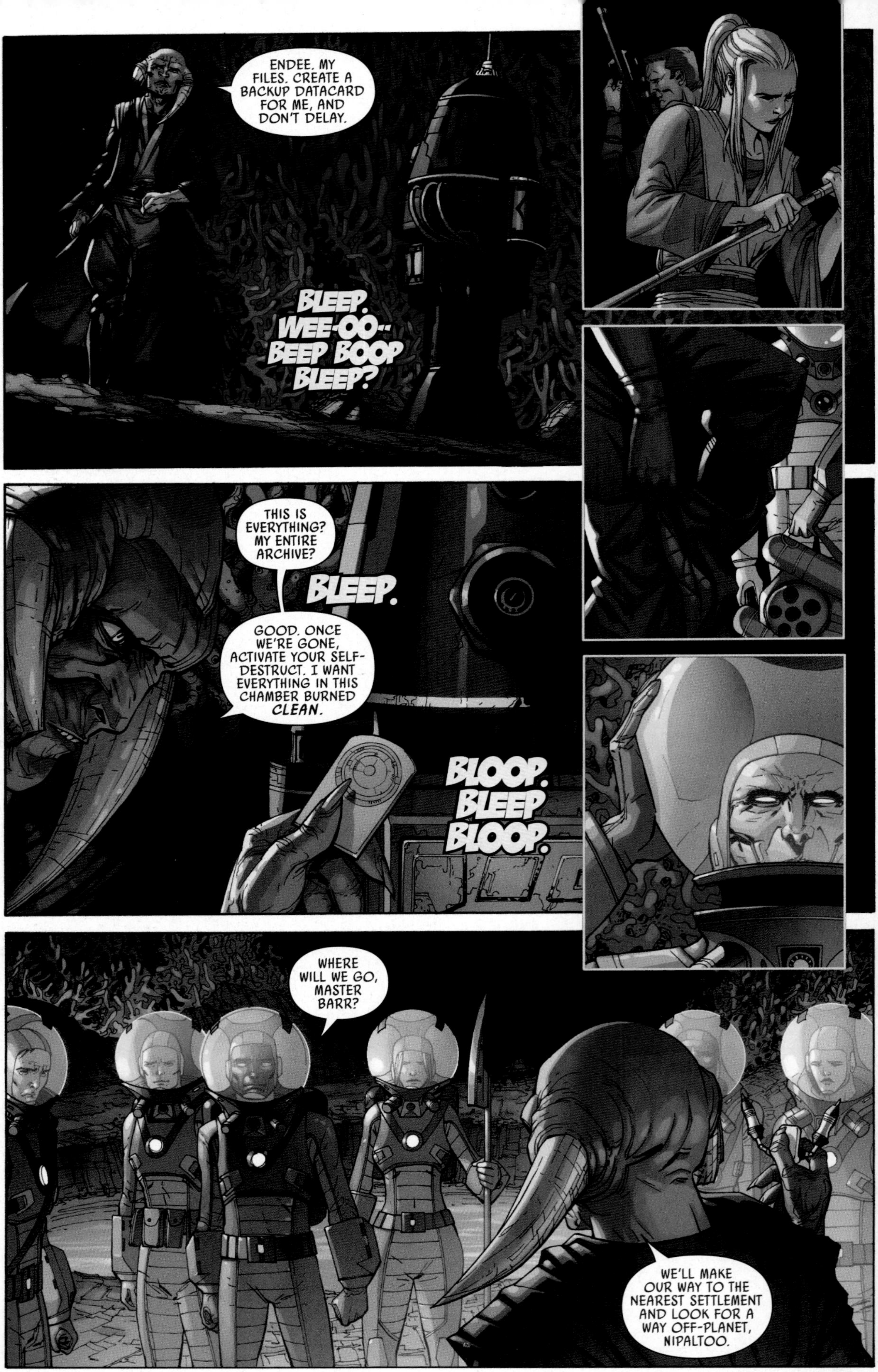
ENDEE. MY FILES. CREATE A BACKUP DATACARD FOR ME, AND DON'T DELAY.
BLEEP. WEE-OO-- BEEP BOOP BLEEP?
THIS IS EVERYTHING? MY ENTIRE ARCHIVE?
BLEEP.
GOOD. ONCE WE'RE GONE, ACTIVATE YOUR SELF-DESTRUCT. I WANT EVERYTHING IN THIS CHAMBER BURNED *CLEAN*.
BLOOP. BLEEP BLOOP.
WHERE WILL WE GO, MASTER BARR?
WE'LL MAKE OUR WAY TO THE NEAREST SETTLEMENT AND LOOK FOR A WAY OFF-PLANET, NIPALTOO.

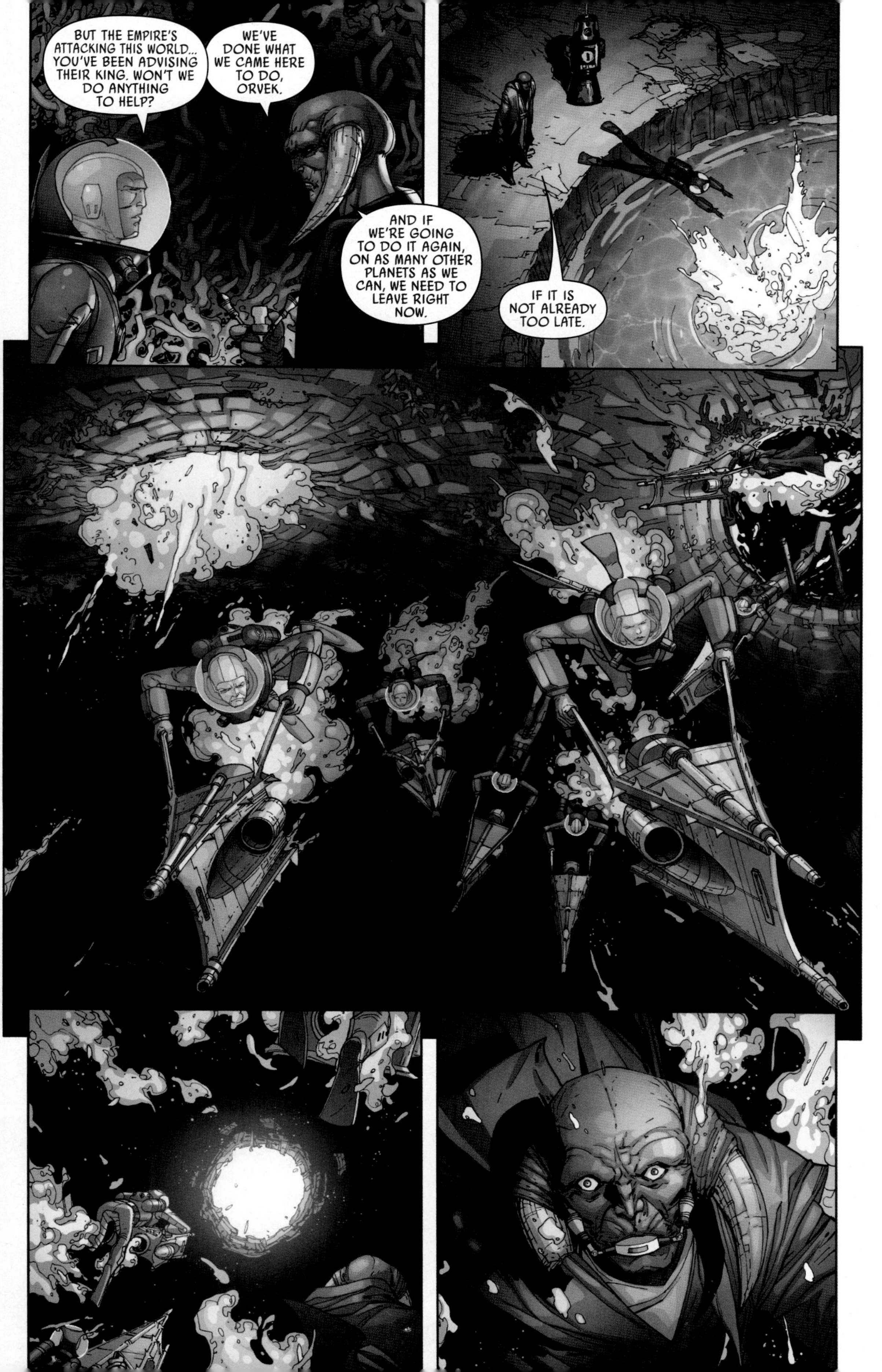
BUT THE EMPIRE'S ATTACKING THIS WORLD... YOU'VE BEEN ADVISING THEIR KING. WON'T WE DO ANYTHING TO HELP?
WE'VE DONE WHAT WE CAME HERE TO DO, ORVEK.
AND IF WE'RE GOING TO DO IT AGAIN, ON AS MANY OTHER PLANETS AS WE CAN, WE NEED TO LEAVE RIGHT NOW.
IF IT IS NOT ALREADY TOO LATE.

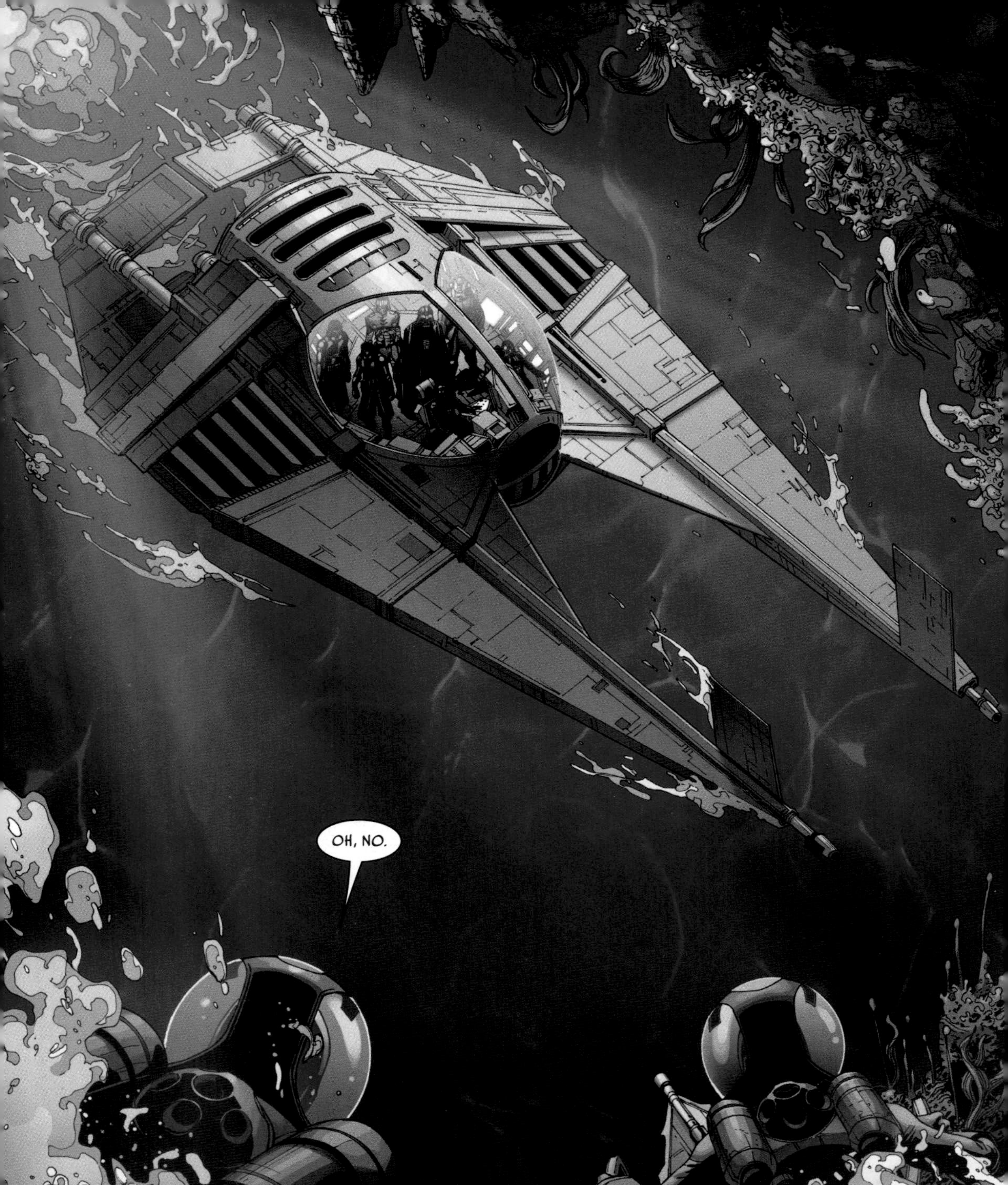
OH, NO.
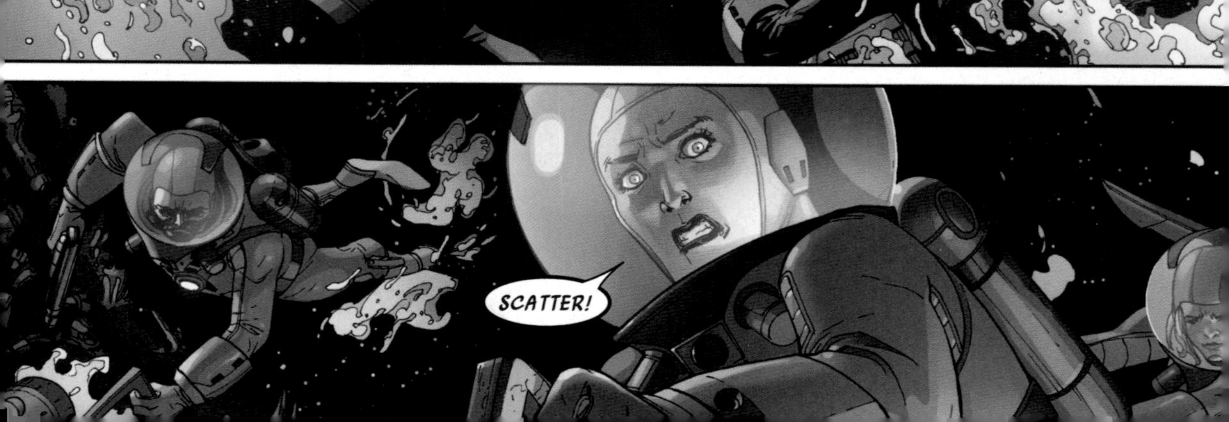
SCATTER!

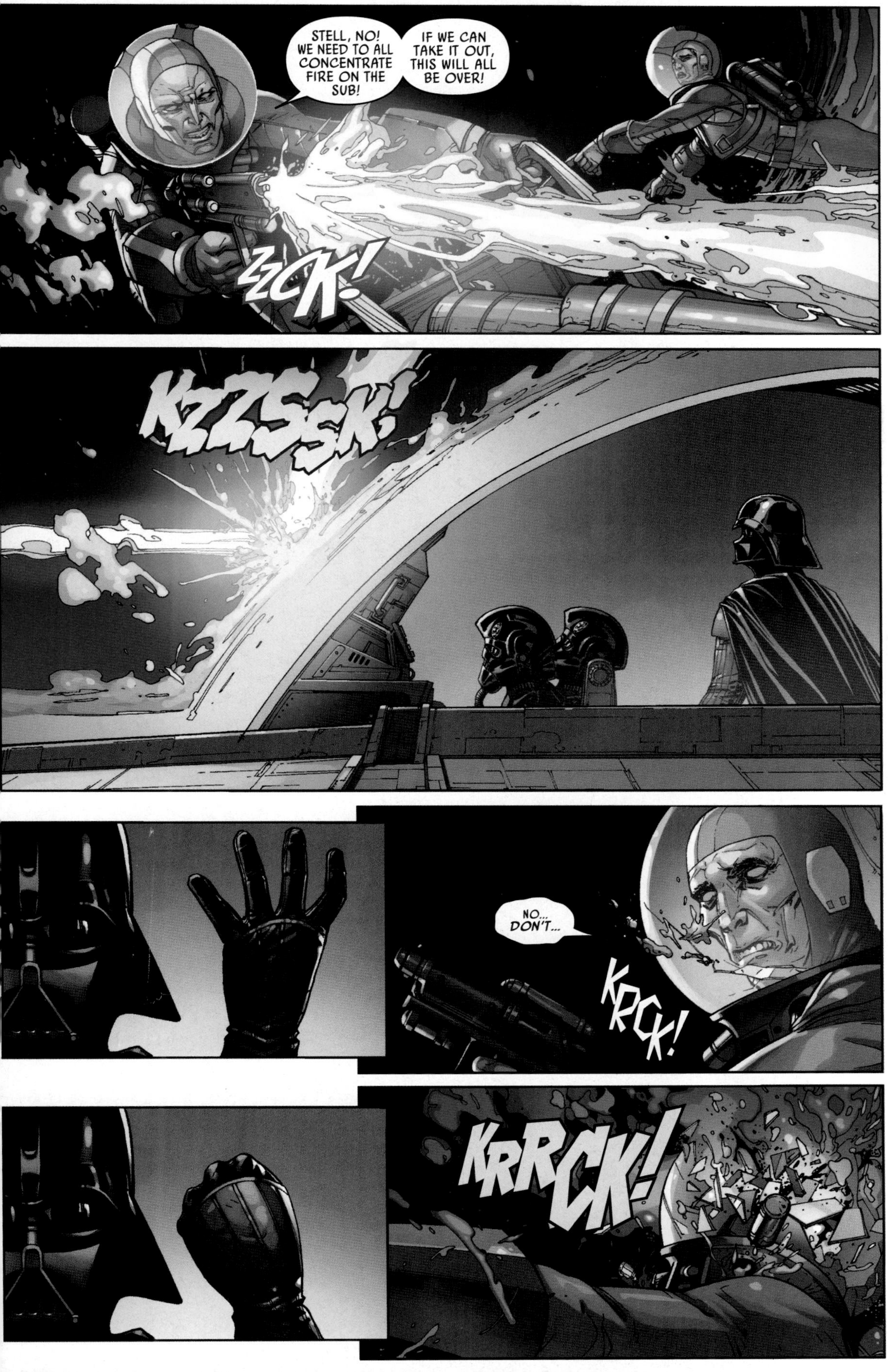

STELL, NO! WE NEED TO ALL CONCENTRATE FIRE ON THE SUB!
IF WE CAN TAKE IT OUT, THIS WILL ALL BE OVER!
ZZZCK!
KZZSSK!
NO... DON'T...
KRCK!
KRRCK!

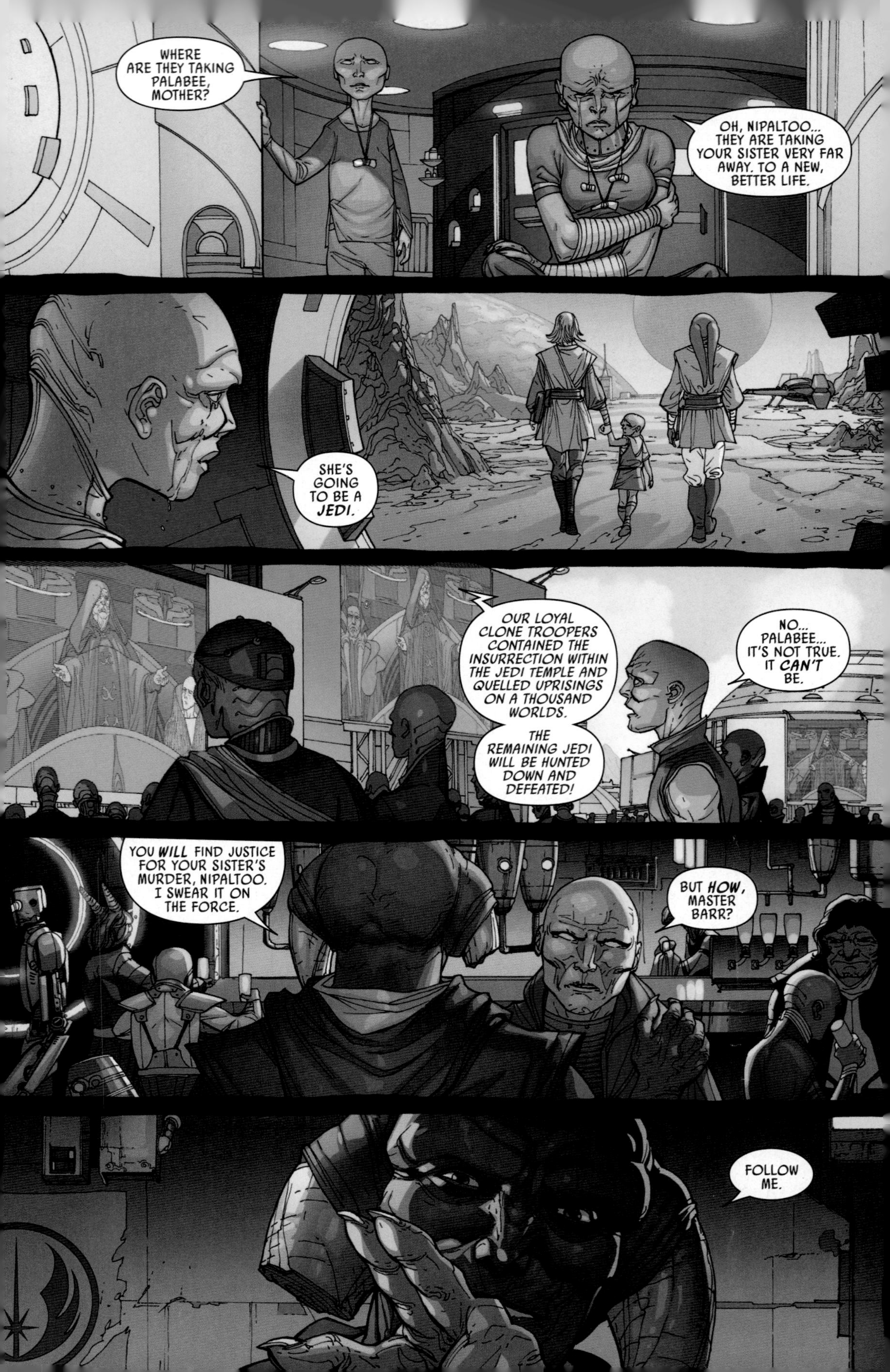
WHERE ARE THEY TAKING PALABEE, MOTHER?
OH, NIPALTOO... THEY ARE TAKING YOUR SISTER VERY FAR AWAY. TO A NEW, BETTER LIFE.
SHE'S GOING TO BE A JEDI.
OUR LOYAL CLONE TROOPERS CONTAINED THE INSURRECTION WITHIN THE JEDI TEMPLE AND QUELLED UPRISINGS ON A THOUSAND WORLDS.
THE REMAINING JEDI WILL BE HUNTED DOWN AND DEFEATED!
NO... PALABEE... IT'S NOT TRUE. IT CAN'T BE.
YOU WILL FIND JUSTICE FOR YOUR SISTER'S MURDER, NIPALTOO. I SWEAR IT ON THE FORCE.
BUT HOW, MASTER BARR?
FOLLOW ME.

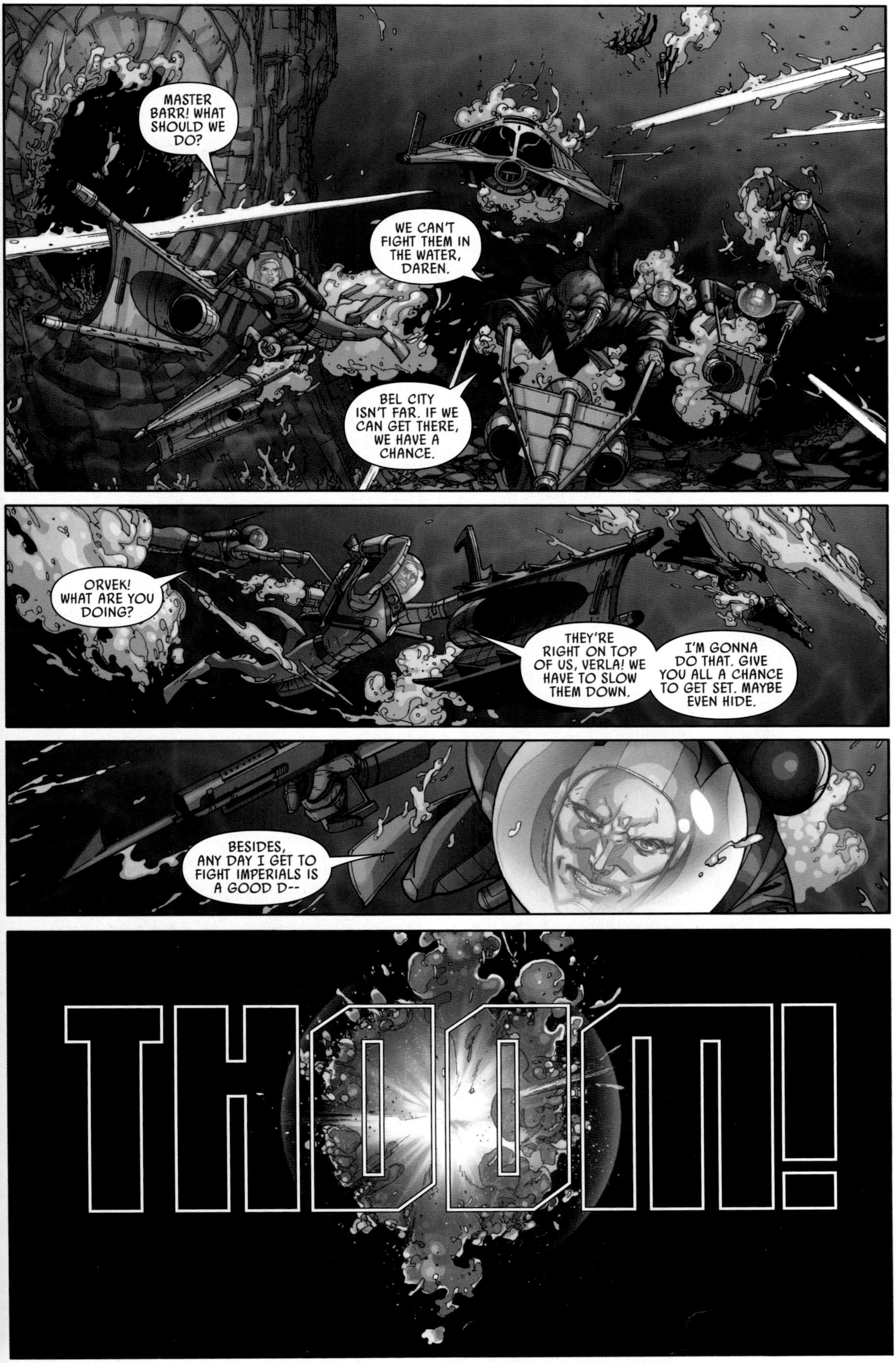
MASTER BARR! WHAT SHOULD WE DO?
WE CAN'T FIGHT THEM IN THE WATER, DAREN.
BEL CITY ISN'T FAR. IF WE CAN GET THERE, WE HAVE A CHANCE.
ORVEK! WHAT ARE YOU DOING?
THEY'RE RIGHT ON TOP OF US, VERLA! WE HAVE TO SLOW THEM DOWN.
I'M GONNA DO THAT. GIVE YOU ALL A CHANCE TO GET SET. MAYBE EVEN HIDE.
BESIDES, ANY DAY I GET TO FIGHT IMPERIALS IS A GOOD D--
THOOM!

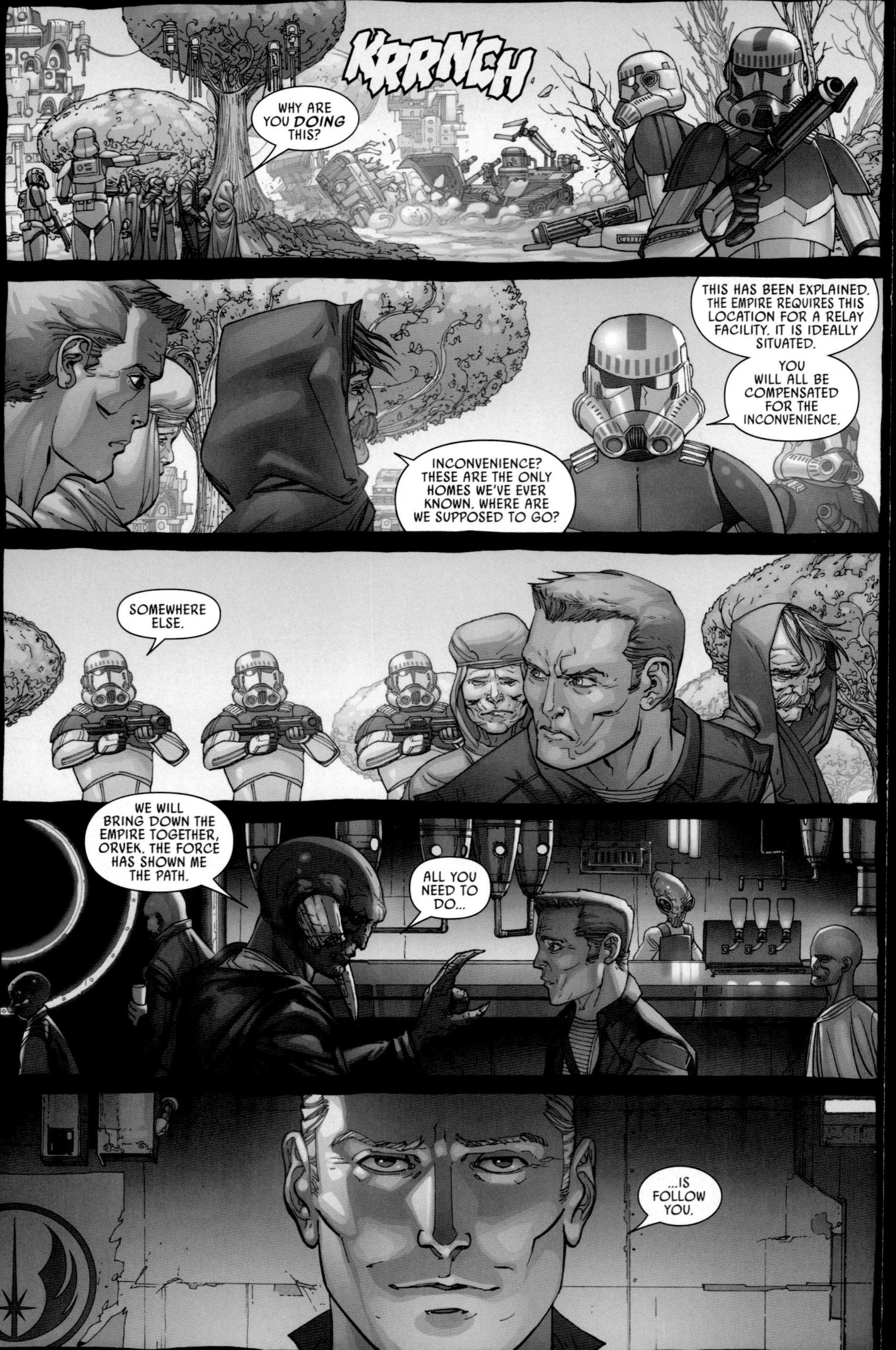
KRRNCH
WHY ARE YOU DOING THIS?
THIS HAS BEEN EXPLAINED. THE EMPIRE REQUIRES THIS LOCATION FOR A RELAY FACILITY. IT IS IDEALLY SITUATED.
YOU WILL ALL BE COMPENSATED FOR THE INCONVENIENCE.
INCONVENIENCE? THESE ARE THE ONLY HOMES WE'VE EVER KNOWN. WHERE ARE WE SUPPOSED TO GO?
SOMEWHERE ELSE.
WE WILL BRING DOWN THE EMPIRE TOGETHER, ORVEK. THE FORCE HAS SHOWN ME THE PATH.
ALL YOU NEED TO DO...
...IS FOLLOW YOU.

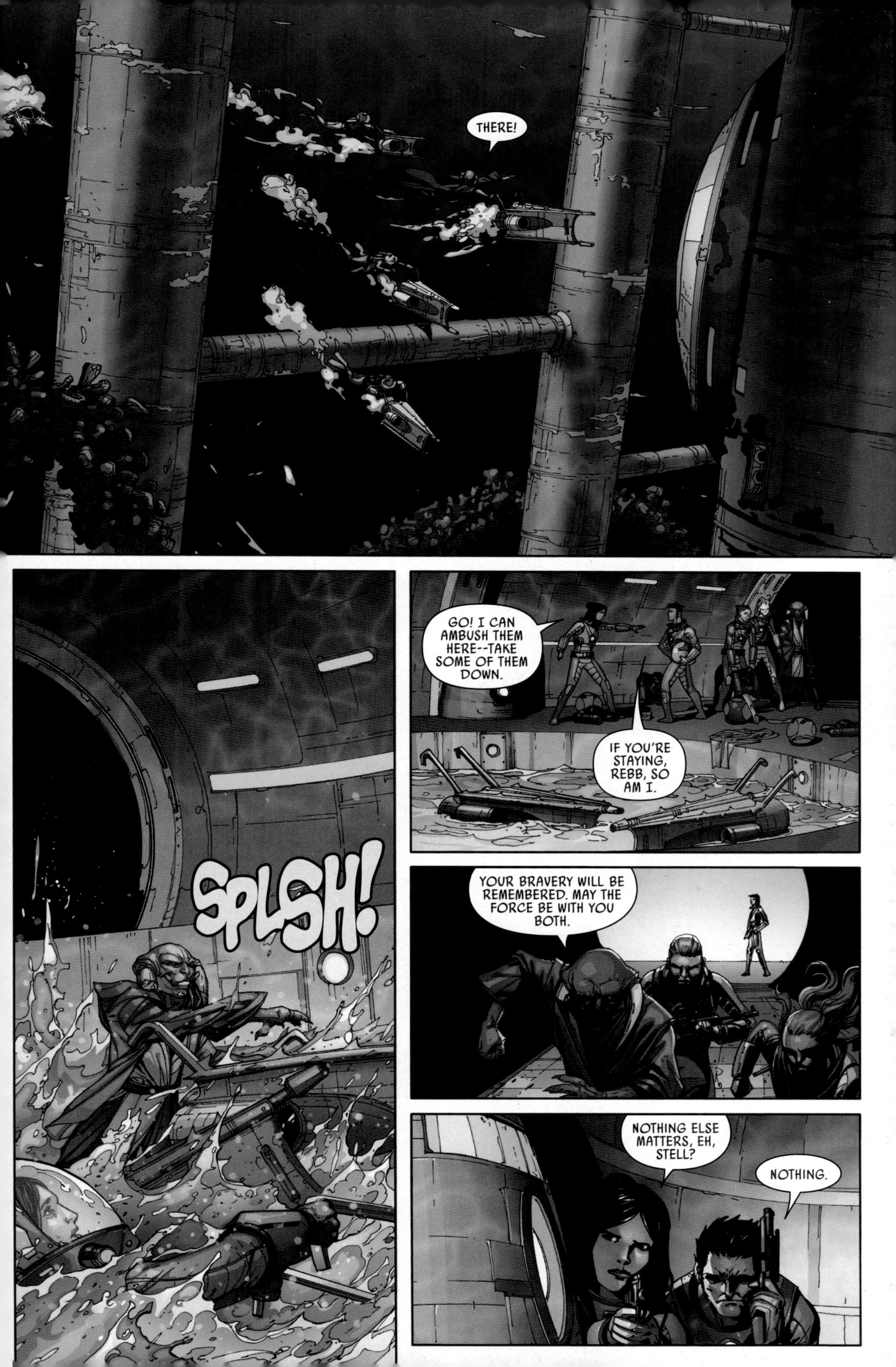
THERE!
SPLSH!
GO! I CAN AMBUSH THEM HERE--TAKE SOME OF THEM DOWN.
IF YOU'RE STAYING, REBB, SO AM I.
YOUR BRAVERY WILL BE REMEMBERED. MAY THE FORCE BE WITH YOU BOTH.
NOTHING ELSE MATTERS, EH, STELL?
NOTHING.

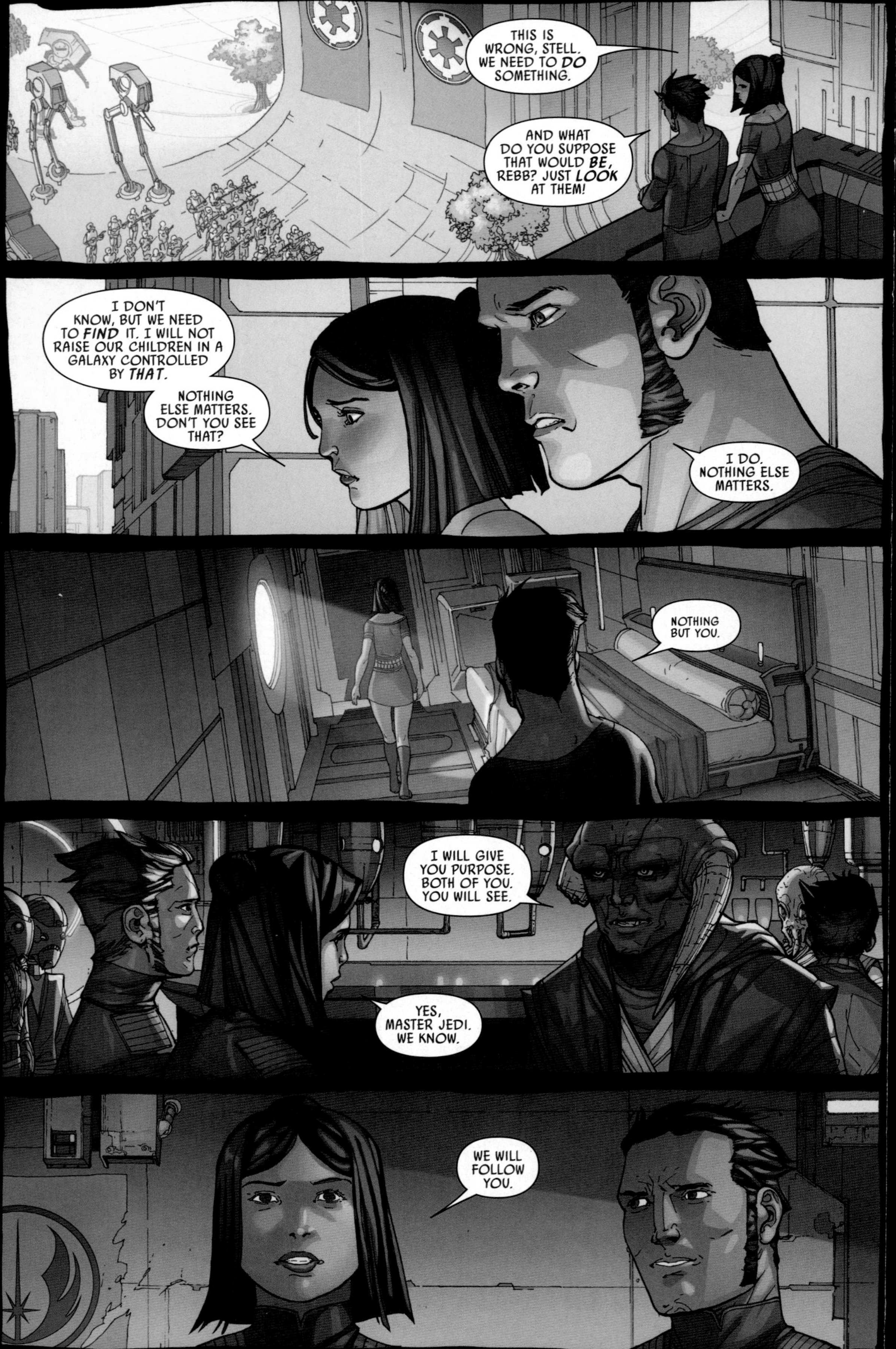
THIS IS WRONG, STELL. WE NEED TO DO SOMETHING.
AND WHAT DO YOU SUPPOSE THAT WOULD BE, REBB? JUST LOOK AT THEM!
I DON'T KNOW, BUT WE NEED TO FIND IT. I WILL NOT RAISE OUR CHILDREN IN A GALAXY CONTROLLED BY THAT.
NOTHING ELSE MATTERS. DON'T YOU SEE THAT?
I DO. NOTHING ELSE MATTERS.
NOTHING BUT YOU.
I WILL GIVE YOU PURPOSE. BOTH OF YOU. YOU WILL SEE.
YES, MASTER JEDI. WE KNOW.
WE WILL FOLLOW YOU.

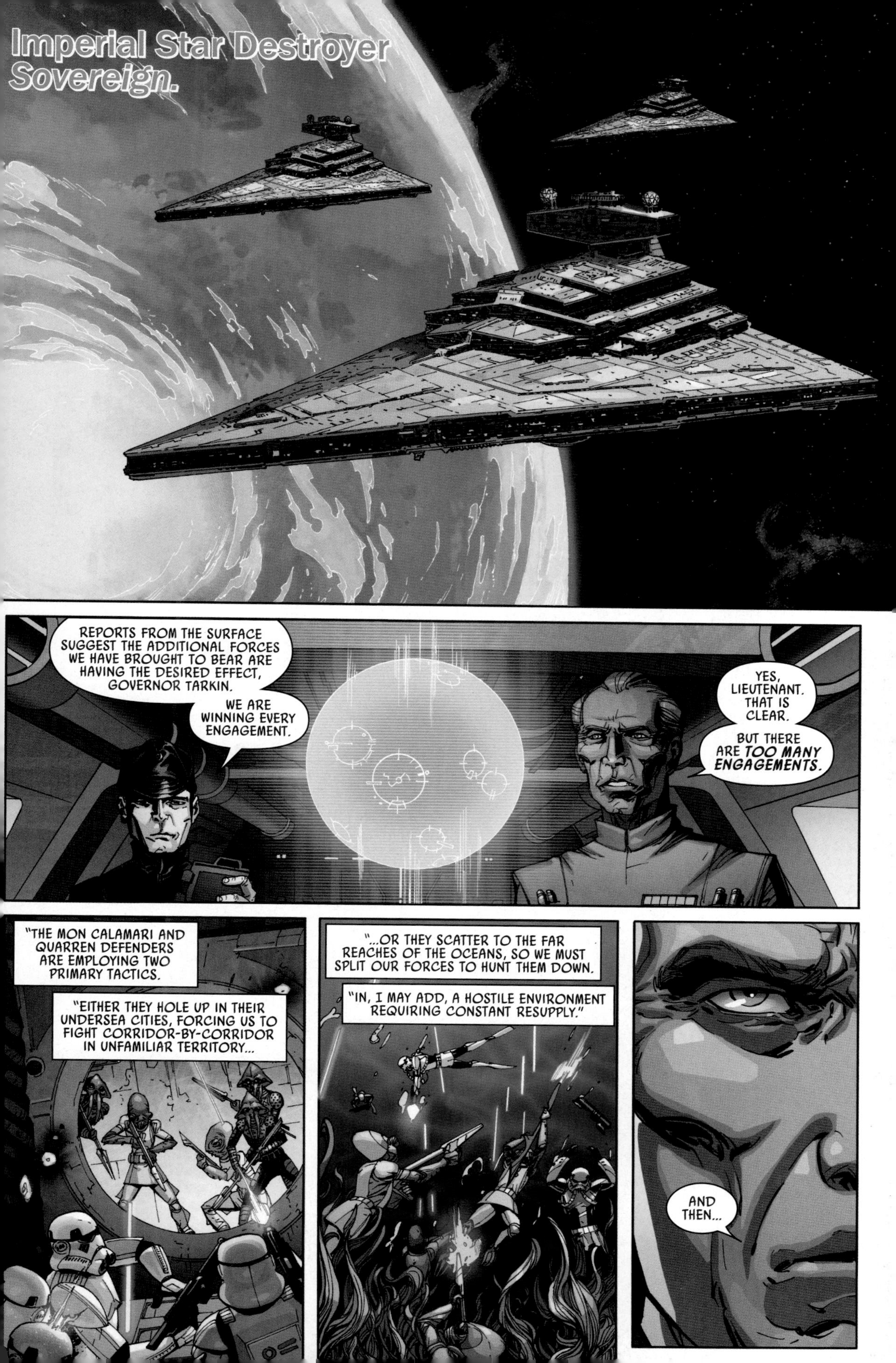
Imperial Star Destroyer Sovereign.
REPORTS FROM THE SURFACE SUGGEST THE ADDITIONAL FORCES WE HAVE BROUGHT TO BEAR ARE HAVING THE DESIRED EFFECT, GOVERNOR TARKIN.
WE ARE WINNING EVERY ENGAGEMENT.
YES, LIEUTENANT. THAT IS CLEAR.
BUT THERE ARE TOO MANY ENGAGEMENTS.
"THE MON CALAMARI AND QUARREN DEFENDERS ARE EMPLOYING TWO PRIMARY TACTICS.
"EITHER THEY HOLE UP IN THEIR UNDERSEA CITIES, FORCING US TO FIGHT CORRIDOR-BY-CORRIDOR IN UNFAMILIAR TERRITORY...
"...OR THEY SCATTER TO THE FAR REACHES OF THE OCEANS, SO WE MUST SPLIT OUR FORCES TO HUNT THEM DOWN.
"IN, I MAY ADD, A HOSTILE ENVIRONMENT REQUIRING CONSTANT RESUPPLY."
AND THEN...

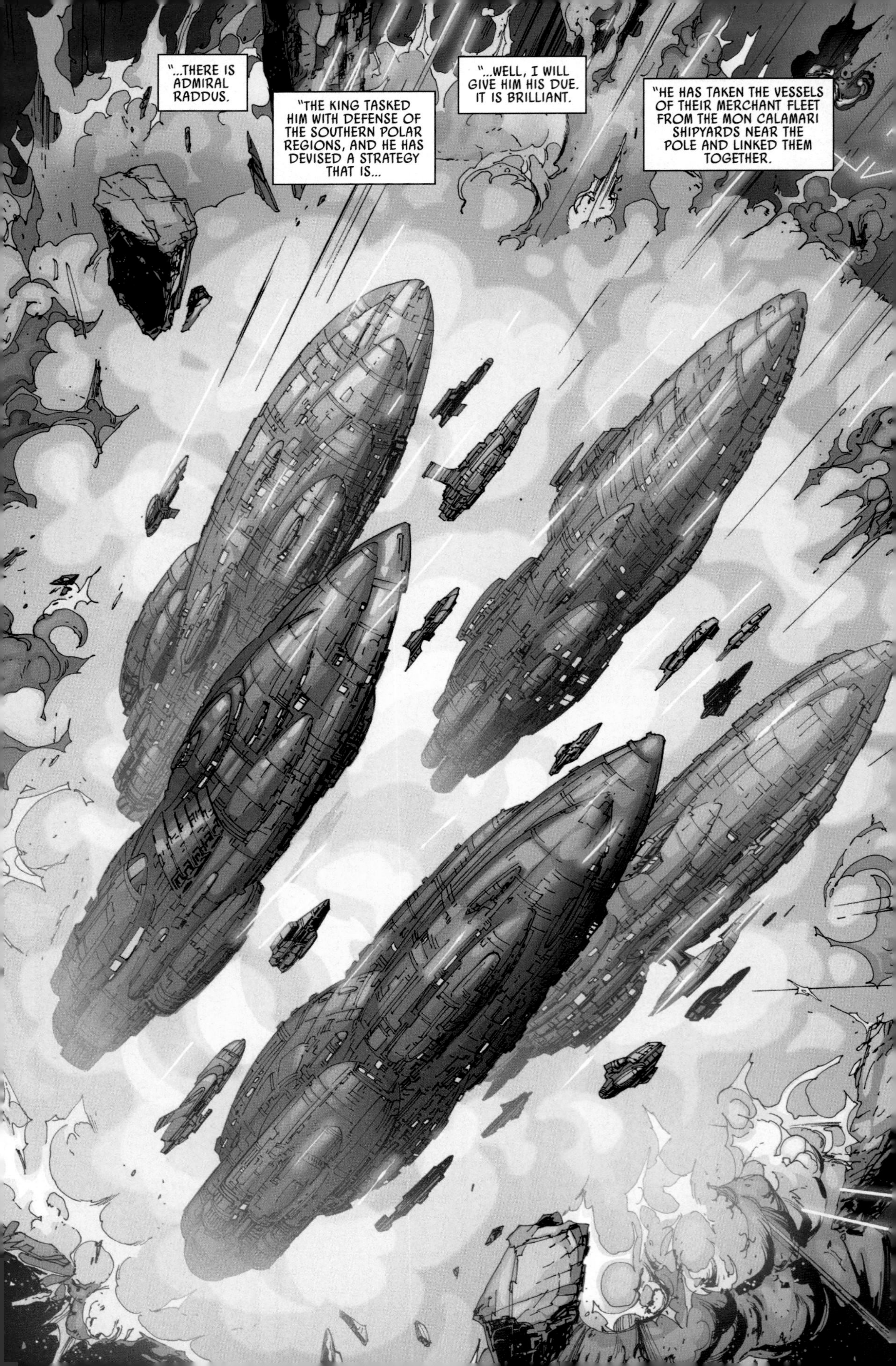
"...THERE IS ADMIRAL RADDUS.
"THE KING TASKED HIM WITH DEFENSE OF THE SOUTHERN POLAR REGIONS, AND HE HAS DEVISED A STRATEGY THAT IS...
"...WELL, I WILL GIVE HIM HIS DUE. IT IS BRILLIANT.
"HE HAS TAKEN THE VESSELS OF THEIR MERCHANT FLEET FROM THE MON CALAMARI SHIPYARDS NEAR THE POLE AND LINKED THEM TOGETHER.

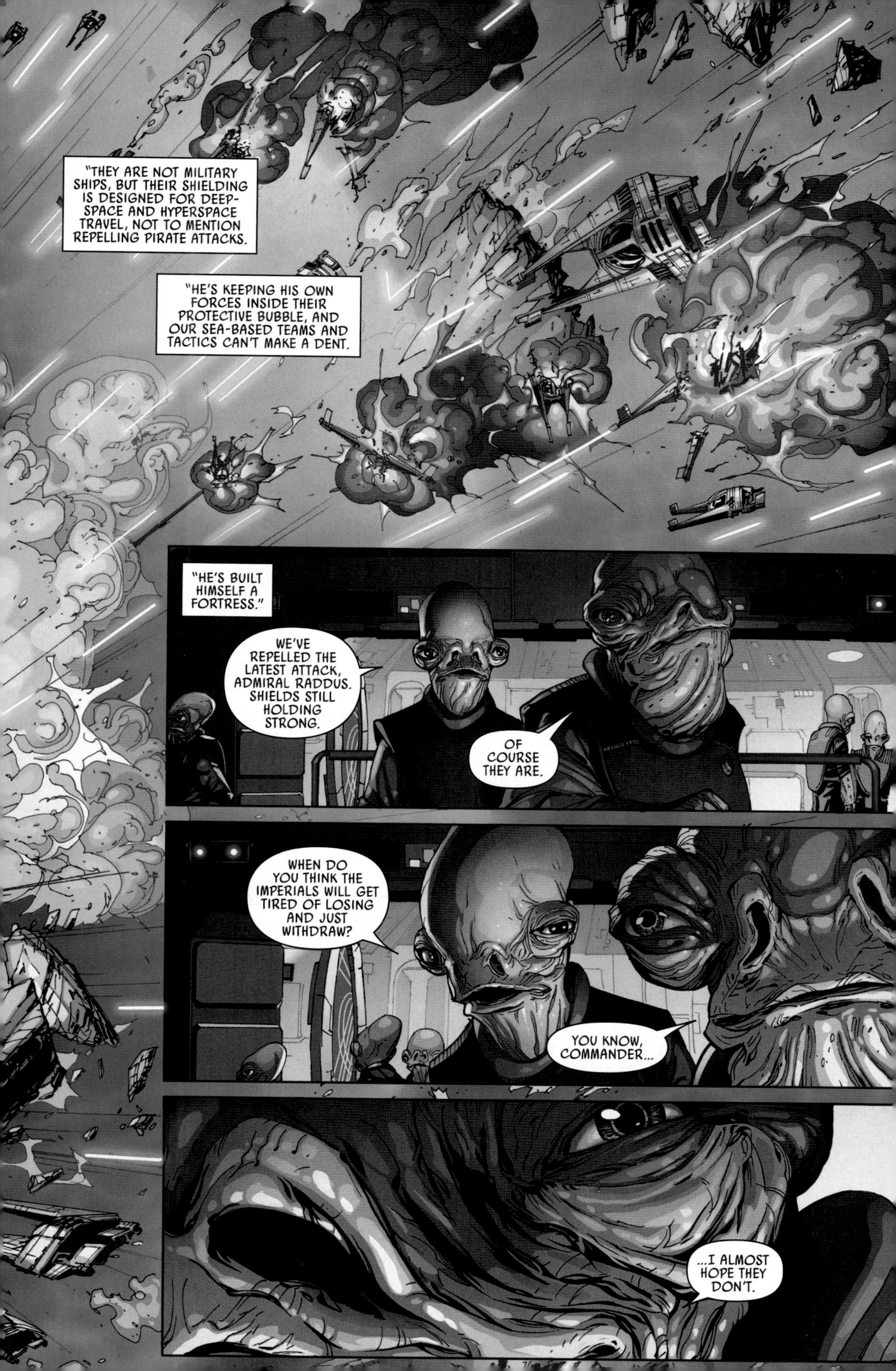
"THEY ARE NOT MILITARY SHIPS, BUT THEIR SHIELDING IS DESIGNED FOR DEEP-SPACE AND HYPERSPACE TRAVEL, NOT TO MENTION REPELLING PIRATE ATTACKS.
"HE'S KEEPING HIS OWN FORCES INSIDE THEIR PROTECTIVE BUBBLE, AND OUR SEA-BASED TEAMS AND TACTICS CAN'T MAKE A DENT.
"HE'S BUILT HIMSELF A FORTRESS."
WE'VE REPELLED THE LATEST ATTACK, ADMIRAL RADDUS. SHIELDS STILL HOLDING STRONG.
OF COURSE THEY ARE.
WHEN DO YOU THINK THE IMPERIALS WILL GET TIRED OF LOSING AND JUST WITHDRAW?
YOU KNOW, COMMANDER...
...I ALMOST HOPE THEY DON'T.

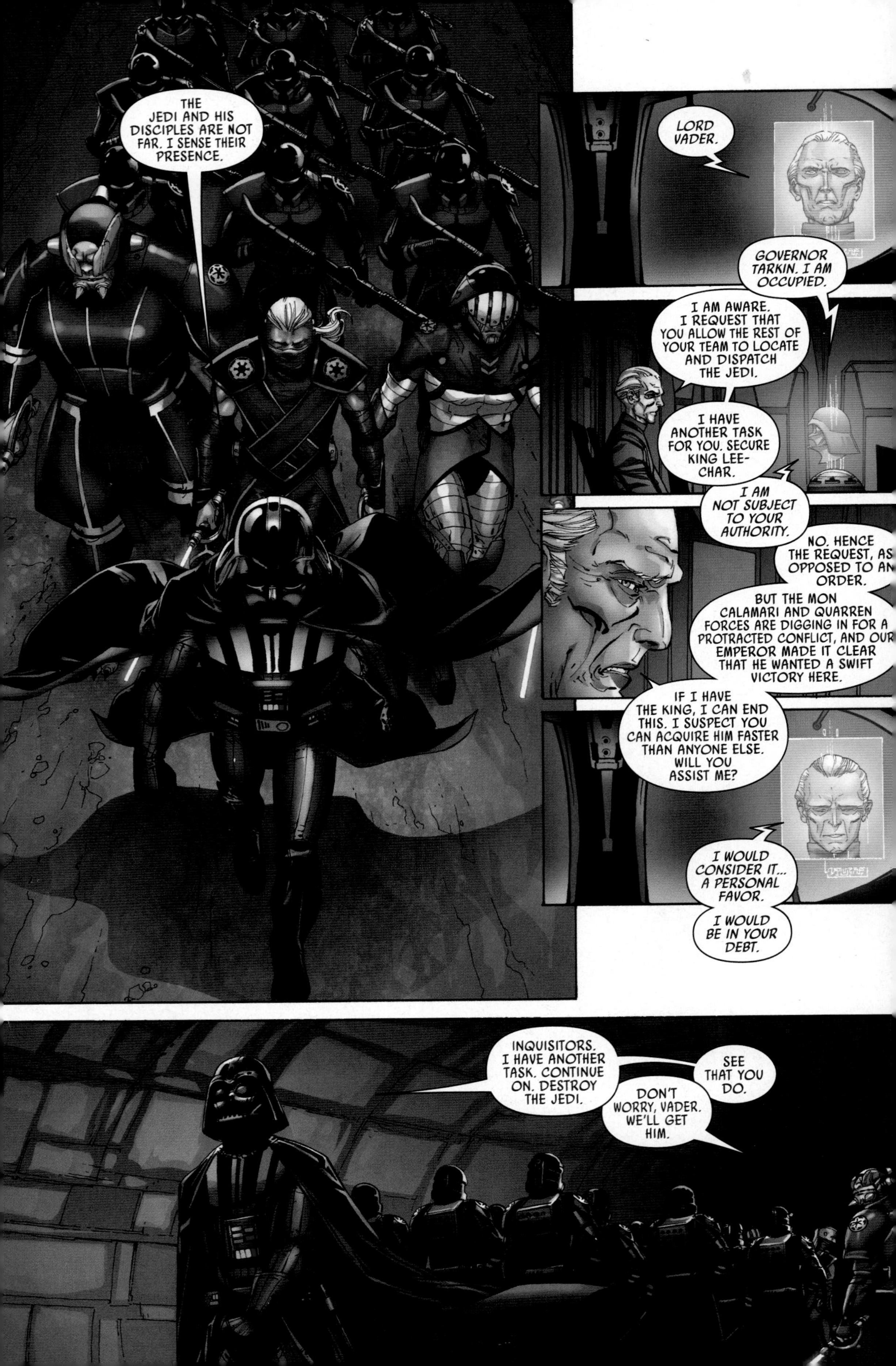
THE JEDI AND HIS DISCIPLES ARE NOT FAR. I SENSE THEIR PRESENCE.
LORD VADER.
GOVERNOR TARKIN. I AM OCCUPIED.
I AM AWARE. I REQUEST THAT YOU ALLOW THE REST OF YOUR TEAM TO LOCATE AND DISPATCH THE JEDI.
I HAVE ANOTHER TASK FOR YOU. SECURE KING LEE-CHAR.
I AM NOT SUBJECT TO YOUR AUTHORITY.
NO. HENCE THE REQUEST, AS OPPOSED TO AN ORDER.
BUT THE MON CALAMARI AND QUARREN FORCES ARE DIGGING IN FOR A PROTRACTED CONFLICT, AND OUR EMPEROR MADE IT CLEAR THAT HE WANTED A SWIFT VICTORY HERE.
IF I HAVE THE KING, I CAN END THIS. I SUSPECT YOU CAN ACQUIRE HIM FASTER THAN ANYONE ELSE. WILL YOU ASSIST ME?
I WOULD CONSIDER IT... A PERSONAL FAVOR.
I WOULD BE IN YOUR DEBT.
INQUISITORS. I HAVE ANOTHER TASK. CONTINUE ON. DESTROY THE JEDI.
SEE THAT YOU DO.
DON'T WORRY, VADER. WE'LL GET HIM.

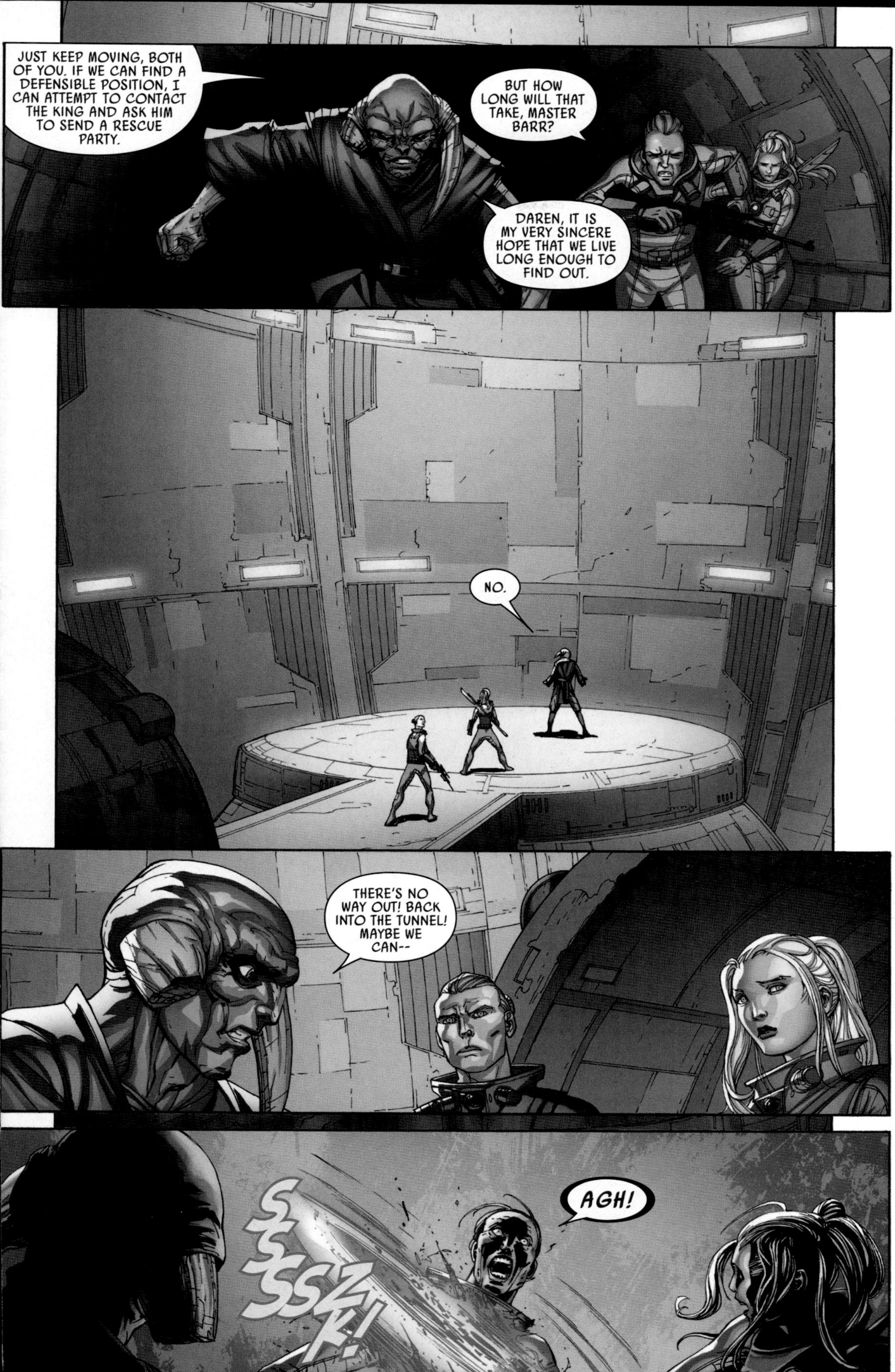
JUST KEEP MOVING, BOTH OF YOU. IF WE CAN FIND A DEFENSIBLE POSITION, I CAN ATTEMPT TO CONTACT THE KING AND ASK HIM TO SEND A RESCUE PARTY.
BUT HOW LONG WILL THAT TAKE, MASTER BARR?
DAREN, IT IS MY VERY SINCERE HOPE THAT WE LIVE LONG ENOUGH TO FIND OUT.
NO.
THERE'S NO WAY OUT! BACK INTO THE TUNNEL! MAYBE WE CAN--
SSSSZK!
AGH!

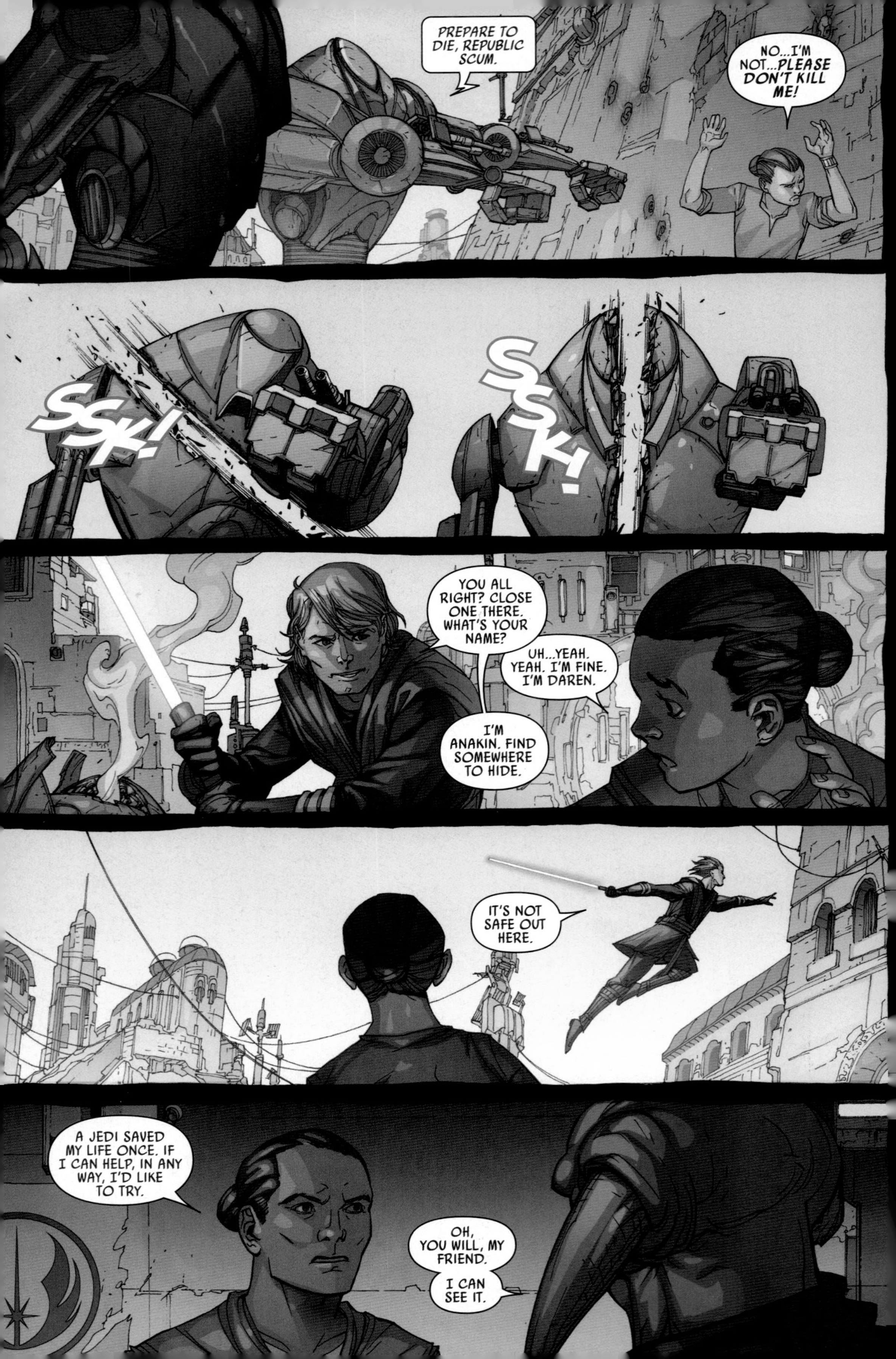
PREPARE TO DIE, REPUBLIC SCUM.
NO...I'M NOT...PLEASE DON'T KILL ME!
SSK!
SSK!
YOU ALL RIGHT? CLOSE ONE THERE. WHAT'S YOUR NAME?
UH...YEAH. YEAH. I'M FINE. I'M DAREN.
I'M ANAKIN. FIND SOMEWHERE TO HIDE.
IT'S NOT SAFE OUT HERE.
A JEDI SAVED MY LIFE ONCE. IF I CAN HELP, IN ANY WAY, I'D LIKE TO TRY.
OH, YOU WILL, MY FRIEND.
I CAN SEE IT.

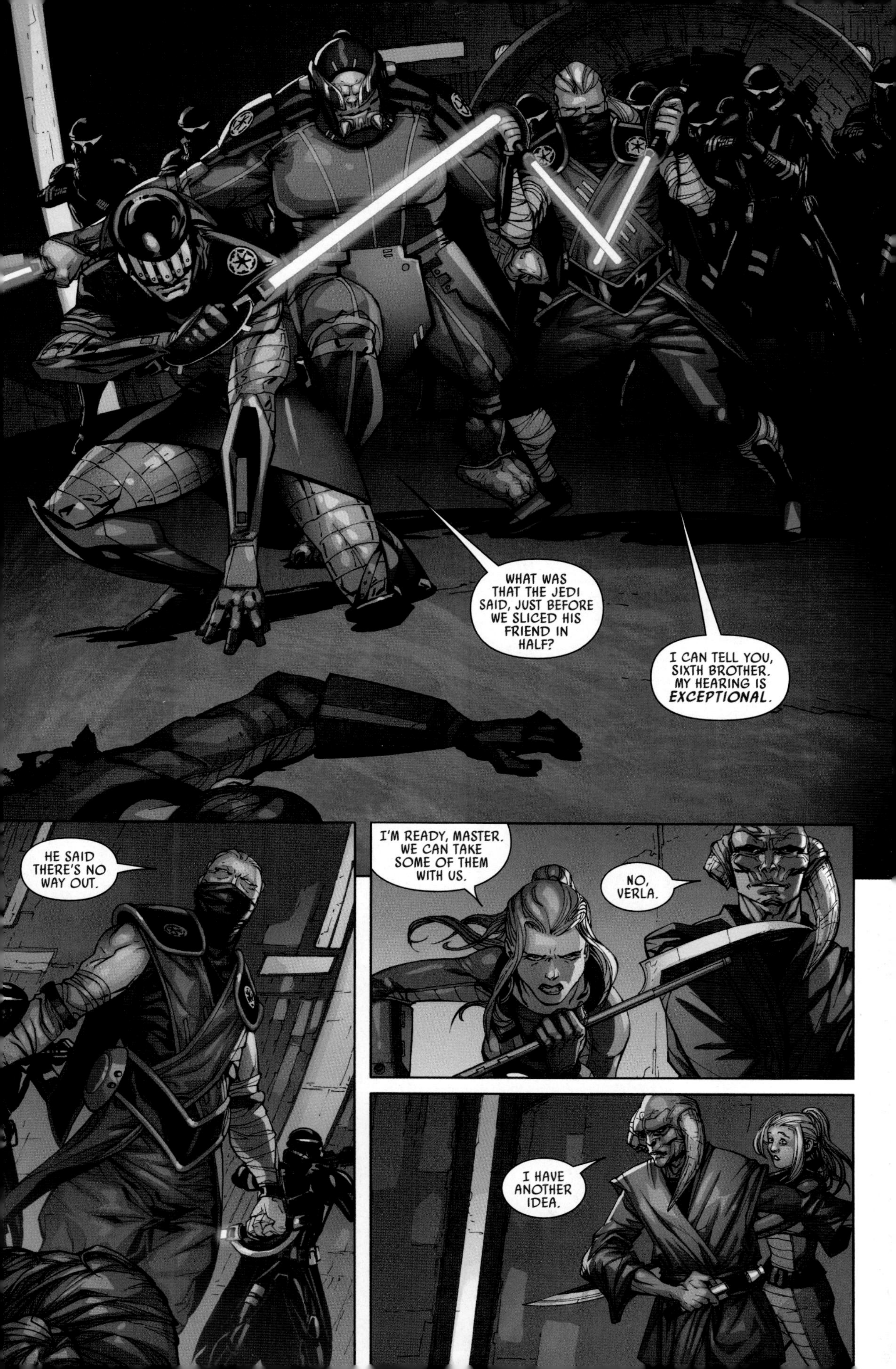
WHAT WAS THAT THE JEDI SAID, JUST BEFORE WE SLICED HIS FRIEND IN HALF?
I CAN TELL YOU, SIXTH BROTHER. MY HEARING IS *EXCEPTIONAL*.
HE SAID THERE'S NO WAY OUT.
I'M READY, MASTER. WE CAN TAKE SOME OF THEM WITH US.
NO, VERLA.
I HAVE ANOTHER IDEA.

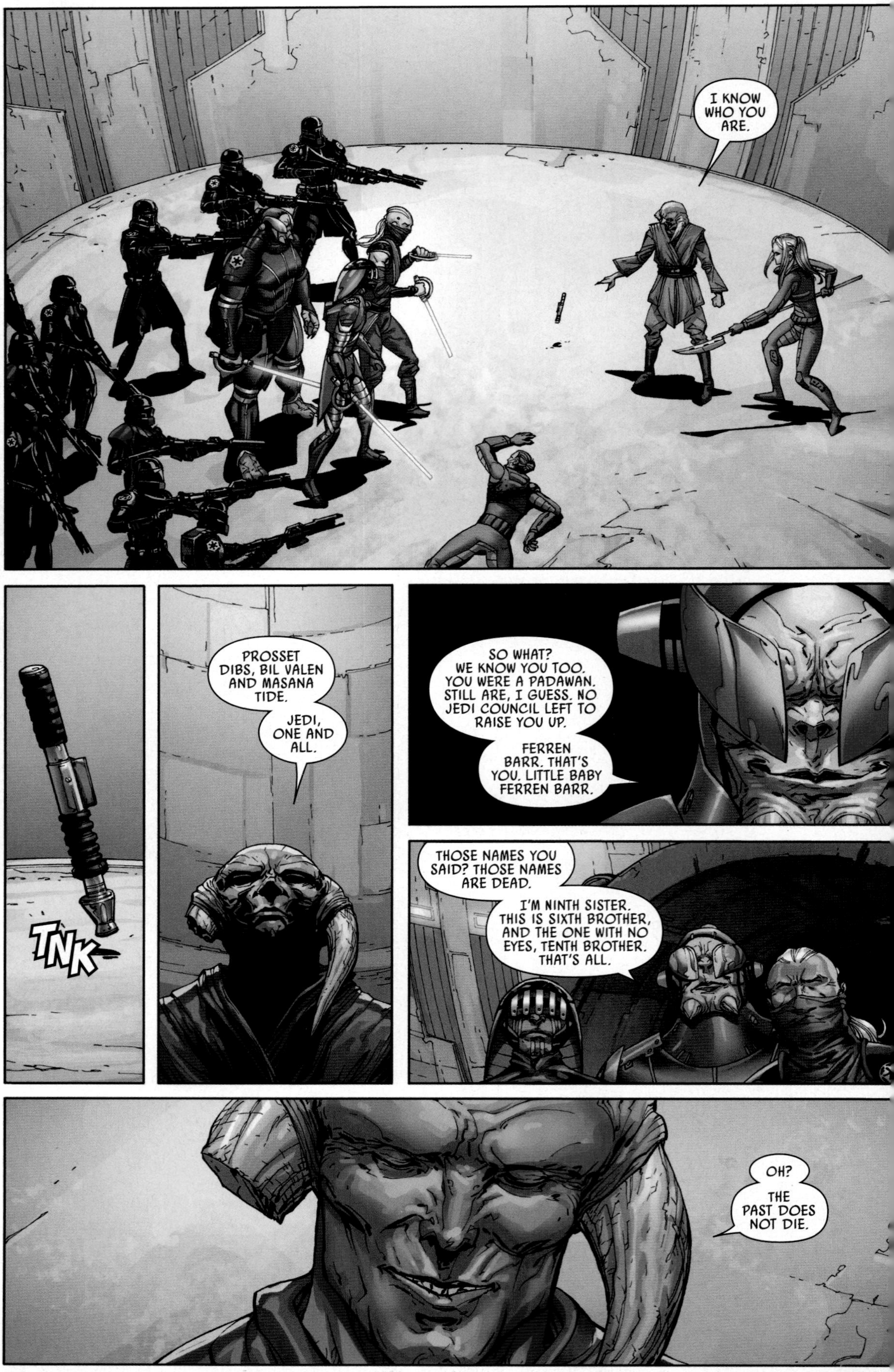

I KNOW WHO YOU ARE.
TNK
PROSSET DIBS, BIL VALEN AND MASANA TIDE.
JEDI, ONE AND ALL.
SO WHAT? WE KNOW YOU TOO. YOU WERE A PADAWAN. STILL ARE, I GUESS. NO JEDI COUNCIL LEFT TO RAISE YOU UP.
FERREN BARR. THAT'S YOU. LITTLE BABY FERREN BARR.
THOSE NAMES YOU SAID? THOSE NAMES ARE DEAD.
I'M NINTH SISTER. THIS IS SIXTH BROTHER, AND THE ONE WITH NO EYES, TENTH BROTHER. THAT'S ALL.
OH?
THE PAST DOES NOT DIE.

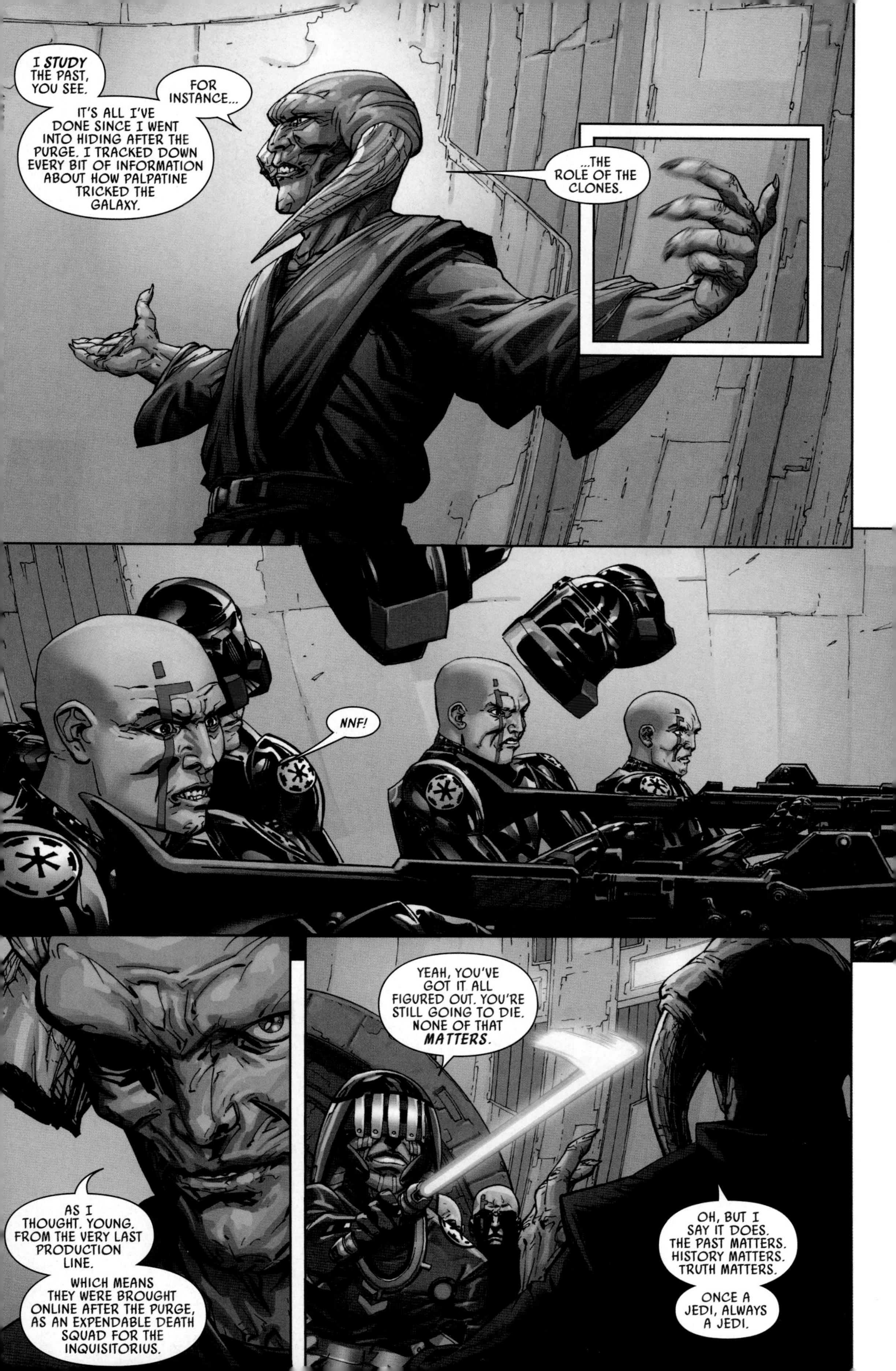
I *STUDY* THE PAST, YOU SEE.
IT'S ALL I'VE DONE SINCE I WENT INTO HIDING AFTER THE PURGE. I TRACKED DOWN EVERY BIT OF INFORMATION ABOUT HOW PALPATINE TRICKED THE GALAXY.
FOR INSTANCE...
...THE ROLE OF THE CLONES.
NNF!
AS I THOUGHT. YOUNG. FROM THE VERY LAST PRODUCTION LINE.
WHICH MEANS THEY WERE BROUGHT ONLINE AFTER THE PURGE, AS AN EXPENDABLE DEATH SQUAD FOR THE INQUISITORIUS.
YEAH, YOU'VE GOT IT ALL FIGURED OUT. YOU'RE STILL GOING TO DIE. NONE OF THAT *MATTERS*.
OH, BUT I SAY IT DOES. THE PAST MATTERS. HISTORY MATTERS. TRUTH MATTERS.
ONCE A JEDI, ALWAYS A JEDI.

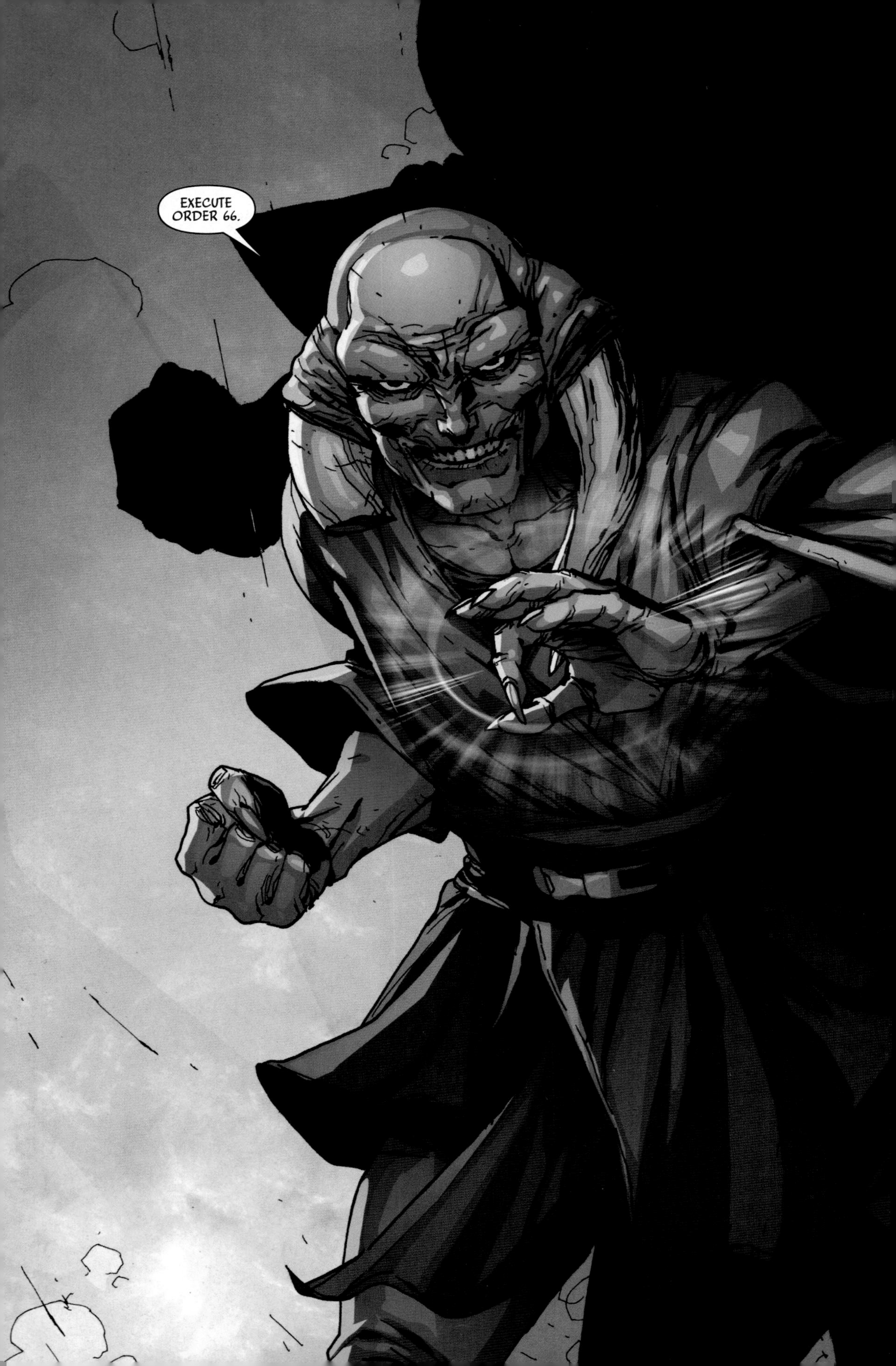
EXECUTE ORDER 66.

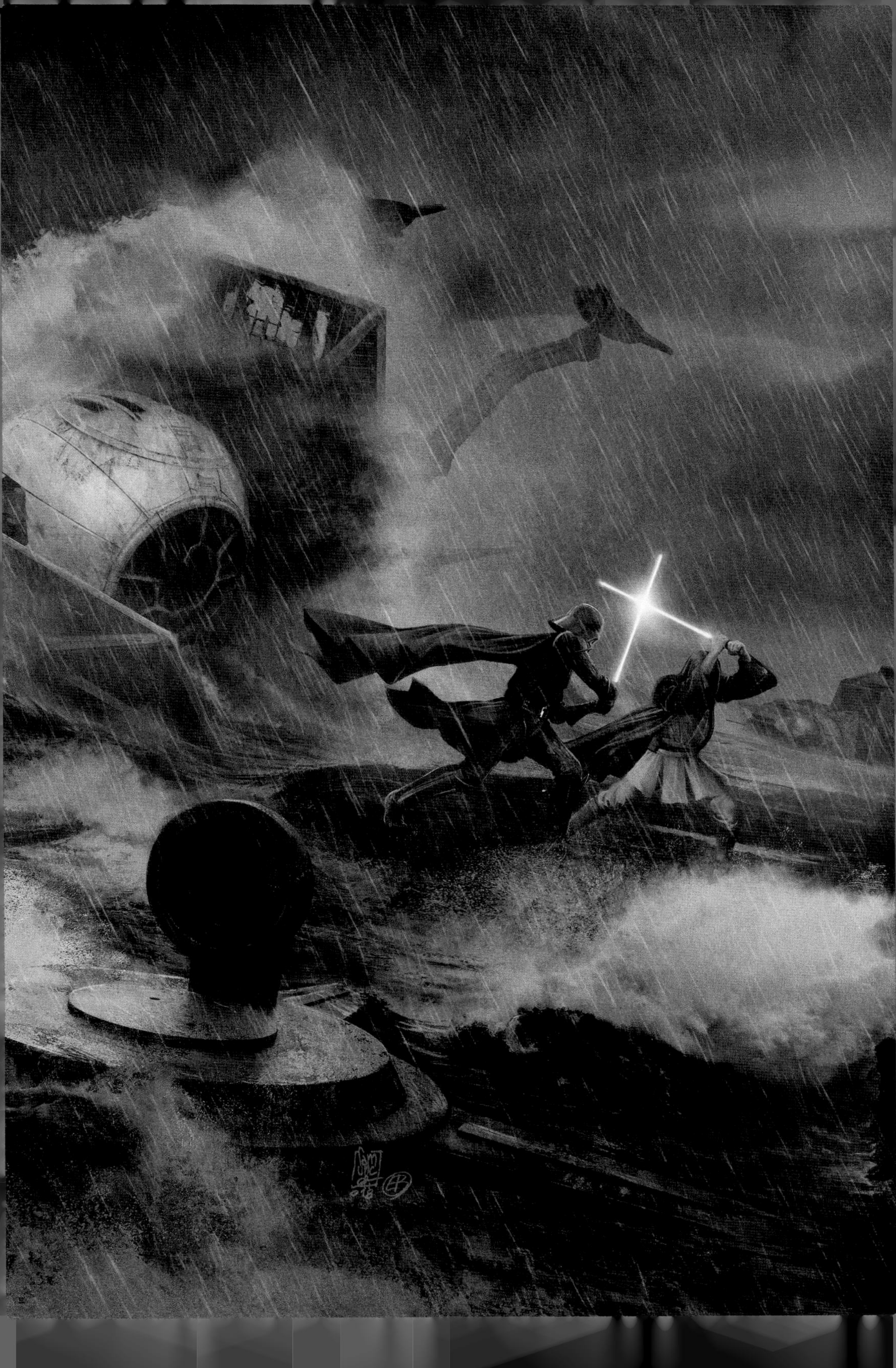

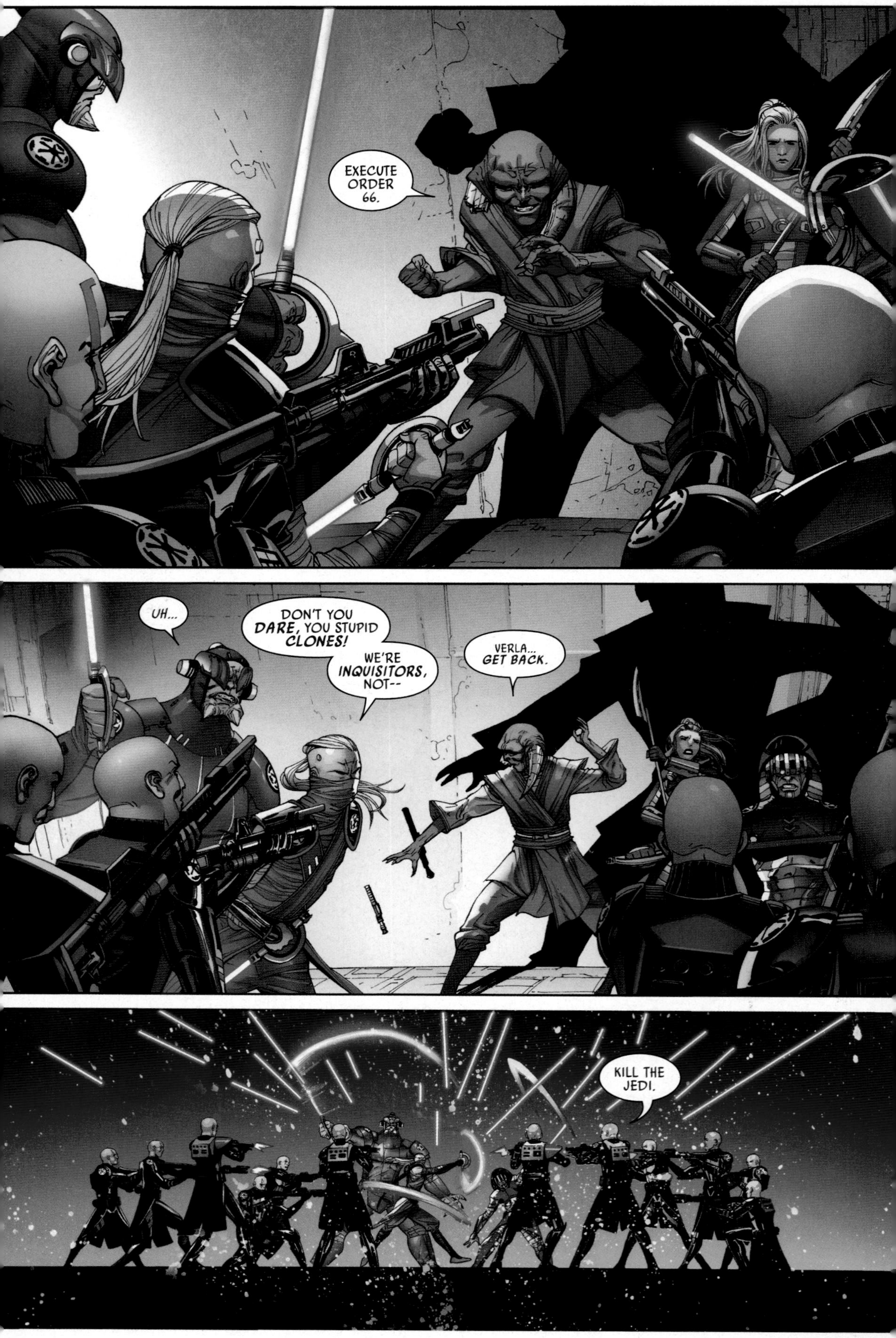
EXECUTE ORDER 66.
UH...
DON'T YOU DARE, YOU STUPID CLONES!
WE'RE INQUISITORS, NOT--
VERLA... GET BACK.
KILL THE JEDI.

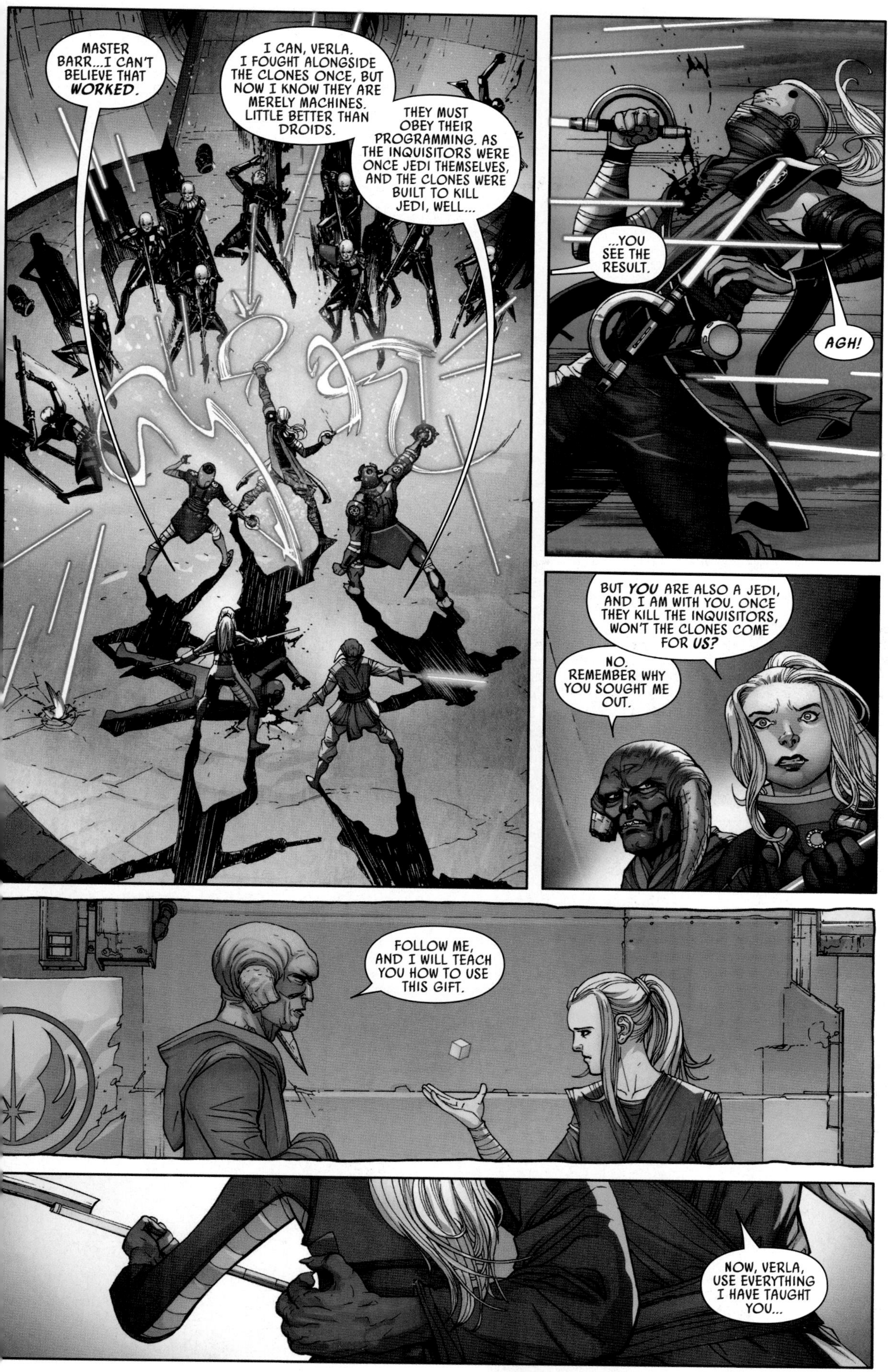
MASTER BARR...I CAN'T BELIEVE THAT WORKED.
I CAN, VERLA. I FOUGHT ALONGSIDE THE CLONES ONCE, BUT NOW I KNOW THEY ARE MERELY MACHINES. LITTLE BETTER THAN DROIDS.
THEY MUST OBEY THEIR PROGRAMMING. AS THE INQUISITORS WERE ONCE JEDI THEMSELVES, AND THE CLONES WERE BUILT TO KILL JEDI, WELL...
...YOU SEE THE RESULT.
AGH!
BUT YOU ARE ALSO A JEDI, AND I AM WITH YOU. ONCE THEY KILL THE INQUISITORS, WON'T THE CLONES COME FOR US?
NO. REMEMBER WHY YOU SOUGHT ME OUT.
FOLLOW ME, AND I WILL TEACH YOU HOW TO USE THIS GIFT.
NOW, VERLA, USE EVERYTHING I HAVE TAUGHT YOU...

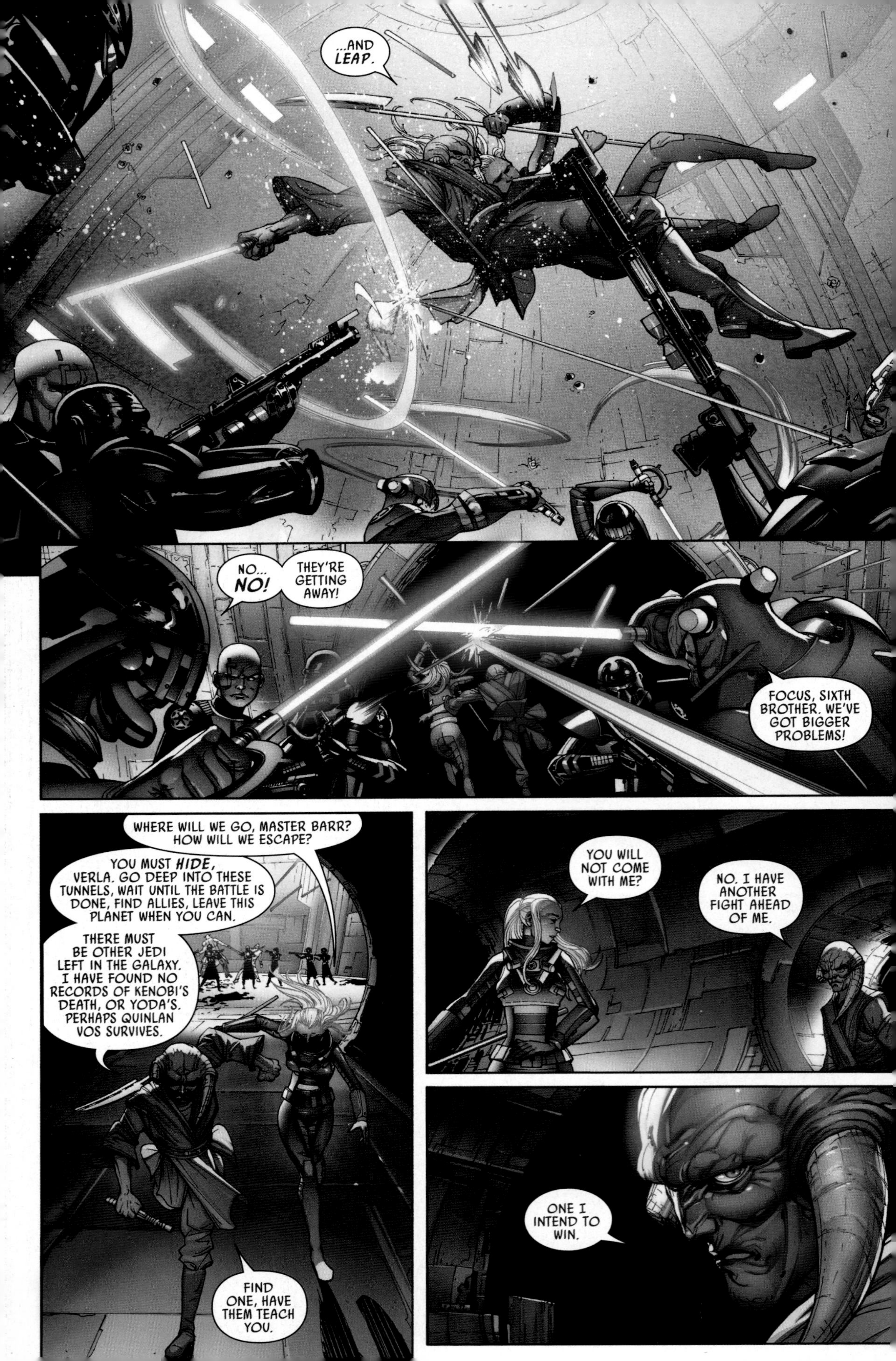
...AND LEAP.
NO... NO!
THEY'RE GETTING AWAY!
FOCUS, SIXTH BROTHER. WE'VE GOT BIGGER PROBLEMS!
WHERE WILL WE GO, MASTER BARR? HOW WILL WE ESCAPE?
YOU MUST HIDE, VERLA. GO DEEP INTO THESE TUNNELS, WAIT UNTIL THE BATTLE IS DONE, FIND ALLIES, LEAVE THIS PLANET WHEN YOU CAN.
THERE MUST BE OTHER JEDI LEFT IN THE GALAXY. I HAVE FOUND NO RECORDS OF KENOBI'S DEATH, OR YODA'S. PERHAPS QUINLAN VOS SURVIVES.
FIND ONE, HAVE THEM TEACH YOU.
YOU WILL NOT COME WITH ME?
NO. I HAVE ANOTHER FIGHT AHEAD OF ME.
ONE I INTEND TO WIN.

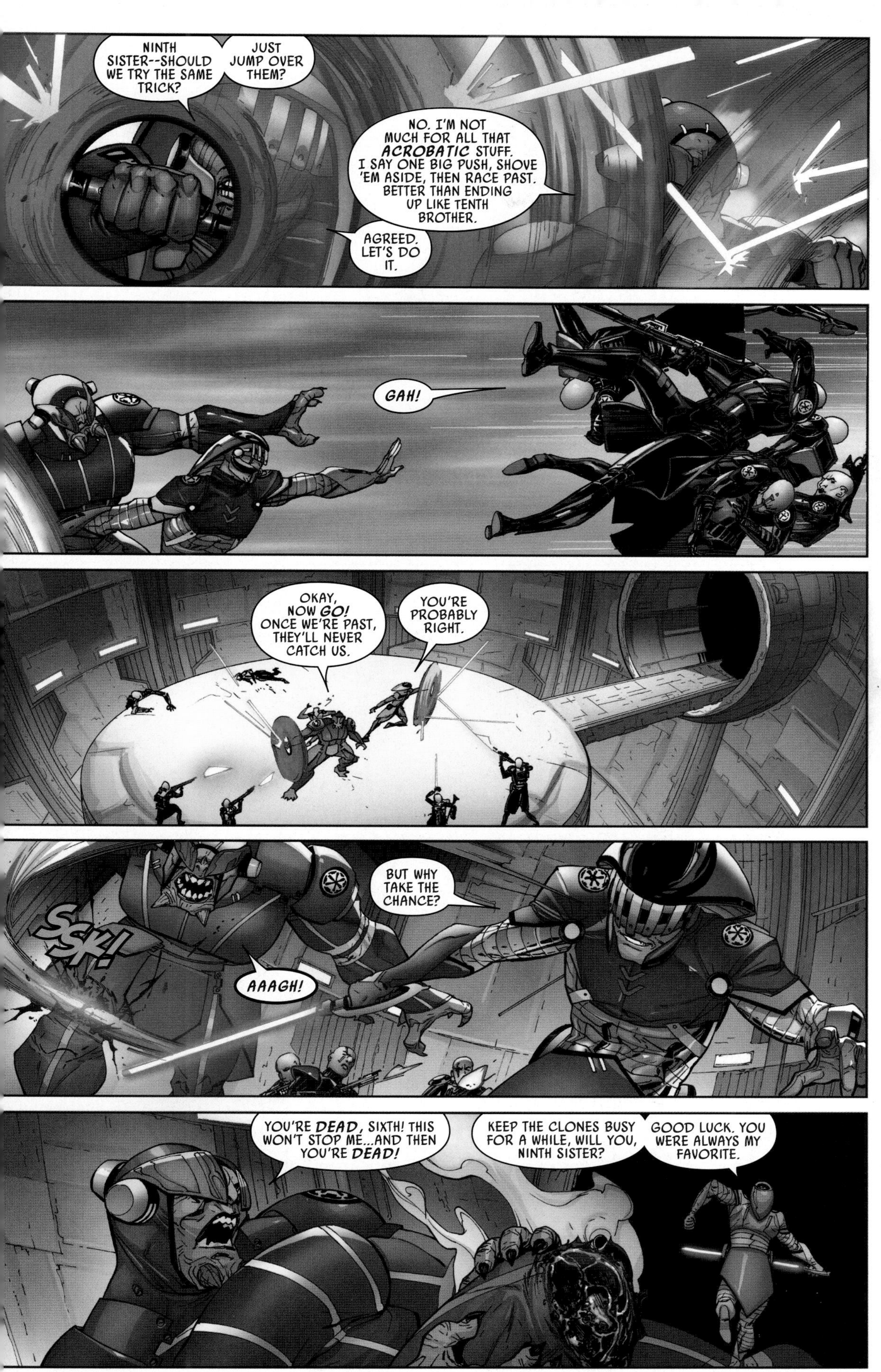
NINTH SISTER--SHOULD WE TRY THE SAME TRICK?
JUST JUMP OVER THEM?
NO. I'M NOT MUCH FOR ALL THAT ACROBATIC STUFF. I SAY ONE BIG PUSH, SHOVE 'EM ASIDE, THEN RACE PAST. BETTER THAN ENDING UP LIKE TENTH BROTHER.
AGREED. LET'S DO IT.
GAH!
OKAY, NOW GO! ONCE WE'RE PAST, THEY'LL NEVER CATCH US.
YOU'RE PROBABLY RIGHT.
BUT WHY TAKE THE CHANCE?
SSK!
AAAGH!
YOU'RE DEAD, SIXTH! THIS WON'T STOP ME...AND THEN YOU'RE DEAD!
KEEP THE CLONES BUSY FOR A WHILE, WILL YOU, NINTH SISTER?
GOOD LUCK. YOU WERE ALWAYS MY FAVORITE.

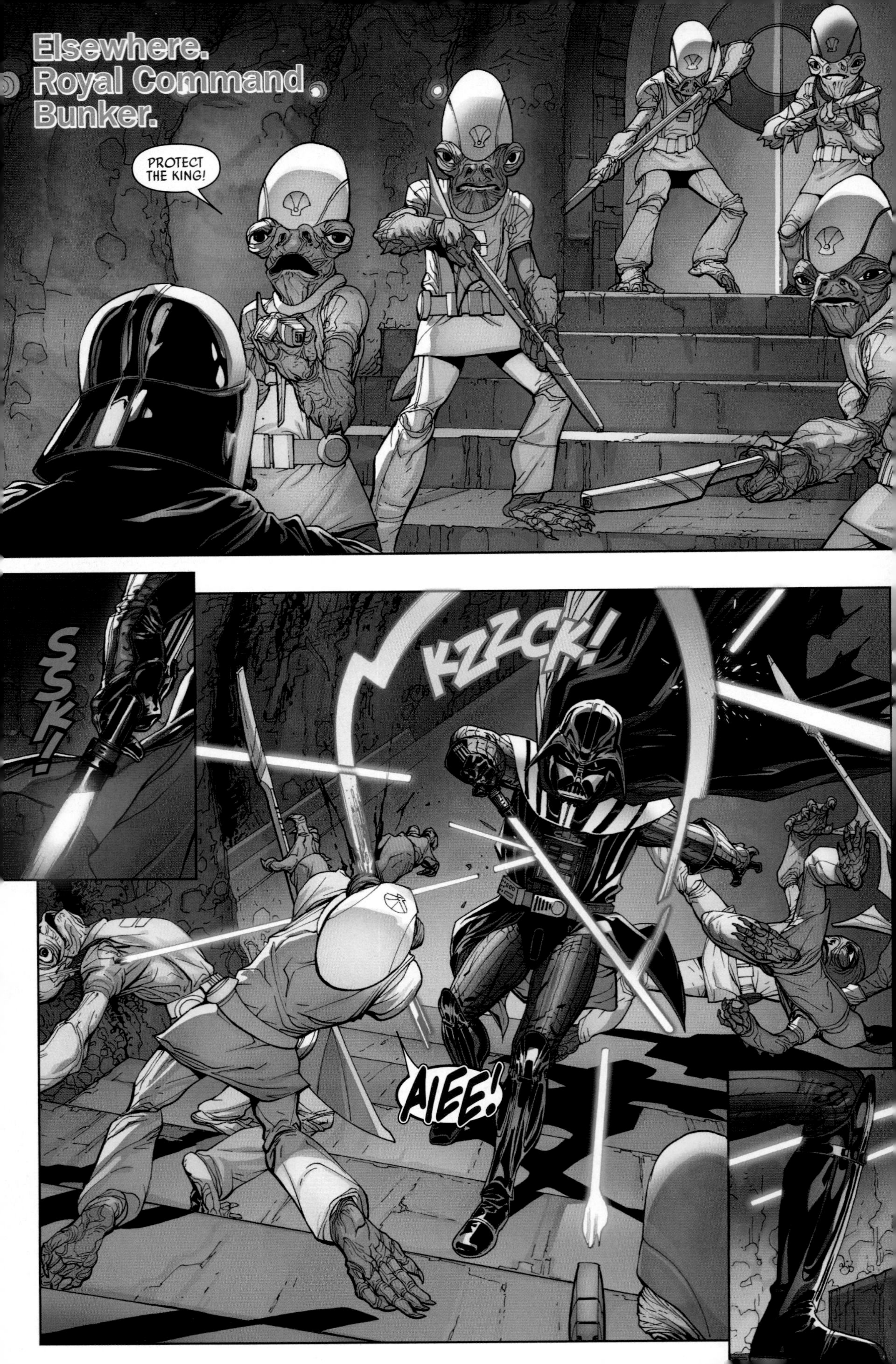

Elsewhere.
Royal Command Bunker.
PROTECT THE KING!
SSK!
KZZCK!
AIEE!

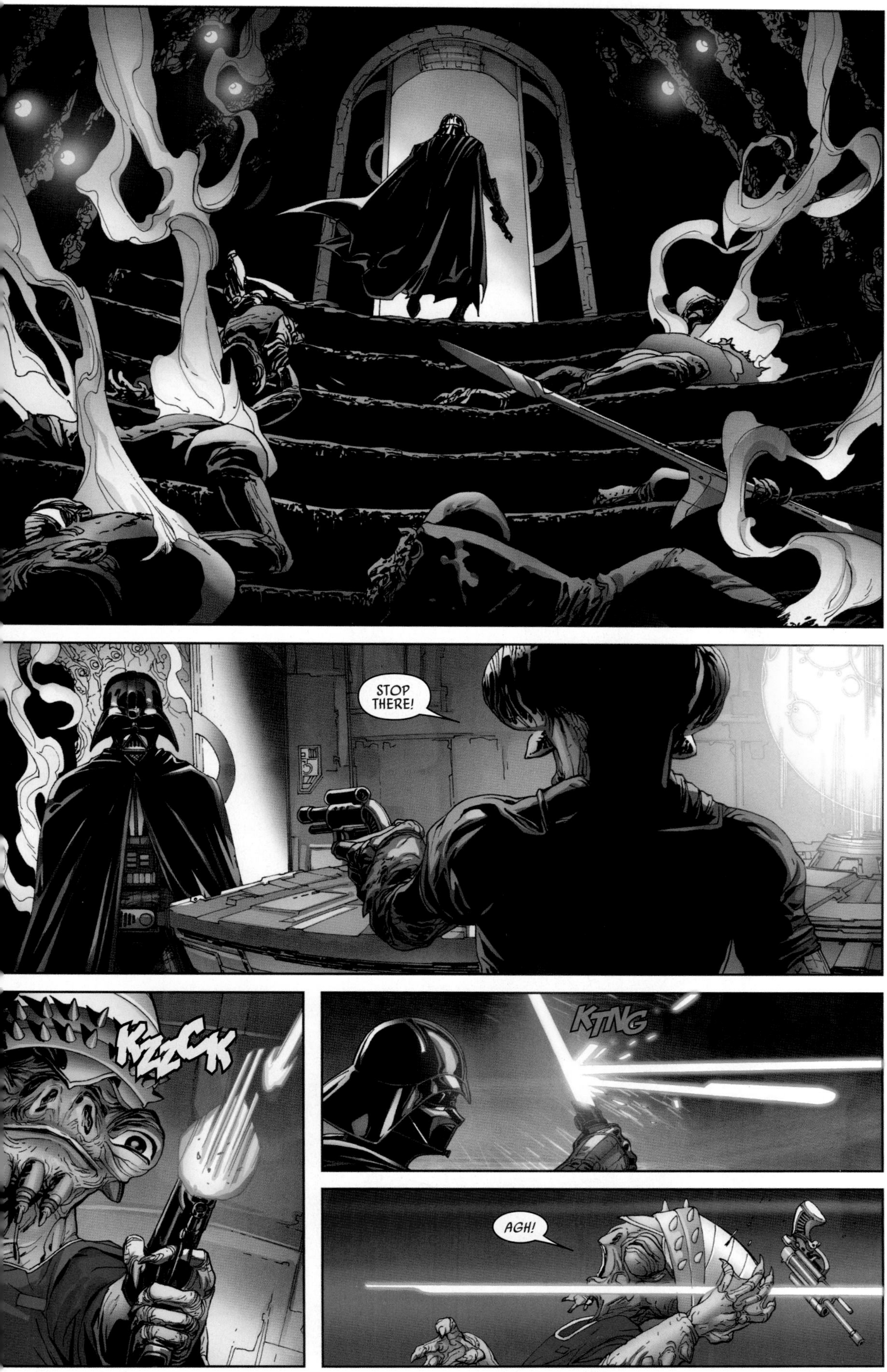
STOP THERE!
KZZCK
KTING
AGH!

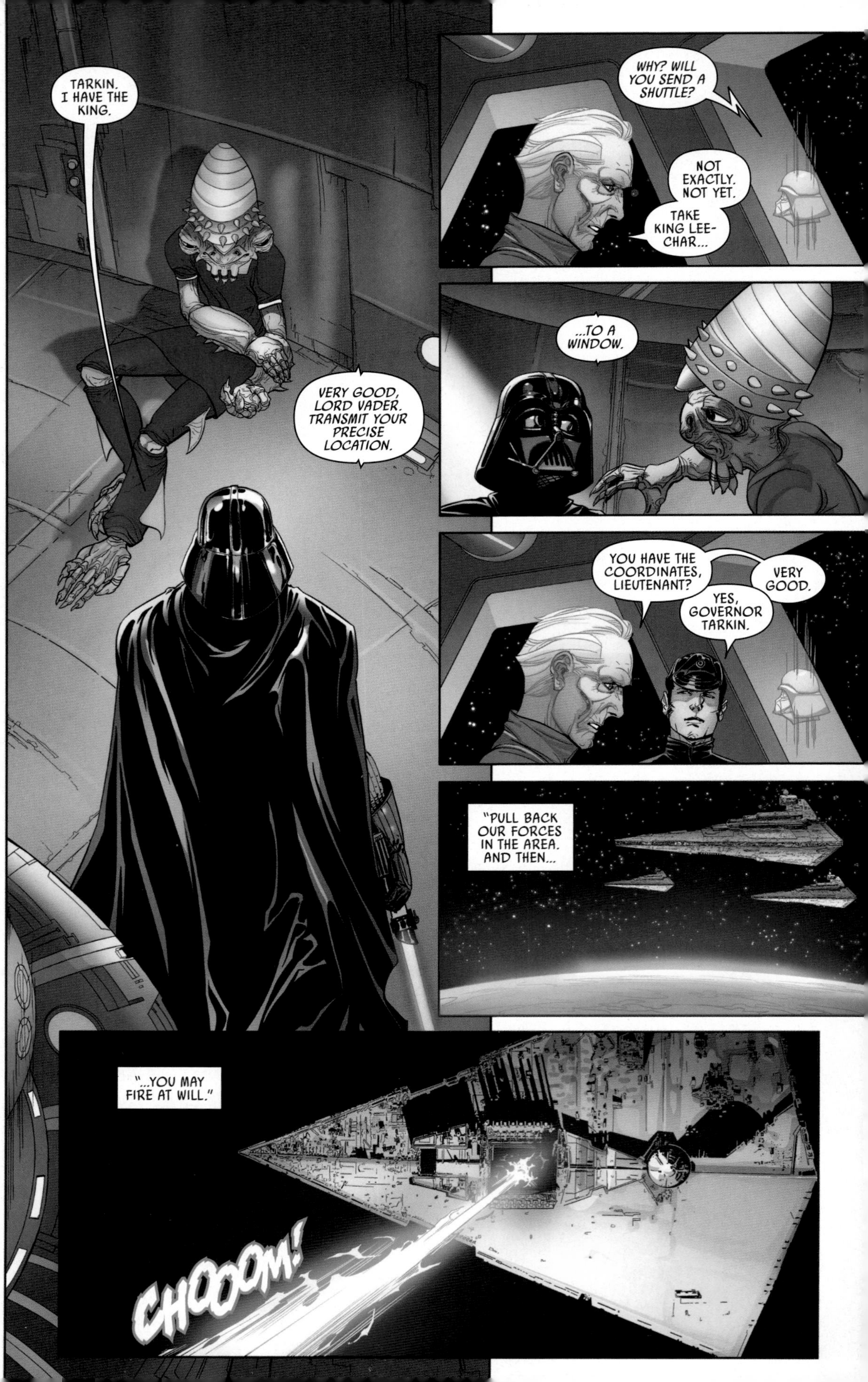
TARKIN. I HAVE THE KING.
VERY GOOD, LORD VADER. TRANSMIT YOUR PRECISE LOCATION.
WHY? WILL YOU SEND A SHUTTLE?
NOT EXACTLY. NOT YET.
TAKE KING LEE-CHAR...
...TO A WINDOW.
YOU HAVE THE COORDINATES, LIEUTENANT?
YES, GOVERNOR TARKIN.
VERY GOOD.
"PULL BACK OUR FORCES IN THE AREA. AND THEN...
"...YOU MAY FIRE AT WILL."
CHOOOM!

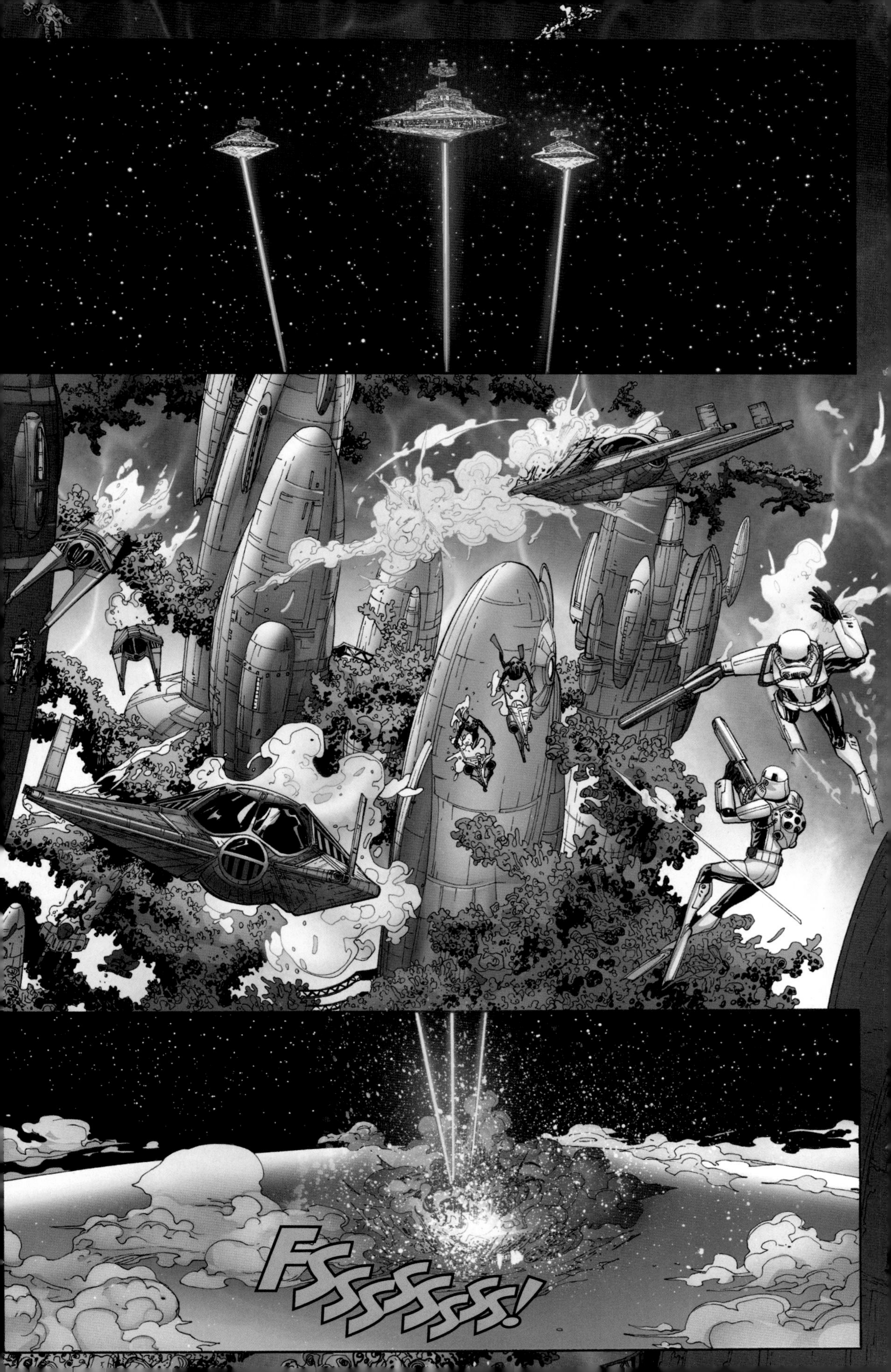
FSSSSSSS!

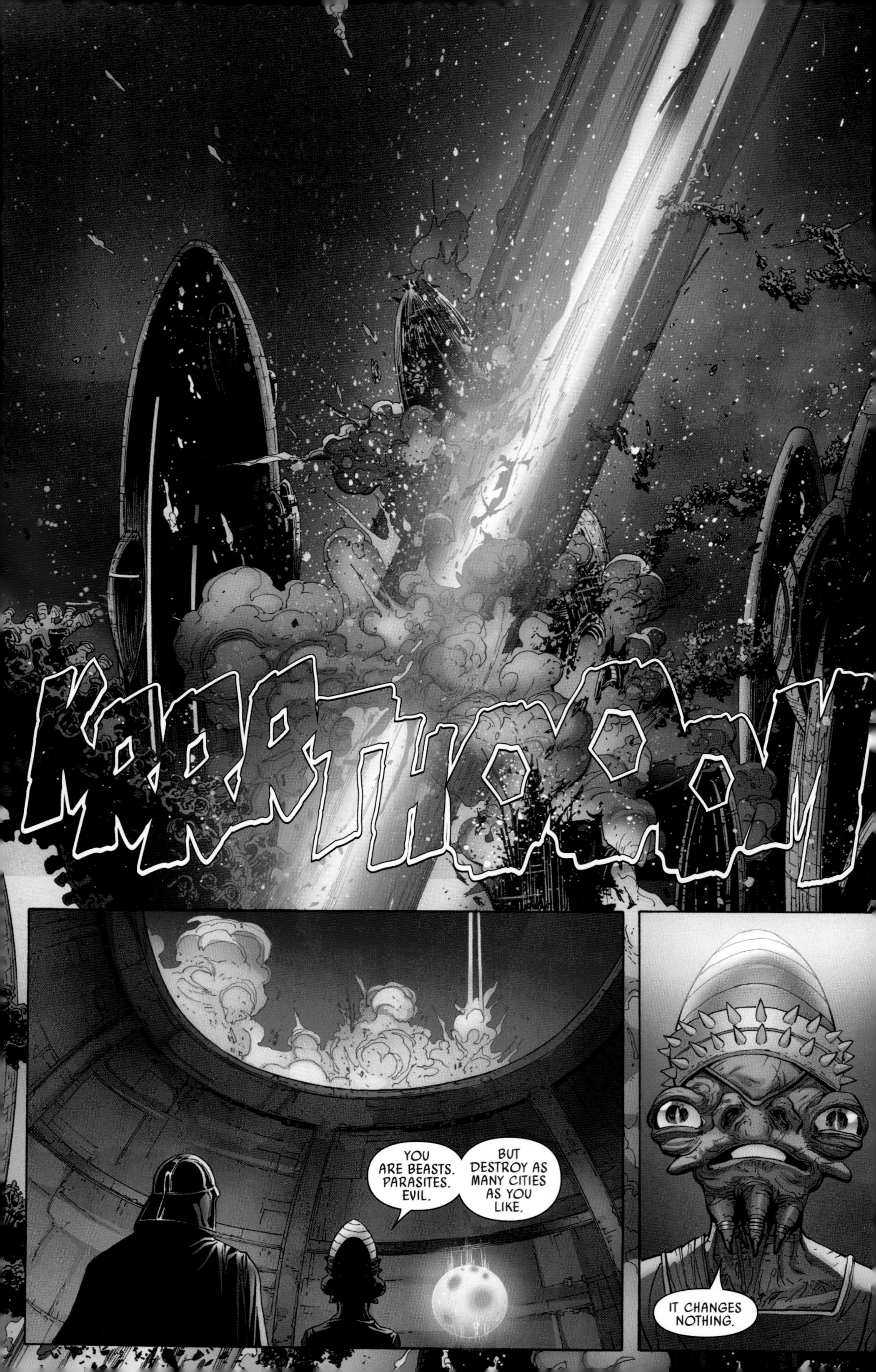
KRRATHOOOOM
YOU ARE BEASTS. PARASITES. EVIL.
BUT DESTROY AS MANY CITIES AS YOU LIKE.
IT CHANGES NOTHING.

I WILL NOT SURRENDER MY PLANET TO YOU. THE GRASPING TENTACLES OF THE EMPIRE WILL *NOT* TAKE UP MON CALA.

IMPRISON ME, EVEN TORTURE ME IF YOU LIKE...IT DOES NOT MATTER.

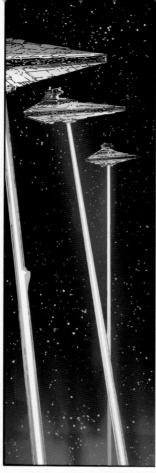

THE MON CALAMARI ARE CENTRAL TO THE DESTRUCTION OF THE EMPIRE, AND IT WILL NOT HAPPEN WITHOUT ME.

I *KNOW* THIS TO BE TRUE.

A TWITCH OF MY FINGER COULD END YOU FOREVER.

YOU ARE CENTRAL TO NOTHING. YOU DO NOT MATTER. YOU HAVE BEEN LIED TO.

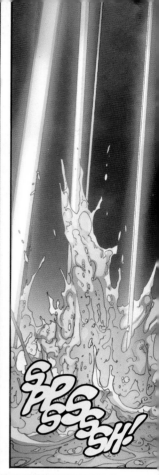

SPSSSSH!

NO, VADER.

SSK!

I TOLD HIM THE TRUTH.

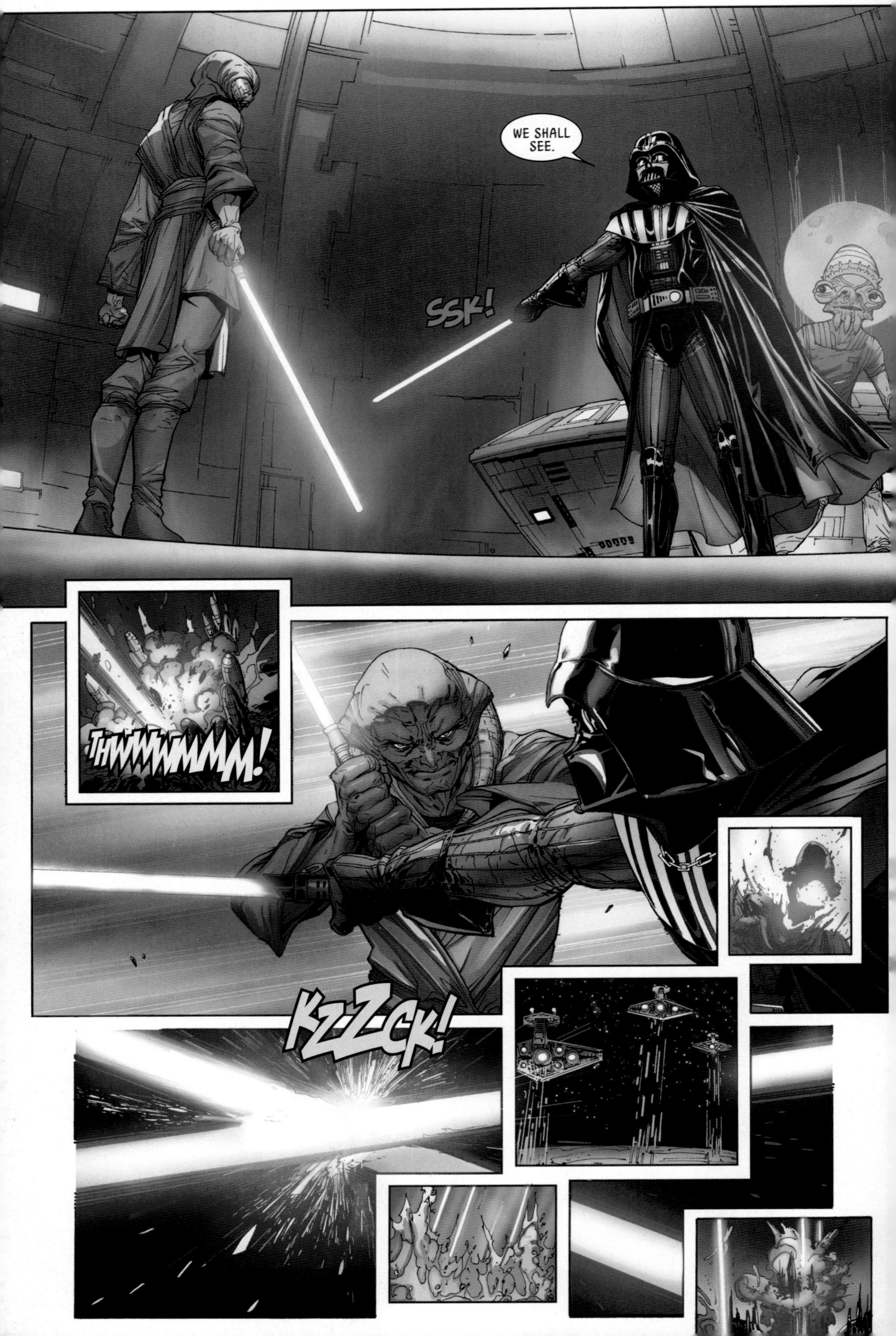
WE SHALL SEE.
SSK!
THWWWMMM!
KZ-ZCK!

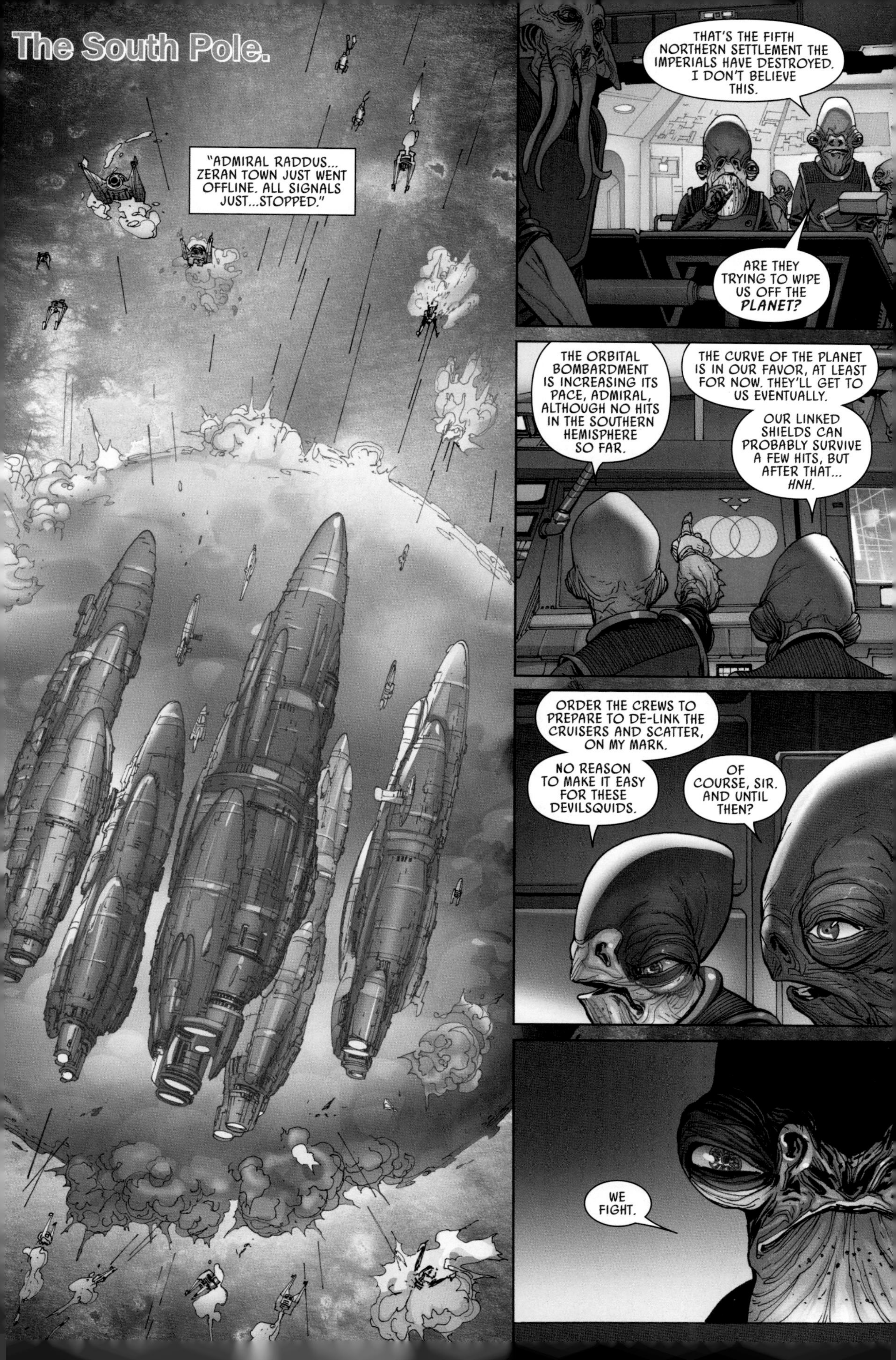
The South Pole.
"ADMIRAL RADDUS... ZERAN TOWN JUST WENT OFFLINE. ALL SIGNALS JUST...STOPPED."
THAT'S THE FIFTH NORTHERN SETTLEMENT THE IMPERIALS HAVE DESTROYED. I DON'T BELIEVE THIS.
ARE THEY TRYING TO WIPE US OFF THE *PLANET?*
THE ORBITAL BOMBARDMENT IS INCREASING ITS PACE, ADMIRAL, ALTHOUGH NO HITS IN THE SOUTHERN HEMISPHERE SO FAR.
THE CURVE OF THE PLANET IS IN OUR FAVOR, AT LEAST FOR NOW. THEY'LL GET TO US EVENTUALLY.
OUR LINKED SHIELDS CAN PROBABLY SURVIVE A FEW HITS, BUT AFTER THAT... *HNH.*
ORDER THE CREWS TO PREPARE TO DE-LINK THE CRUISERS AND SCATTER, ON MY MARK.
NO REASON TO MAKE IT EASY FOR THESE DEVILSQUIDS.
OF COURSE, SIR. AND UNTIL THEN?
WE FIGHT.

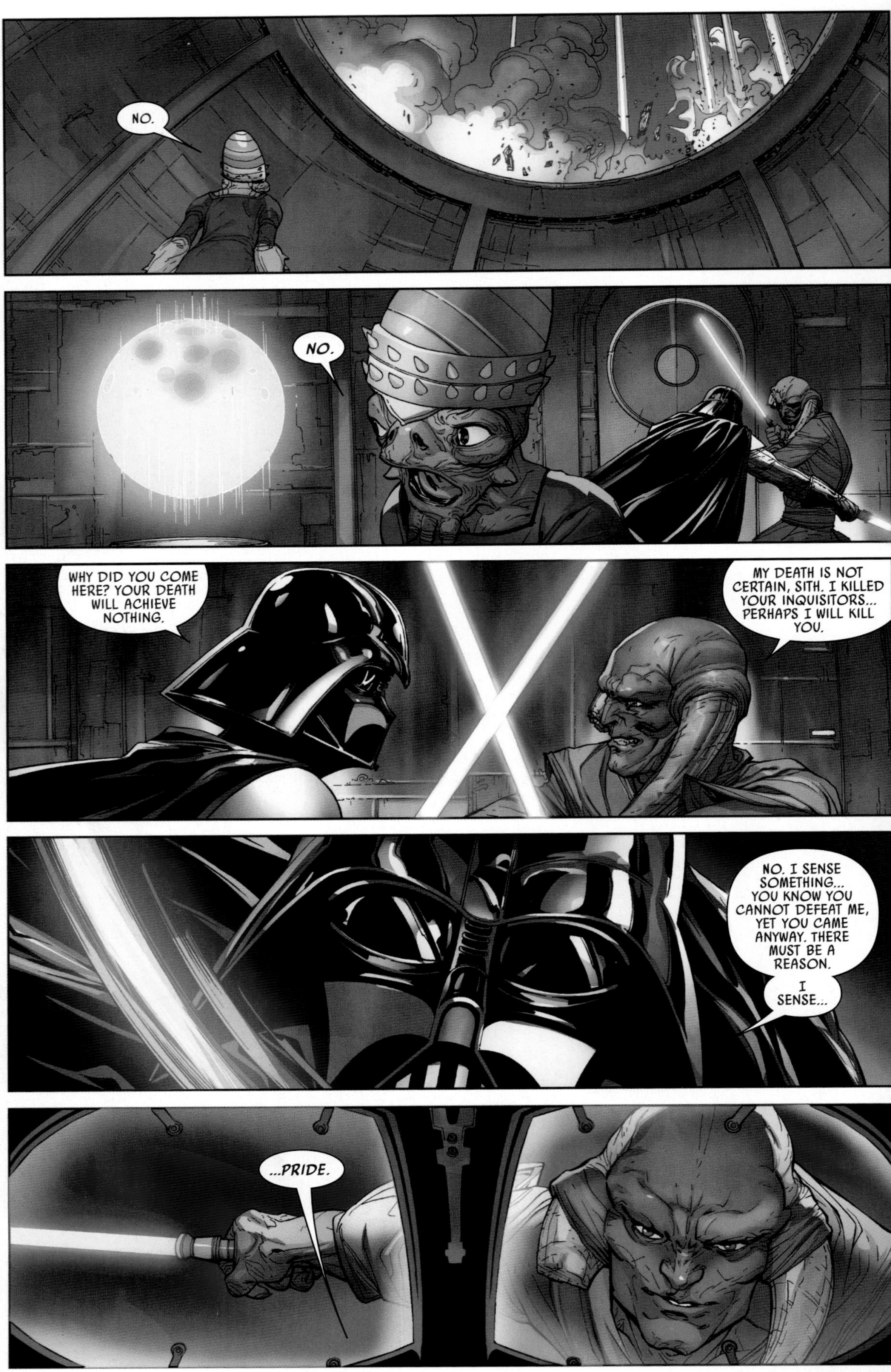
NO.
NO.
WHY DID YOU COME HERE? YOUR DEATH WILL ACHIEVE NOTHING.
MY DEATH IS NOT CERTAIN, SITH. I KILLED YOUR INQUISITORS... PERHAPS I WILL KILL YOU.
NO. I SENSE SOMETHING... YOU KNOW YOU CANNOT DEFEAT ME, YET YOU CAME ANYWAY. THERE MUST BE A REASON.
I SENSE...
...PRIDE.

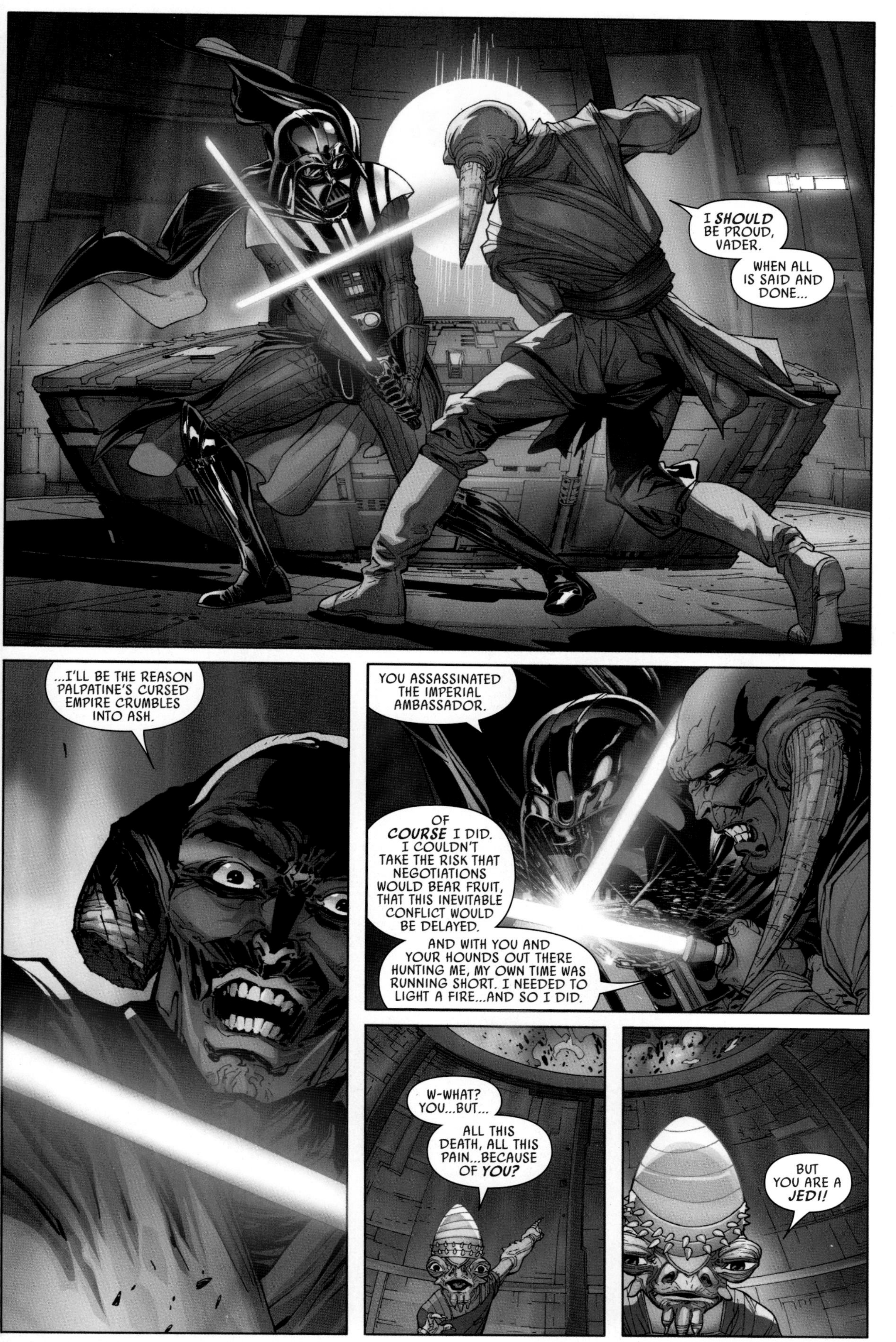
I SHOULD BE PROUD, VADER.
WHEN ALL IS SAID AND DONE...
...I'LL BE THE REASON PALPATINE'S CURSED EMPIRE CRUMBLES INTO ASH.
YOU ASSASSINATED THE IMPERIAL AMBASSADOR.
OF COURSE I DID. I COULDN'T TAKE THE RISK THAT NEGOTIATIONS WOULD BEAR FRUIT, THAT THIS INEVITABLE CONFLICT WOULD BE DELAYED.
AND WITH YOU AND YOUR HOUNDS OUT THERE HUNTING ME, MY OWN TIME WAS RUNNING SHORT. I NEEDED TO LIGHT A FIRE...AND SO I DID.
W-WHAT? YOU...BUT...
ALL THIS DEATH, ALL THIS PAIN...BECAUSE OF YOU?
BUT YOU ARE A JEDI!

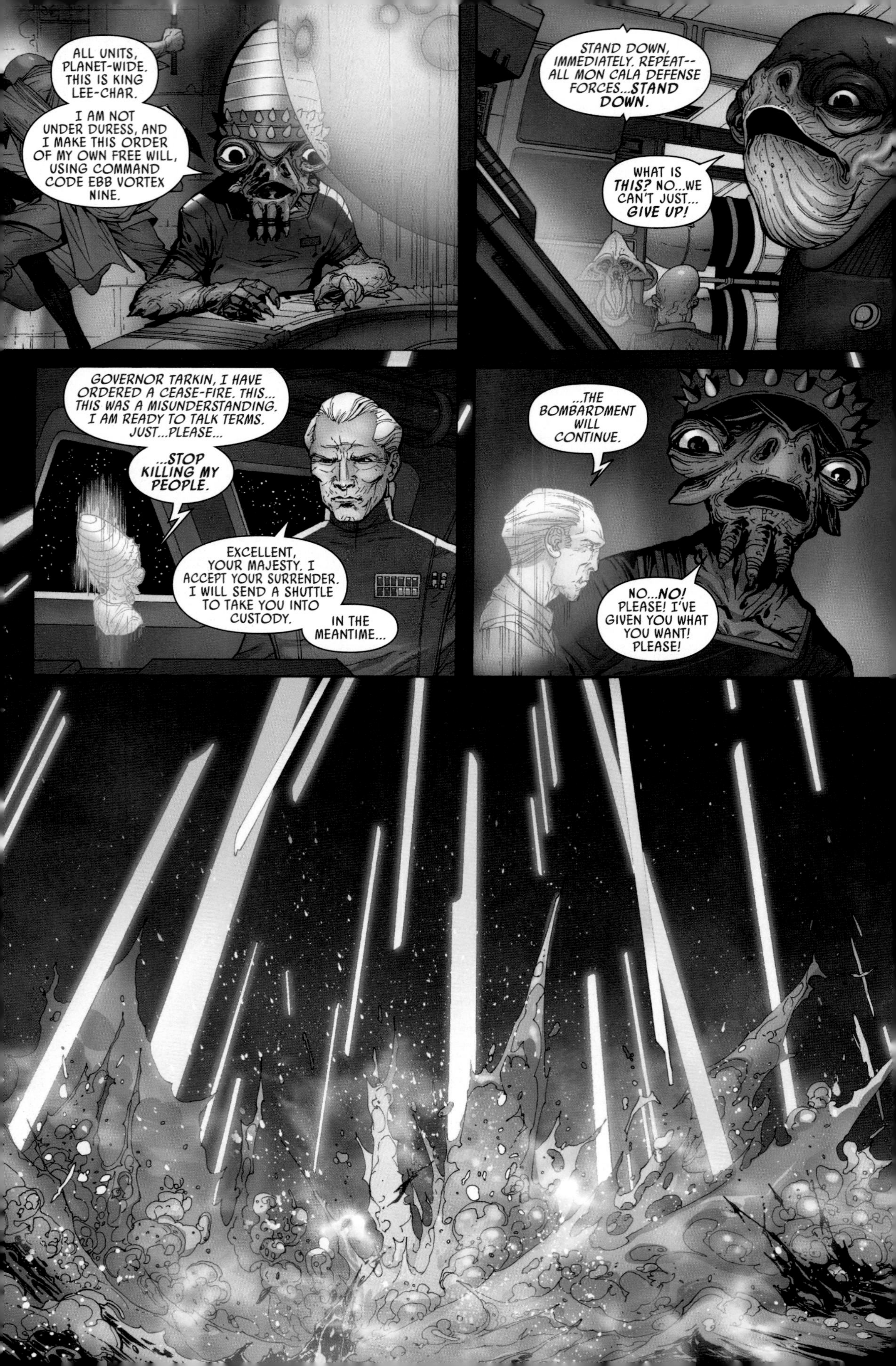
ALL UNITS, PLANET-WIDE. THIS IS KING LEE-CHAR.
I AM NOT UNDER DURESS, AND I MAKE THIS ORDER OF MY OWN FREE WILL, USING COMMAND CODE EBB VORTEX NINE.
STAND DOWN, IMMEDIATELY. REPEAT-- ALL MON CALA DEFENSE FORCES...STAND DOWN.
WHAT IS THIS? NO...WE CAN'T JUST... GIVE UP!
GOVERNOR TARKIN, I HAVE ORDERED A CEASE-FIRE. THIS... THIS WAS A MISUNDERSTANDING. I AM READY TO TALK TERMS. JUST...PLEASE...
...STOP KILLING MY PEOPLE.
EXCELLENT, YOUR MAJESTY. I ACCEPT YOUR SURRENDER. I WILL SEND A SHUTTLE TO TAKE YOU INTO CUSTODY.
IN THE MEANTIME...
...THE BOMBARDMENT WILL CONTINUE.
NO...NO! PLEASE! I'VE GIVEN YOU WHAT YOU WANT! PLEASE!

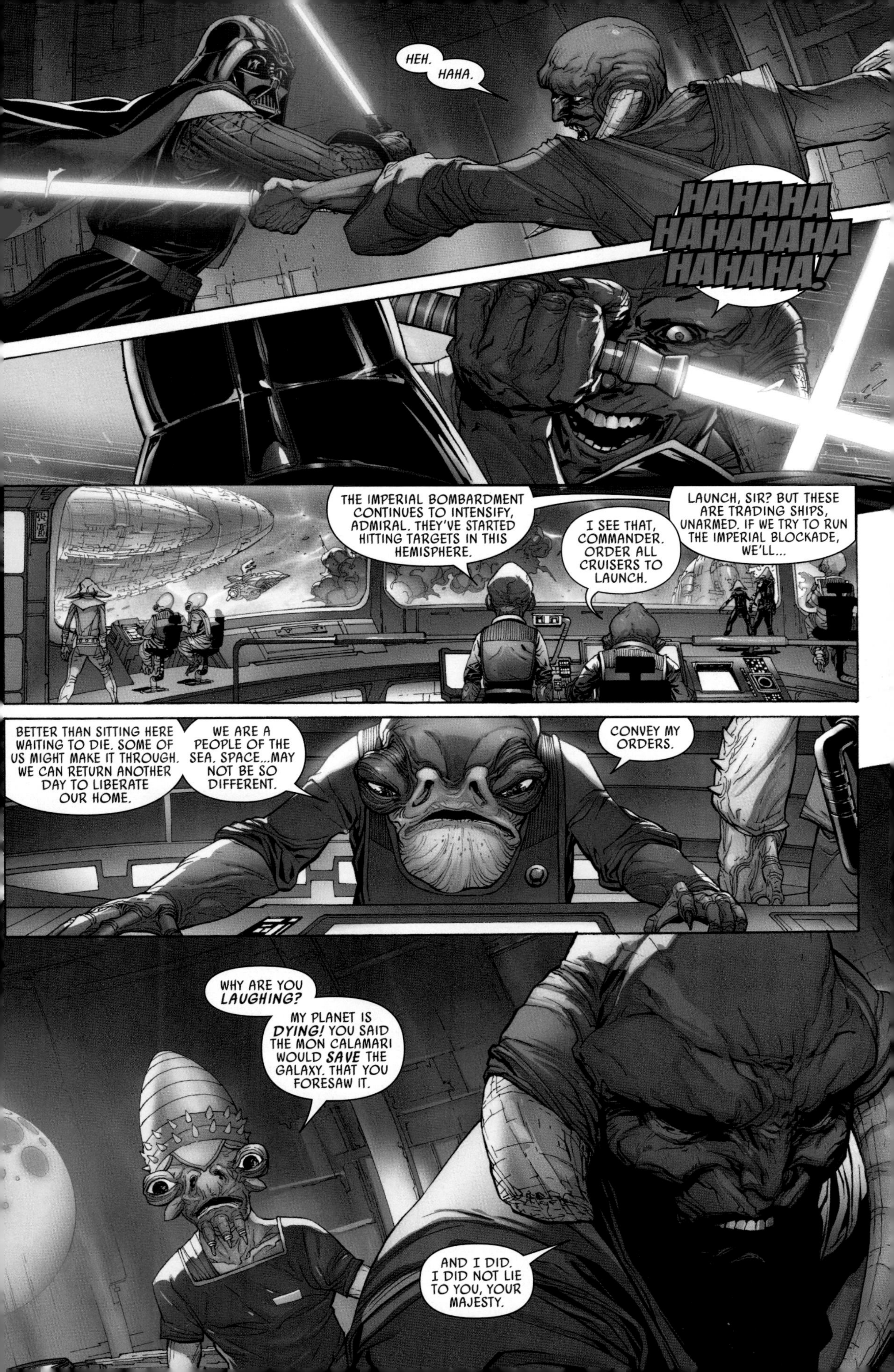
HEH. HAHA.
HAHAHA HAHAHAHA HAHAHA!
THE IMPERIAL BOMBARDMENT CONTINUES TO INTENSIFY, ADMIRAL. THEY'VE STARTED HITTING TARGETS IN THIS HEMISPHERE.
I SEE THAT, COMMANDER. ORDER ALL CRUISERS TO LAUNCH.
LAUNCH, SIR? BUT THESE ARE TRADING SHIPS, UNARMED. IF WE TRY TO RUN THE IMPERIAL BLOCKADE, WE'LL...
BETTER THAN SITTING HERE WAITING TO DIE. SOME OF US MIGHT MAKE IT THROUGH. WE CAN RETURN ANOTHER DAY TO LIBERATE OUR HOME.
WE ARE A PEOPLE OF THE SEA. SPACE...MAY NOT BE SO DIFFERENT.
CONVEY MY ORDERS.
WHY ARE YOU *LAUGHING?*
MY PLANET IS *DYING!* YOU SAID THE MON CALAMARI WOULD *SAVE* THE GALAXY. THAT YOU FORESAW IT.
AND I DID. I DID NOT LIE TO YOU, YOUR MAJESTY.

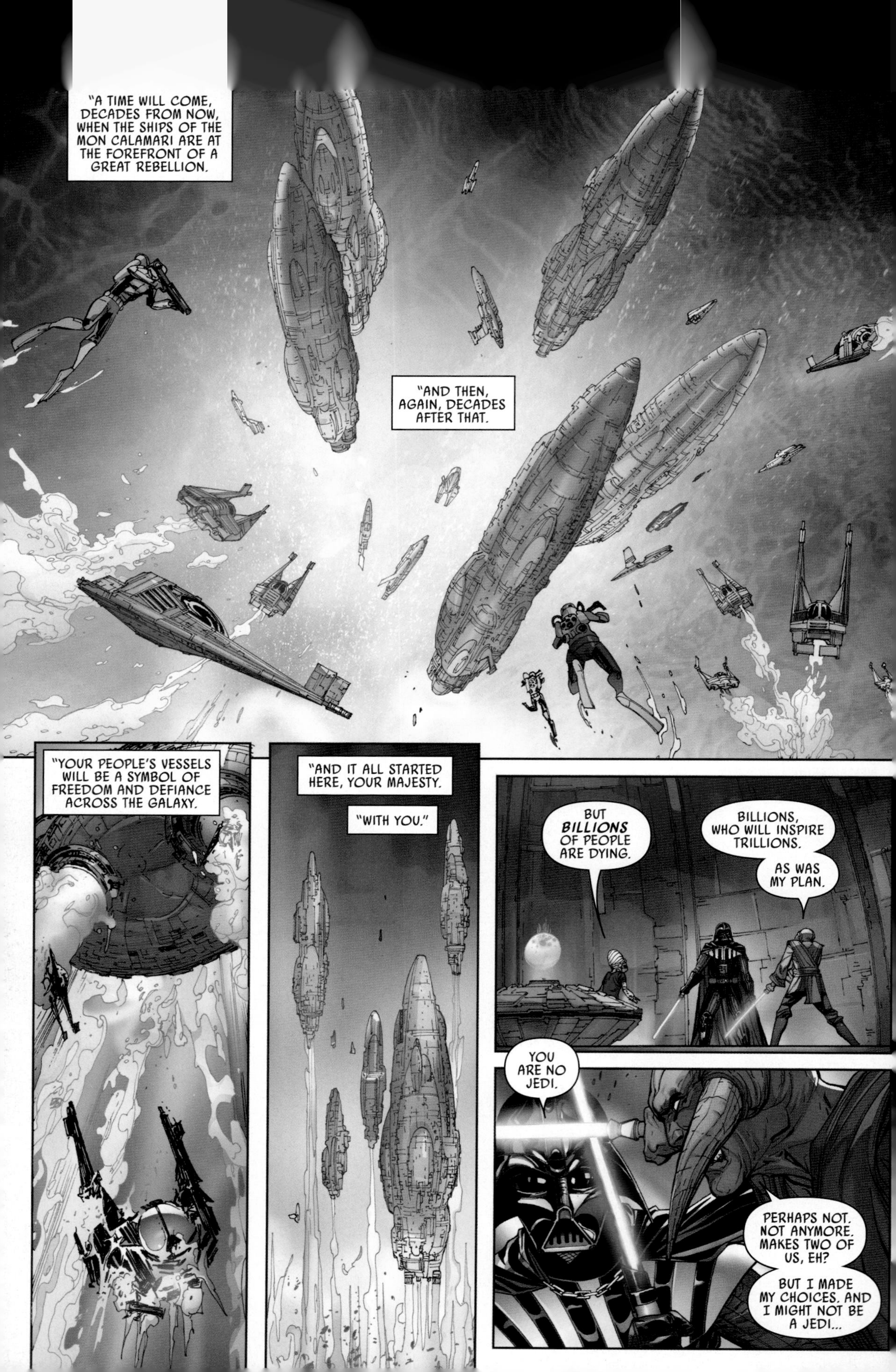
"A TIME WILL COME, DECADES FROM NOW, WHEN THE SHIPS OF THE MON CALAMARI ARE AT THE FOREFRONT OF A GREAT REBELLION.
"AND THEN, AGAIN, DECADES AFTER THAT.
"YOUR PEOPLE'S VESSELS WILL BE A SYMBOL OF FREEDOM AND DEFIANCE ACROSS THE GALAXY.
"AND IT ALL STARTED HERE, YOUR MAJESTY.
"WITH YOU."
BUT ***BILLIONS*** OF PEOPLE ARE DYING.
BILLIONS, WHO WILL INSPIRE TRILLIONS.
AS WAS MY PLAN.
YOU ARE NO JEDI.
PERHAPS NOT. NOT ANYMORE. MAKES TWO OF US, EH?
BUT I MADE MY CHOICES. AND I MIGHT NOT BE A JEDI...

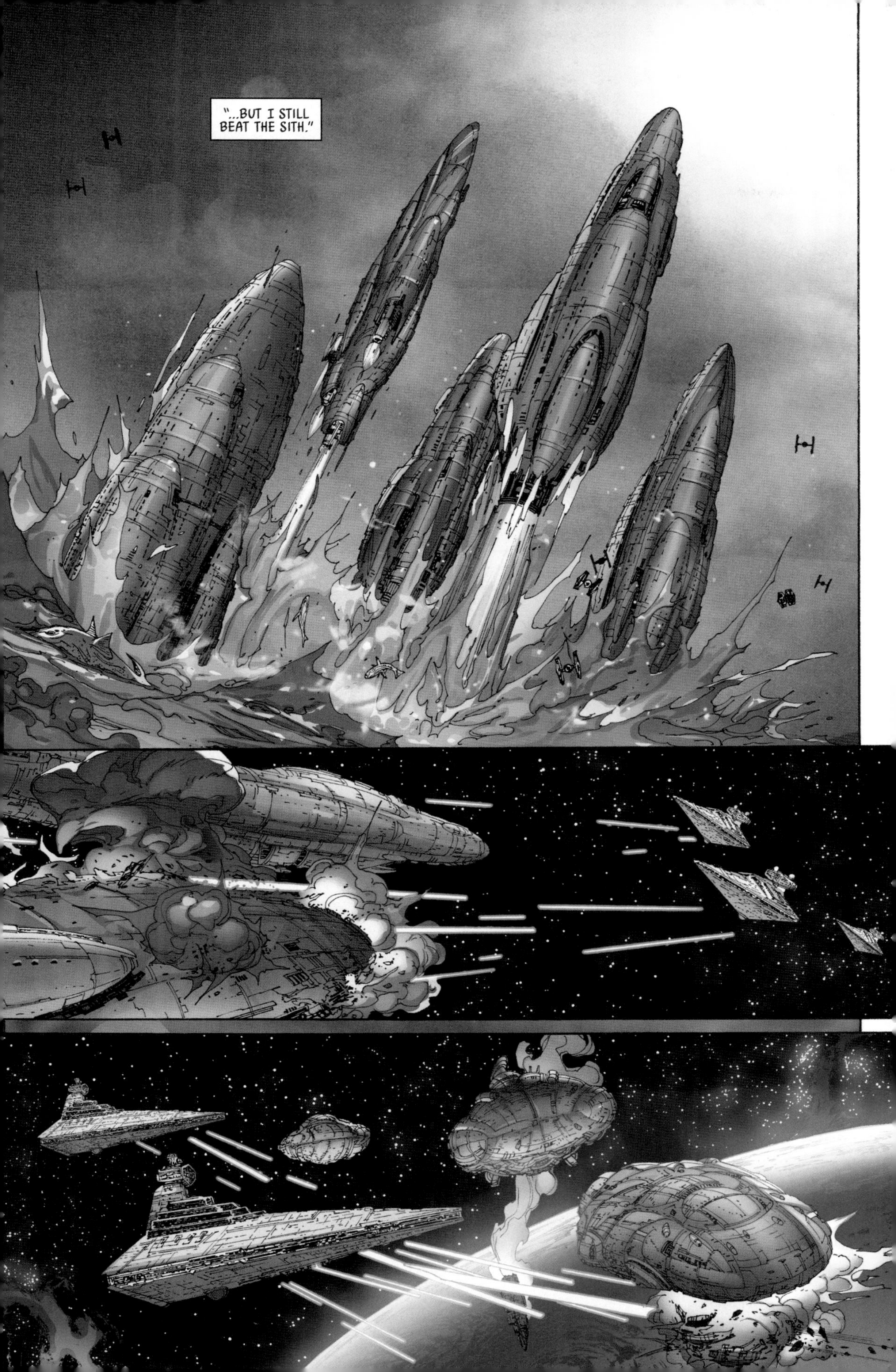
"...BUT I STILL BEAT THE SITH."

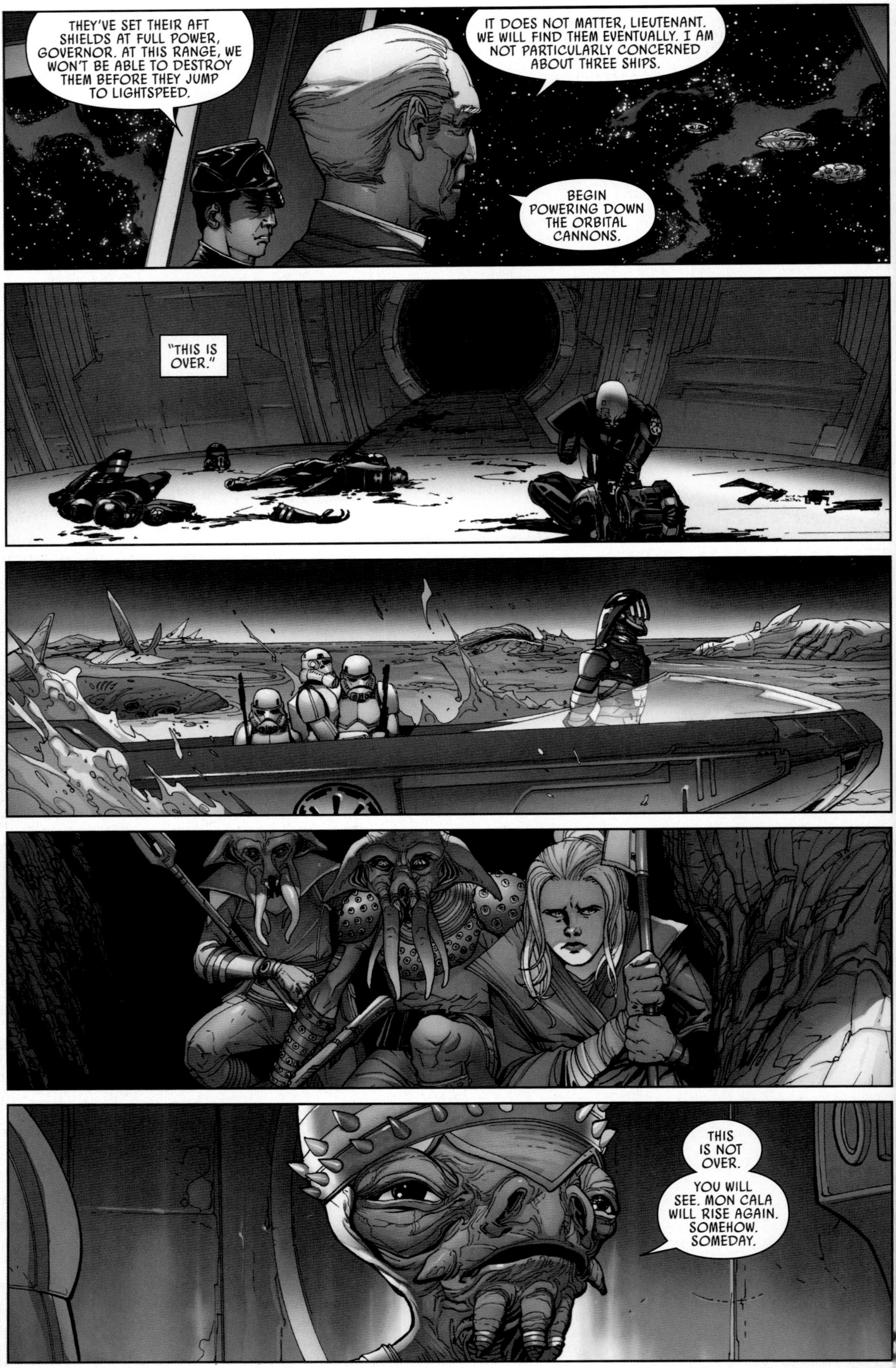
THEY'VE SET THEIR AFT SHIELDS AT FULL POWER, GOVERNOR. AT THIS RANGE, WE WON'T BE ABLE TO DESTROY THEM BEFORE THEY JUMP TO LIGHTSPEED.
IT DOES NOT MATTER, LIEUTENANT. WE WILL FIND THEM EVENTUALLY. I AM NOT PARTICULARLY CONCERNED ABOUT THREE SHIPS.
BEGIN POWERING DOWN THE ORBITAL CANNONS.
"THIS IS OVER."
THIS IS NOT OVER.
YOU WILL SEE. MON CALA WILL RISE AGAIN. SOMEHOW. SOMEDAY.

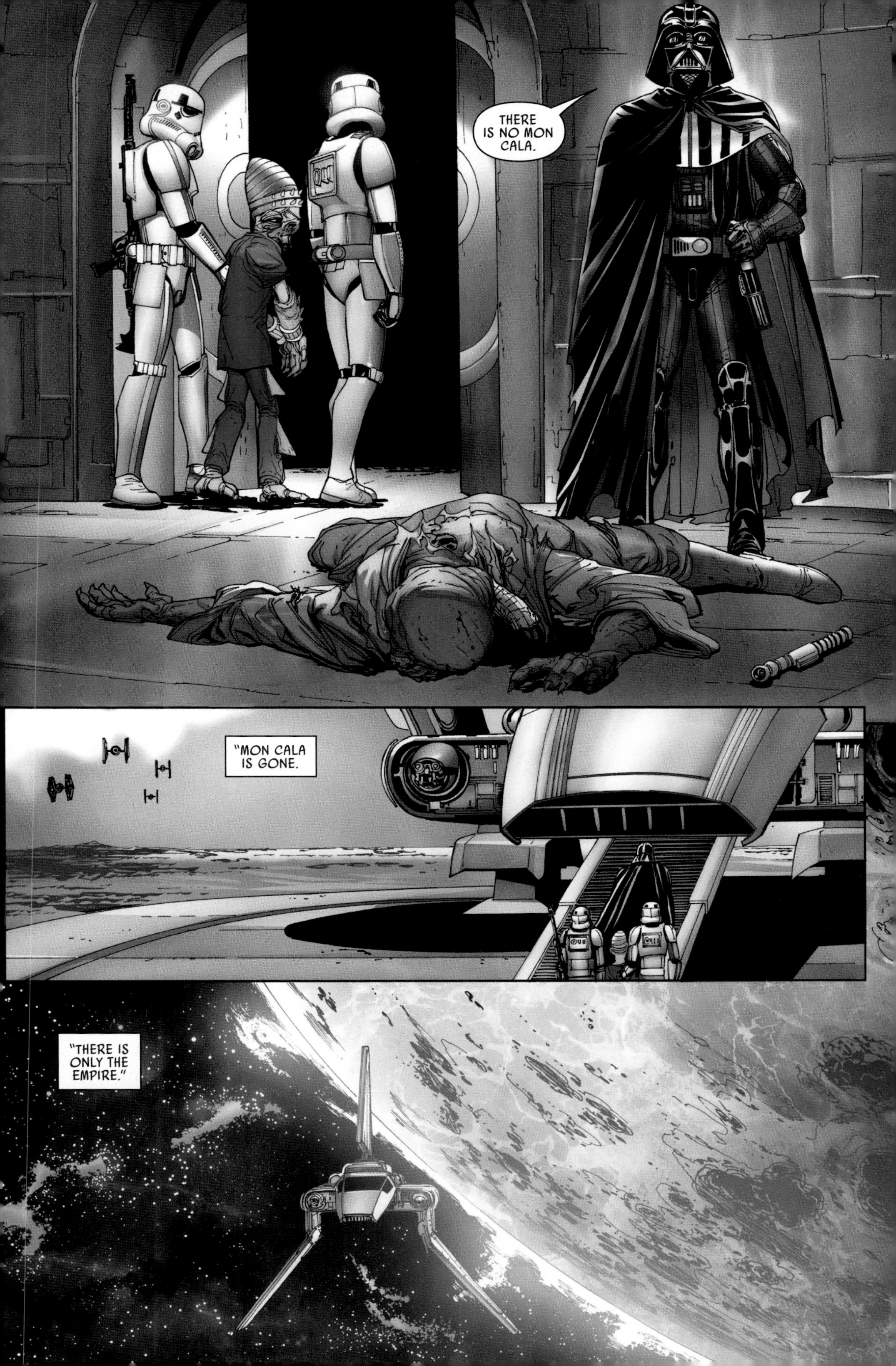
THERE IS NO MON CALA.
"MON CALA IS GONE.
"THERE IS ONLY THE EMPIRE."

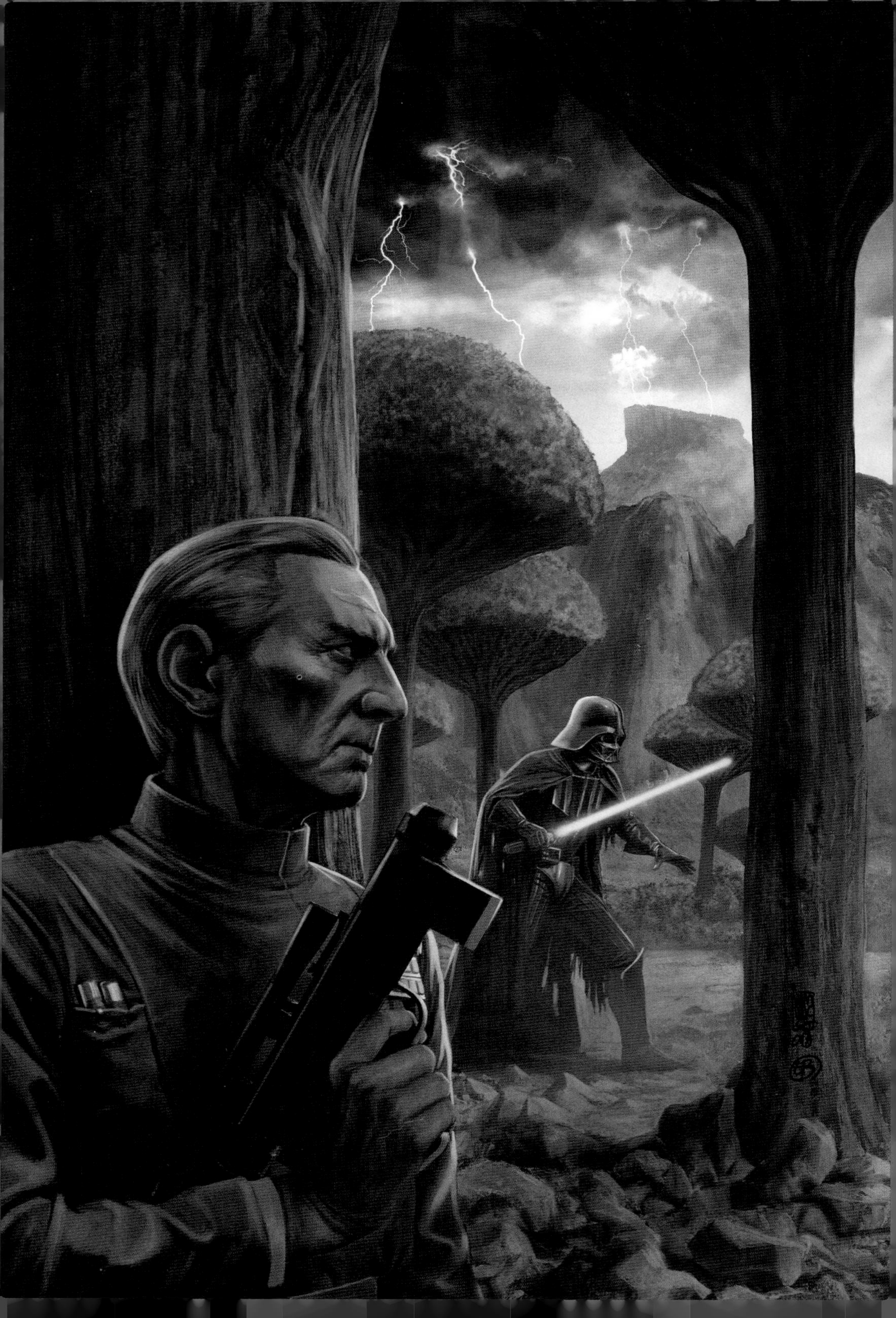

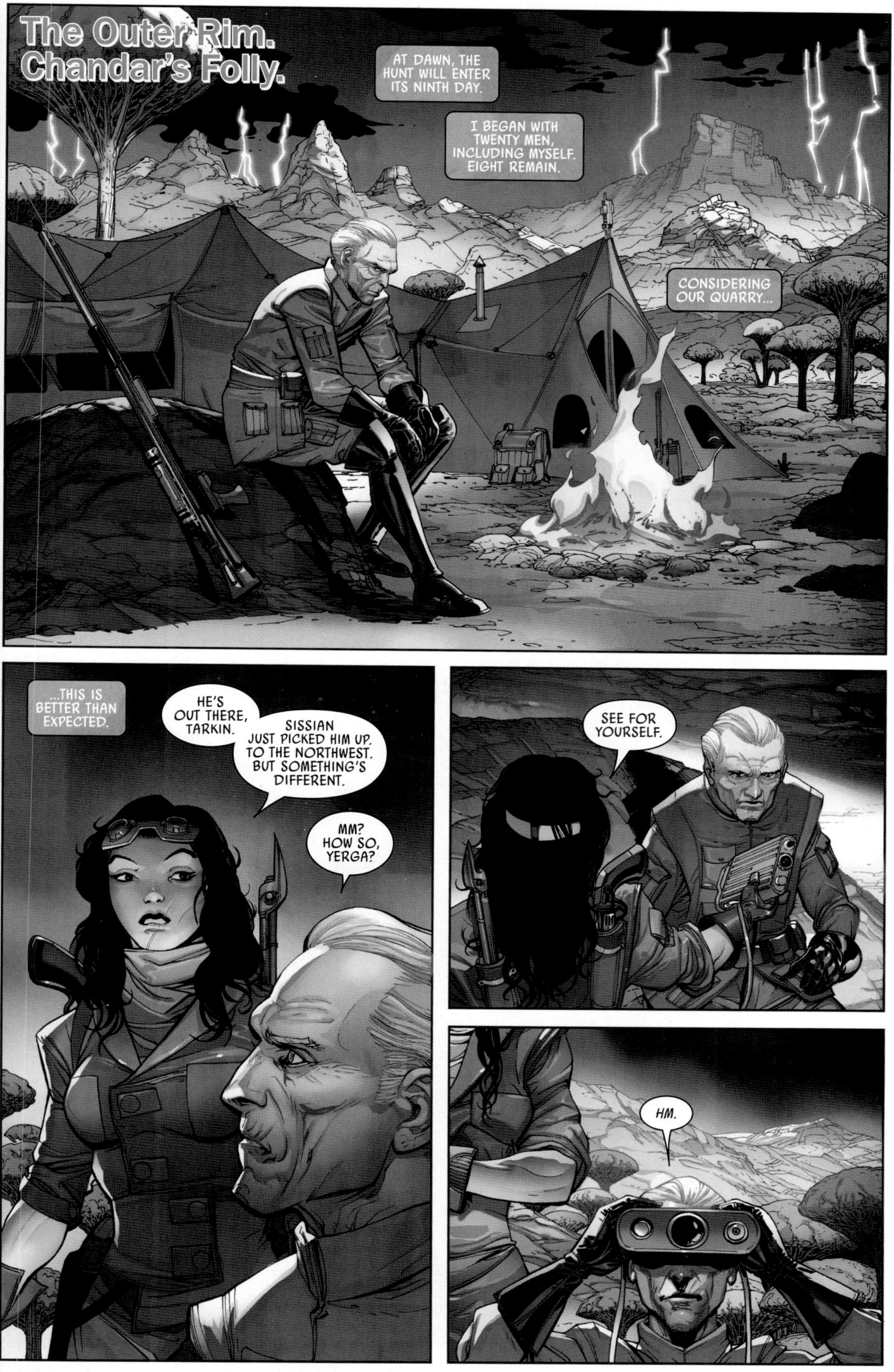
The Outer Rim.
Chandar's Folly.
AT DAWN, THE HUNT WILL ENTER ITS NINTH DAY.
I BEGAN WITH TWENTY MEN, INCLUDING MYSELF. EIGHT REMAIN.
CONSIDERING OUR QUARRY...
...THIS IS BETTER THAN EXPECTED.
HE'S OUT THERE, TARKIN.
SISSIAN JUST PICKED HIM UP. TO THE NORTHWEST. BUT SOMETHING'S DIFFERENT.
MM? HOW SO, YERGA?
SEE FOR YOURSELF.
HM.

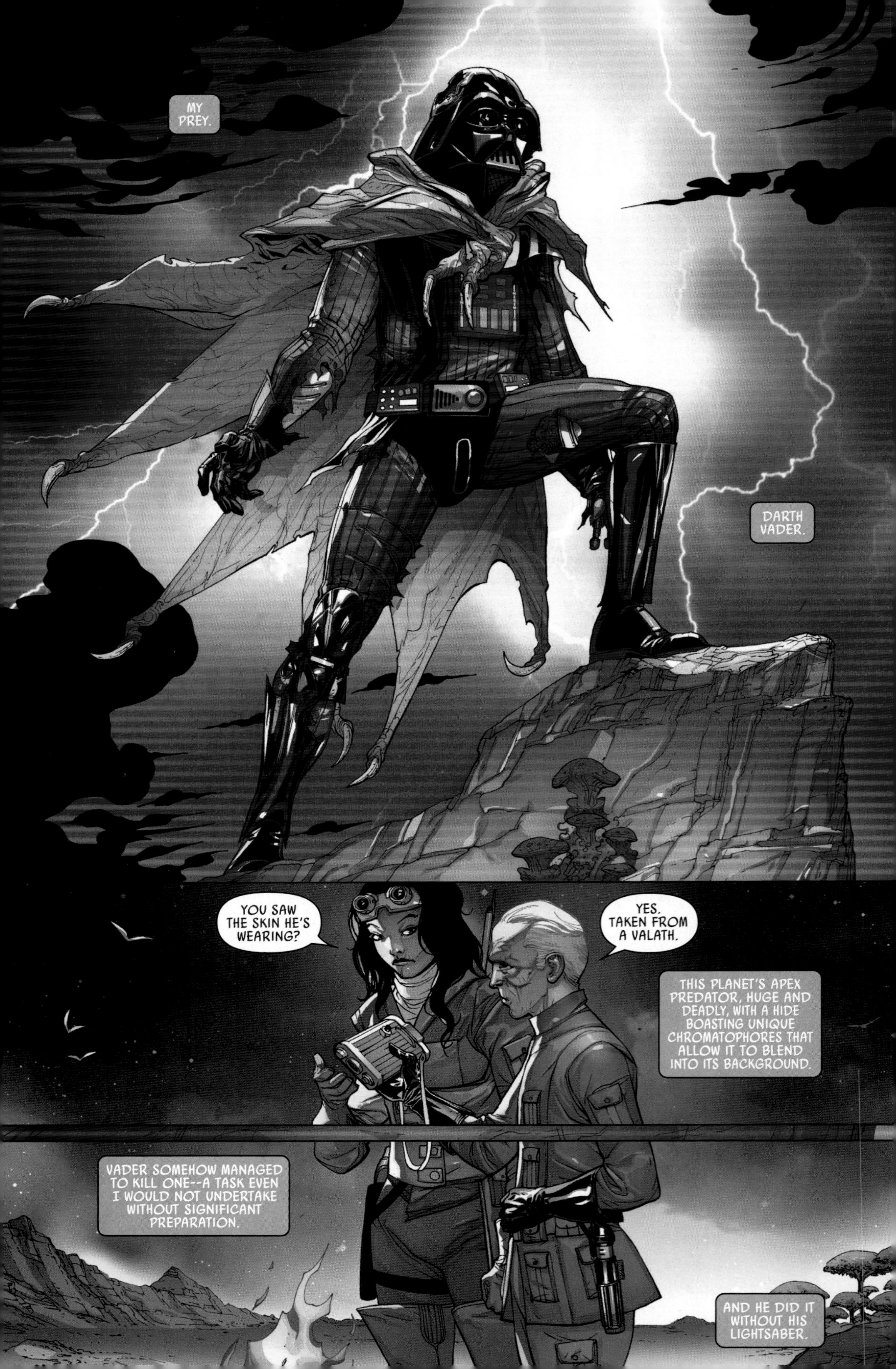
MY PREY.
DARTH VADER.
YOU SAW THE SKIN HE'S WEARING?
YES. TAKEN FROM A VALATH.
THIS PLANET'S APEX PREDATOR, HUGE AND DEADLY, WITH A HIDE BOASTING UNIQUE CHROMATOPHORES THAT ALLOW IT TO BLEND INTO ITS BACKGROUND.
VADER SOMEHOW MANAGED TO KILL ONE--A TASK EVEN I WOULD NOT UNDERTAKE WITHOUT SIGNIFICANT PREPARATION.
AND HE DID IT WITHOUT HIS LIGHTSABER.

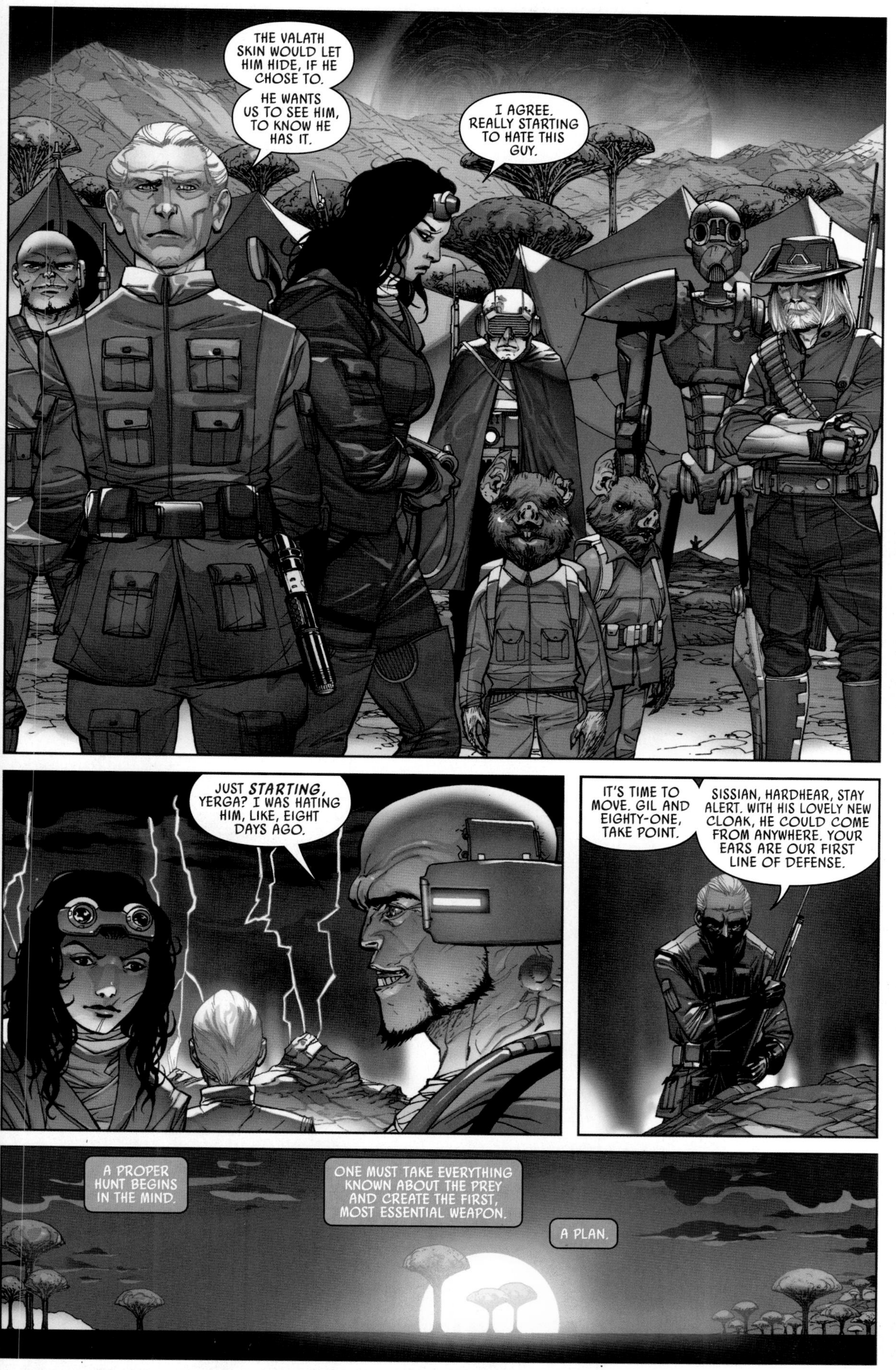
THE VALATH SKIN WOULD LET HIM HIDE, IF HE CHOSE TO.
HE WANTS US TO SEE HIM, TO KNOW HE HAS IT.
I AGREE. REALLY STARTING TO HATE THIS GUY.
JUST *STARTING*, YERGA? I WAS HATING HIM, LIKE, EIGHT DAYS AGO.
IT'S TIME TO MOVE. GIL AND EIGHTY-ONE, TAKE POINT.
SISSIAN, HARDHEAR, STAY ALERT. WITH HIS LOVELY NEW CLOAK, HE COULD COME FROM ANYWHERE. YOUR EARS ARE OUR FIRST LINE OF DEFENSE.
A PROPER HUNT BEGINS IN THE MIND.
ONE MUST TAKE EVERYTHING KNOWN ABOUT THE PREY AND CREATE THE FIRST, MOST ESSENTIAL WEAPON.
A PLAN.

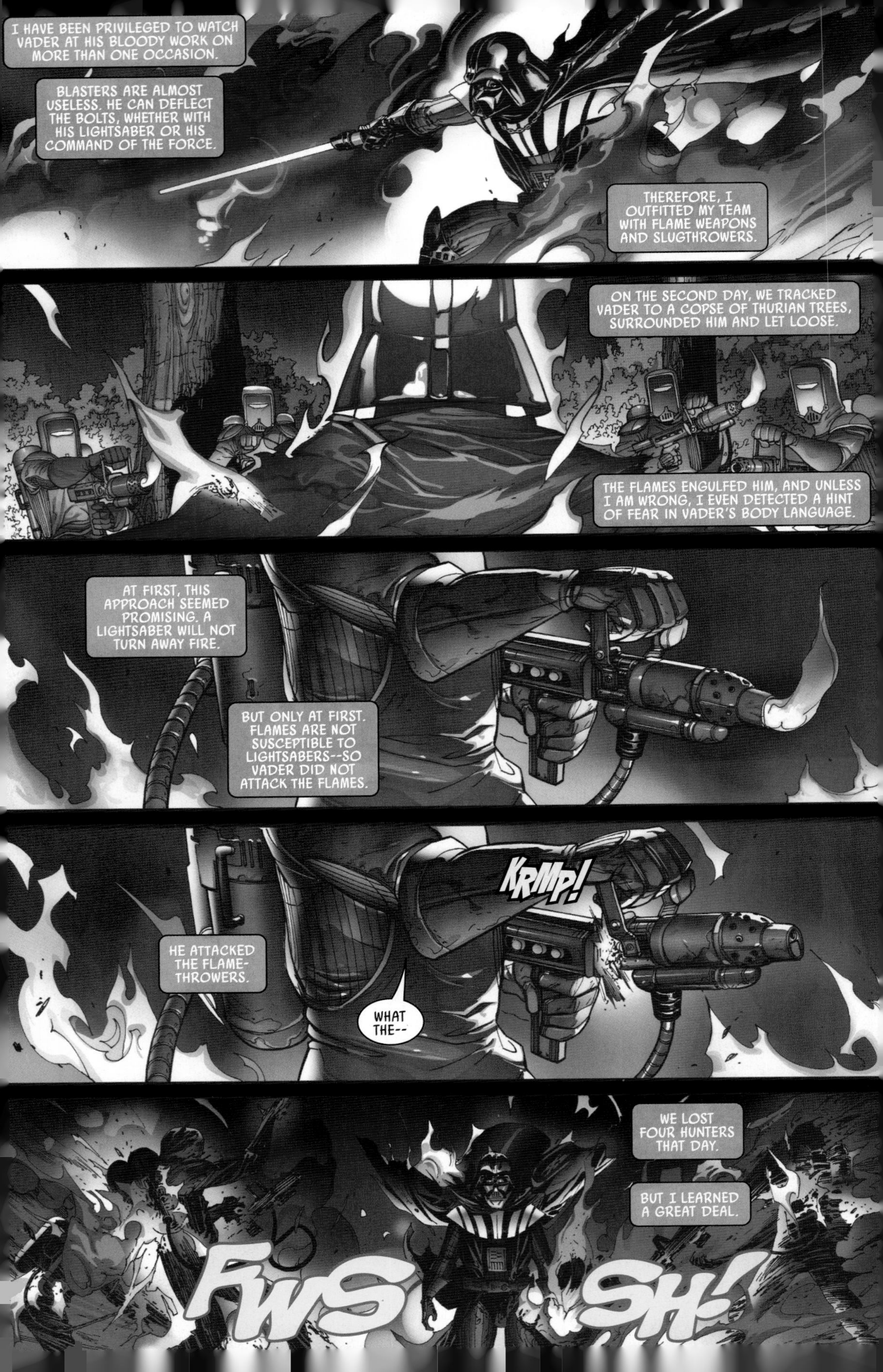

I HAVE BEEN PRIVILEGED TO WATCH VADER AT HIS BLOODY WORK ON MORE THAN ONE OCCASION.
BLASTERS ARE ALMOST USELESS. HE CAN DEFLECT THE BOLTS, WHETHER WITH HIS LIGHTSABER OR HIS COMMAND OF THE FORCE.
THEREFORE, I OUTFITTED MY TEAM WITH FLAME WEAPONS AND SLUGTHROWERS.
ON THE SECOND DAY, WE TRACKED VADER TO A COPSE OF THURIAN TREES, SURROUNDED HIM AND LET LOOSE.
THE FLAMES ENGULFED HIM, AND UNLESS I AM WRONG, I EVEN DETECTED A HINT OF FEAR IN VADER'S BODY LANGUAGE.
AT FIRST, THIS APPROACH SEEMED PROMISING. A LIGHTSABER WILL NOT TURN AWAY FIRE.
BUT ONLY AT FIRST. FLAMES ARE NOT SUSCEPTIBLE TO LIGHTSABERS--SO VADER DID NOT ATTACK THE FLAMES.
KRMP!
HE ATTACKED THE FLAME-THROWERS.
WHAT THE--
WE LOST FOUR HUNTERS THAT DAY.
BUT I LEARNED A GREAT DEAL.

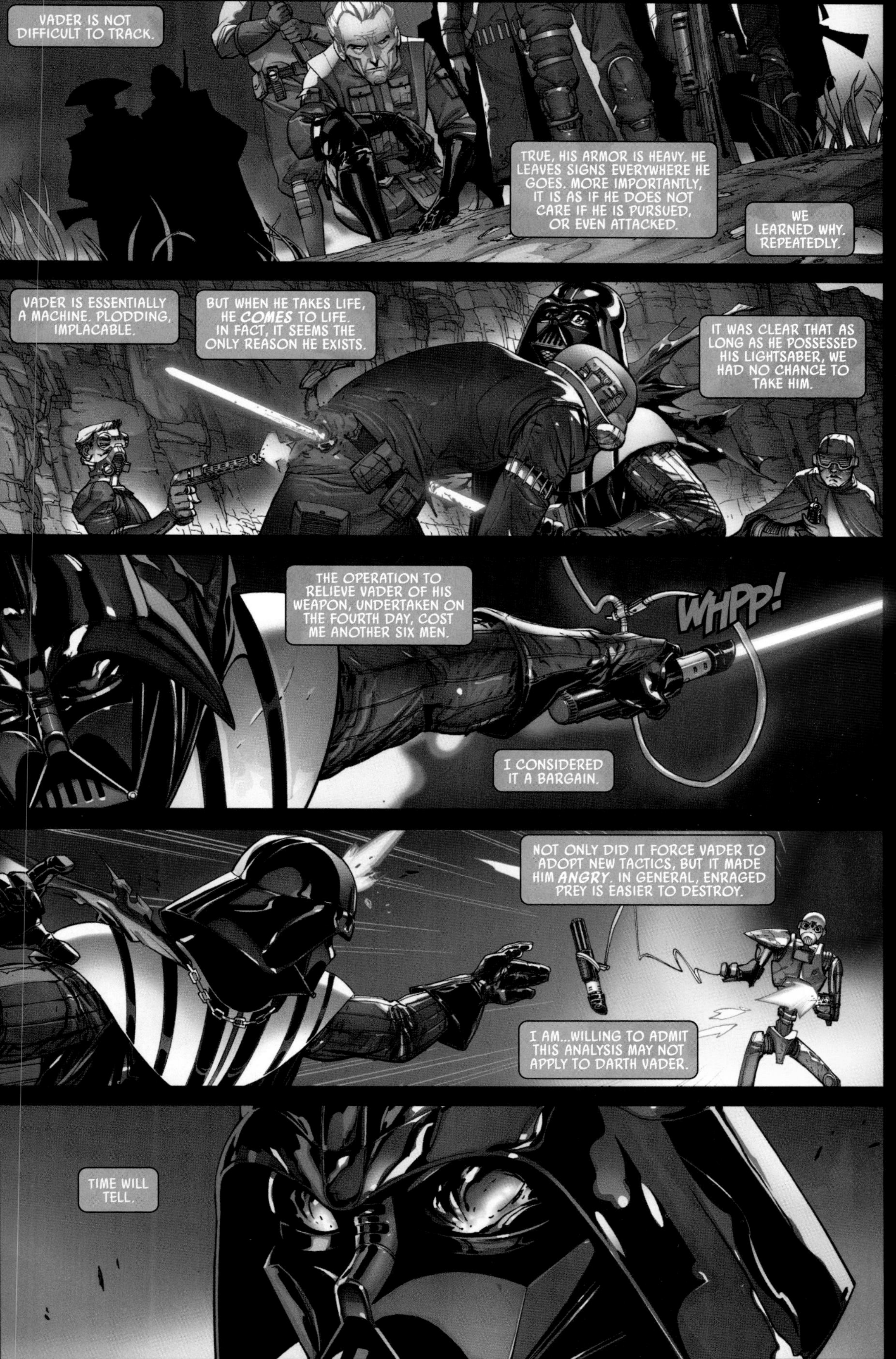
VADER IS NOT DIFFICULT TO TRACK.
TRUE, HIS ARMOR IS HEAVY. HE LEAVES SIGNS EVERYWHERE HE GOES. MORE IMPORTANTLY, IT IS AS IF HE DOES NOT CARE IF HE IS PURSUED, OR EVEN ATTACKED.
WE LEARNED WHY. REPEATEDLY.
VADER IS ESSENTIALLY A MACHINE. PLODDING, IMPLACABLE.
BUT WHEN HE TAKES LIFE, HE *COMES* TO LIFE. IN FACT, IT SEEMS THE ONLY REASON HE EXISTS.
IT WAS CLEAR THAT AS LONG AS HE POSSESSED HIS LIGHTSABER, WE HAD NO CHANCE TO TAKE HIM.
THE OPERATION TO RELIEVE VADER OF HIS WEAPON, UNDERTAKEN ON THE FOURTH DAY, COST ME ANOTHER SIX MEN.
WHPP!
I CONSIDERED IT A BARGAIN.
NOT ONLY DID IT FORCE VADER TO ADOPT NEW TACTICS, BUT IT MADE HIM *ANGRY*. IN GENERAL, ENRAGED PREY IS EASIER TO DESTROY.
I AM...WILLING TO ADMIT THIS ANALYSIS MAY NOT APPLY TO DARTH VADER.
TIME WILL TELL.

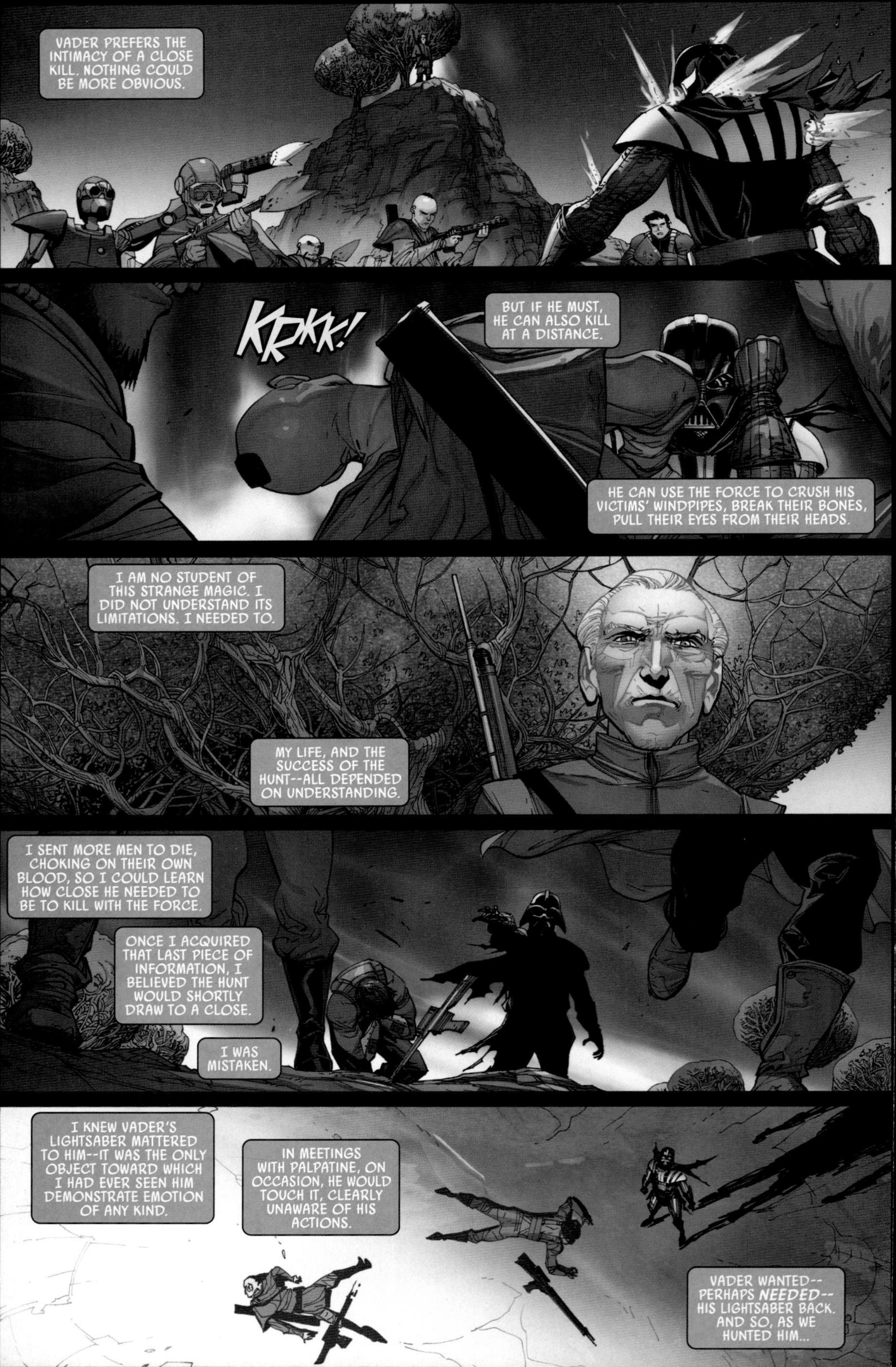
VADER PREFERS THE INTIMACY OF A CLOSE KILL. NOTHING COULD BE MORE OBVIOUS.
KRKK!
BUT IF HE MUST, HE CAN ALSO KILL AT A DISTANCE.
HE CAN USE THE FORCE TO CRUSH HIS VICTIMS' WINDPIPES, BREAK THEIR BONES, PULL THEIR EYES FROM THEIR HEADS.
I AM NO STUDENT OF THIS STRANGE MAGIC. I DID NOT UNDERSTAND ITS LIMITATIONS. I NEEDED TO.
MY LIFE, AND THE SUCCESS OF THE HUNT--ALL DEPENDED ON UNDERSTANDING.
I SENT MORE MEN TO DIE, CHOKING ON THEIR OWN BLOOD, SO I COULD LEARN HOW CLOSE HE NEEDED TO BE TO KILL WITH THE FORCE.
ONCE I ACQUIRED THAT LAST PIECE OF INFORMATION, I BELIEVED THE HUNT WOULD SHORTLY DRAW TO A CLOSE.
I WAS MISTAKEN.
I KNEW VADER'S LIGHTSABER MATTERED TO HIM--IT WAS THE ONLY OBJECT TOWARD WHICH I HAD EVER SEEN HIM DEMONSTRATE EMOTION OF ANY KIND.
IN MEETINGS WITH PALPATINE, ON OCCASION, HE WOULD TOUCH IT, CLEARLY UNAWARE OF HIS ACTIONS.
VADER WANTED--PERHAPS ***NEEDED***--HIS LIGHTSABER BACK. AND SO, AS WE HUNTED HIM...

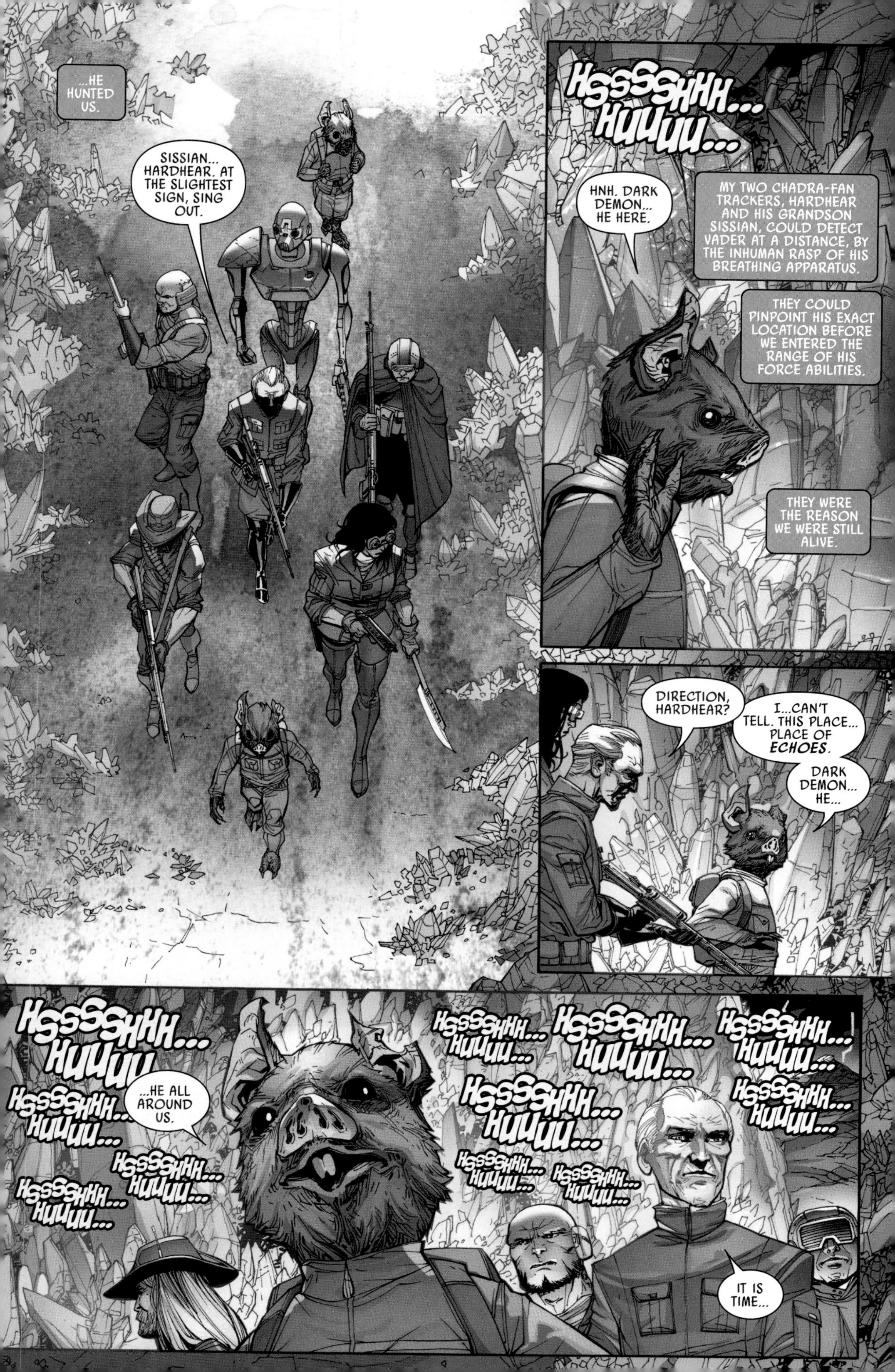

...HE HUNTED US.
SISSIAN... HARDHEAR. AT THE SLIGHTEST SIGN, SING OUT.
HSSSSHHH... HUUUU...
HNH. DARK DEMON... HE HERE.
MY TWO CHADRA-FAN TRACKERS, HARDHEAR AND HIS GRANDSON SISSIAN, COULD DETECT VADER AT A DISTANCE, BY THE INHUMAN RASP OF HIS BREATHING APPARATUS.
THEY COULD PINPOINT HIS EXACT LOCATION BEFORE WE ENTERED THE RANGE OF HIS FORCE ABILITIES.
THEY WERE THE REASON WE WERE STILL ALIVE.
DIRECTION, HARDHEAR?
I...CAN'T TELL. THIS PLACE... PLACE OF *ECHOES*.
DARK DEMON... HE...
HSSSSHHH... HUUUU...
...HE ALL AROUND US.
HSSSSHHH... HUUUU...
IT IS TIME...

...TO RUN.

THERE IS NO PANIC. JUST A RACE TO ESCAPE WHAT WE HAVE REALIZED IS A KILL BOX.

BUT IT IS DISCIPLINED. *THERE IS NO PANIC.*

MY HUNTERS ARE GOOD AT WHAT THEY DO. I HIRED WELL.

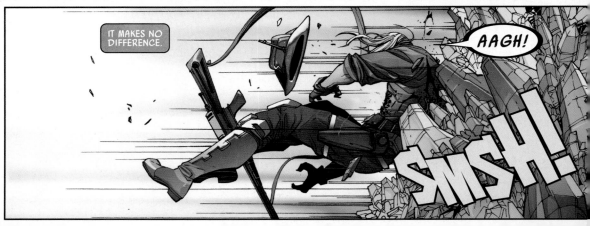

IT MAKES NO DIFFERENCE.

AAGH!

SMSH!

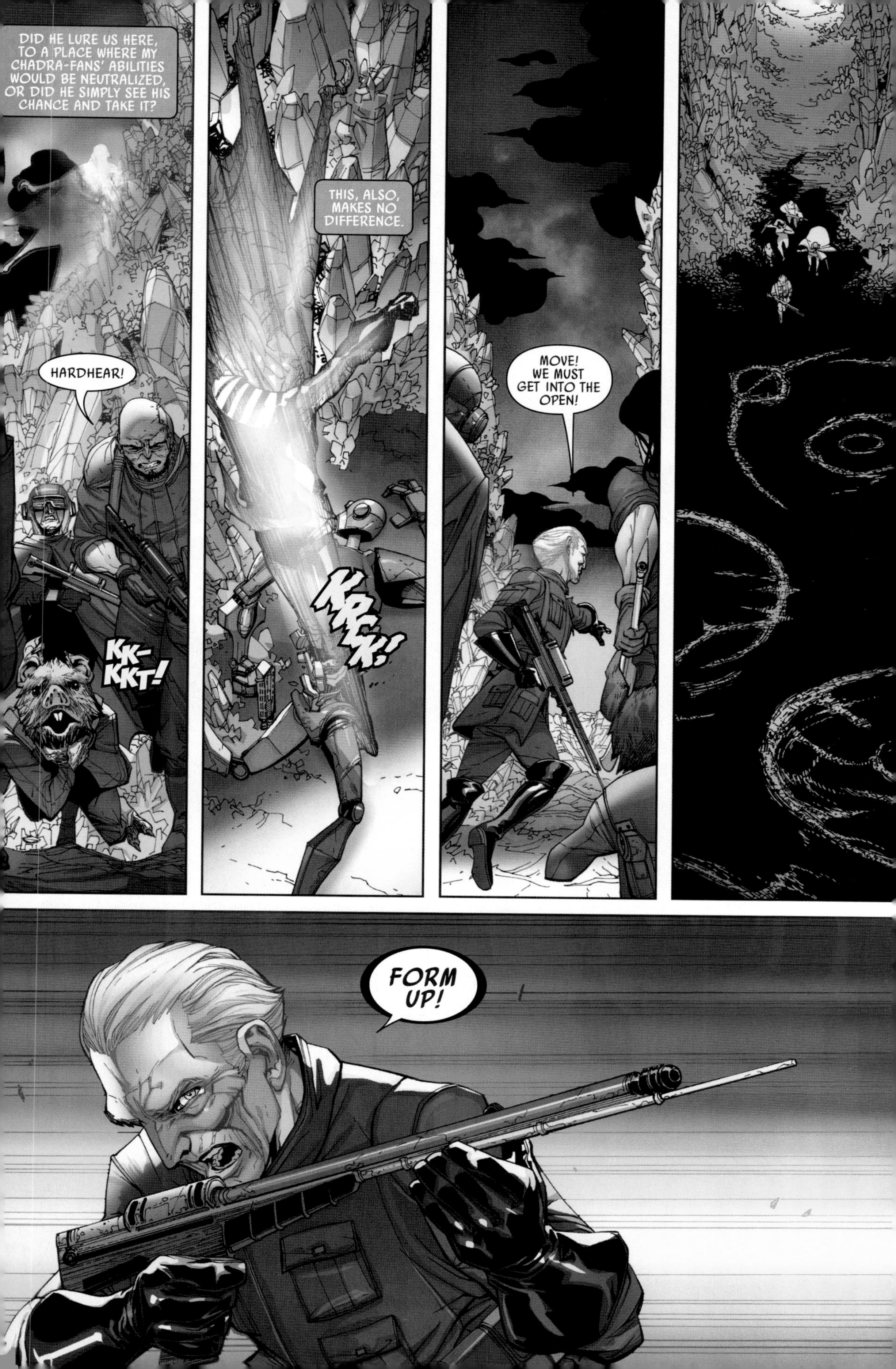
DID HE LURE US HERE, TO A PLACE WHERE MY CHADRA-FANS' ABILITIES WOULD BE NEUTRALIZED, OR DID HE SIMPLY SEE HIS CHANCE AND TAKE IT?
HARDHEAR!
KK-KKT!
THIS, ALSO, MAKES NO DIFFERENCE.
KRCK!
MOVE! WE MUST GET INTO THE OPEN!
FORM UP!

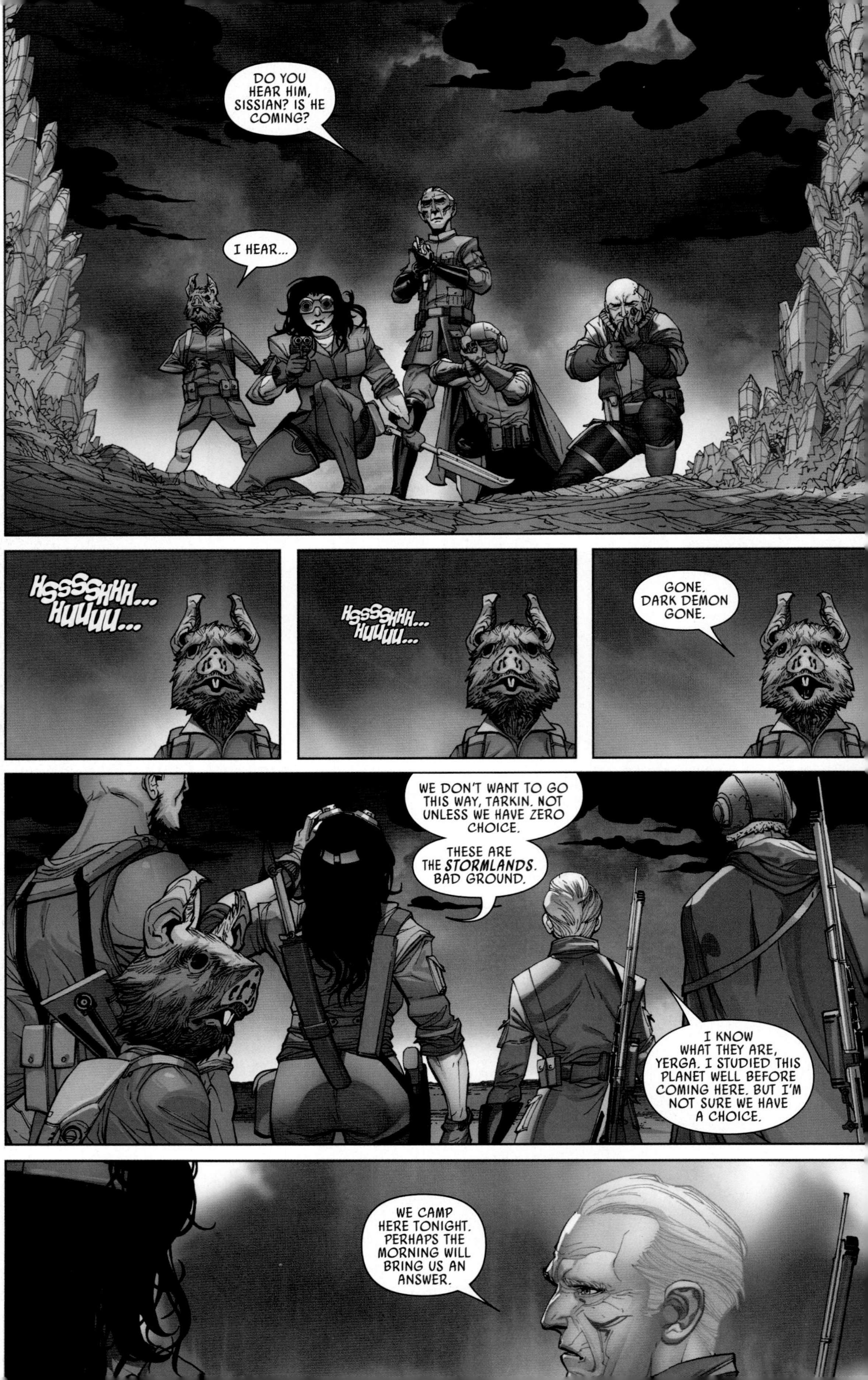
DO YOU HEAR HIM, SISSIAN? IS HE COMING?
I HEAR...
HSSSSHHH... HUUUU...
HSSSSHHH... HUUUU...
GONE. DARK DEMON GONE.
WE DON'T WANT TO GO THIS WAY, TARKIN. NOT UNLESS WE HAVE ZERO CHOICE.
THESE ARE THE STORMLANDS. BAD GROUND.
I KNOW WHAT THEY ARE, YERGA. I STUDIED THIS PLANET WELL BEFORE COMING HERE. BUT I'M NOT SURE WE HAVE A CHOICE.
WE CAMP HERE TONIGHT. PERHAPS THE MORNING WILL BRING US AN ANSWER.

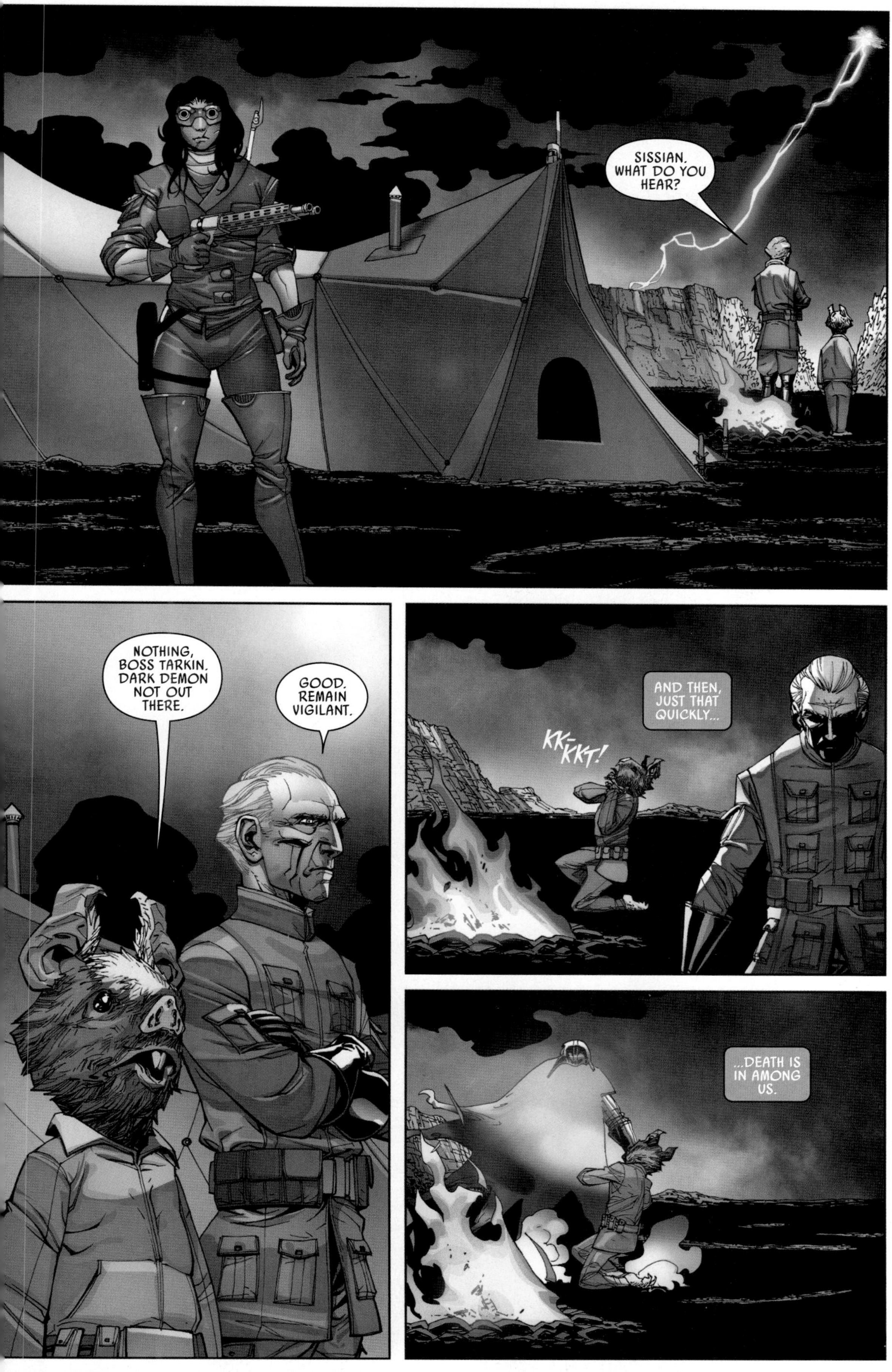
SISSIAN. WHAT DO YOU HEAR?
NOTHING, BOSS TARKIN. DARK DEMON NOT OUT THERE.
GOOD. REMAIN VIGILANT.
AND THEN, JUST THAT QUICKLY...
KK-KKT!
...DEATH IS IN AMONG US.

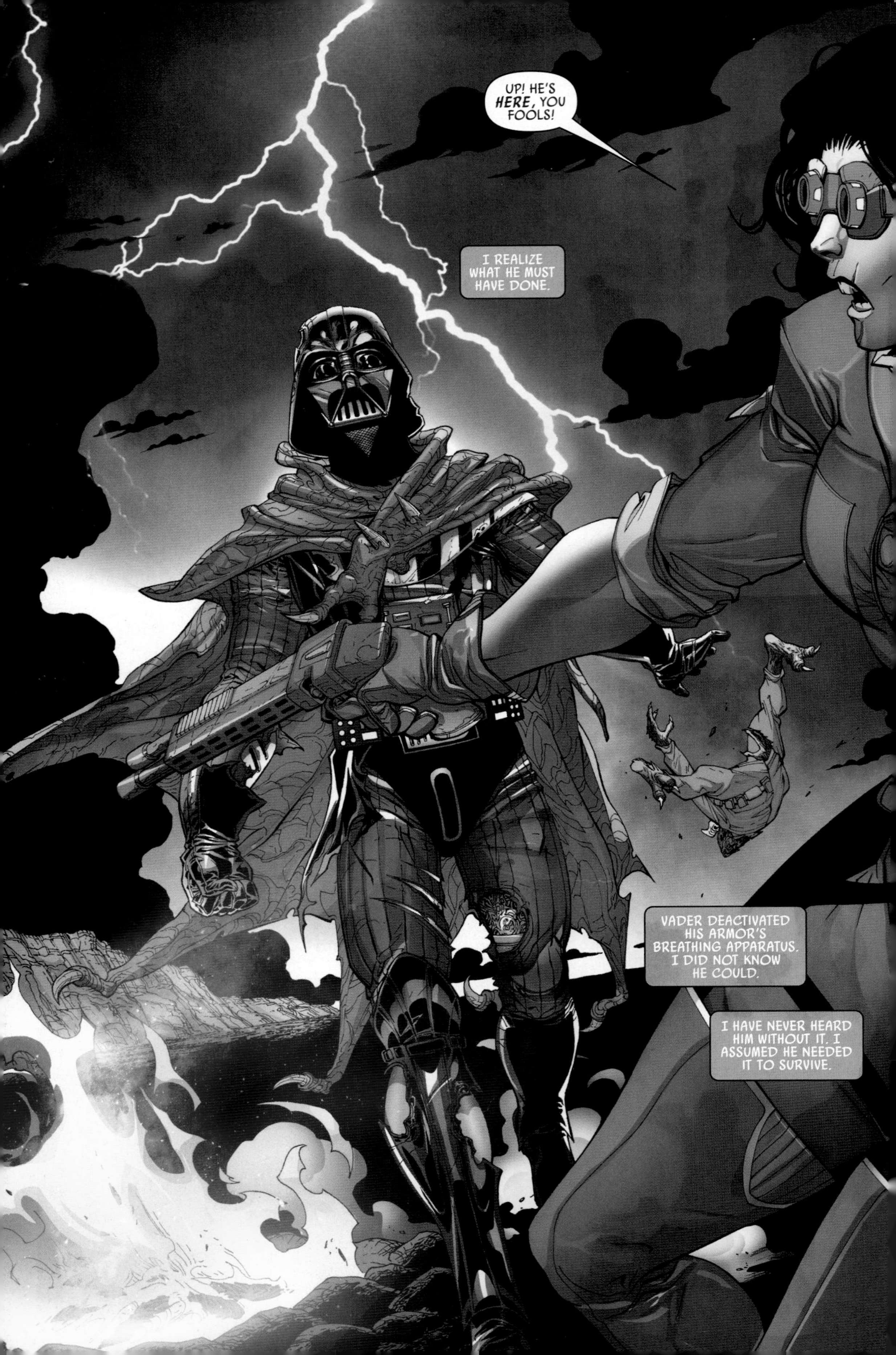
UP! HE'S HERE, YOU FOOLS!
I REALIZE WHAT HE MUST HAVE DONE.
VADER DEACTIVATED HIS ARMOR'S BREATHING APPARATUS. I DID NOT KNOW HE COULD.
I HAVE NEVER HEARD HIM WITHOUT IT. I ASSUMED HE NEEDED IT TO SURVIVE.

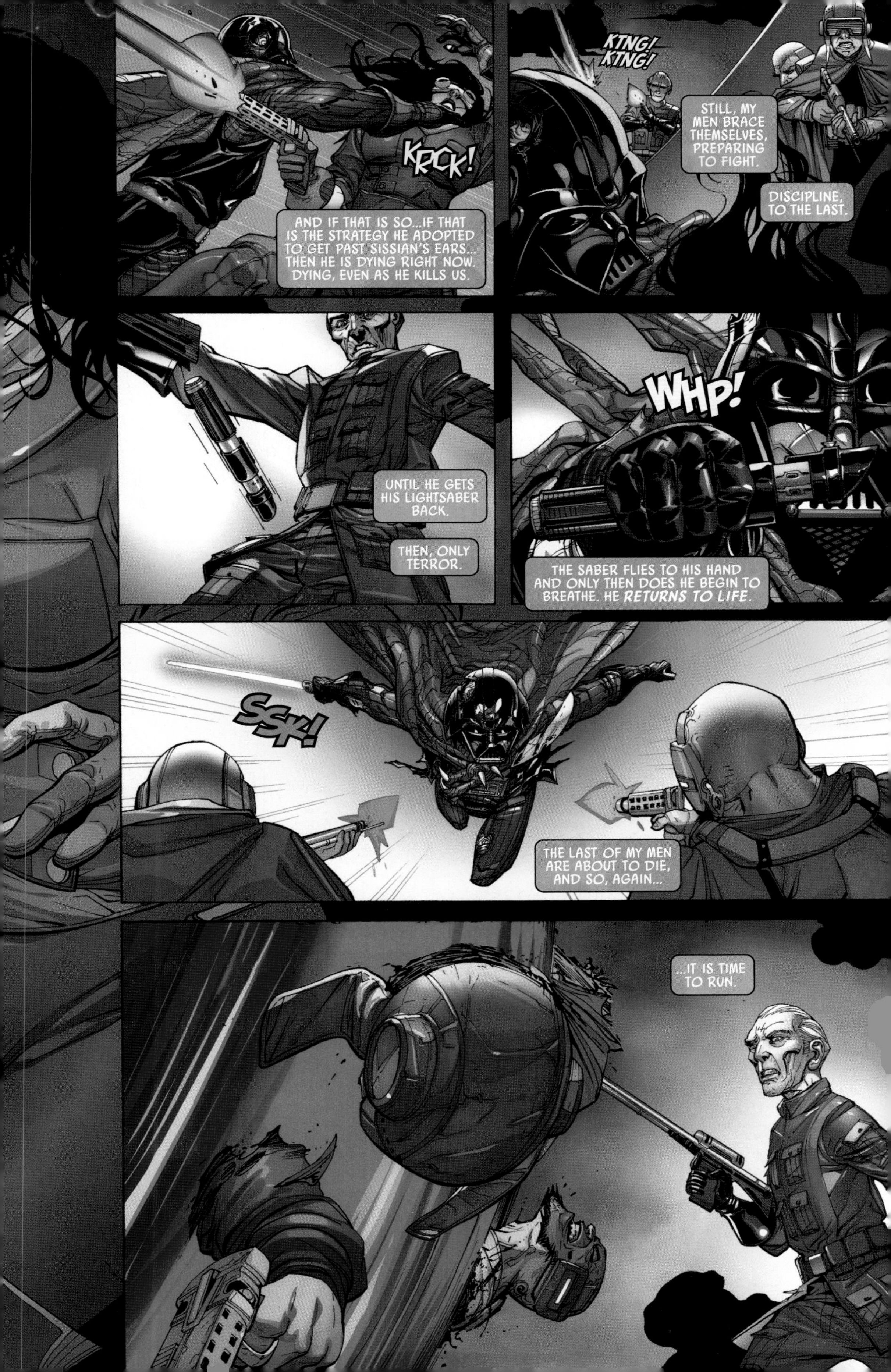
KRCK!
AND IF THAT IS SO...IF THAT IS THE STRATEGY HE ADOPTED TO GET PAST SISSIAN'S EARS... THEN HE IS DYING RIGHT NOW. DYING, EVEN AS HE KILLS US.
KTNG! KTNG!
STILL, MY MEN BRACE THEMSELVES, PREPARING TO FIGHT.
DISCIPLINE, TO THE LAST.
UNTIL HE GETS HIS LIGHTSABER BACK.
THEN, ONLY TERROR.
WHP!
THE SABER FLIES TO HIS HAND AND ONLY THEN DOES HE BEGIN TO BREATHE. HE RETURNS TO LIFE.
SSK!
THE LAST OF MY MEN ARE ABOUT TO DIE, AND SO, AGAIN...
...IT IS TIME TO RUN.

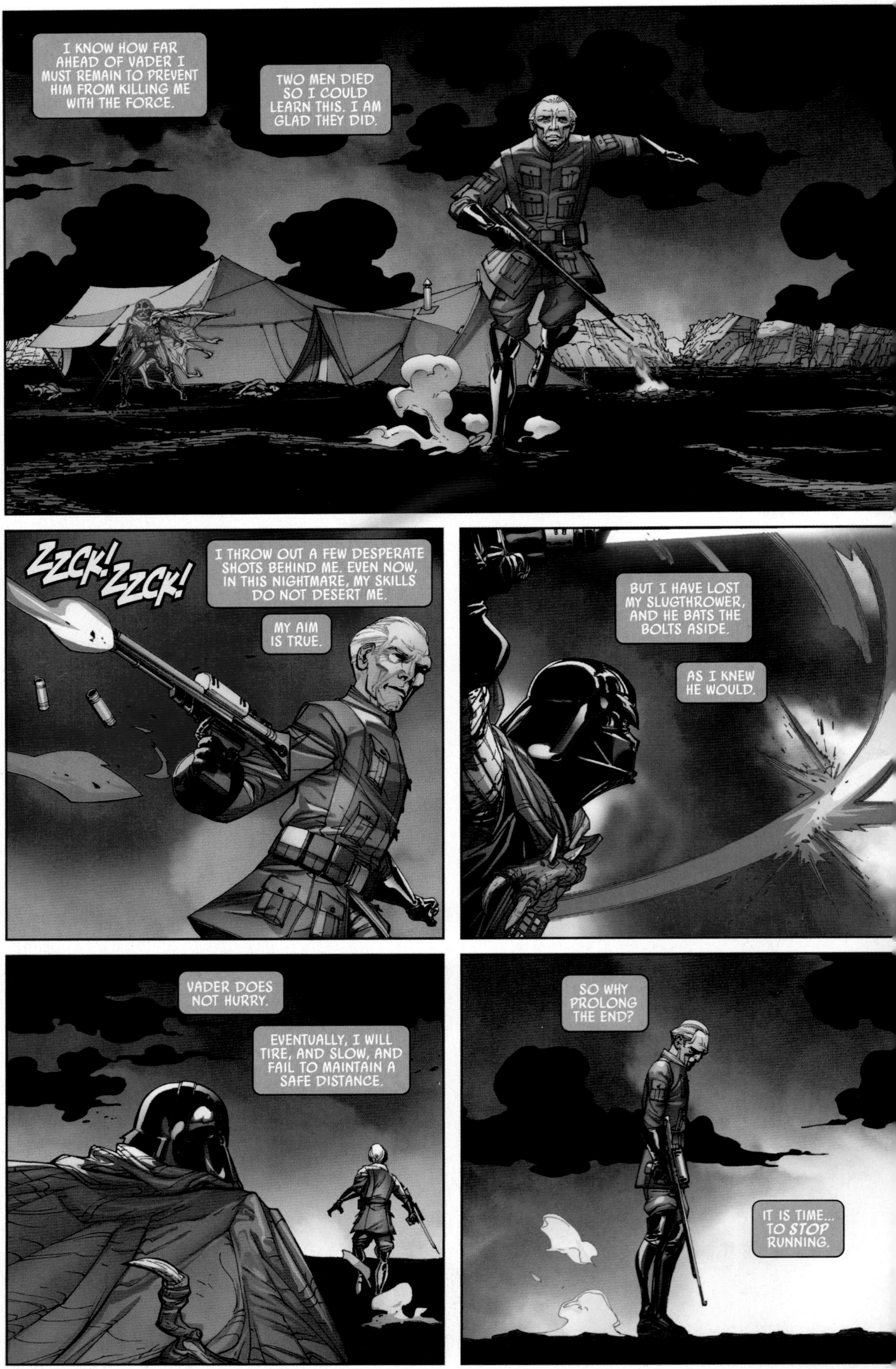
I KNOW HOW FAR AHEAD OF VADER I MUST REMAIN TO PREVENT HIM FROM KILLING ME WITH THE FORCE.
TWO MEN DIED SO I COULD LEARN THIS. I AM GLAD THEY DID.
ZZCK! ZZCK!
I THROW OUT A FEW DESPERATE SHOTS BEHIND ME. EVEN NOW, IN THIS NIGHTMARE, MY SKILLS DO NOT DESERT ME.
MY AIM IS TRUE.
BUT I HAVE LOST MY SLUGTHROWER, AND HE BATS THE BOLTS ASIDE.
AS I KNEW HE WOULD.
VADER DOES NOT HURRY.
EVENTUALLY, I WILL TIRE, AND SLOW, AND FAIL TO MAINTAIN A SAFE DISTANCE.
SO WHY PROLONG THE END?
IT IS TIME... TO STOP RUNNING.

VADER HAS DESTROYED ALL OF THE KILLERS I BROUGHT TO THIS WORLD. I AM THE LAST.

HE HAS WON.

HE KNOWS IT.

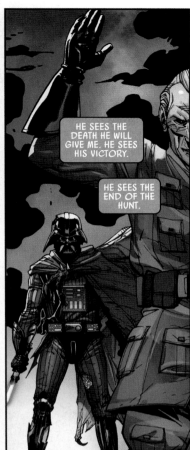

HE SEES THE DEATH HE WILL GIVE ME. HE SEES HIS VICTORY.

HE SEES THE END OF THE HUNT.

SO DO I.

VADER SAVORS MY IMMINENT MURDER--HE CAN ALREADY FEEL IT. HE *WANTS* IT.

AND SO HE DOES NOT CONSIDER THE LAND, THE SKIES, THIS PLACE TO WHICH I HAVE LED HIM, OR THIS MOMENT, PLANNED BEFORE THIS HUNT BEGAN.

FOR THESE ARE THE STORMLANDS. THIS IS *BAD GROUND*.

AND HERE, THE TALLER YOU STAND...

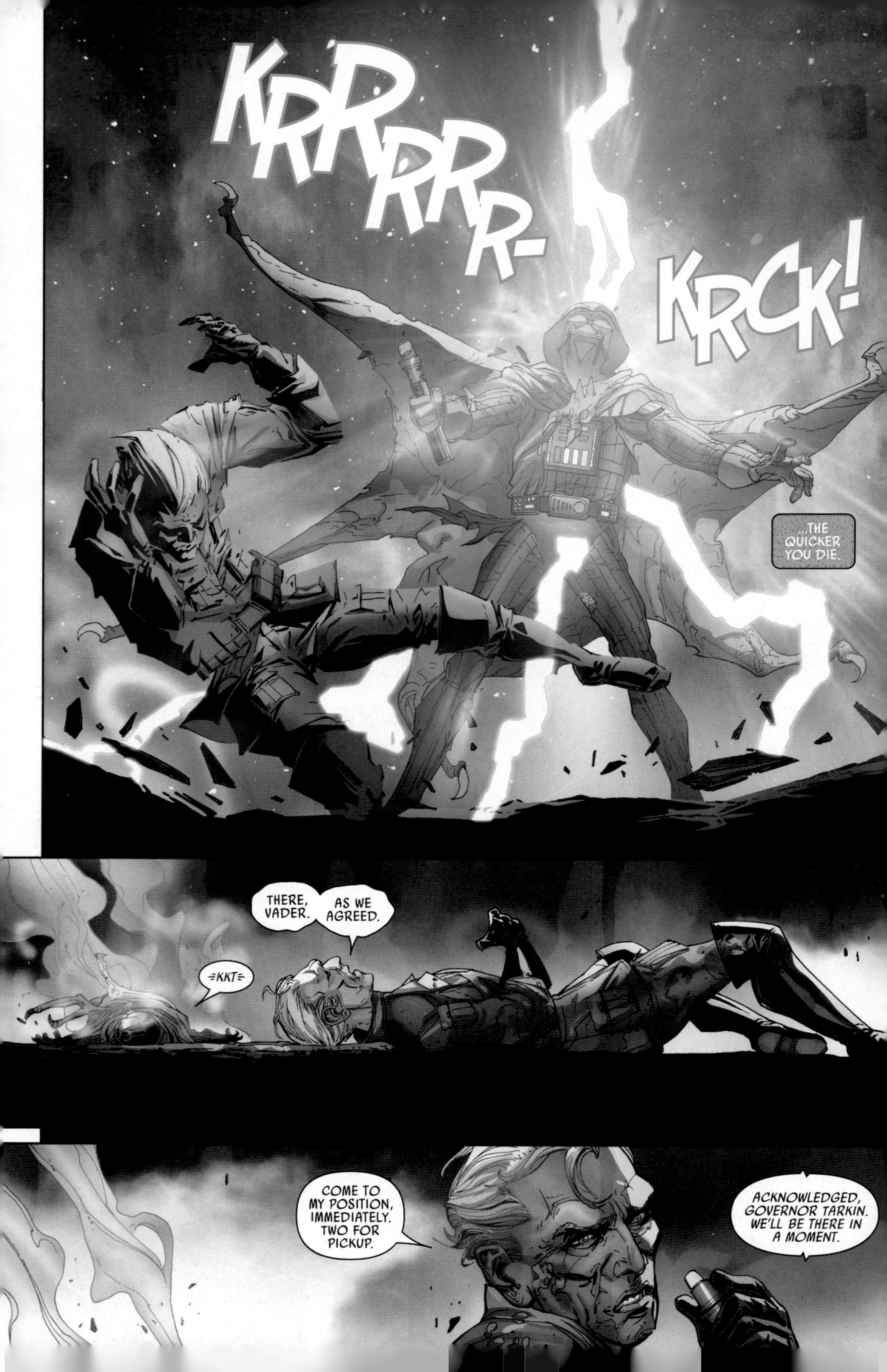
KRRRRRR-
KRCK!
...THE QUICKER YOU DIE.
THERE, VADER.
AS WE AGREED.
=KKT=
COME TO MY POSITION, IMMEDIATELY. TWO FOR PICKUP.
ACKNOWLEDGED, GOVERNOR TARKIN. WE'LL BE THERE IN A MOMENT.

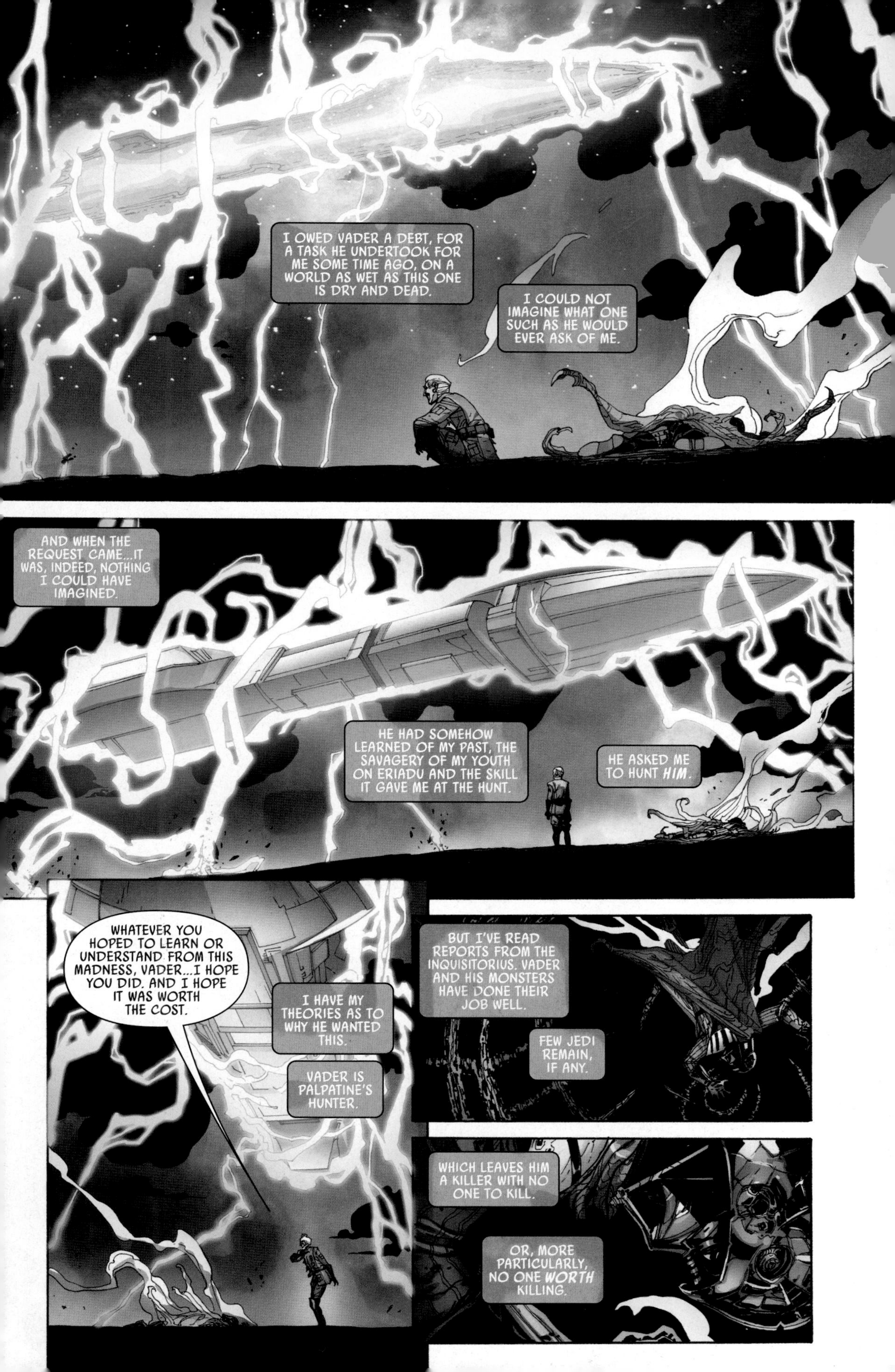
I OWED VADER A DEBT, FOR A TASK HE UNDERTOOK FOR ME SOME TIME AGO, ON A WORLD AS WET AS THIS ONE IS DRY AND DEAD.
I COULD NOT IMAGINE WHAT ONE SUCH AS HE WOULD EVER ASK OF ME.
AND WHEN THE REQUEST CAME...IT WAS, INDEED, NOTHING I COULD HAVE IMAGINED.
HE HAD SOMEHOW LEARNED OF MY PAST, THE SAVAGERY OF MY YOUTH ON ERIADU AND THE SKILL IT GAVE ME AT THE HUNT.
HE ASKED ME TO HUNT *HIM*.
WHATEVER YOU HOPED TO LEARN OR UNDERSTAND FROM THIS MADNESS, VADER...I HOPE YOU DID. AND I HOPE IT WAS WORTH THE COST.
I HAVE MY THEORIES AS TO WHY HE WANTED THIS.
VADER IS PALPATINE'S HUNTER.
BUT I'VE READ REPORTS FROM THE INQUISITORIUS. VADER AND HIS MONSTERS HAVE DONE THEIR JOB WELL.
FEW JEDI REMAIN, IF ANY.
WHICH LEAVES HIM A KILLER WITH NO ONE TO KILL.
OR, MORE PARTICULARLY, NO ONE *WORTH* KILLING.

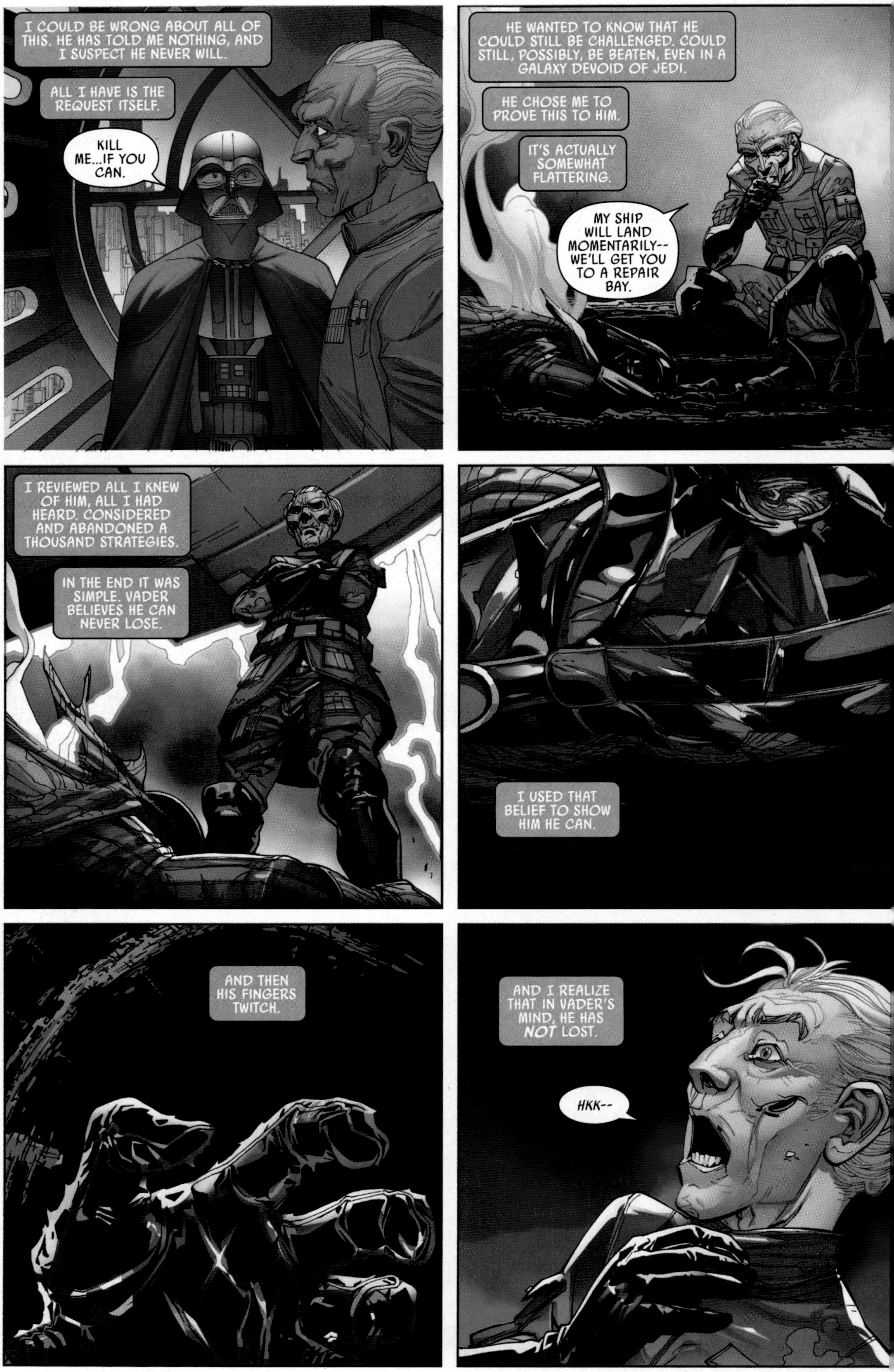
I COULD BE WRONG ABOUT ALL OF THIS. HE HAS TOLD ME NOTHING, AND I SUSPECT HE NEVER WILL.
ALL I HAVE IS THE REQUEST ITSELF.
KILL ME...IF YOU CAN.
HE WANTED TO KNOW THAT HE COULD STILL BE CHALLENGED. COULD STILL, POSSIBLY, BE BEATEN, EVEN IN A GALAXY DEVOID OF JEDI.
HE CHOSE ME TO PROVE THIS TO HIM.
IT'S ACTUALLY SOMEWHAT FLATTERING.
MY SHIP WILL LAND MOMENTARILY-- WE'LL GET YOU TO A REPAIR BAY.
I REVIEWED ALL I KNEW OF HIM, ALL I HAD HEARD. CONSIDERED AND ABANDONED A THOUSAND STRATEGIES.
IN THE END IT WAS SIMPLE. VADER BELIEVES HE CAN NEVER LOSE.
I USED THAT BELIEF TO SHOW HIM HE CAN.
AND THEN HIS FINGERS TWITCH.
AND I REALIZE THAT IN VADER'S MIND, HE HAS *NOT* LOST.
HKK--

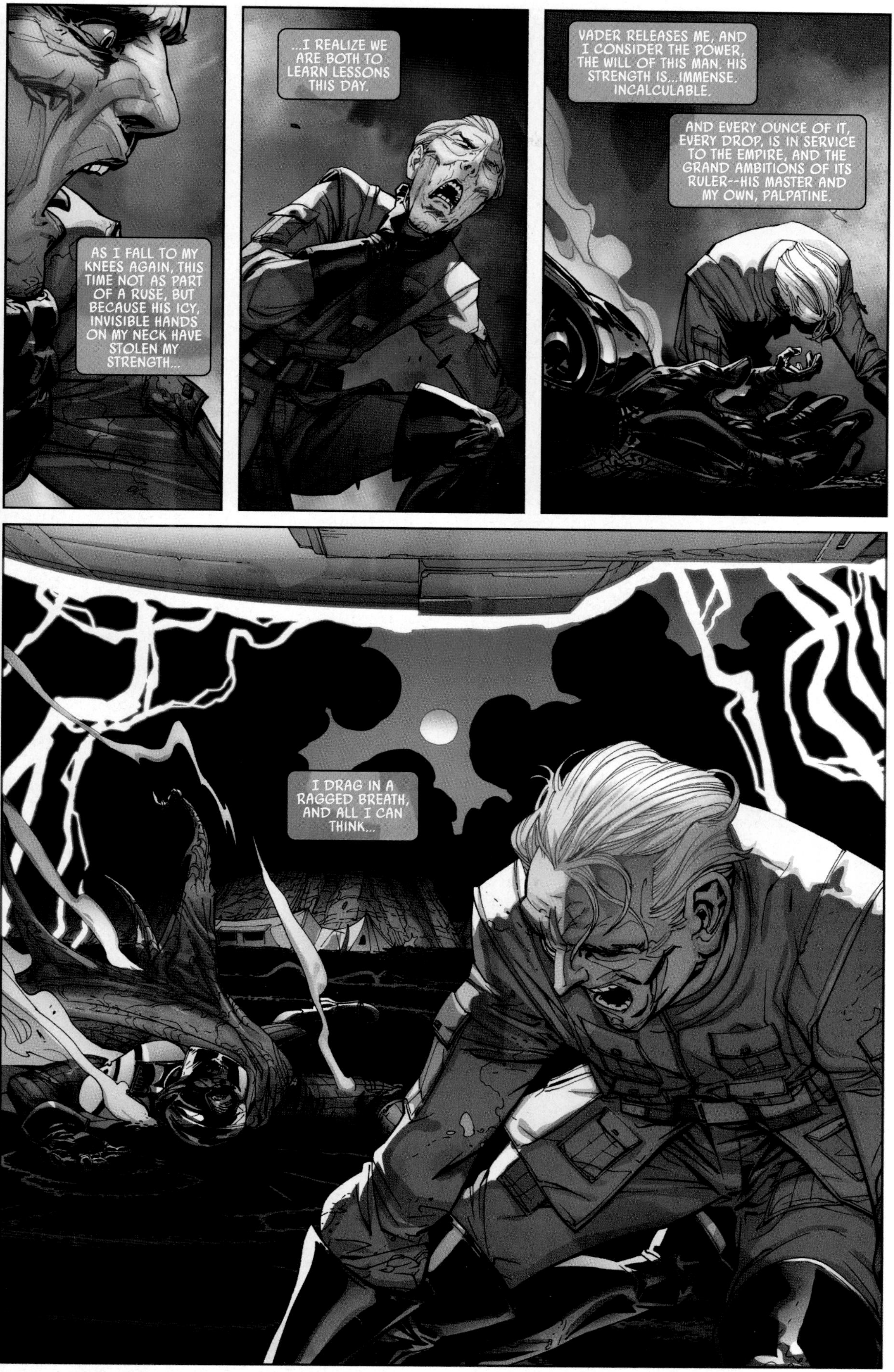
AS I FALL TO MY KNEES AGAIN, THIS TIME NOT AS PART OF A RUSE, BUT BECAUSE HIS ICY, INVISIBLE HANDS ON MY NECK HAVE STOLEN MY STRENGTH...
...I REALIZE WE ARE BOTH TO LEARN LESSONS THIS DAY.
VADER RELEASES ME, AND I CONSIDER THE POWER, THE WILL OF THIS MAN. HIS STRENGTH IS...IMMENSE. INCALCULABLE.
AND EVERY OUNCE OF IT, EVERY DROP, IS IN SERVICE TO THE EMPIRE, AND THE GRAND AMBITIONS OF ITS RULER--HIS MASTER AND MY OWN, PALPATINE.
I DRAG IN A RAGGED BREATH, AND ALL I CAN THINK...

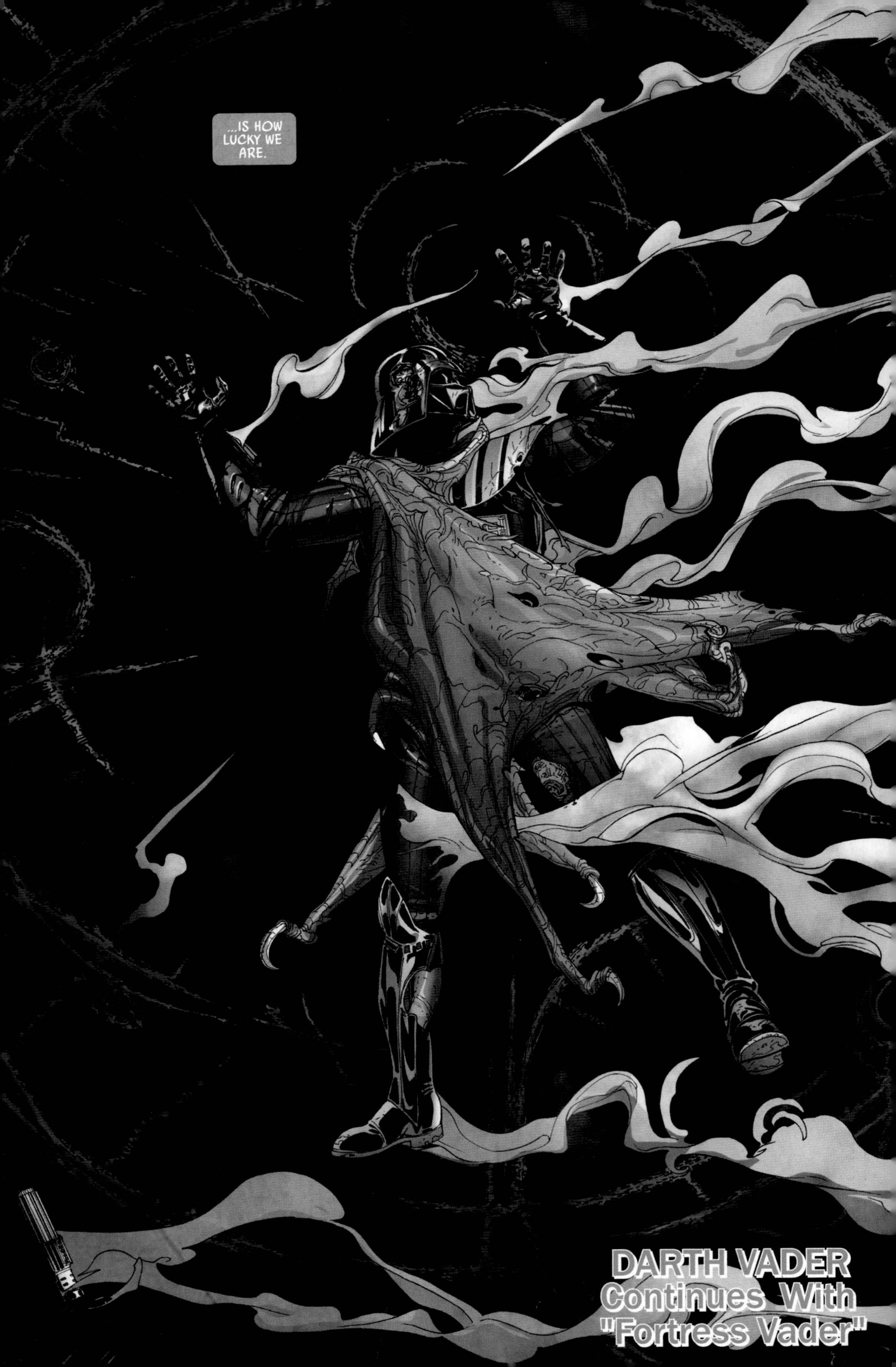
...IS HOW LUCKY WE ARE.
DARTH VADER Continues With "Fortress Vader"

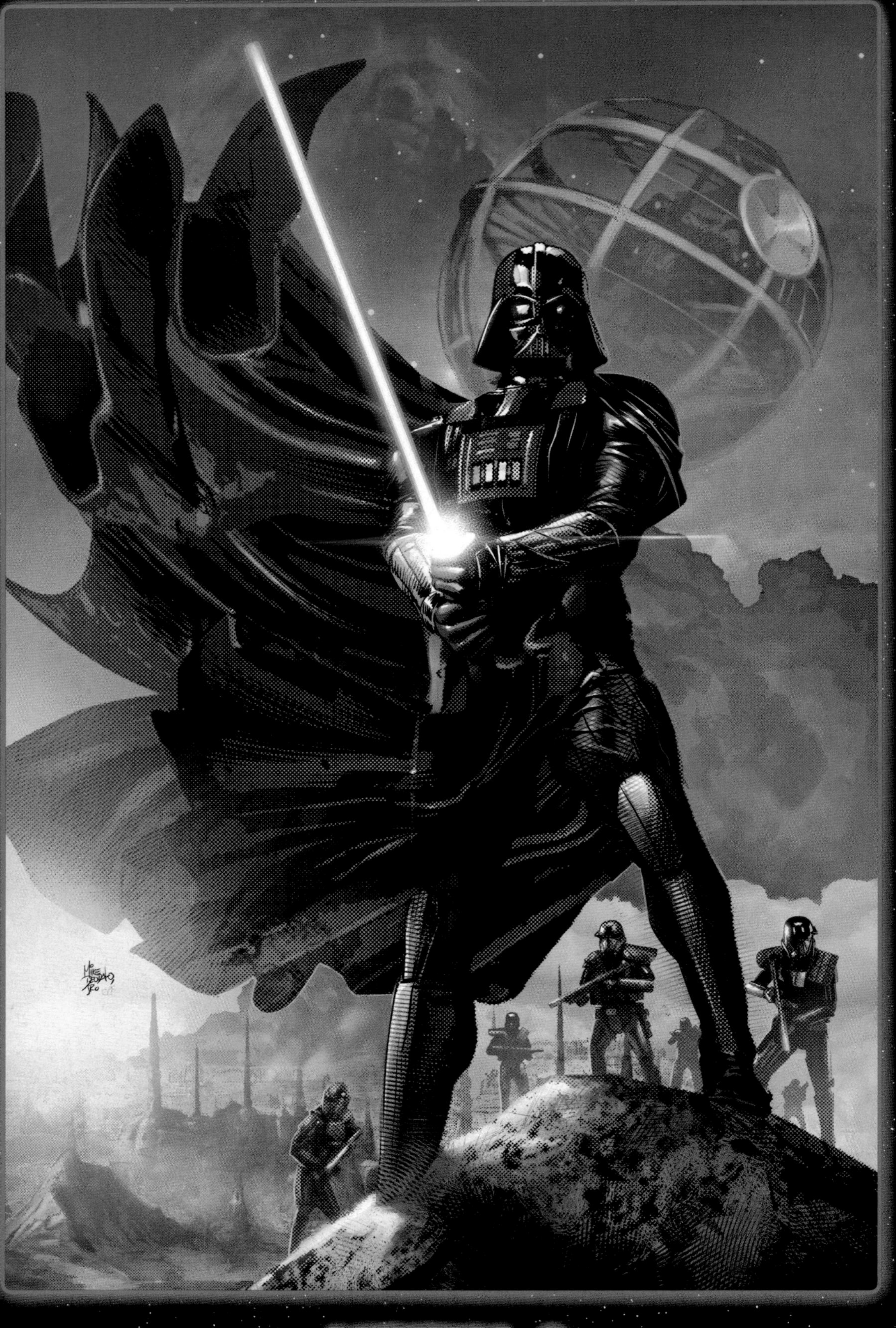

ANNUAL 2

TECHNOLOGICAL TERROR

The Republic is overthrown and the Jedi defeated. Emperor Palpatine, Dark Lord of the Sith, rules the galaxy with an iron fist.

Order and security is bloodily maintained by Palpatine's apprentice, the fearsome Darth Vader, whose fall to the dark side of the Force and defeat at the hands of Obi-Wan Kenobi leaves him confined to a suit of cybernetic armor to preserve his life.

Now, Vader lives only to serve his master's Empire — but he isn't Palpatine's only weapon. The Emperor has many loyal servants, such as Governor Wilhuff Tarkin, whose plans to safeguard the New Order could threaten even Darth Vader's powerful position....

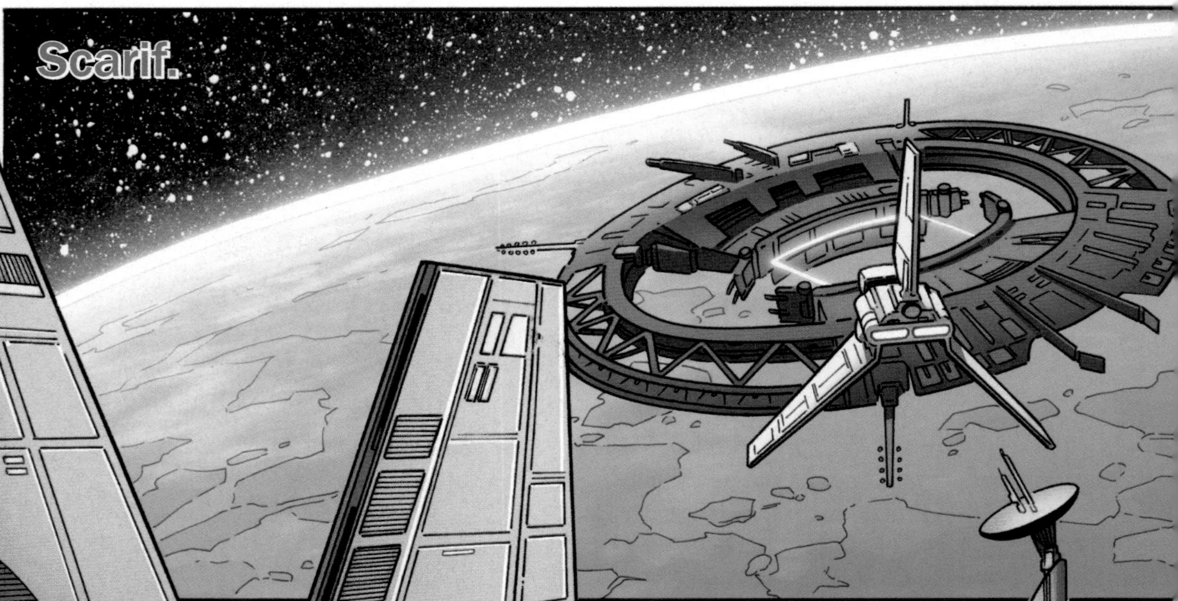
Scarif.

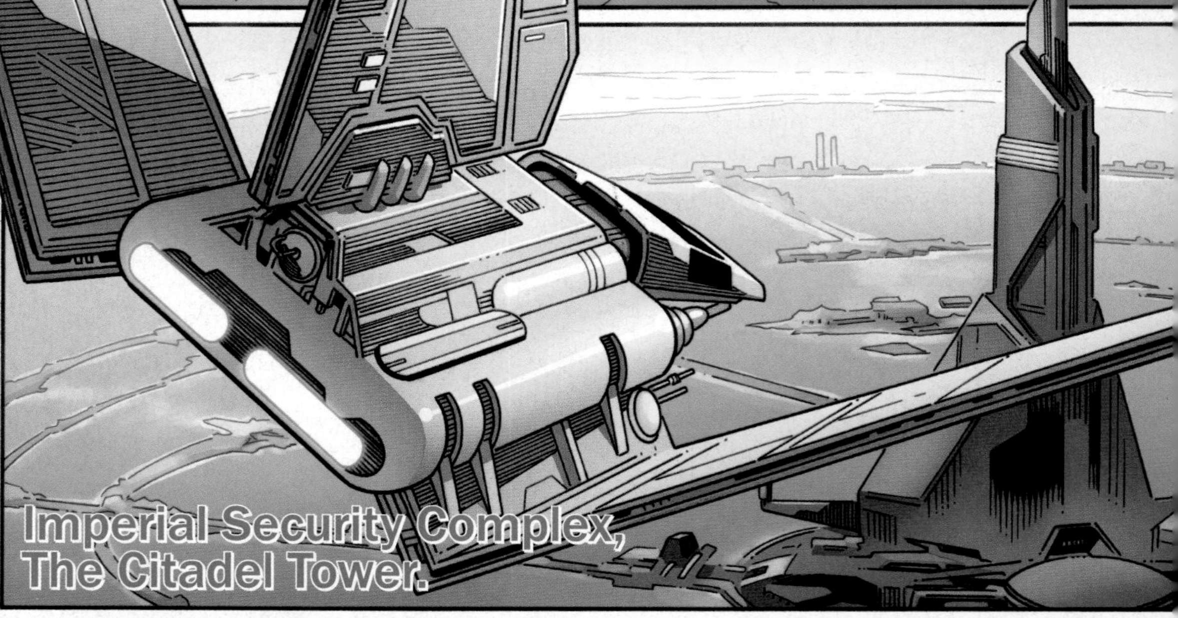
Imperial Security Complex,
The Citadel Tower.

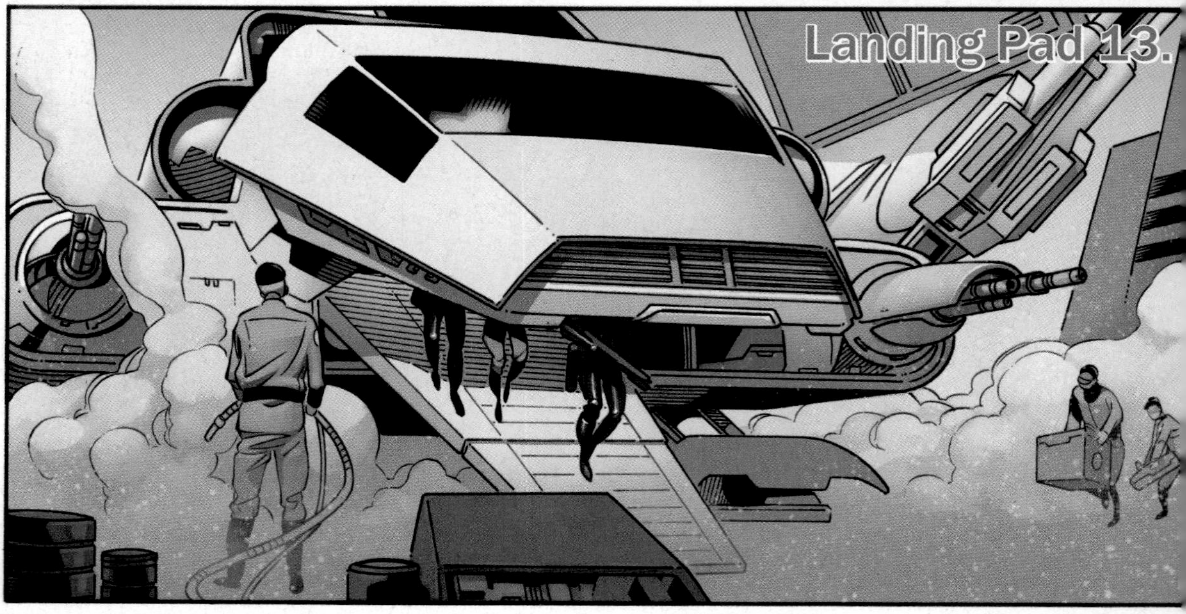
Landing Pad 13.

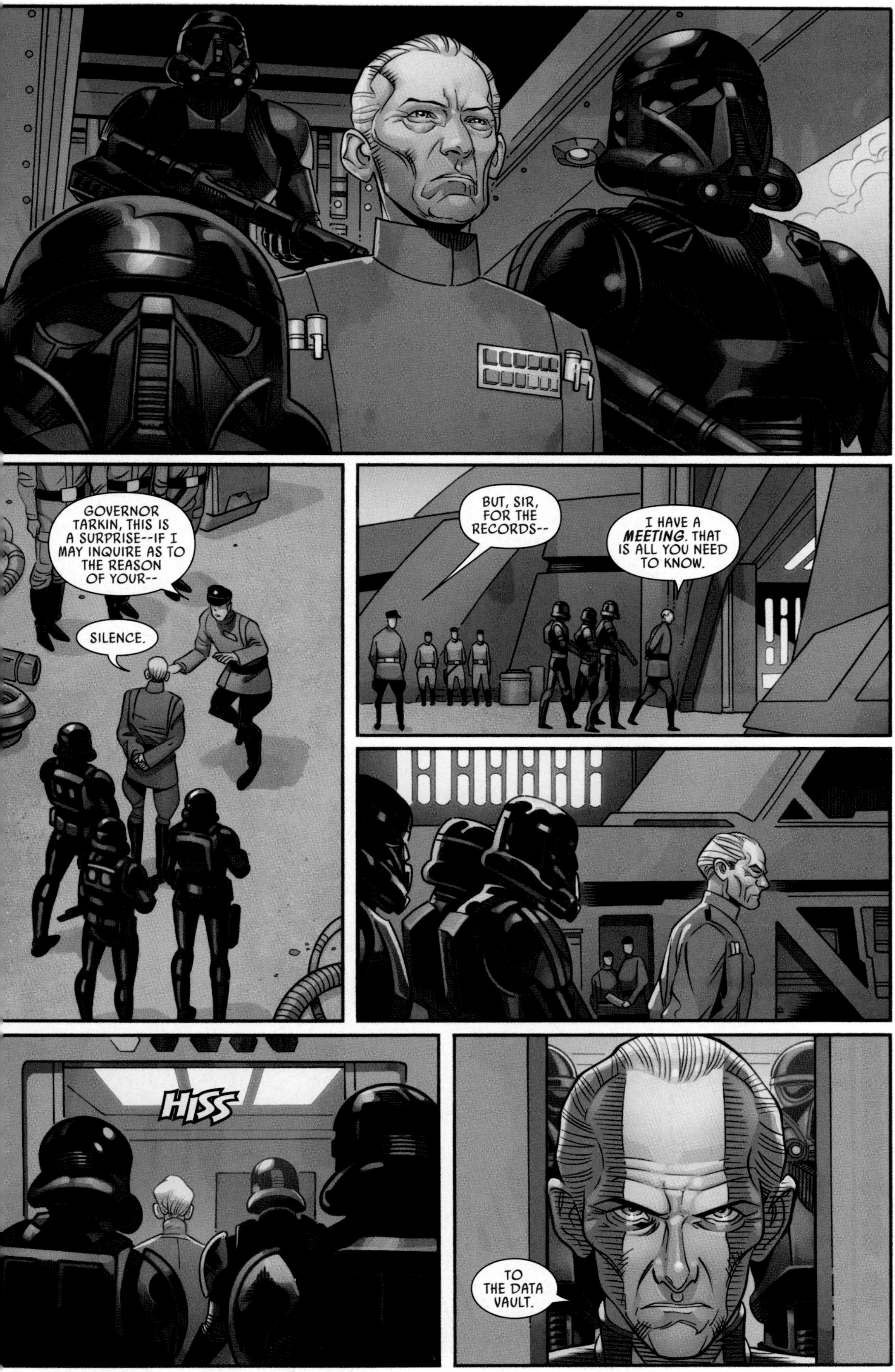
GOVERNOR TARKIN, THIS IS A SURPRISE--IF I MAY INQUIRE AS TO THE REASON OF YOUR--
SILENCE.
BUT, SIR, FOR THE RECORDS--
I HAVE A MEETING. THAT IS ALL YOU NEED TO KNOW.
HISS
TO THE DATA VAULT.

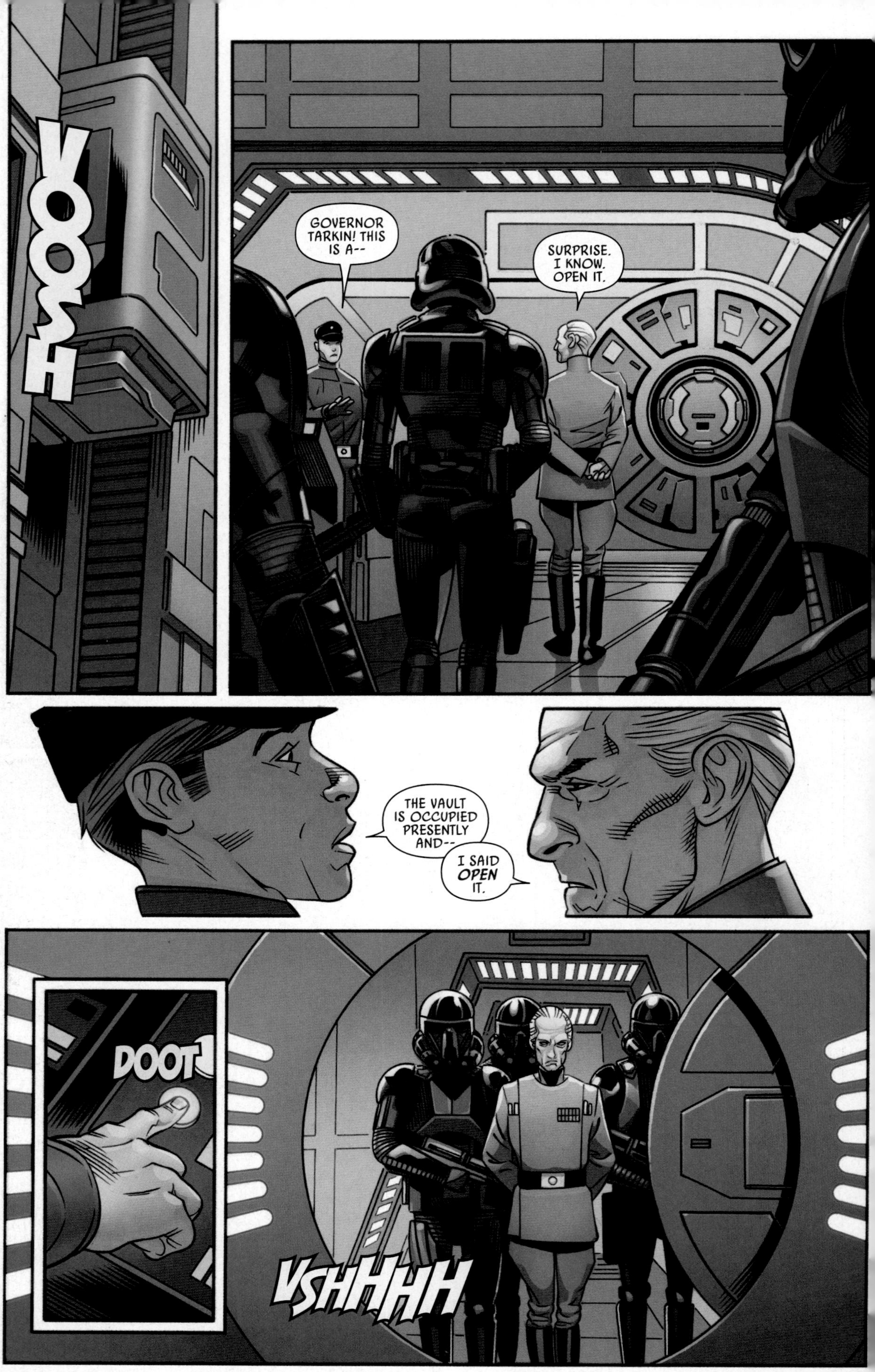
VOOSH
GOVERNOR TARKIN! THIS IS A--
SURPRISE. I KNOW. OPEN IT.
THE VAULT IS OCCUPIED PRESENTLY AND--
I SAID OPEN IT.
DOOT
VSHHHH

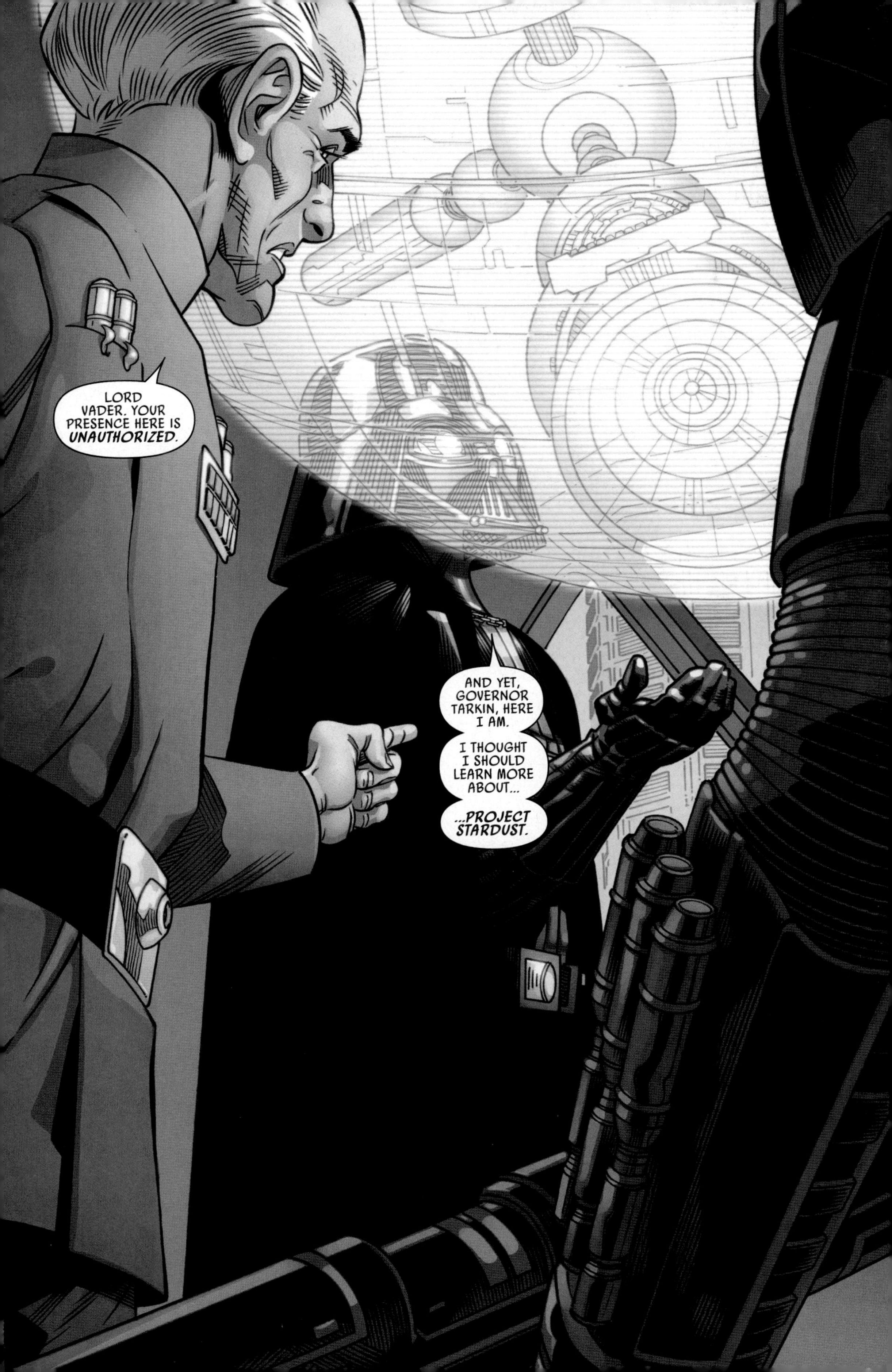
LORD VADER. YOUR PRESENCE HERE IS *UNAUTHORIZED*.
AND YET, GOVERNOR TARKIN, HERE I AM.
I THOUGHT I SHOULD LEARN MORE ABOUT...
...PROJECT STARDUST.

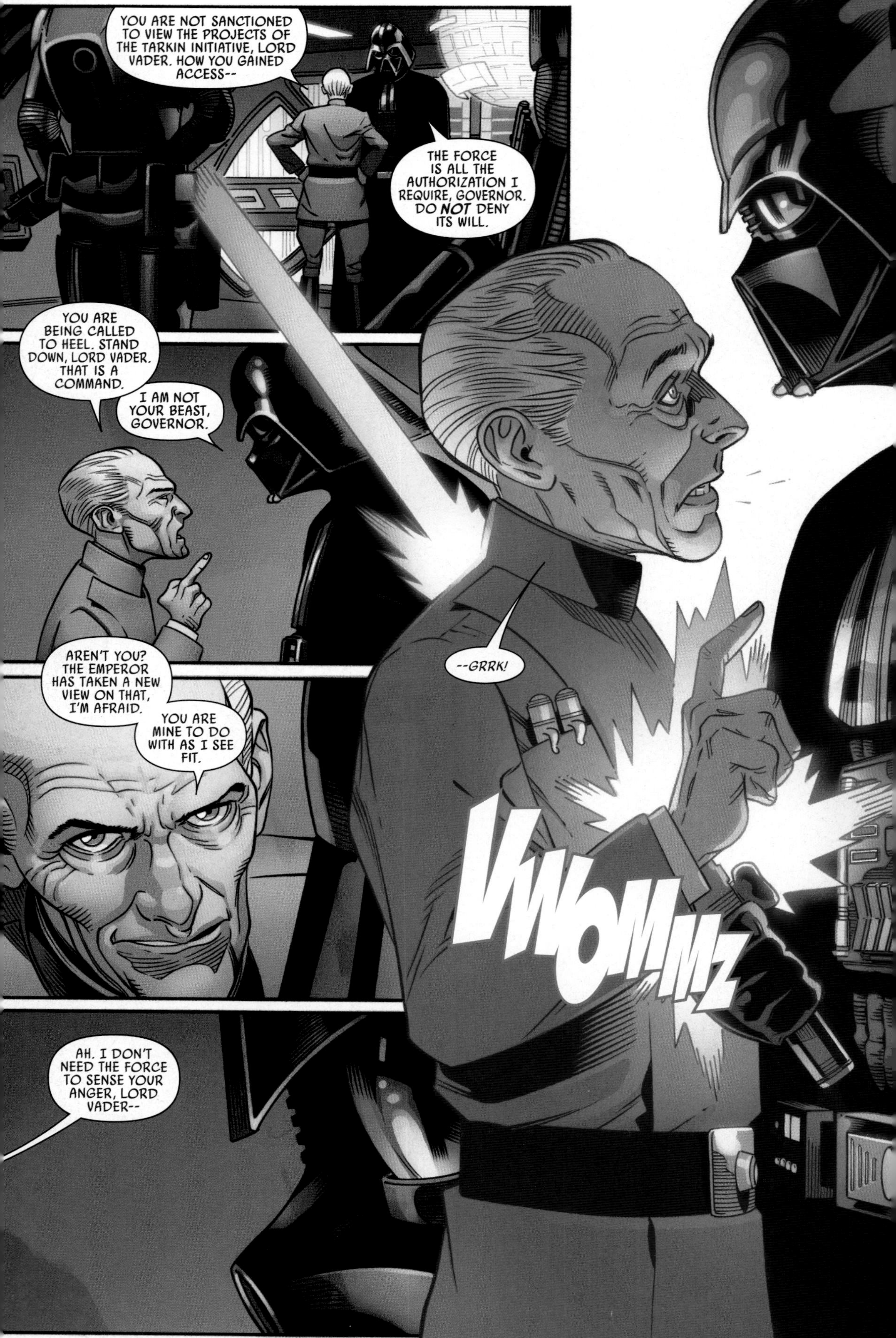
YOU ARE NOT SANCTIONED TO VIEW THE PROJECTS OF THE TARKIN INITIATIVE, LORD VADER. HOW YOU GAINED ACCESS--
THE FORCE IS ALL THE AUTHORIZATION I REQUIRE, GOVERNOR. DO **NOT** DENY ITS WILL.
YOU ARE BEING CALLED TO HEEL. STAND DOWN, LORD VADER. THAT IS A COMMAND.
I AM NOT YOUR BEAST, GOVERNOR.
AREN'T YOU? THE EMPEROR HAS TAKEN A NEW VIEW ON THAT, I'M AFRAID.
YOU ARE MINE TO DO WITH AS I SEE FIT.
AH. I DON'T NEED THE FORCE TO SENSE YOUR ANGER, LORD VADER--
--GRRK!
VWOMMZ

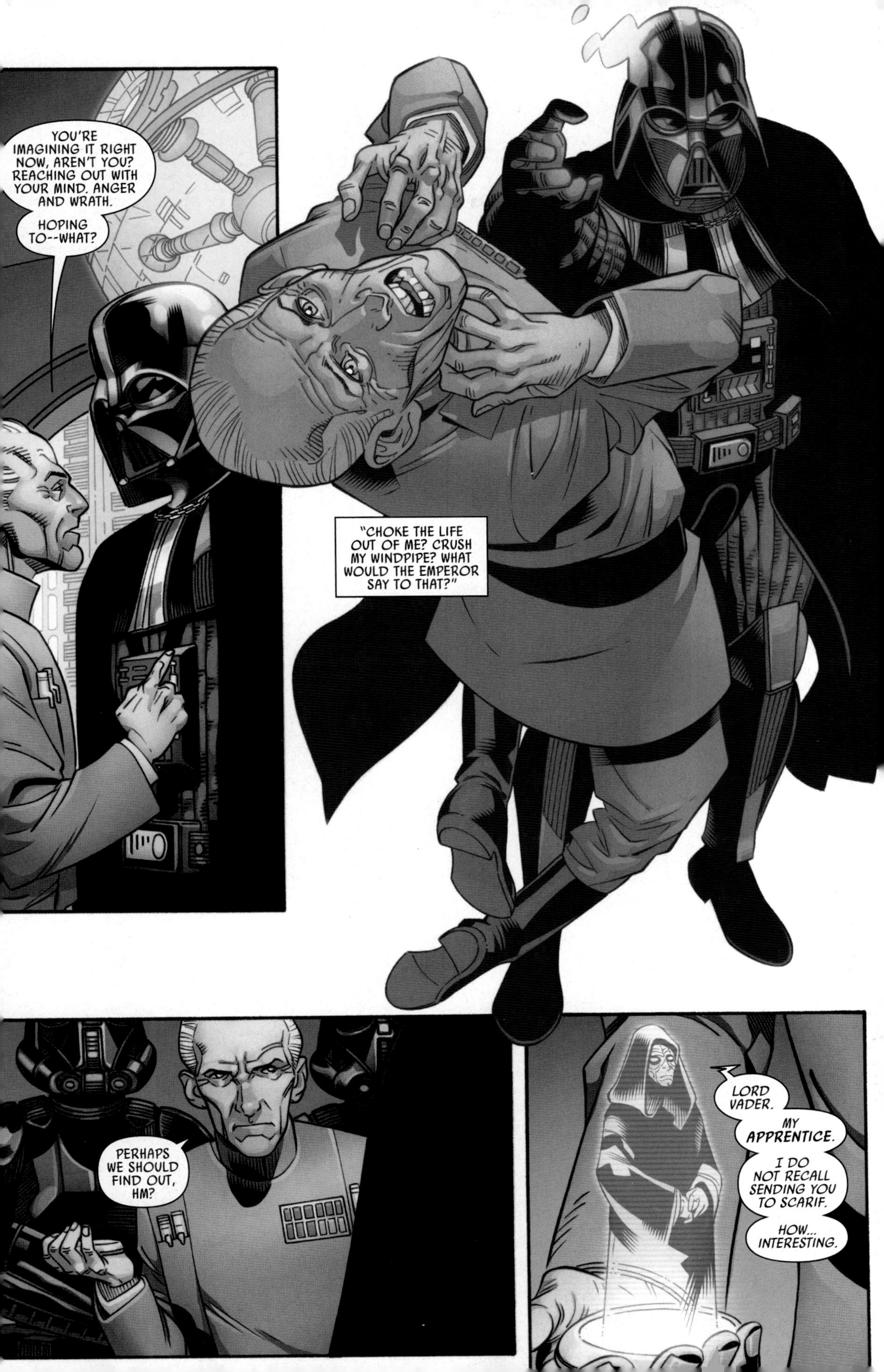
YOU'RE IMAGINING IT RIGHT NOW, AREN'T YOU? REACHING OUT WITH YOUR MIND. ANGER AND WRATH.
HOPING TO--WHAT?
"CHOKE THE LIFE OUT OF ME? CRUSH MY WINDPIPE? WHAT WOULD THE EMPEROR SAY TO THAT?"
PERHAPS WE SHOULD FIND OUT, HM?
LORD VADER.
MY APPRENTICE.
I DO NOT RECALL SENDING YOU TO SCARIF.
HOW... INTERESTING.

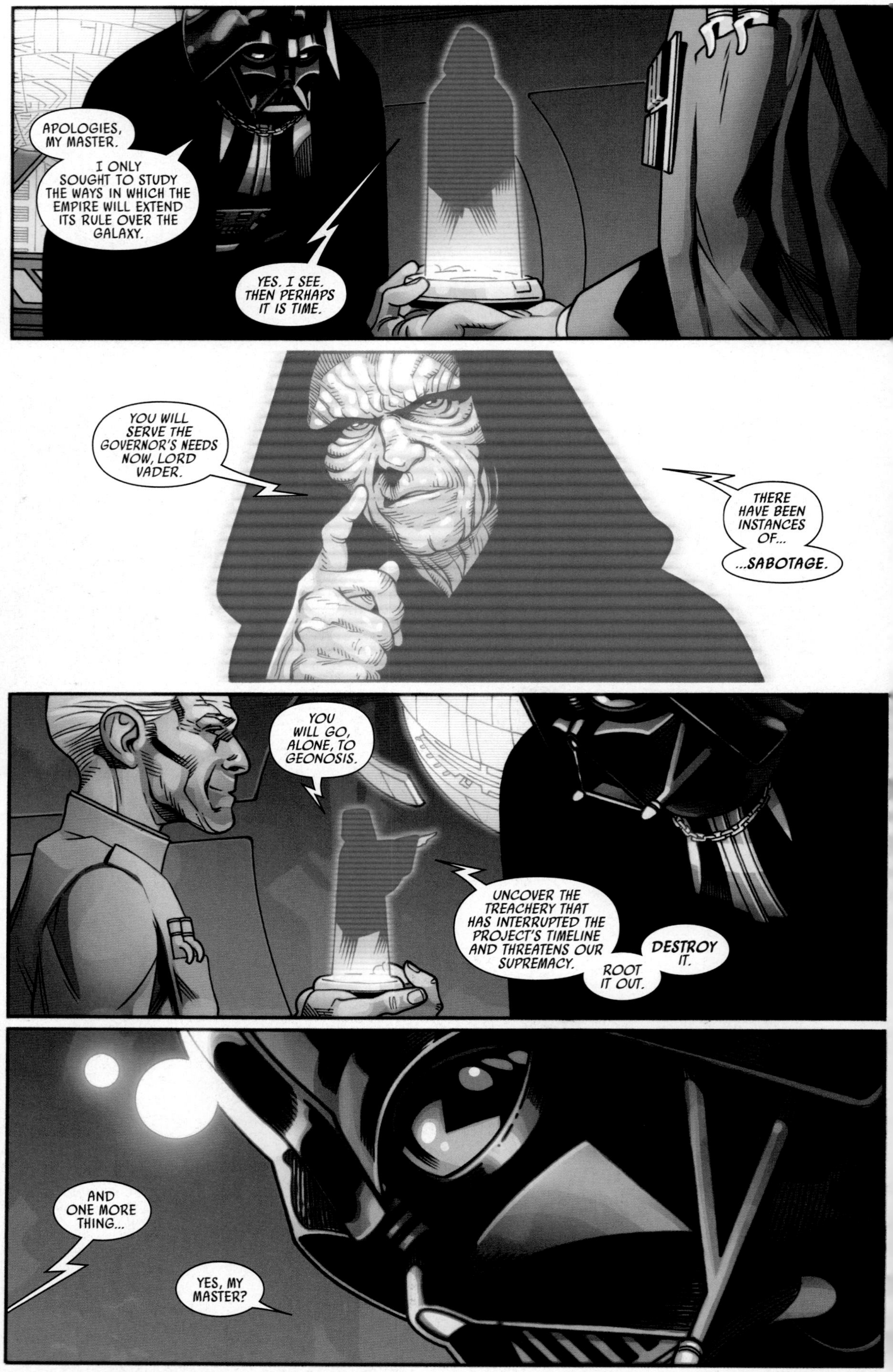
APOLOGIES, MY MASTER.
I ONLY SOUGHT TO STUDY THE WAYS IN WHICH THE EMPIRE WILL EXTEND ITS RULE OVER THE GALAXY.
YES. I SEE. THEN PERHAPS IT IS TIME.
YOU WILL SERVE THE GOVERNOR'S NEEDS NOW, LORD VADER.
THERE HAVE BEEN INSTANCES OF...
...SABOTAGE.
YOU WILL GO, ALONE, TO GEONOSIS.
UNCOVER THE TREACHERY THAT HAS INTERRUPTED THE PROJECT'S TIMELINE AND THREATENS OUR SUPREMACY.
ROOT IT OUT.
DESTROY IT.
AND ONE MORE THING...
YES, MY MASTER?

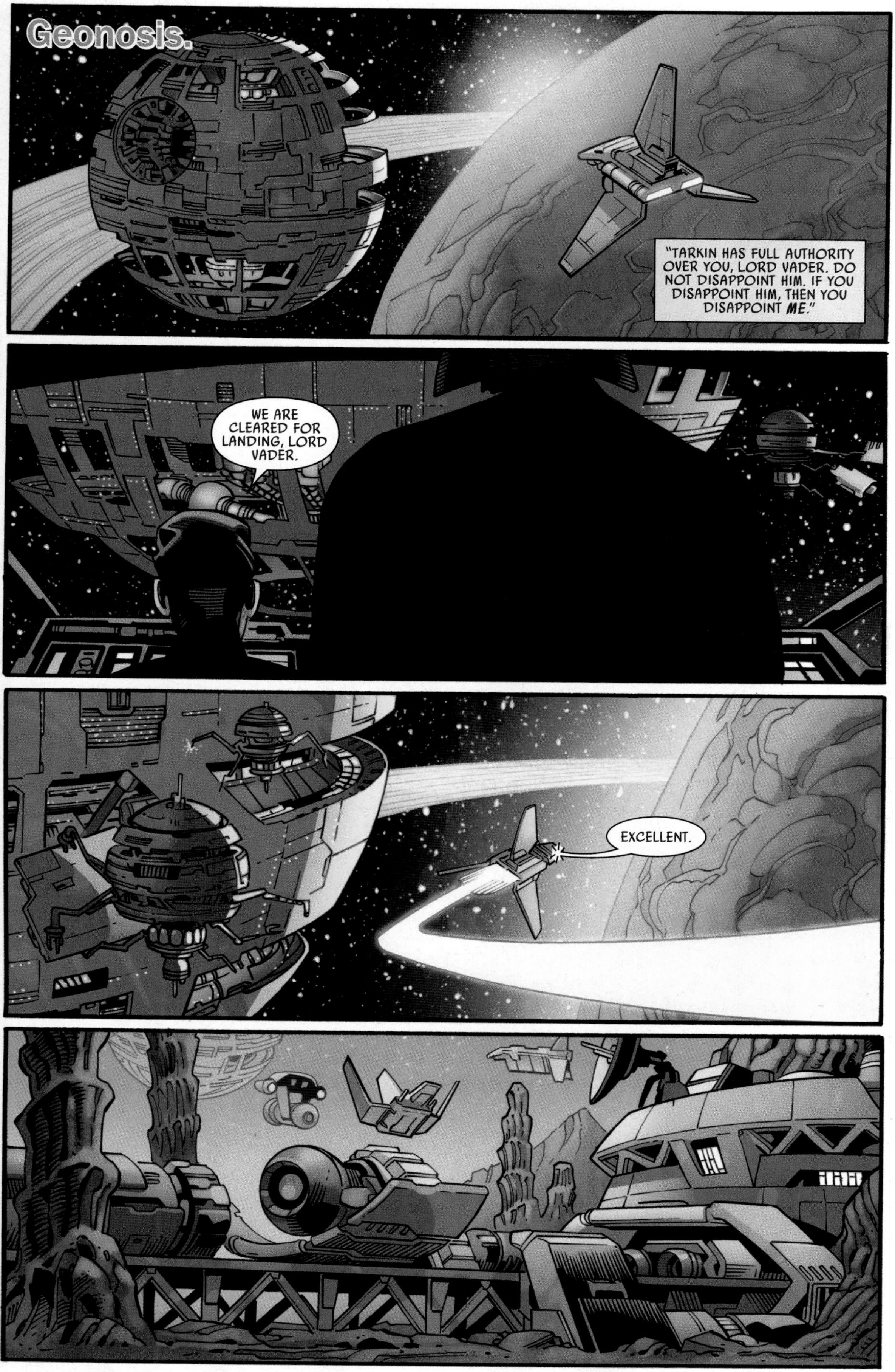
Geonosis.
"TARKIN HAS FULL AUTHORITY OVER YOU, LORD VADER. DO NOT DISAPPOINT HIM. IF YOU DISAPPOINT HIM, THEN YOU DISAPPOINT *ME*."
WE ARE CLEARED FOR LANDING, LORD VADER.
EXCELLENT.

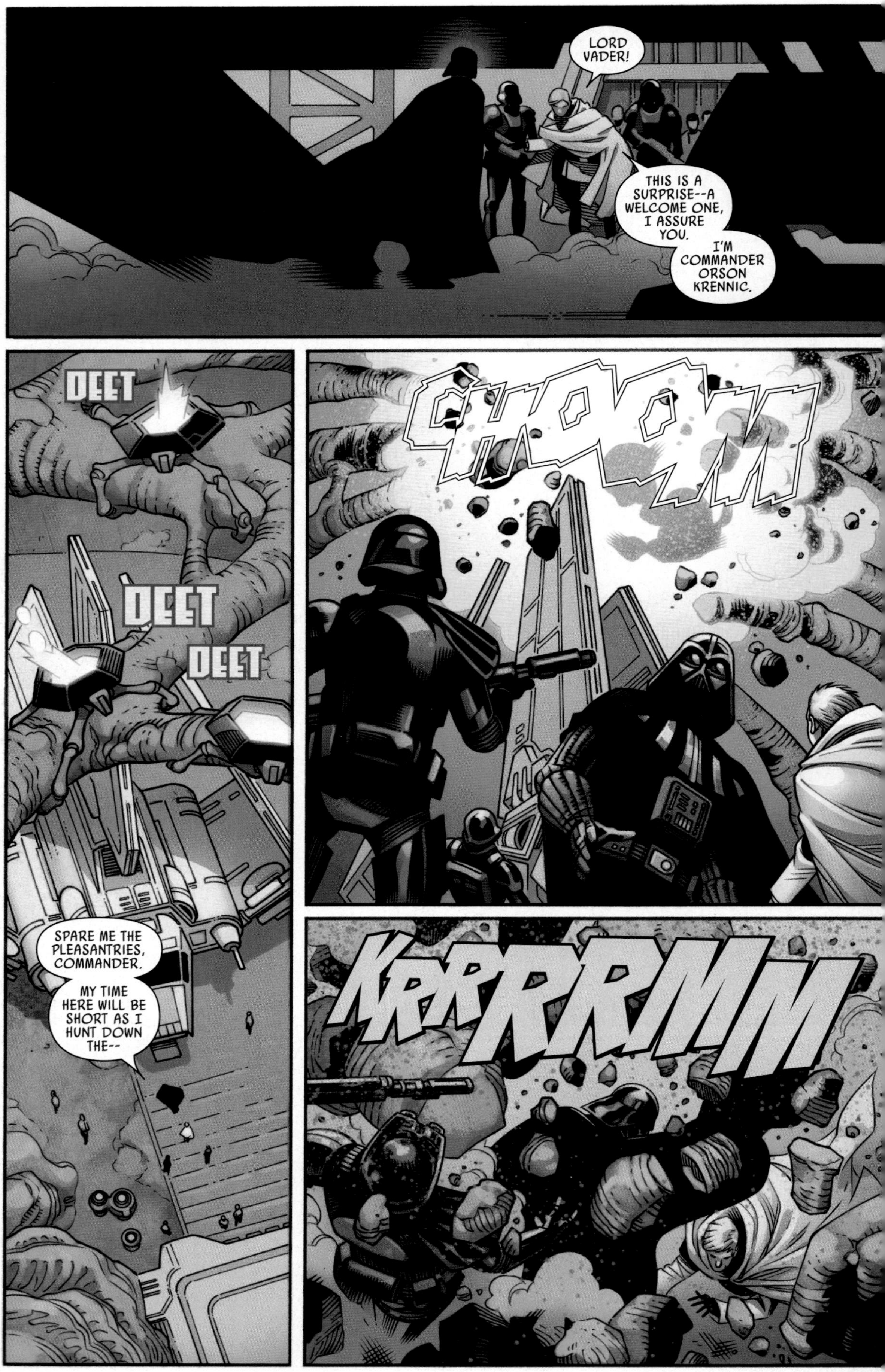

LORD VADER!
THIS IS A SURPRISE--A WELCOME ONE, I ASSURE YOU.
I'M COMMANDER ORSON KRENNIC.
DEET
DEET
DEET
SPARE ME THE PLEASANTRIES, COMMANDER.
MY TIME HERE WILL BE SHORT AS I HUNT DOWN THE--
CHOOM
KRRRRMM

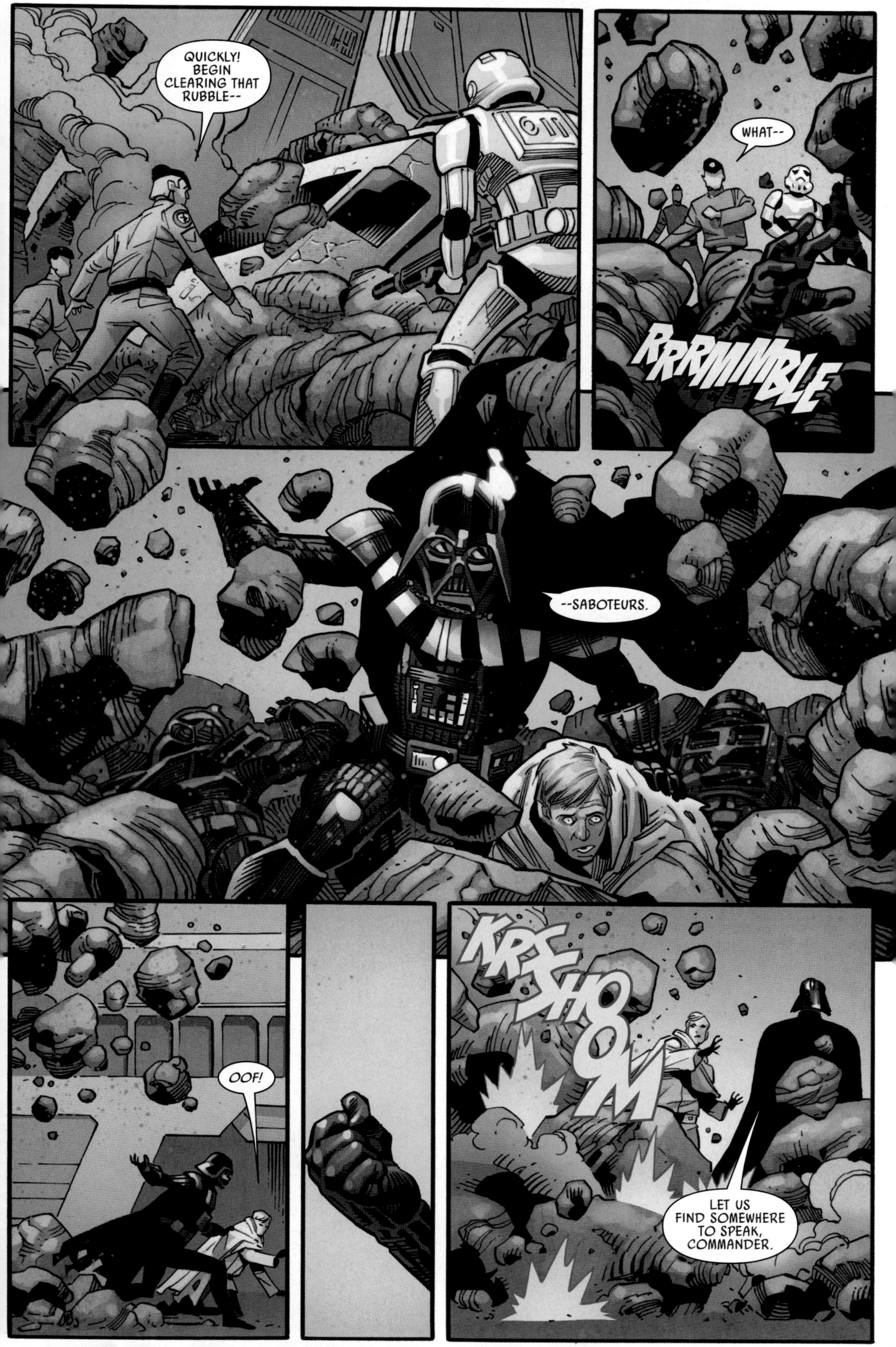
QUICKLY! BEGIN CLEARING THAT RUBBLE--
WHAT--
RRRMMBLE
--SABOTEURS.
OOF!
KRESHOOM
LET US FIND SOMEWHERE TO SPEAK, COMMANDER.

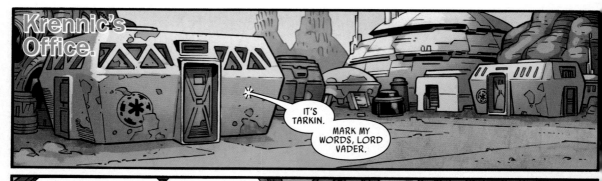

IT'S TARKIN.

MARK MY WORDS, LORD VADER.

NOW, I DON'T MEAN TO SPEAK OUT OF TURN, BUT WHAT HAPPENED THERE ON THE LANDING PAD--AGAIN, THANK YOU FOR SAVING ME-- WAS AN ASSASSINATION ATTEMPT.

NOT AN ACCIDENT. AN ATTEMPT TO MURDER THE **BOTH** OF US.

TARKIN...HE HAS A HISTORY WITH THIS PROJECT. HE'S LONG TRIED TO TAKE CONTROL OF IT.

I'VE FOILED HIS ATTEMPTS SO FAR. BUT PERHAPS HE'LL...ESCALATE HIS EFFORTS?

I'M JUST *SPECULATING*, OF COURSE.

HE DOESN'T LIKE YOU, YOU KNOW. TARKIN. YOU'RE CLOSE TO THE EMPEROR. YOU HAVE HIS EAR.

TARKIN'S AN OUTSIDER. A SECTOR HEAD. A POLITICIAN!

I CARE NOT FOR SUCH BASELESS ACCUSATIONS, COMMANDER. IF YOU HAVE PROOF, GIVE IT.

...

AS I THOUGHT. TELL ME--

I'M A BUILDER-- AN *ARCHITECT*. BUT YOU KNOW ALL THIS ALREADY...

--WHAT OTHER ACTS OF SABOTAGE HAVE TAKEN PLACE ON THIS NASCENT BATTLE STATION?

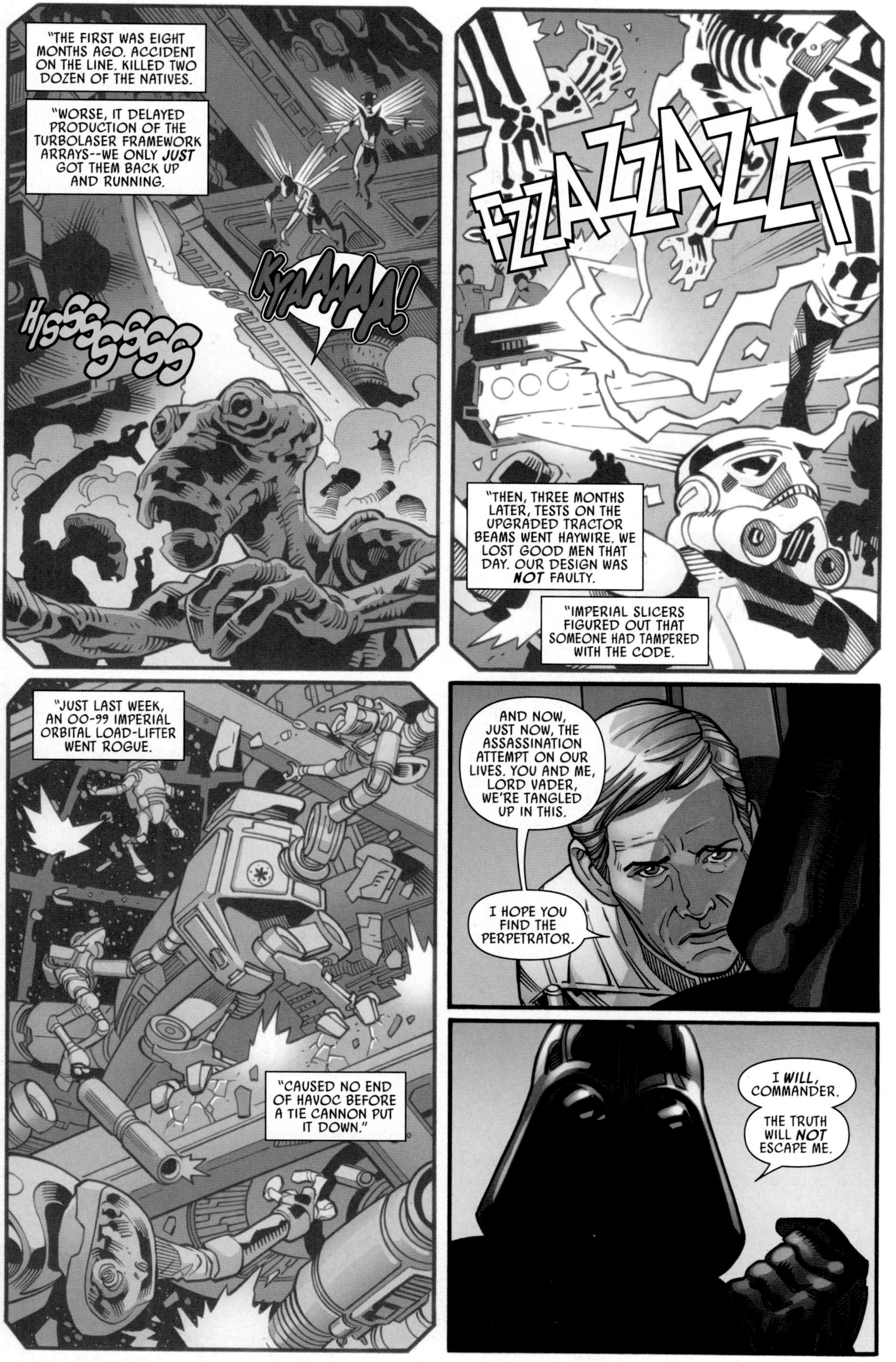
"THE FIRST WAS EIGHT MONTHS AGO. ACCIDENT ON THE LINE. KILLED TWO DOZEN OF THE NATIVES.
"WORSE, IT DELAYED PRODUCTION OF THE TURBOLASER FRAMEWORK ARRAYS--WE ONLY JUST GOT THEM BACK UP AND RUNNING.
KYAAAAA!
HISSSSSSS
FZZAZZAZZT
"THEN, THREE MONTHS LATER, TESTS ON THE UPGRADED TRACTOR BEAMS WENT HAYWIRE. WE LOST GOOD MEN THAT DAY. OUR DESIGN WAS NOT FAULTY.
"IMPERIAL SLICERS FIGURED OUT THAT SOMEONE HAD TAMPERED WITH THE CODE.
"JUST LAST WEEK, AN OO-99 IMPERIAL ORBITAL LOAD-LIFTER WENT ROGUE.
"CAUSED NO END OF HAVOC BEFORE A TIE CANNON PUT IT DOWN."
AND NOW, JUST NOW, THE ASSASSINATION ATTEMPT ON OUR LIVES. YOU AND ME, LORD VADER, WE'RE TANGLED UP IN THIS.
I HOPE YOU FIND THE PERPETRATOR.
I WILL, COMMANDER.
THE TRUTH WILL NOT ESCAPE ME.

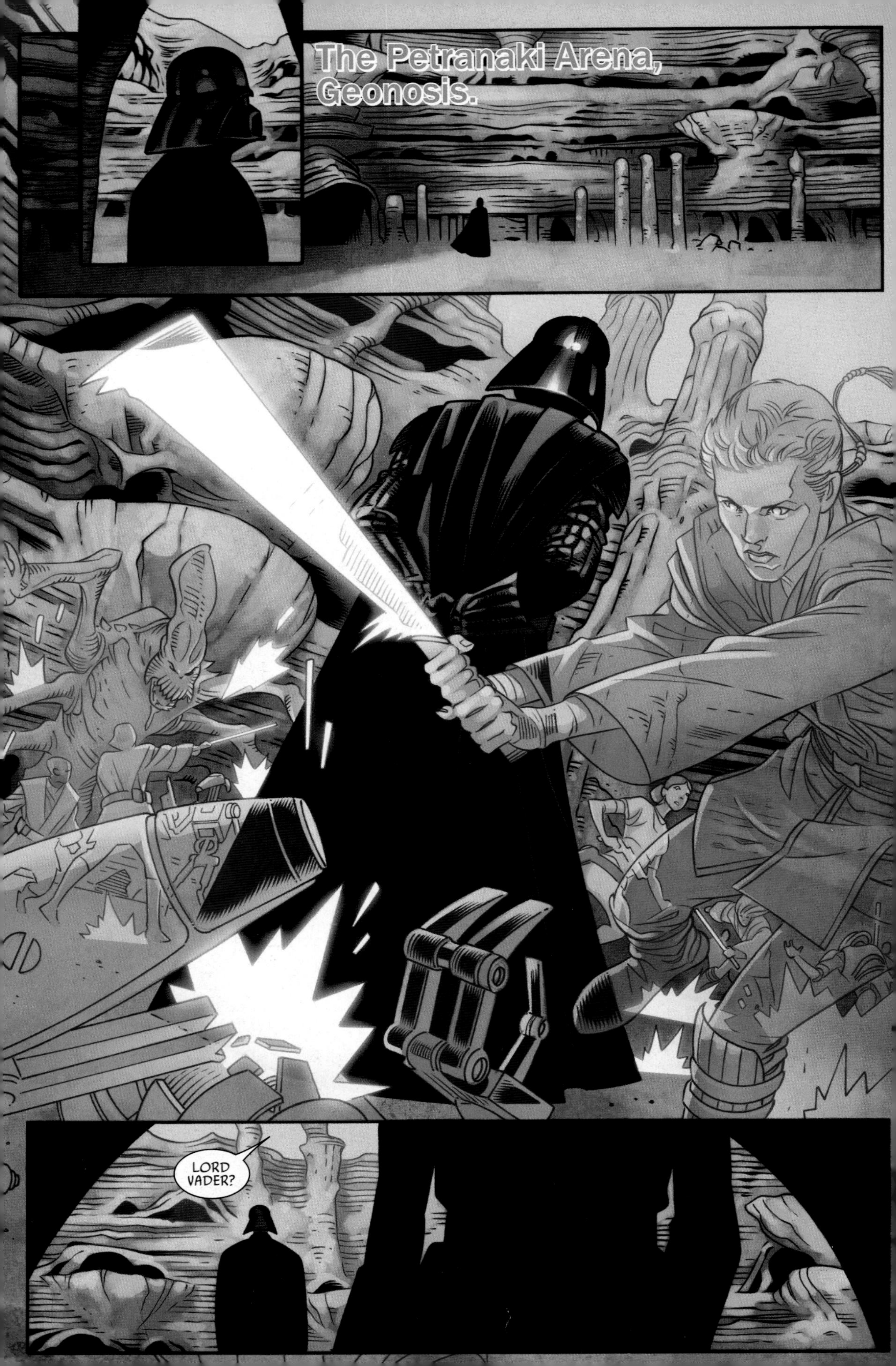
The Petranaki Arena, Geonosis.
LORD VADER?

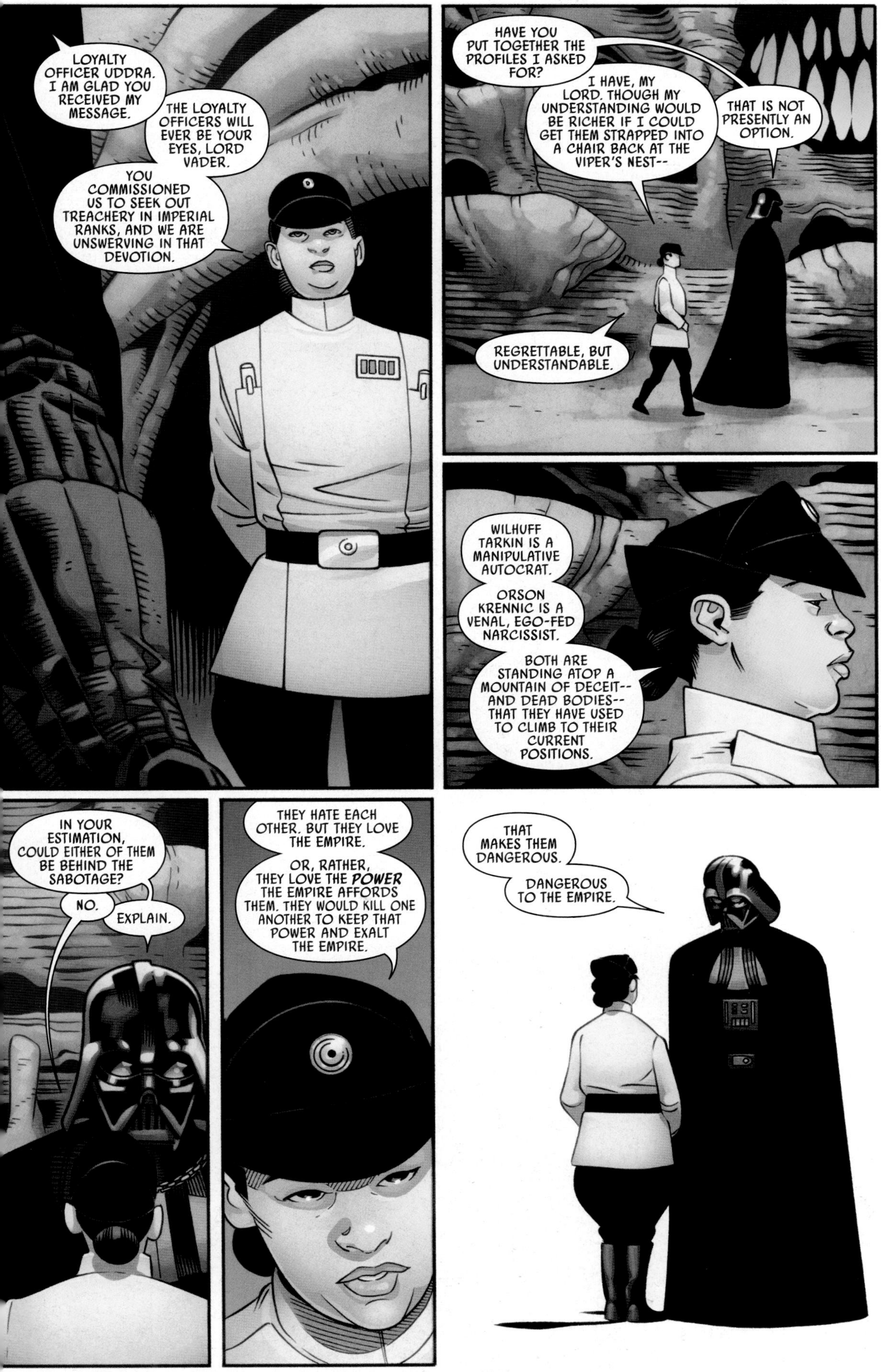
LOYALTY OFFICER UDDRA. I AM GLAD YOU RECEIVED MY MESSAGE.
THE LOYALTY OFFICERS WILL EVER BE YOUR EYES, LORD VADER.
YOU COMMISSIONED US TO SEEK OUT TREACHERY IN IMPERIAL RANKS, AND WE ARE UNSWERVING IN THAT DEVOTION.
HAVE YOU PUT TOGETHER THE PROFILES I ASKED FOR?
I HAVE, MY LORD. THOUGH MY UNDERSTANDING WOULD BE RICHER IF I COULD GET THEM STRAPPED INTO A CHAIR BACK AT THE VIPER'S NEST--
THAT IS NOT PRESENTLY AN OPTION.
REGRETTABLE, BUT UNDERSTANDABLE.
WILHUFF TARKIN IS A MANIPULATIVE AUTOCRAT.
ORSON KRENNIC IS A VENAL, EGO-FED NARCISSIST.
BOTH ARE STANDING ATOP A MOUNTAIN OF DECEIT--AND DEAD BODIES--THAT THEY HAVE USED TO CLIMB TO THEIR CURRENT POSITIONS.
IN YOUR ESTIMATION, COULD EITHER OF THEM BE BEHIND THE SABOTAGE?
NO.
EXPLAIN.
THEY HATE EACH OTHER. BUT THEY LOVE THE EMPIRE.
OR, RATHER, THEY LOVE THE *POWER* THE EMPIRE AFFORDS THEM. THEY WOULD KILL ONE ANOTHER TO KEEP THAT POWER AND EXALT THE EMPIRE.
THAT MAKES THEM DANGEROUS.
DANGEROUS TO THE EMPIRE.

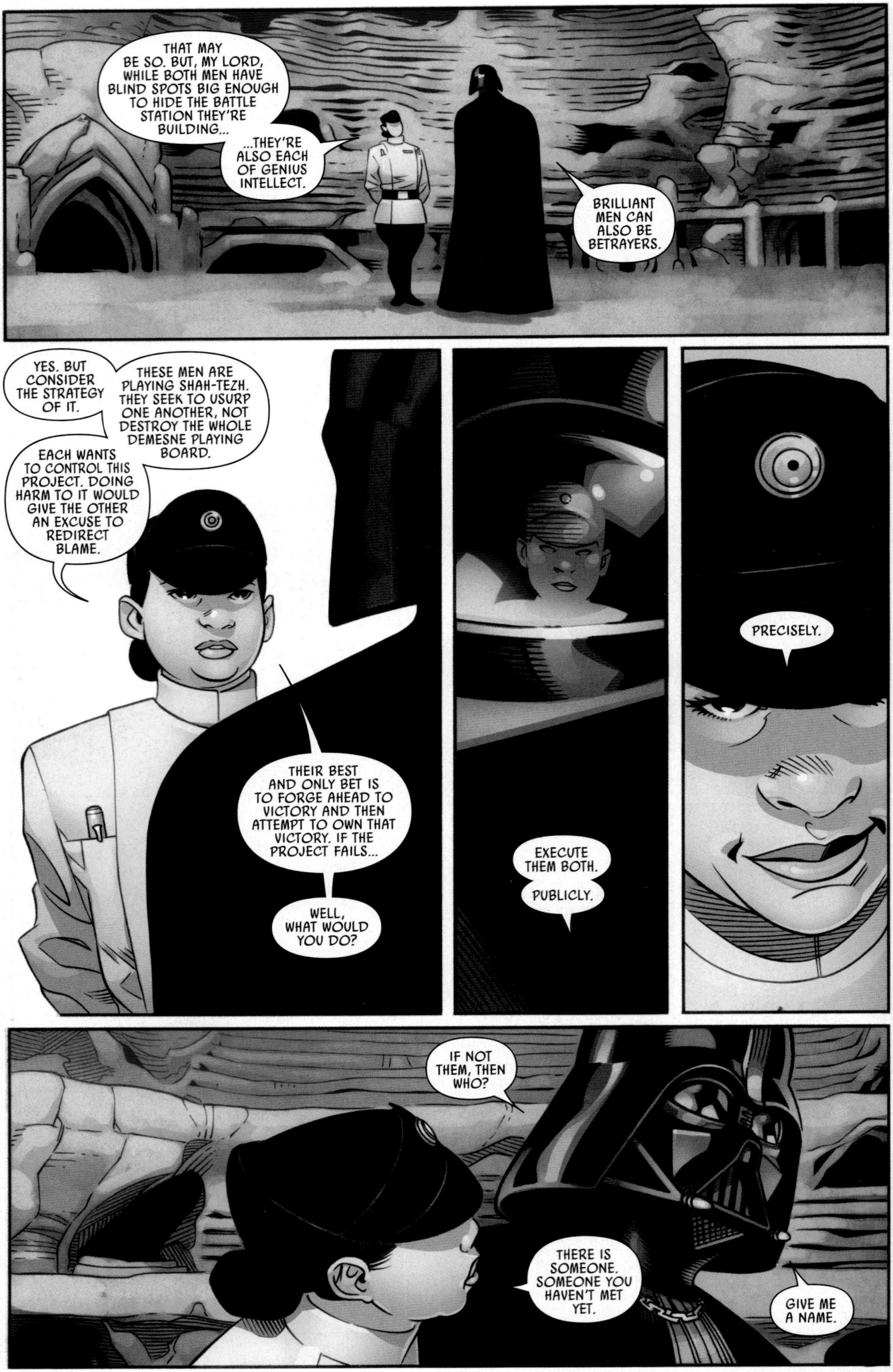
THAT MAY BE SO. BUT, MY LORD, WHILE BOTH MEN HAVE BLIND SPOTS BIG ENOUGH TO HIDE THE BATTLE STATION THEY'RE BUILDING...
...THEY'RE ALSO EACH OF GENIUS INTELLECT.
BRILLIANT MEN CAN ALSO BE BETRAYERS.
YES. BUT CONSIDER THE STRATEGY OF IT.
THESE MEN ARE PLAYING SHAH-TEZH. THEY SEEK TO USURP ONE ANOTHER, NOT DESTROY THE WHOLE DEMESNE PLAYING BOARD.
EACH WANTS TO CONTROL THIS PROJECT. DOING HARM TO IT WOULD GIVE THE OTHER AN EXCUSE TO REDIRECT BLAME.
THEIR BEST AND ONLY BET IS TO FORGE AHEAD TO VICTORY AND THEN ATTEMPT TO OWN THAT VICTORY. IF THE PROJECT FAILS...
WELL, WHAT WOULD YOU DO?
EXECUTE THEM BOTH.
PUBLICLY.
PRECISELY.
IF NOT THEM, THEN WHO?
THERE IS SOMEONE. SOMEONE YOU HAVEN'T MET YET.
GIVE ME A NAME.

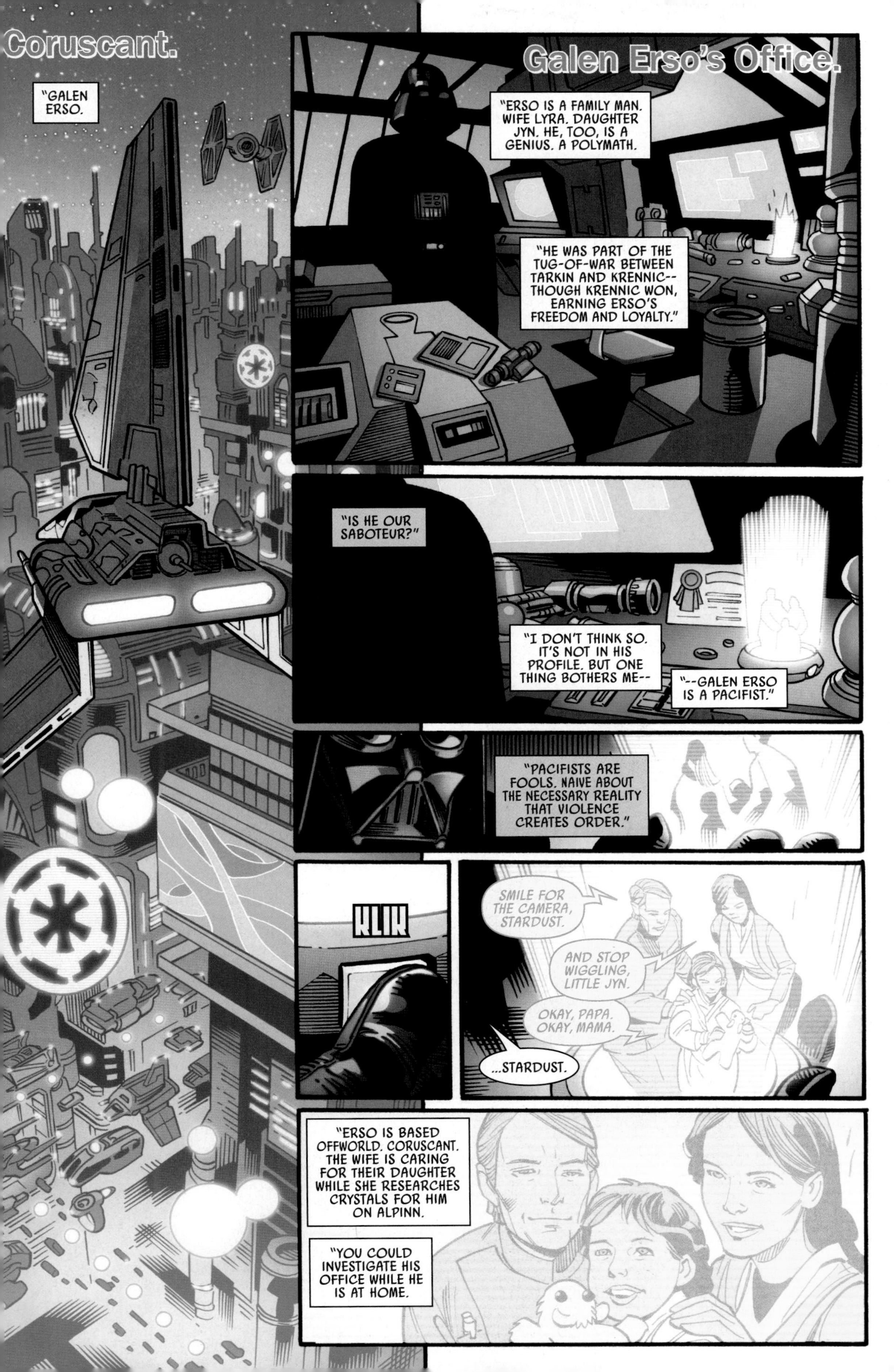

Coruscant.
"GALEN ERSO.
Galen Erso's Office.
"ERSO IS A FAMILY MAN. WIFE LYRA. DAUGHTER JYN. HE, TOO, IS A GENIUS. A POLYMATH.
"HE WAS PART OF THE TUG-OF-WAR BETWEEN TARKIN AND KRENNIC--THOUGH KRENNIC WON, EARNING ERSO'S FREEDOM AND LOYALTY."
"IS HE OUR SABOTEUR?"
"I DON'T THINK SO. IT'S NOT IN HIS PROFILE. BUT ONE THING BOTHERS ME--
"--GALEN ERSO IS A PACIFIST."
"PACIFISTS ARE FOOLS. NAIVE ABOUT THE NECESSARY REALITY THAT VIOLENCE CREATES ORDER."
KLIK
SMILE FOR THE CAMERA, STARDUST.
AND STOP WIGGLING, LITTLE JYN.
OKAY, PAPA. OKAY, MAMA.
...STARDUST.
"ERSO IS BASED OFFWORLD. CORUSCANT. THE WIFE IS CARING FOR THEIR DAUGHTER WHILE SHE RESEARCHES CRYSTALS FOR HIM ON ALPINN.
"YOU COULD INVESTIGATE HIS OFFICE WHILE HE IS AT HOME.

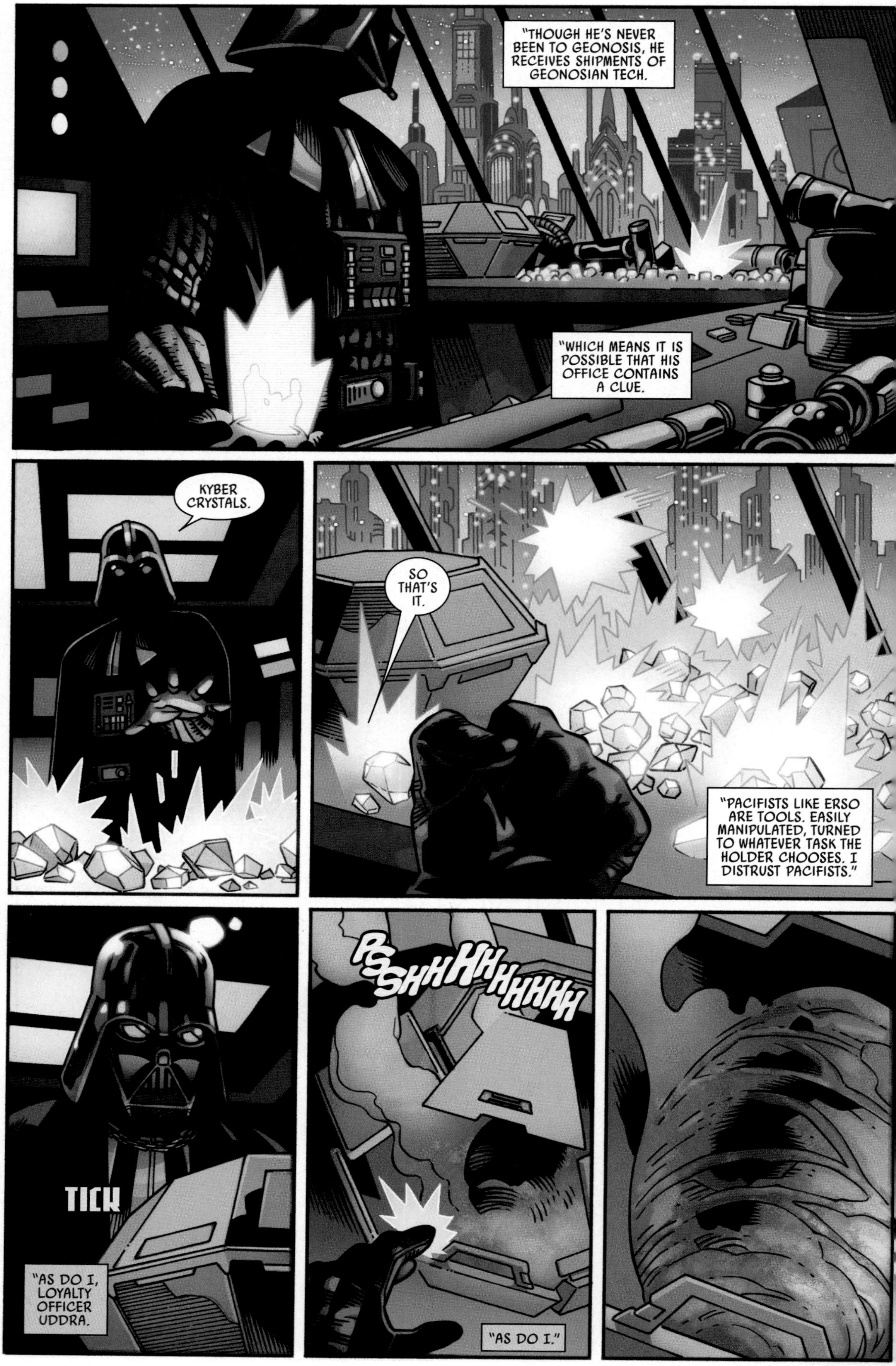
"THOUGH HE'S NEVER BEEN TO GEONOSIS, HE RECEIVES SHIPMENTS OF GEONOSIAN TECH.
"WHICH MEANS IT IS POSSIBLE THAT HIS OFFICE CONTAINS A CLUE.
KYBER CRYSTALS.
SO THAT'S IT.
"PACIFISTS LIKE ERSO ARE TOOLS. EASILY MANIPULATED, TURNED TO WHATEVER TASK THE HOLDER CHOOSES. I DISTRUST PACIFISTS."
TICK
"AS DO I, LOYALTY OFFICER UDDRA.
PSSHHHHHHHHH
"AS DO I."

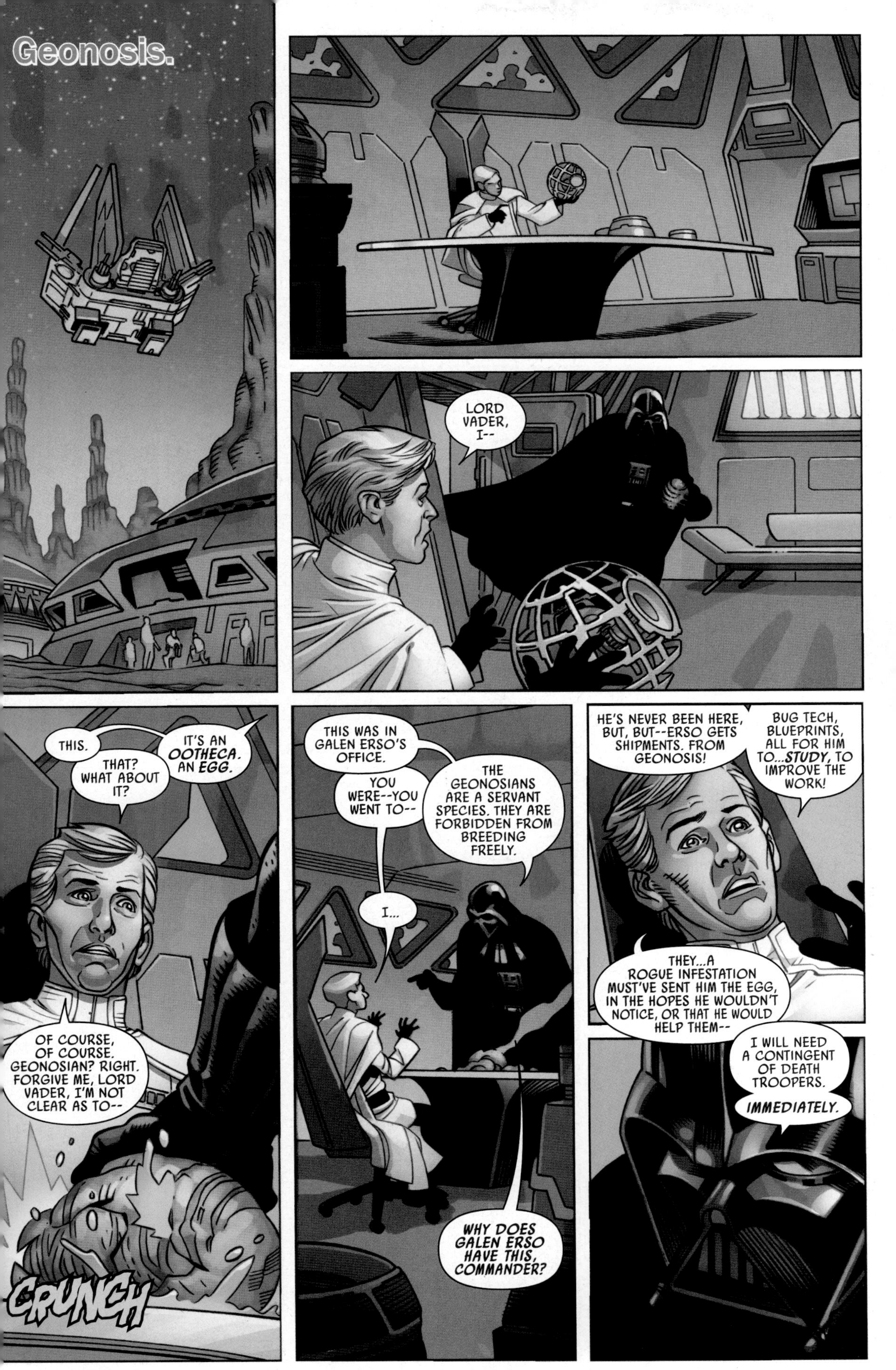

Geonosis.
LORD VADER, I--
THIS.
THAT? WHAT ABOUT IT?
IT'S AN *OOTHECA*. AN *EGG*.
OF COURSE, OF COURSE. GEONOSIAN? RIGHT. FORGIVE ME, LORD VADER, I'M NOT CLEAR AS TO--
CRUNCH
THIS WAS IN GALEN ERSO'S OFFICE.
YOU WERE--YOU WENT TO--
THE GEONOSIANS ARE A SERVANT SPECIES. THEY ARE FORBIDDEN FROM BREEDING FREELY.
I...
WHY DOES GALEN ERSO HAVE THIS, COMMANDER?
HE'S NEVER BEEN HERE, BUT, BUT--ERSO GETS SHIPMENTS. FROM GEONOSIS!
BUG TECH, BLUEPRINTS, ALL FOR HIM TO...*STUDY*, TO IMPROVE THE WORK!
THEY...A ROGUE INFESTATION MUST'VE SENT HIM THE EGG, IN THE HOPES HE WOULDN'T NOTICE, OR THAT HE WOULD HELP THEM--
I WILL NEED A CONTINGENT OF DEATH TROOPERS.
IMMEDIATELY.

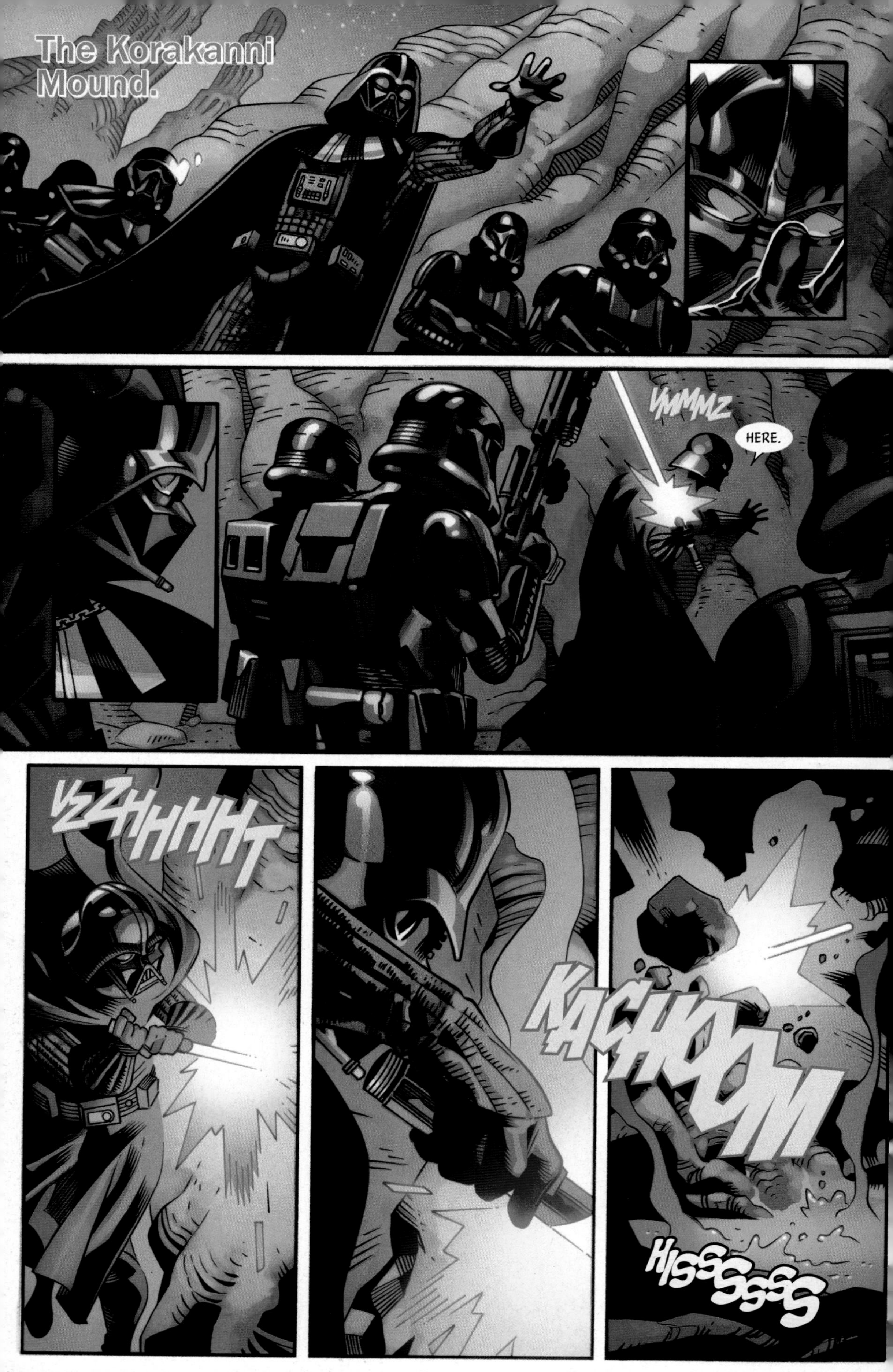
The Korakanni Mound.
VMMMZ
HERE.
VZZHHHHT
KACHOOM
HISSSSSSS

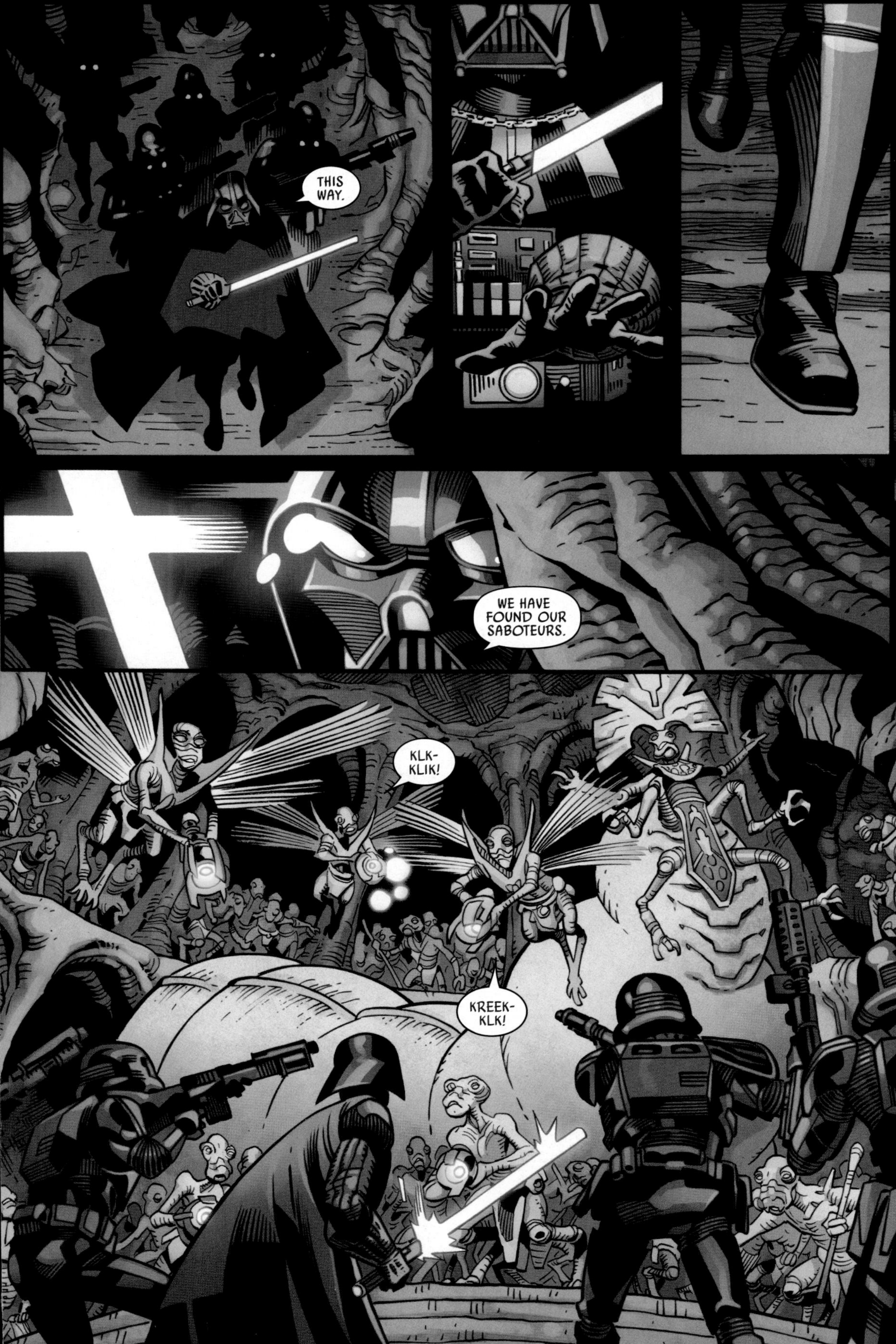
THIS WAY.
WE HAVE FOUND OUR SABOTEURS.
KLK-KLIK!
KREEK-KLK!

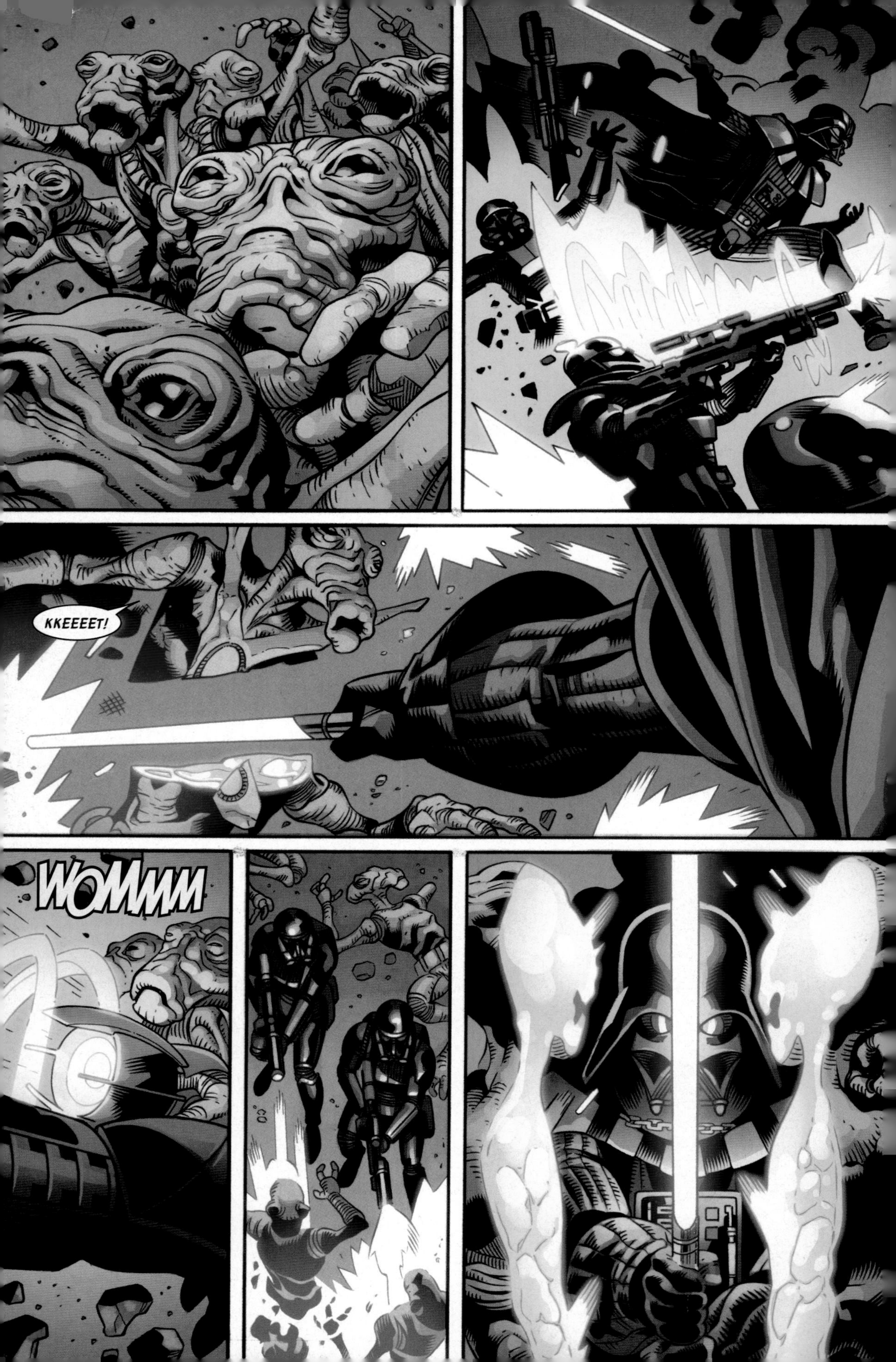
KKEEEET!
WOMMM

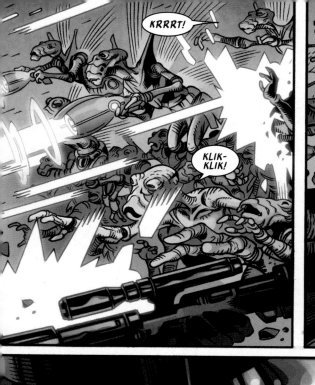

KRRRT!

KLIK-KLIK!

SHKREEEEE!

A ROGUE QUEEN. UNSANCTIONED BREEDING. AND SABOTAGE.

FOR YOUR TREACHERY AGAINST THE EMPIRE...

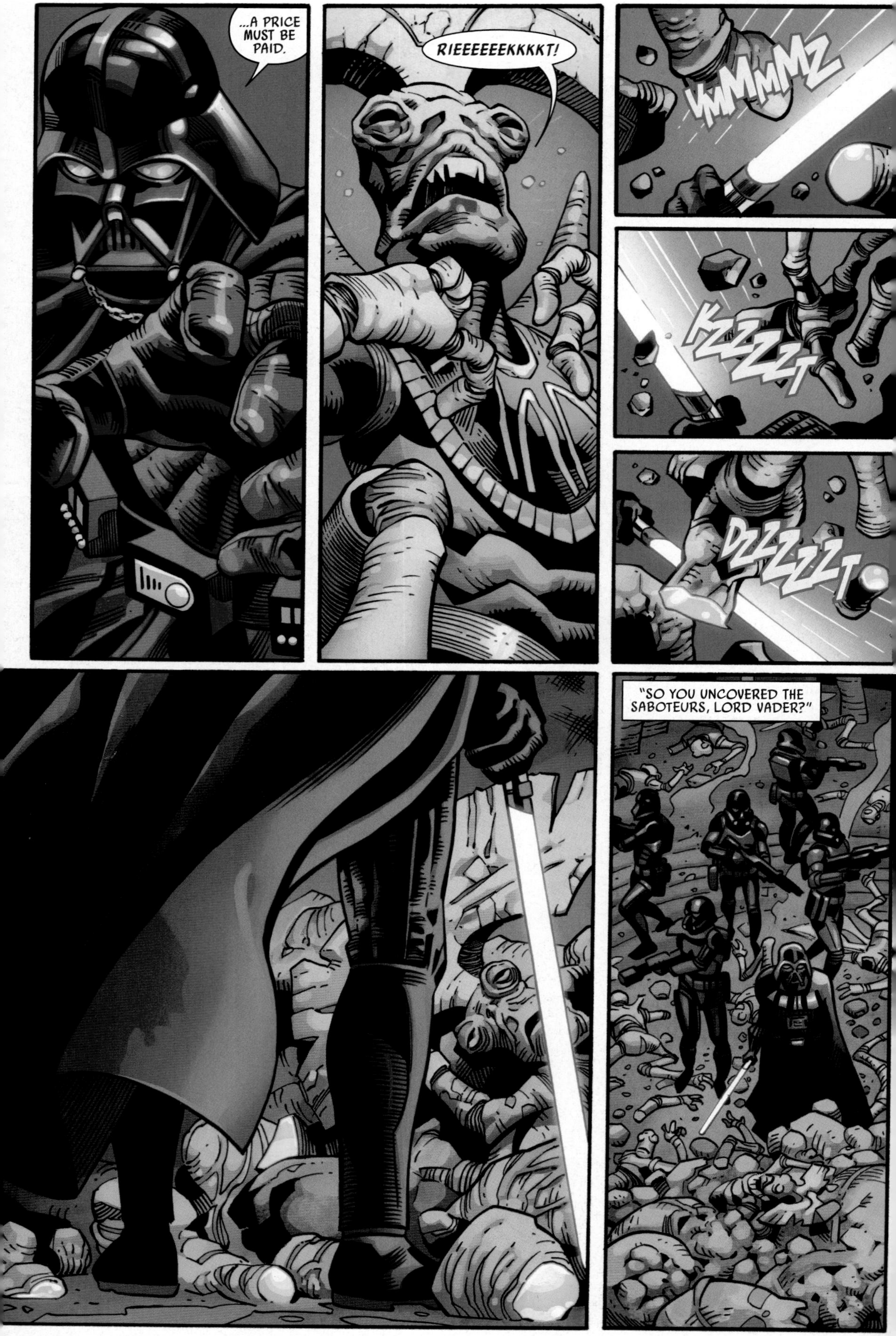
...A PRICE MUST BE PAID.
RIEEEEEEKKKKT!
VMMMMMZ
KZZZZZT
DZZZZZZZT
"SO YOU UNCOVERED THE SABOTEURS, LORD VADER?"

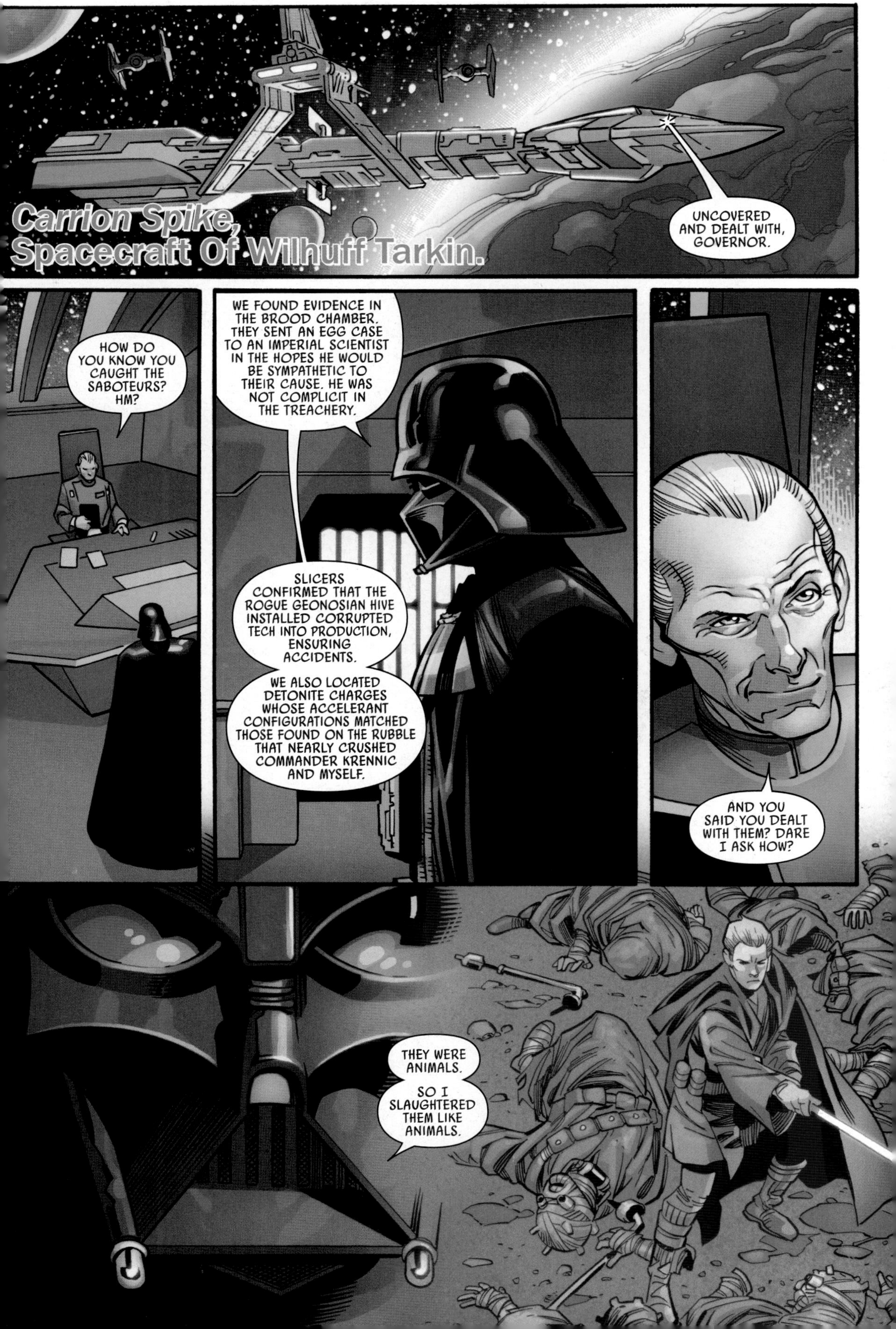
Carrion Spike, Spacecraft Of Wilhuff Tarkin.
UNCOVERED AND DEALT WITH, GOVERNOR.
HOW DO YOU KNOW YOU CAUGHT THE SABOTEURS? HM?
WE FOUND EVIDENCE IN THE BROOD CHAMBER. THEY SENT AN EGG CASE TO AN IMPERIAL SCIENTIST IN THE HOPES HE WOULD BE SYMPATHETIC TO THEIR CAUSE. HE WAS NOT COMPLICIT IN THE TREACHERY.
SLICERS CONFIRMED THAT THE ROGUE GEONOSIAN HIVE INSTALLED CORRUPTED TECH INTO PRODUCTION, ENSURING ACCIDENTS.
WE ALSO LOCATED DETONITE CHARGES WHOSE ACCELERANT CONFIGURATIONS MATCHED THOSE FOUND ON THE RUBBLE THAT NEARLY CRUSHED COMMANDER KRENNIC AND MYSELF.
AND YOU SAID YOU DEALT WITH THEM? DARE I ASK HOW?
THEY WERE ANIMALS.
SO I SLAUGHTERED THEM LIKE ANIMALS.

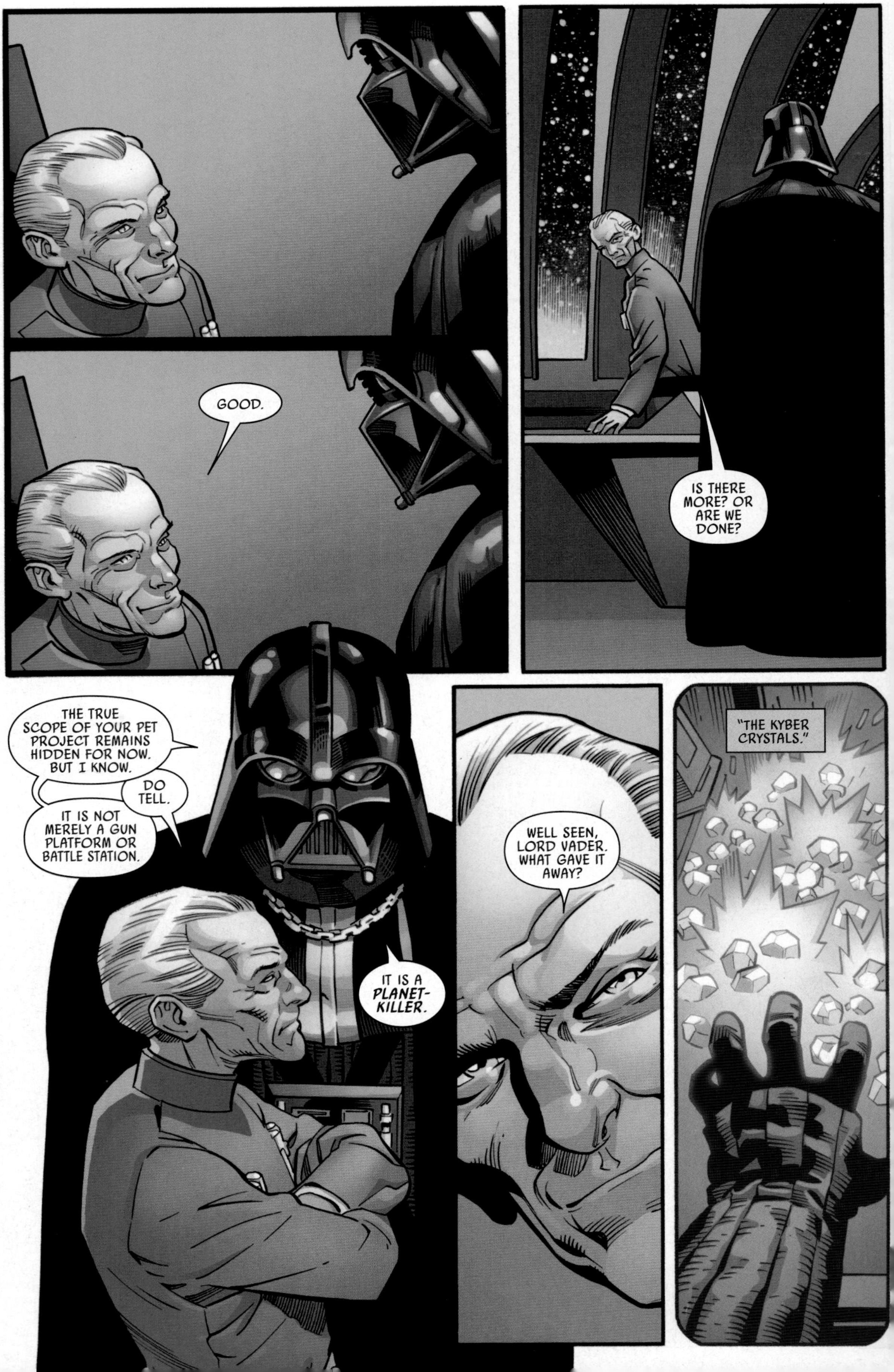
GOOD.
IS THERE MORE? OR ARE WE DONE?
THE TRUE SCOPE OF YOUR PET PROJECT REMAINS HIDDEN FOR NOW. BUT I KNOW.
DO TELL.
IT IS NOT MERELY A GUN PLATFORM OR BATTLE STATION.
IT IS A *PLANET-KILLER*.
WELL SEEN, LORD VADER. WHAT GAVE IT AWAY?
"THE KYBER CRYSTALS."

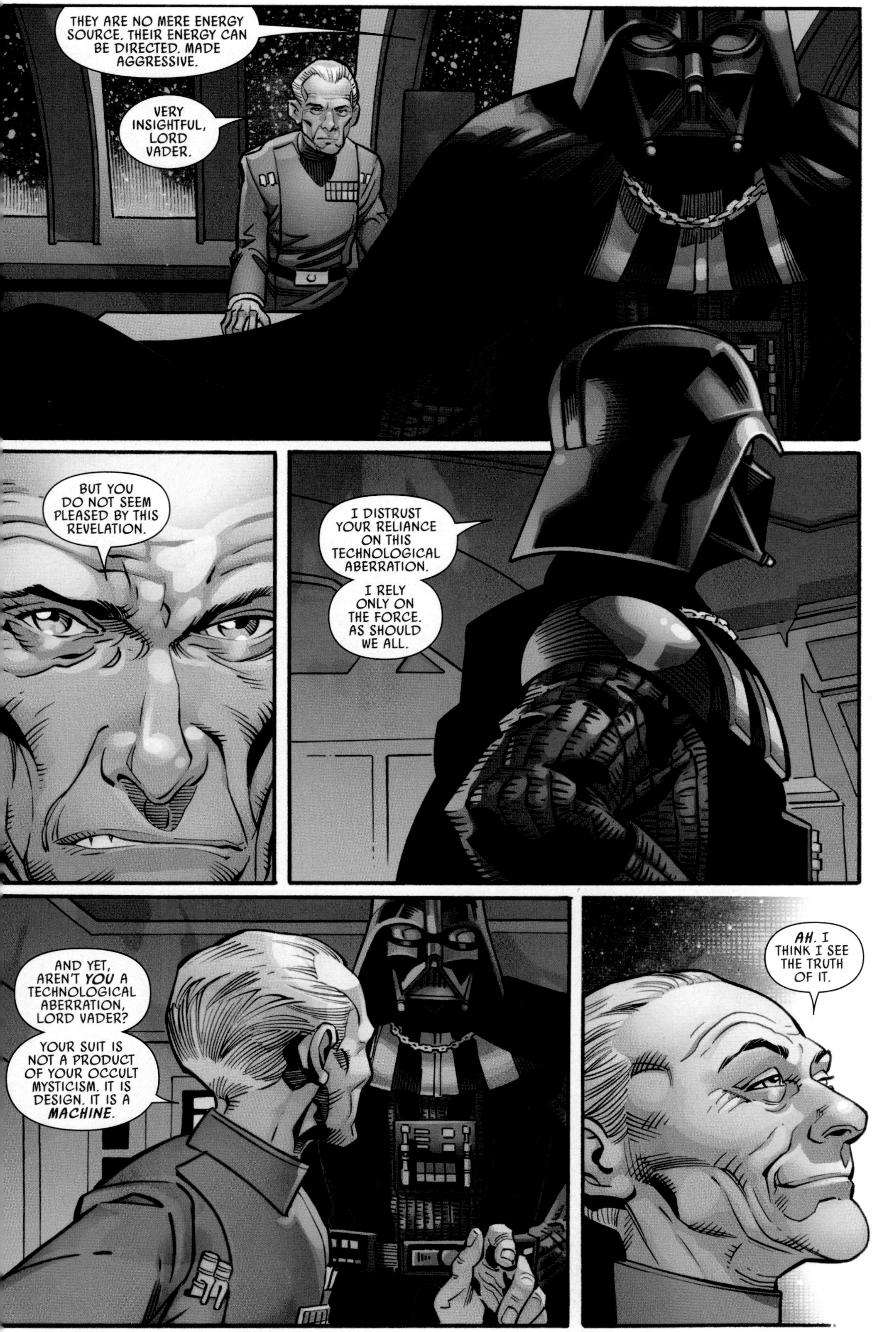
THEY ARE NO MERE ENERGY SOURCE. THEIR ENERGY CAN BE DIRECTED. MADE AGGRESSIVE.
VERY INSIGHTFUL, LORD VADER.
BUT YOU DO NOT SEEM PLEASED BY THIS REVELATION.
I DISTRUST YOUR RELIANCE ON THIS TECHNOLOGICAL ABERRATION.
I RELY ONLY ON THE FORCE. AS SHOULD WE ALL.
AND YET, AREN'T *YOU* A TECHNOLOGICAL ABERRATION, LORD VADER?
YOUR SUIT IS NOT A PRODUCT OF YOUR OCCULT MYSTICISM. IT IS DESIGN. IT IS A ***MACHINE***.
AH. I THINK I SEE THE TRUTH OF IT.

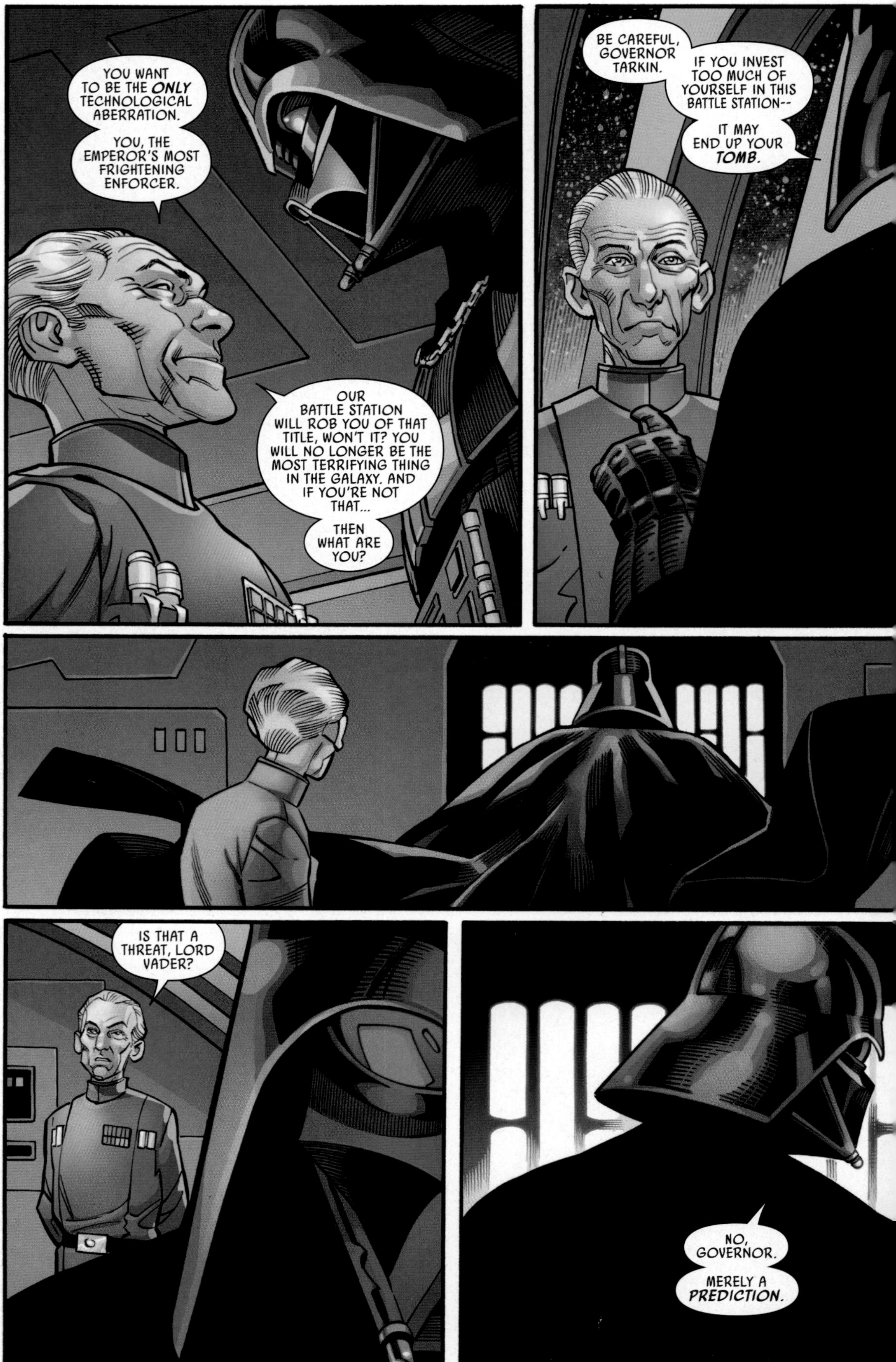
YOU WANT TO BE THE ONLY TECHNOLOGICAL ABERRATION.
YOU, THE EMPEROR'S MOST FRIGHTENING ENFORCER.
OUR BATTLE STATION WILL ROB YOU OF THAT TITLE, WON'T IT? YOU WILL NO LONGER BE THE MOST TERRIFYING THING IN THE GALAXY. AND IF YOU'RE NOT THAT...
THEN WHAT ARE YOU?
BE CAREFUL, GOVERNOR TARKIN.
IF YOU INVEST TOO MUCH OF YOURSELF IN THIS BATTLE STATION--
IT MAY END UP YOUR TOMB.
IS THAT A THREAT, LORD VADER?
NO, GOVERNOR.
MERELY A PREDICTION.

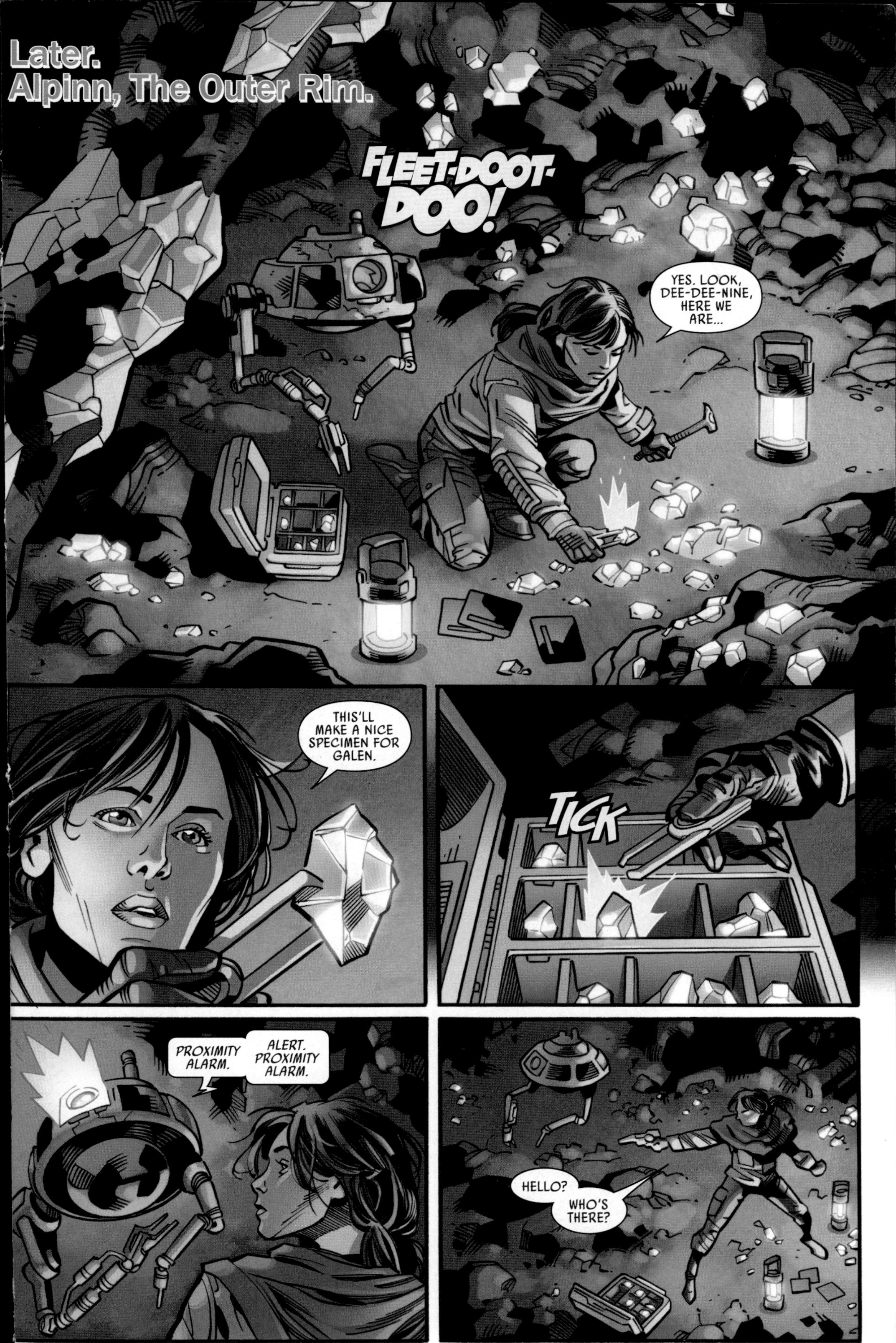
Later.
Alpinn, The Outer Rim.
FLEET-DOOT-DOO!
YES. LOOK, DEE-DEE-NINE, HERE WE ARE...
THIS'LL MAKE A NICE SPECIMEN FOR GALEN.
TICK
PROXIMITY ALARM.
ALERT. PROXIMITY ALARM.
HELLO?
WHO'S THERE?

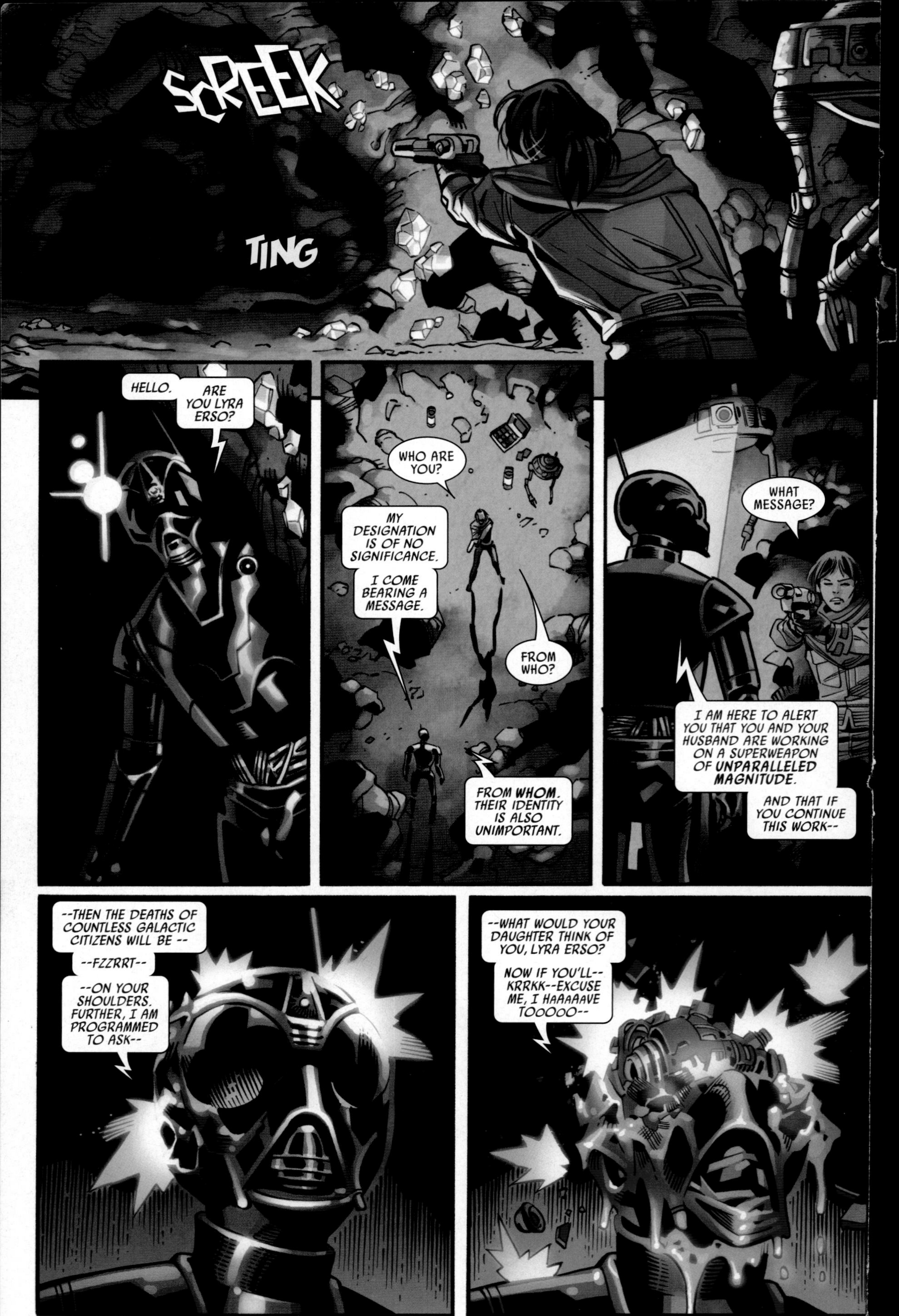
SCREEK
TING
HELLO.
ARE YOU LYRA ERSO?
WHO ARE YOU?
MY DESIGNATION IS OF NO SIGNIFICANCE.
I COME BEARING A MESSAGE.
FROM WHO?
FROM WHOM. THEIR IDENTITY IS ALSO UNIMPORTANT.
WHAT MESSAGE?
I AM HERE TO ALERT YOU THAT YOU AND YOUR HUSBAND ARE WORKING ON A SUPERWEAPON OF UNPARALLELED MAGNITUDE.
AND THAT IF YOU CONTINUE THIS WORK--
--THEN THE DEATHS OF COUNTLESS GALACTIC CITIZENS WILL BE --
--FZZRRT--
--ON YOUR SHOULDERS. FURTHER, I AM PROGRAMMED TO ASK--
--WHAT WOULD YOUR DAUGHTER THINK OF YOU, LYRA ERSO?
NOW IF YOU'LL--KRRKK--EXCUSE ME, I HAAAAAVE TOOOOO--

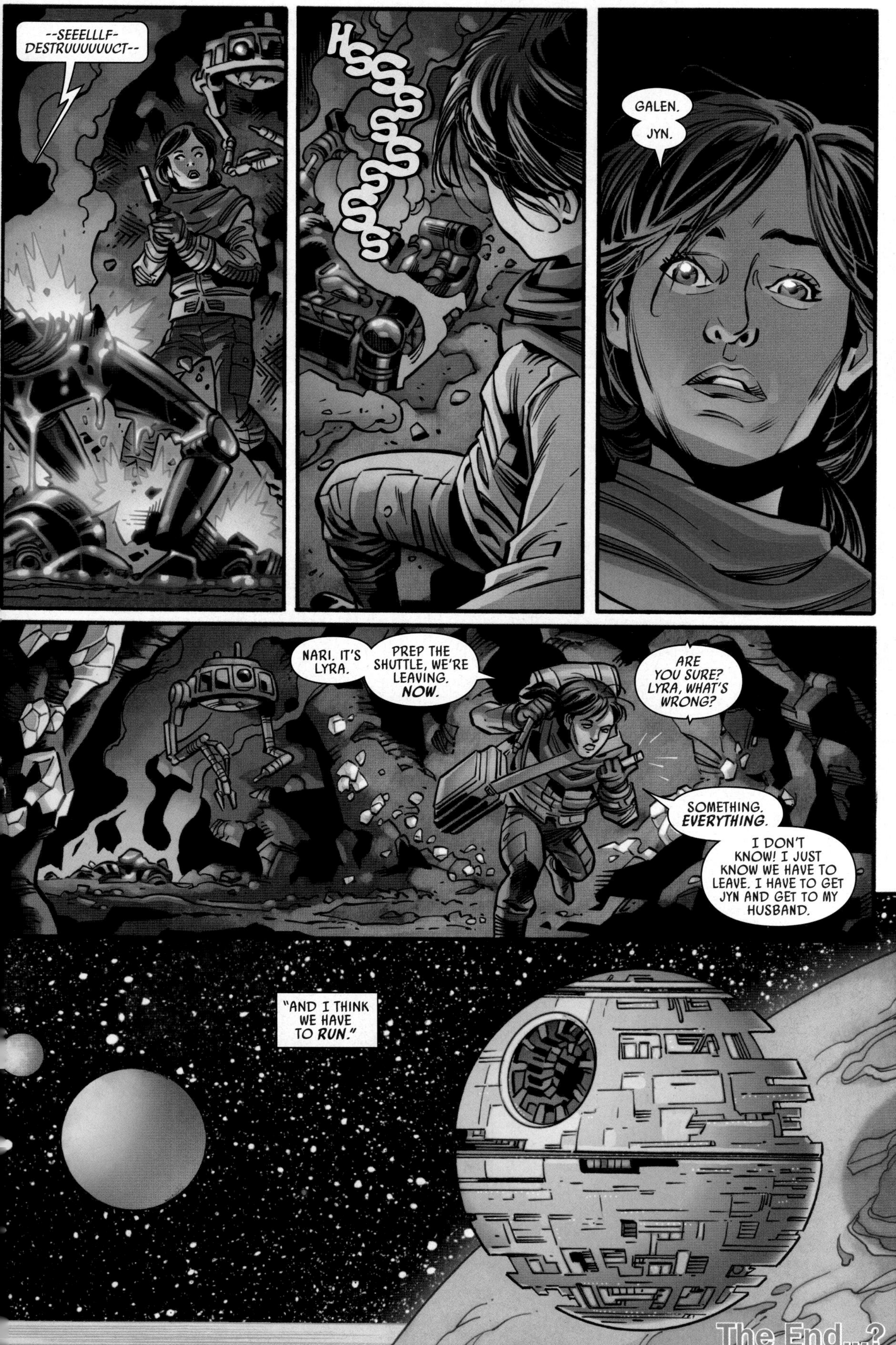
--SEEELLLF-DESTRUUUUUUCT--
HSSSSSSSSS
GALEN.
JYN.
NARI. IT'S LYRA.
PREP THE SHUTTLE, WE'RE LEAVING. NOW.
ARE YOU SURE? LYRA, WHAT'S WRONG?
SOMETHING. EVERYTHING.
I DON'T KNOW! I JUST KNOW WE HAVE TO LEAVE. I HAVE TO GET JYN AND GET TO MY HUSBAND.
"AND I THINK WE HAVE TO RUN."
The End...?

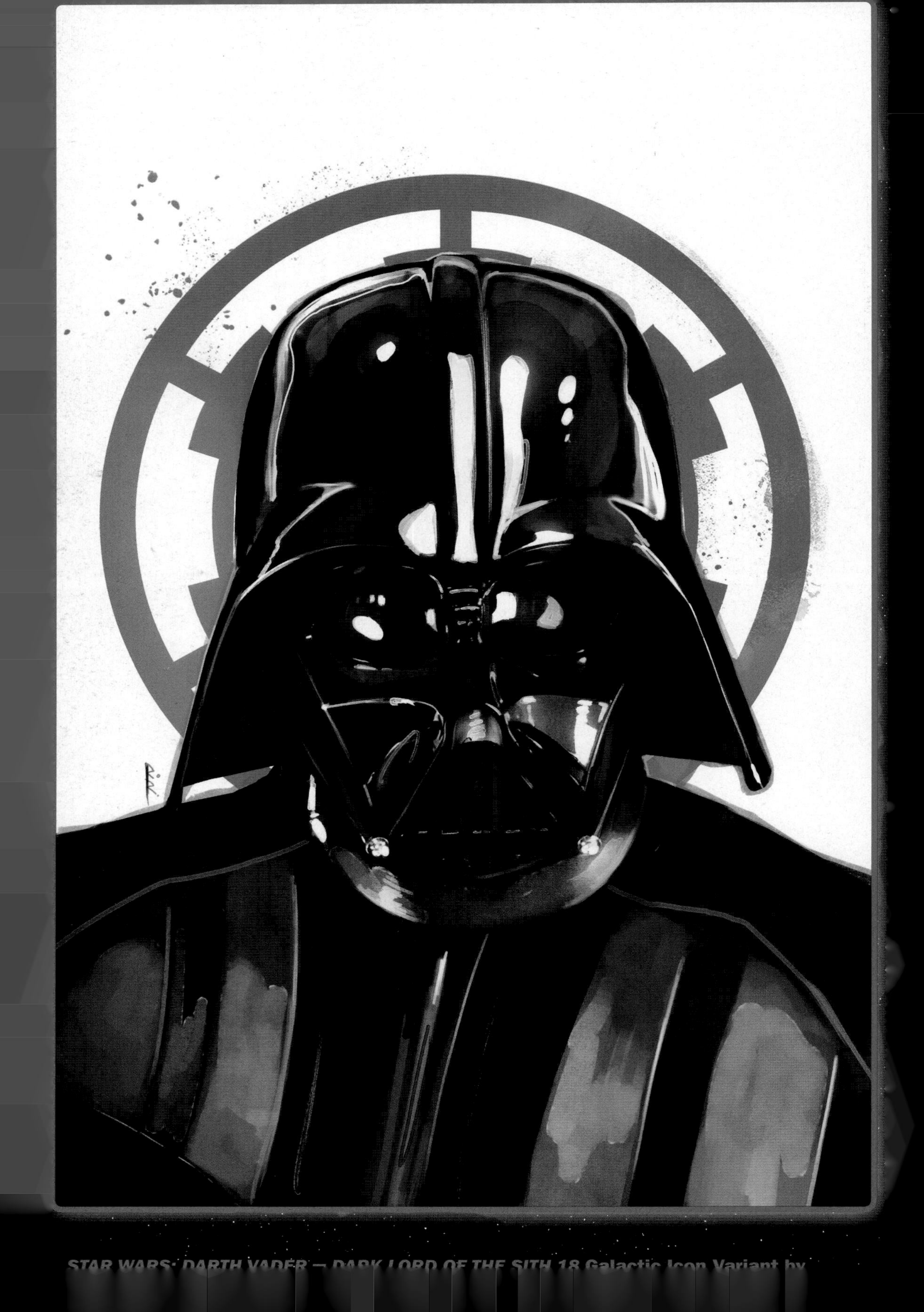

STAR WARS: DARTH VADER — DARK LORD OF THE SITH 18 Galactic Icon Variant by

AFTER BARELY ESCAPING DARTH VADER WITH HER LIFE, DOCTOR APHRA SETS OFF IN SEARCH OF RARE AND DEADLY ARTIFACTS!

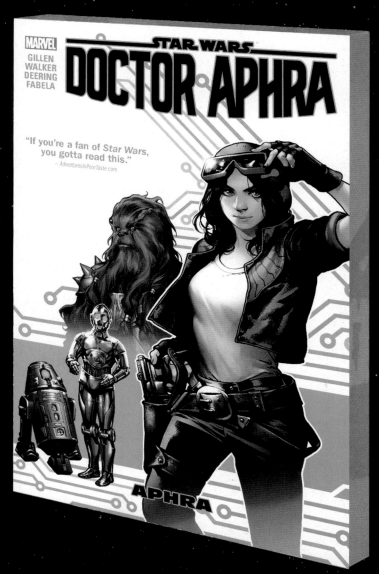

STAR WARS: DOCTOR APHRA VOL. 1 — APHRA TPB
978-1302906771

ON SALE NOW
AVAILABLE IN PRINT AND DIGITAL WHEREVER BOOKS ARE SOLD

TO FIND A COMIC SHOP NEAR YOU, VISIT COMICSHOPLOCATOR.COM

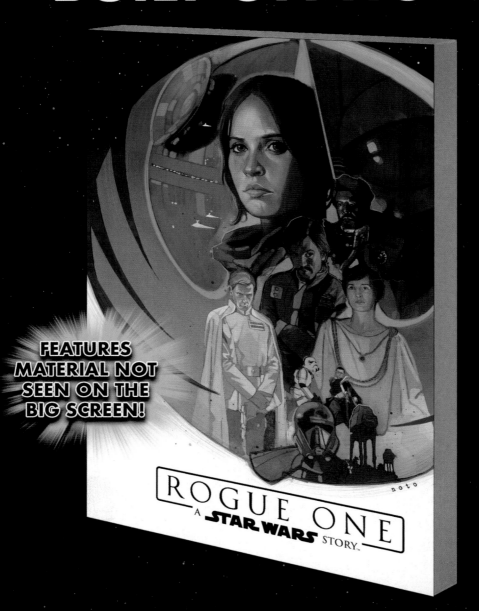

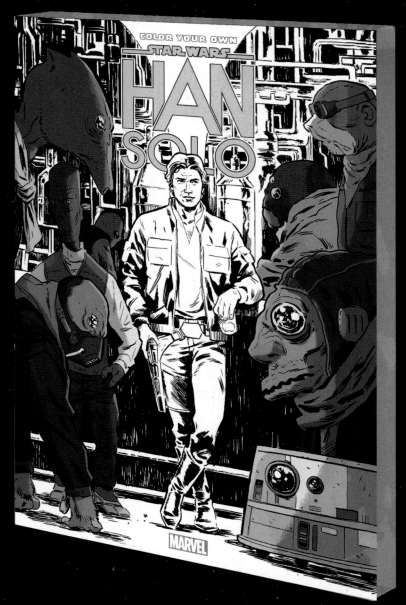

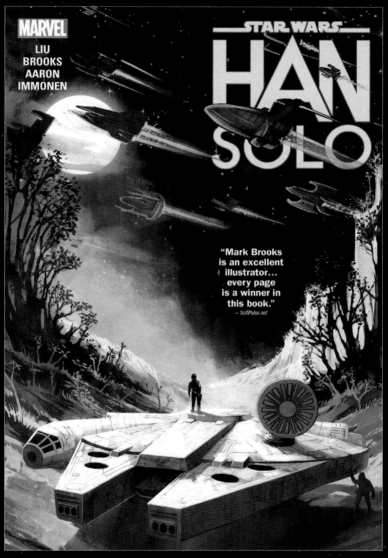

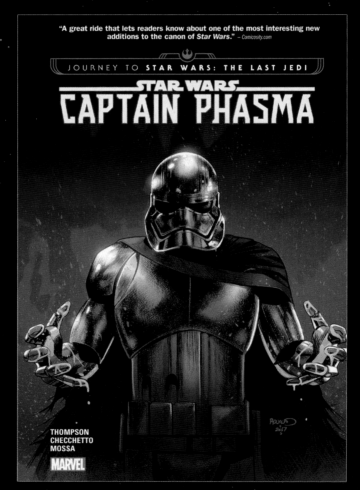

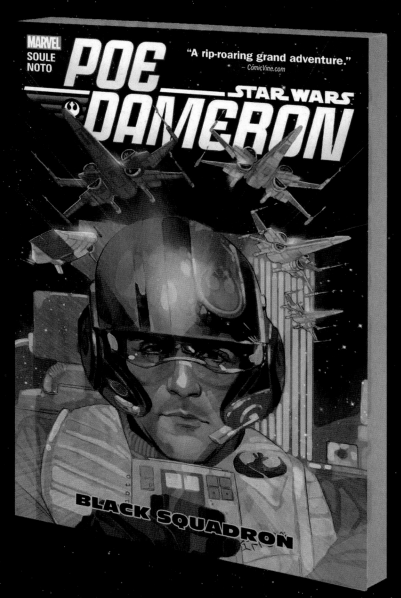